MEXICO
IN
CRISIS

MEXICO IN CRISIS

Second Edition

JUDITH
ADLER
HELLMAN

HOLMES & MEIER PUBLISHERS
New York   London

Published in the United States of America 1983 by
Holmes & Meier Publishers, Inc.
30 Irving Place
New York, N.Y. 10003

Great Britain:
Holmes & Meier Publishers, Ltd.
131 Trafalgar Road
Greenwich, London SE10 9TX

Second Edition 1983

Book design by Stephanie Barton

Library of Congress Cataloging in Publication Data

Hellman, Judith Adler.
Mexico in Crisis.

Bibliography: p.
Includes index.
1. Mexico—Politics and government—1970–
2. Mexico—Politics and government—1946–1970.
3. Mexico—Politics and government—1910–1946.
I. Title.
JL1231.H44   1983   972.08′3   83-8485
ISBN 0-8419-0840-0(c)
ISBN 0-8419-0895-8 (pa)

Manufactured in the United States of America

**TO
MY
PARENTS**

TABLE OF CONTENTS

PREFACE TO THE SECOND EDITION

It seems that the convention in prefaces to second editions is for the author to assert that he or she has "resisted the temptation" to thoroughly rewrite, or at least to totally reorganize the material presented in the original version. I confess that I wasn't much tempted at the outset, but a careful rethinking of what I had presented years ago broke down my resistance—at least in part. The original book was written with a series of modest goals in mind. I had hoped to outline the historical processes that prompted a particular form of economic development in Mexico. I attempted to offer an explanation for the institutionalization in Mexico of certain peculiar political forms. I tried to provide an analysis that would account for the remarkable stability of the Mexican system in the face of rapid and dramatic changes in the world economy, major geopolitical crises, unprecedented population growth and demographic shifts, and a variety of other transformations that would have shattered a less resilient political order. I was also intent on examining why "Mexico" had prospered, but Mexicans—the majority of them, at least—had not.

Writing in 1983, I find that the broad analysis I originally posed still holds, although, needless to say, there are aspects of that analysis which now seem to me inadequate. Still, notwithstanding oil riches and patchwork political reform, despite the entry of new actors into the political process and shifts in the relative strength of longer-term participants, in spite of successive economic crises and the nationalization of the banks, I find that the system responds today in the 1980s to the same *basic* forces that moved it in the 1960s and 1970s. Perhaps the most significant changes in the last decade have been the emergence of new militancy among organized workers in the urban areas, and the deterioration of the condition of peasants with the decline of agricultural productivity in the countryside.

If the central argument of this book has not been altered, certainly new data have prompted me to pose some new interpretations. Furthermore, a range of new events and phenomena that have come to the fore

ix

in the last six years require careful examination and analysis: the impact of oil on economic development and on politics, the proletarianization of the peasantry and the flow of rural migrants both to the cities and to the U.S. borderland region, the consolidation of opposition on the left, the fiscal crisis and the devaluation of the peso, and the reinforcement of dependency ties to the United States. In addition, the level of conflict and division among different elements or factions within both the economic and the political elite has been clarified by the successive crises of the 1970s. I have also incorporated recent research on Mexican political economy and offered some suggestion of the stimulating debates which have unfolded in the last several years as Latin American, North American, and European analysts have grappled with the role of the state and social classes in Mexican development. Finally, in bringing this work up to date, I have not only treated the crisis of 1981–1983, but attempted to show how the collapse of the economy in this period grew out of development priorities in place since the 1940s.

In addition to the colleagues, friends, and relations to whom I expressed my appreciation in the first preface, I would like to thank Susan Eckstein, who, as an anonymous assessor of the first edition, made many helpful suggestions. Sam Lanfranco provided very useful feedback on the revisions for chapters 3 and 8. Richard Roman generously shared with me documents collected in his recent fieldwork and offered comments on the conclusions. I also thank Virginia Brisbin and Richard Westra who assisted me in gathering updated economic data. Kalowatie Deonandan gave both moral support and invaluable help with the countless small but niggling details that go into the final preparation of a manuscript. Anne Cook was very solidary and generous with her time and help. Thanks are also due to Naomi Lipman for her skilled editorial work. The staff of Secretarial Services of York University performed on this occasion, as on every other, with the blend of professionalism and human kindness that for me has always made finishing a piece of writing an unmixed pleasure. I would also like to acknowledge the receipt of a York University Small Research Grant and a Social Sciences and Humanities Research Council of Canada Travel Grant which made possible additional fieldwork. Finally, my husband, Stephen Hellman, deserves a renewed note of special thanks: his unfaltering support and encouragement of this project have made all the difference.

PREFACE TO THE FIRST EDITION

Over the past few years, many people who learn that I have lived in Mexico and carried out research in the countryside have immediately put to me a series of hard-to-answer questions. Those who have traveled in Mexico, even as casual tourists, could not fail to note the contrast between modern urban centers and an apparently backward countryside; between the affluence of some Mexicans and the obvious misery of so many others. During their stay in Mexico City, these travelers have been duly impressed with the skyscrapers, elegant hotels, palatial villas, the broad, tree-lined boulevards filled with late model cars, and the shiny new metro. At the same time they are dismayed to find only a short distance from this attractive, modern core all the sights, sounds, and odors of poverty. For some tourists the contrast is underlined when they are approached by a constant stream of beggars as they make their way along a promenade of shops filled with gay paper flowers, straw donkeys, and marionettes who play guitars and wear oversized sombreros. Often visitors who have taken in this series of contrasting impressions are puzzled and want to know why such dramatic disparities of wealth have accompanied economic development in Mexico.

Another set of questions is posed by those who have studied the Mexican Revolution and have always believed that it represented an example of a triumphant peasant revolution. Such people often ask, "What has happened here? Was the Mexican Revolution betrayed? Why is it that there are more landless peasants in Mexico today than before the revolution?"

Yet another series of questions is raised by students of politics who have been led by their readings to regard Mexico as an outstanding example of a functioning democracy with a one-party system. These students ask, "How does 'democracy' work in Mexico? How does the dominant party maintain itself in power? What is the meaning of elections in a one-party system? How do various interest groups make their demands known to the country's leaders? And, finally, how can a ruling party 'institutionalize' a revolution?"

In 1968 an outbreak of student unrest and a brutal government response made headlines in newspapers around the globe. With world attention focused on Mexico as the site of the nineteenth Olympics, and the international press on hand to record the Games, newspaper readers were shocked to learn from their own correspondents that in a single evening more than 300 unarmed demonstrators had been mowed down by army machine guns and that hundreds more had "disappeared" during a summer of violent conflict. What had happened to Mexico's much admired "political stability"? What were the forces involved in this conflict? What were the "grave national problems" that the students were shouting about? Why had the government found it necessary to call in the army? Why was so much force required to put down a student movement?

Obviously these are complex questions, and to find reasonable answers or explanations we need to take a careful look at Mexican political development over the last seventy years. We begin by going back to the revolution of 1910 to analyze the forces and interests at play in that struggle, focusing not only on the participants and the goals for which they fought, but also on the groups that emerged with power at the end of that conflict. In chapter 2 we look at this new political elite, its economic base, its interests, and the political party it established. We then analyze the structure of the party both as it appears on paper and as it functions in reality. The third chapter concerns the development policy the ruling elite has formulated and implemented since 1940, how that policy has shaped the agricultural sector, and how the discovery of vast oil reserves affects the overall strategy for development. Chapter 4 concerns the consequences this policy has had in human terms. In chapters 5 and 6 case studies of a peasant and a student movement highlight the mechanisms employed by the ruling party to maintain itself in power, and the ways in which opposition to the system is expressed. The seventh chapter is an examination of the reformist administration of President Luis Echeverría and his efforts to reorient the course of Mexican development. The final chapter details and explains the economic crisis of 1981–1982 and weighs the prospects for change through the 1980s.

When I began work on this book in 1970, there were few sources in English which addressed these issues in a straightforward way and attempted to cut through the elaborate mythology which surrounds the Mexican Revolution and the Mexican political system. Much of what North Americans had written about contemporary Mexico was laudatory and focused on the political stability and economic growth facilitated by the one-party system.[1] Flattering comparisons were made with the disorder and stagnation that characterized other Latin American countries, and the persistent economic inequalities and social injustice in Mexico tended to be downplayed with references to the "incomplete" or, even more positively, the "ongoing" nature of the Mexican Revolution. Reading these studies, one wonders if these observers were afraid of offending their Mexican friends or the Mexican government, or if their perception of the Mexican situation was such that they actually found little to criticize. In either event, the violent explosion of 1968 generally caught these scholars in an intellectual bind because nothing they had written about Mexican politics suggested either the possibility or the cause of an outbreak of this dimension, nor the naked armed repression and mass imprisonment of political opposition that followed.

Since 1968, students of Mexican politics appear to have been emboldened, and there is a much greater tendency to "tell it like it is." This is what I have attempted to do. In so doing, I have no fear of offending gracious and respected Mexican friends because it has been their expressed desire that I write about these issues as objectively and revealingly as I can.

I would like to thank Eric Wolf and Gerrit Huizer who long ago encouraged me to undertake this project. My friend and colleague, Liisa North, contributed invaluable comments and advice on the first draft. Giorgio Cingolani provided provocative criticism and showed me how research on Mexico can be carried forward while sitting for a summer in a library in Italy. I am very grateful to Professor Mario Einaudi and to the directors and staff of the Fondázione Einaudi in Turin for affording me the opportunity to proceed with my work while my husband carried out his own research at that institute. I want to express special appreciation to Cynthia Hewitt de Alcántara and Sergio Alcántara Ferrer who introduced me to rural Mexican politics in 1967, and read and criticized the early chapters of this book in 1973. Russell Chace provided valuable comments on the section dealing with the revolution of 1910. Through every stage of this work I relied heavily on the analytic skills, theoretical knowledge, common sense, and encouragement of my husband, Stephen Hellman. All these people have been extremely generous with their time and their help, but are in no way responsible for the instances when I was too stubborn to heed their advice.

My greatest debt is to countless Mexicans who, with patience and tolerance, have allowed me to interview them. Men and women inside the government and engaged in opposition, individuals above and underground, members of elite groups as well as peasants and workers, have all contributed to this book by their interest in my project and their willingness, and, in some cases, eagerness, to have their point of view included in this study of Mexican politics.

MEXICO
IN
CRISIS

THE REVOLUTION

> ... If for the ardour of an easy triumph, if for
> wanting to abbreviate the struggle, we cut out of
> our program the radicalism which makes it in-
> compatible with the program of the specifically
> bourgeois and conservative parties, then we will
> have done the work of bandits and assassins, be-
> cause the blood spilled will only serve to give
> greater strength to the bourgeoisie. . . .
>
> Ricardo Flores Magón
> January 19, 1910

The Mexican Revo-
lution was a brutally violent political and social upheaval that ravaged
the Mexican countryside for more than a decade. The revolution still
stands as the bloodiest conflict ever witnessed in the Western Hemisphere. Until the recent years of carnage in Cambodia, in terms of the
proportion of population lost, this was the most violent revolutionary
struggle ever. For in 1910 Mexico counted a population of only 14.5
million people. And during the struggle that followed the outbreak of
fighting in October 1910, as many as one and a half million Mexicans
lost their lives. The appalling death toll on the battlefield, the lack of
medical care for the wounded, and the routine execution of captured
soldiers decimated the revolutionary armies.

The civilian population suffered grievously. For nearly a million
"noncombatants" the revolution brought death by starvation, disease,
exposure, or execution. Villages were burned or flooded by federal
troops. Crops were destroyed and peasants were taken as hostages or
summarily shot as "examples" to their fellow villagers. Thousands fled
across the northern border into the United States never to return to
their native land. By 1920, a total of 8,000 different villages had completely disappeared from the map as a direct result of the revolution.[1]

The revolution was touched off by a group of landowners and intellectuals centered in the North of Mexico. These men sought to overthrow Porfirio Díaz, the general who had seized power by military coup
in 1876 and ruled Mexico as a dictator for more than thirty years. In his
place they hoped to establish a liberal democracy in which presidential
succession would be determined by the principle of "effective suffrage

and no reelection." Led by Francisco Madero, a politically progressive landowner, the northern revolutionaries were a heterogeneous conglomeration of sectors of a number of different social classes, each with its own grievances against the Díaz regime and its own set of demands to press.

Both the style and substance of Díaz's politics had provoked deepseated resentment among substantial portions of the northern elite. These landowners, industrialists, mine owners, and merchants were prepared to take up arms in 1910 because their economic and political advancement had been thwarted by the Díaz dictatorship. The penetration of the Mexican economy by foreign capital had been pushed by Díaz to the degree that on the eve of the revolution more than two-thirds of all investment came from foreign sources.[2] The banks were 94 percent foreign owned, and electric power, most large mining enterprises, and the railroads were all under foreign control.[3] Indeed, Díaz had invited foreign capital to finance the construction of Mexico's railroad system and had offered all kinds of monetary inducements to reduce the risk of investment. "In sweeping away the web of resistance which had inhibited foreign capital in the past and in enforcing the peace and security for such capital, Díaz assigned a role to foreigners in Mexico's internal economy which has very few parallels in the history of modern states."[4] American ownership of land, railroads, mines, banks, and industries was particularly marked in the North of Mexico, a situation that frustrated the economic ambitions of the northern Mexican bourgeoisie.[5] And apart from Díaz's encouragement and generous concessions to foreigners, the president had reserved economic and political opportunity at the top for a small, favored elite made up of the men who had come to power with him in the 1870s and their descendants. Members of the northern bourgeoisie who were shut out of this closed circle felt economically and politically excluded. As the dictatorship provided them no institutional means by which to effect a transfer of power to themselves, these men readily aligned themselves with the intellectuals who called the overthrow of the regime.[6] Thus the revolutionary armies of the North included this elite component of men who were fighting to oust the narrow group of Mexican and foreign capitalists in whose hands economic and political power had concentrated.

The northern armies also incorporated members of the middle classes—clerks, teachers, professionals, small businessmen, small- and medium-sized farmers, estate overseers, and ranch foremen—a group whose advancement was also blocked by entrenched elites. Opportunities for employment for the educated middle class had not expanded during the Díaz years at a rate rapid enough to absorb those seeking white collar and professional jobs.[7] And middle-class northerners resented their exclusion from the closed circle of government where all appointments were controlled by Díaz and his henchmen. Furthermore, the economic recession which began in 1905 and reached crisis proportions in 1909 heightened middle-class discontent as it caused further contraction of the already limited opportunities for social and economic mobility open to these people. Thus when the call to revolution came, a substantial proportion of this middle sector cast its lot with the revolutionary forces.

The mass base of the revolution in the North was formed by workers, miners, agricultural laborers, peasants, cowboys, shepherds, muleteers, and drifters. Before the revolution, this sector had been characterized by a pattern of horizontal mobility; according to the work available, men moved back and forth among various jobs on the estates, in the mines, in the factories, or across the border in the United States. But the years of recession and depression immediately prior to 1910 simultaneously eliminated most of these alternative work opportunities. And the northern working class and peasantry, whose economic condition was already precarious at best, found themselves squeezed even harder.[8]

The goals articulated by the revolutionary leaders of the North were as diverse as the social classes participating in the struggle. The middle- and upper-class liberals were calling for political reforms to broaden the base of political participation, for anticlerical legislation to curb the power of the Catholic church, and for nationalistic legislation to impose state control over foreign investment and ownership. They were concerned with putting an end to some of the more glaring abuses of the Díaz regime: forced military conscription, suppression of the press, the total neglect of public education, and the maintenance of order through the use of the brutal *rurales*, a militia of mercenary soldiers.

While the call for "social justice" and "democracy" articulated by liberal politicians appealed to the mass base of revolutionary soldiers, the peasant and worker combatants had goals of their own. These goals corresponded to the workers' and peasants' needs and experiences and were not always well understood by their middle- and upper-class leaders. Workers were concerned with winning the right to organize, guarantees of decent working conditions, adequate pay and job security, the abolition of the company store, and other basic labor rights. Peasants had demands that varied according to the type of work they did and their relationship to the land. Agricultural laborers who worked for wages on commercial estates had grievances that closely resembled those of workers: demands for higher pay, better working conditions, and so forth. Sharecroppers and renters wanted land of their own. They wished to be free of the obligation to return to a landlord in cash or kind a large proportion of their produce. And those peasants who were tied to traditional estates sought relief from the burdens of debt peonage.

At the same time that we can identify separate sets of demands made by elite, middle, and mass sectors incorporated within the revolutionary movement of the North, we must also distinguish this ideologically heterogeneous northern movement from the clearly peasant revolution that developed in the south-central region of Mexico in the state of Morelos. The revolutionary front that emerged in Morelos was a unified, ideologically coherent movement of landless peasants fighting under the leadership of men and women of peasant origin.[9] In this area of Mexico, peasant villages had held title to communal lands from the period of the Spanish conquest until well into the second half of the nineteenth century. The "Liberal Reforms" of the 1850s and 1860s were designed to transform these peasants into yeoman farmers working individual family farms. But the reforms had the effect of permitting large commerical landowners to gain control over the communal village holdings. Deprived of the basis of their livelihood, the peasants of Morelos and other central Mexican states were forced to relinquish their status as independent small holders and attach themselves as peons or serfs to the large estates of the commercial landowners who had gained control of the village lands. This process of land alienation had greatly accelerated during the Díaz years. Thus, when word of the outbreak of revolution in the North reached Morelos, the peasants quickly rallied to the cause. The fight to overthrow the Díaz regime promised to provide the opportunity to reclaim land from the Díaz favorites who had progressively usurped the peasants' holdings. In this respect the goal of the southern revolutionary front was a radical one in that its implementation would have required the total transformation of the land tenure system that existed in 1910. Yet, at the same time, the southerners' demand was an archaic one: the peasants of Morelos were fighting for the restoration of village lands and the return to a traditional order of communal agricultural exploitation. Their vision of revolution had little to do with the demands of the northern elite or middle classes. It did not even comprehend the aspirations of industrial or agricultural workers who had never had any land of their own either to lose or have "restored." It was a limited vision of revolution, but despite its narrow focus, it was a compelling vision for the tens of thousands of peasant men and women who left their wretched homes to join the revolution in Morelos.

THE ARMIES OF THE REVOLUTION

The revolutionary armies that formed in the northern and south-central regions of Mexico are customarily identified by the names of their principal leaders. This convention reflects the degree to which personal charisma rather than ideological commitment was the element that drew and held together each of the revolutionary armies. Political adhesion to one army or another was linked to personal loyalties to the leader and his network of allies. It is particularly difficult to discuss the armies of the North without reference to the general who mustered and led the troops, because these movements were so heterogeneous in composition and ideology that, at times, the only common motivation shared by comrades-in-arms derived from personal attachment to their revolutionary chief. Even on the southern front where the revolution had a clear and coherent ideology, the movement was shaped by the charismatic qualities of its undisputed leader, Emiliano Zapata, whose name came to represent all that the southern peasants, or *zapatistas,* were fighting for.

Born in a peasant village in the state of Morelos, Zapata himself was a horse trainer and trader, rather than a peasant farmer, but his movement fully embodied the aspirations of the peasants of his home region. At the head of an army of 70,000 landless men and women organized in small, highly mobile guerrilla bands, Zapata used the mountains and forests of Morelos as his base of operations. From this tactically advantageous position, he led the fight for the restoration of village lands. As occurs in cases of successful guerrilla warfare, Zapata's followers were not so much an army as a fully mobilized population. The peasant fighters struck swiftly at the federal forces sent into the region to suppress their rebellion, and then retired to their villages, buried their rifles beneath the mud floor of their huts, and resumed their everyday life in the fields. When the enemy penetrated Morelos in search of the "rebel army," they found only peaceful peasants humbly plowing the tiny parcels of land that were all that was left of their once extensive village holdings. Because Zapata's force was supplied directly from the small villages of Morelos, the entire state was devastated in the course of the revolution by federal armies using search-and-destroy techniques to flush out the peasant guerrillas.

The loyalty of Zapata's troops was unique in the history of the revolution. The guerrilla leader lived with a price on his head for ten years. But his followers regarded him with such esteem and affection that no one within his movement gave in to the temptation to betray his leader in return for the cash reward. The passionate loyalty Zapata commanded seemed to grow from his direct and earthy way of dealing with his supporters, and from the fact that he never asked nor accepted any material benefits for himself.

As one peasant who fought for Zapata explained:

> In my judgment, what Zapata was fighting for was just. Porfirio's government took everything away from us. Everything went to the rich, the *hacendados*, those with the power were the masters, and we had nothing. We were their servants because we could not plant or make use of any lands that did not belong to the *hacienda*. So they had us subjugated. We were completely enslaved by the *hacendados*. That is what Zapata fought to set right. . . .
>
> I liked Zapata's plan and that's why, when he came to my village, I went to him. I still hadn't joined but I went up in the hills with *tortillas* and water. . . . I went to see Zapata in his camp. He was in a little house but they wouldn't let me go in. They were suspicious. There were two guards right in front of the door. I stood at a distance, watching. He was sitting inside with his general staff. And he calls out to me, "What do you have there, friend?"
>
> "Nothing, señor. Just my *tortillas*."
>
> "Come in."
>
> "Let's see your *tortillas*. Take them out."
>
> And I gave them all to him. How he liked my *tortillas!*
>
> He and his staff finished them off.
>
> "And what do you have in your gourd? *Pulque?*"
>
> "No, señor, water." And he drank it.[10]

While Zapata's leadership was charismatic, and the goals of his movement compelling to his peasant followers, the revolution of the South never succeeded in attracting any sizable degree of nonpeasant support. Throughout the years of struggle, Zapata was able to count upon the adhesion and collaboration of a group of urban and rural radical intellectuals. These men helped Zapata formulate his *Plan de Ayala* and other proclamations and programs calling for the breakup of the large estates and the restoration of lands to the peasant villages. But apart from these intellectuals, Zapata seemed unable to understand or reach urban Mexicans. Thus a serious limitation of *zapatismo* lay in the movement's inability to broaden its appeal or move beyond the land question to other issues that concerned industrial workers. Another limitation was that Zapata and his people constituted an effective fighting force only when they fought on their home ground, the mountains of Morelos. When they ventured beyond their own territory, the *zapatistas* were like fish out of water. This is what happened when they marched on Mexico City. Cut off from their supply base, the guerrillas could not hold the capital, and so they returned to their mountains to continue the struggle to defend the lands they had already won.

While the *zapatista* guerrillas held off federal troops in Morelos, on the northern front Díaz's soldiers clashed with a large number of different "revolutionary armies," each with its own charismatic leader who gave his movement a specific social and political character. Among these armies, three in particular played determining roles in the course of the revolution.

The army led by Venustiano Carranza, a large landowner, was a conservative force among the revolutionaries. During the Díaz years, Carranza had served as a senator of the republic. But when the call to revolution came, Carranza armed the peons of his own *hacienda*, put together a small army, and joined the fight on the side of Madero. Carranza's force was called the Constitutionalist Army, and its leadership was provided almost entirely by middle-class liberals. These men fought for political reforms that would alter the worst aspects of the Díaz dictatorship, and would replace the despotism of Díaz with a narrowly based "constitutional democracy." But the *carrancista* leaders hated and feared the revolutionary groups that fought for radical social change just as much as they had resented the oppressions of the Díaz regime.[11]

Fighting on the same side with Carranza were the troops of General Alvaro Obregón. Obregón was the son of a once wealthy rancher who had fallen on hard times. As a young man the general worked at a variety of trades—mechanic, salesman, sugar miller, and others—before returning to ranching. This background gave Obregón experience with people, places, and ideas somewhat outside his own social milieu, and helped him to identify with some of the more radical social goals of the revolution. In particular, his experiences enabled him to understand the grievances and aspirations of workers, and his ability to attract a working-class following would eventually alter the course of the revolution. "Obregón was by no means a socialist, but favored nationalist legislation and agrarian and labor reforms which would, at one and the same time, curtail United States encroachment, break the power of the great landed families, and widen the opportunities in the market for both labor and his kind of middle class."[12]

In 1912, inspired by the ideas of Madero, the liberals, and the radical intellectuals, Obregón gathered a group of 300 fellow ranchers into a fighting force "that came to be known as the Rich Man's Battalion."[13] Apart from the small- and middle-scale commercial farmers who joined this band, teachers, tradesmen, white-collar professionals, and a variety of other middle-class elements were attracted to Obregón's cause. The ranks of Obregón's force, as elsewhere in the North, were filled out with miners, cowboys, industrial and agricultural workers, and peons from the huge *haciendas* of the northern states.

Undoubtedly the most able of all the northern generals, Obregón was a student of military strategy and in the course of the war proved himself a master tactician. He studied the progress of the Great War in Europe, and applied in battle what he had learned of modern trench warfare. Of all the northern generals, Obregón was perhaps the man best qualified for leadership.[14] He was a flexible, well-disciplined person who was able to understand goals beyond his own self-interest.

The last of the most important revolutionary armies was the "Northern Division" led by the famous bandit-turned-revolutionary, General Pancho Villa. Villa's origins were as humble as Zapata's. He spent his youth laboring as a peon on a large *hacienda;* then, after a brief career as a mule driver, Villa lived for twenty-two years as a cattle rustler and bandit. By the time the revolution broke out, he already enjoyed a widespread reputation as a Robin Hood who stole from the rich landowner to give to the poor peon. Villa was not an ideologically sophisticated man. But in a good fight between the old dictator in Mexico City—supported by the rich landowners—and the new liberal leaders from the North, Pancho Villa cast his lot with Francisco Madero and the revolutionaries.

John Reed, the American journalist who traveled with Villa's army as a war correspondent, described the bandit this way:

His reckless and romantic bravery is the subject of countless poems. They tell, for example, how one of his band named Reza was captured by the *rurales* and bribed to betray Villa. Villa heard of it and sent word into the city of Chihuahua that he was coming for Reza. In broad daylight he entered the city on horse-back, took ice cream in the Plaza—the ballad is very explicit on this point—and rode up and down the streets until he found Reza strolling with his sweetheart in the Sunday crowd on the Paseo Bolívar, where he shot him and escaped. In time of famine he fed whole districts, and took care of entire villages evicted by the soldiers under Porfirio Díaz's outrageous land law. Everywhere he was known as The Friend of the Poor. He was the Mexican Robin Hood.[15]

Villa recruited his forces from the cowboys, miners, small ranchers, bandits, gamblers, and drifters of Chihuahua State. In the other armies of the revolution, the women and children of soldiers normally traveled along with the troops, often because their homes had been destroyed, or their lives so totally uprooted that they had nowhere else to go. As a result, the movement of revolutionary forces often resembled the migrations of whole populations rather than an army on the march. But Villa often persuaded his troops to leave their women and children behind, and he instituted a technique of rapid, forced marches and surprise attacks that were the key to his military success. Most of Villa's troops were men who had lived half their lives in the saddle, and 40,000 strong, the Northern Division comprised a formidable cavalry. Indeed Villa's most impressive military victories were achieved with daring cavalry maneuvers, while his most disastrous defeats, toward the end of the revolution, came when he failed to understand the limitations of a cavalry attack used against an entrenched army protected by barbed wire and machine guns.[16]

The social goal closest to Villa's heart was free public schooling. Unlike Zapata, who enjoyed the benefits of two years of primary education, Villa was illiterate until the age of forty-six when socialist intellectuals, imprisoned with him in the Mexico City penitentiary, taught the passionately eager general the rudiments of reading and writing. Villa never lost the illiterate's overwhelming faith in the power of education to erase injustice and social inequality. From the Villa camp John Reed wrote, "Often I have heard him say: 'When I passed such and such street this morning I saw a lot of kids. Let's put a school there.' "[17] In this haphazard fashion Villa established more than fifty primary schools during his reign as military governor of Chihuahua State.

Apart from his commitment to education, Villa's concern with social reform was sporadic and ill-defined. His movement had no clear political ideology and his army was so amorphous that it provided a home for any opportunist who sought to penetrate its ranks.

> More a force of nature than of politics, the villista party was commotion rampant. These northern drifters could give their populism no real point. Cowboys, muleskinners, bandits, railroad laborers, peddlers, refugee peons, the villistas had no definite class interests or local attachments. And to certain ambitious operators . . . this disorder was an opportunity. . . . Villa was the very incarnation of irregularity, and his men took him as a model.[18]

Although his movement was originally allied with the forces of Carranza and Obregón, distrust, rivalry, and, ultimately, betrayal by Carranza led Villa to break with the conservative and moderate northern generals and to identify himself with the radical demands of the zapatistas. Nevertheless, we cannot say that Villa's concept of revolution was as fully developed or as radical as Zapata's. For, even at the height of his military strength, Villa never attempted to seize landholdings and distribute them to the landless in a systematic fashion as Zapata had done in the South. Villa often gave away tracts of land in the same generous spirit that he distributed thousands of pesos of the currency he printed himself in the basement of the Governor's Palace in Chihuahua City. But neither Villa nor the generals who fought under him were much interested in establishing the legal bases or the mechanisms for a full scale land reform program. For one thing, the arid expanses of the North did not lend themselves to parcelization and distribution in small lots. For another, given the low level of political consciousness that characterized Villa's officers and troops, the large estates that were seized by the *villistas* tended to remain in the hands of Villa's generals. These men used the estates to create an upper-class way of life for themselves, becoming a landed elite in their own right with interests directly opposed to those who demanded land reform.[19]

YEARS OF CONFLICT AND BLOODSHED

These were the principal forces that made the revolution against the old regime. Díaz's institutional structure, sclerotic and decayed after so many years of rule, fell to pieces more quickly than any of the protagonists would have thought possible. And only a year after the fighting began, Francisco Madero, head of the liberals, took office as the revolution's first president.

The Revolution Comes to Power

Sadly, Madero proved incapable of controlling the forces he had unleashed. A weak-willed, inconsistent idealist, Madero was unable to provide firm leadership or to reconcile the contradictions between conservatives like Carranza and radicals like Zapata. In all fairness, it is difficult to imagine that the strongest and most able of politicians could have satisfied the demands of so many different forces fighting for so many different goals. Madero certainly was unable to play this role, although he struggled bravely. Unfortunately he never really understood the passions he had kindled with his call to revolution. He never understood the overpowering hunger for land that had filled the ranks of Zapata's army with desperate, landless men and women. Madero wanted to give full democratic rights to the people at a time when such niceties as votes and electoral contests were largely irrelevant. He expected that he could govern with mercy and humility at the moment that the reactionary forces were plotting his overthrow.[20] Madero did not appreciate that he needed the armed support of the revolutionary forces to consolidate his control over the Mexican state. For Madero the struggle had successfully concluded when he took his seat in the presidential chair. Díaz's army, administration, and Senate were left intact while the new president attempted to delimit the content of the revolution and to contain the revolutionary forces that had emerged.[21] Madero implored his allies to lay down their arms and accept the revolution that he would construct. But none of the principal generals had enough confidence in the new regime to disband his army without some concrete assurance that the new revolution would reflect his own concept of what a revolution ought to be.

Madero also faced strong opposition from the United States government. President William Howard Taft was initially sympathetic to Madero's government, but as soon as he realized that Madero had no intention of granting special concessions to American capital or taking measures to protect American property in Mexico, Taft withdrew his support.[22] To make matters worse, the American ambassador to Mexico, Henry Lane Wilson, was closely linked to American financial interests which were in direct competition with those of the Madero family. Accordingly, Wilson became "a fanatical enemy of the government to which he was accredited," and did everything in his power—which was considerable—to bring that government down.[23]

Ambassador Wilson proceeded to create panic among American citizens in Mexico, sending thousands fleeing from the republic, and on the Ambassador's advice, 100,000 American troops were massed on the Mexican border. Wilson then brought to the embassy the leading counterrevolutionary conspirators, Felix Díaz, nephew of the deposed dictator, Bernardo Reyes, and Victoriano Huerta, and assisted them in formulating their plot against Madero. Four days later Madero and his closest associates were dead, the sinister Huerta had assumed the presidency, and Wilson gleefully dispatched the news to Washington that "a wicked despotism has fallen."[24]

But the United States government was now headed by Woodrow Wilson. And the new American president was reluctant to recognize Huerta because it was clear even in Washington that Huerta's government was despotic.[25] Ambassador Wilson was recalled and replaced, and a new type of U.S. intervention began. The new American policy in Mexico involved arms sales to favored revolutionary factions, arms embargoes against revolutionary forces unacceptable to U.S. business interests, and the seizure of the port of Veracruz at the cost of some two hundred Mexican lives.[26]

With Madero gone, the fighting began anew. In March 1913, Carranza sent forth the call to rebellion to avenge the death of Madero and overthrow Huerta. The revolutionary armies united to crush the counterrevolution of Huerta, and their strength was such that Huerta's reign in Mexico City was relatively short-lived. He managed to control Mexico for eighteen months, from February 1913 to July 1914. Then Huerta was driven from power by General Carranza who had finally emerged as the dominant force among the armies of the revolution.

Political, Economic, and Social Dislocation

Another six years of bloodshed followed. Carranza's appropriation of the revolution was challenged by Zapata and Villa and later by

Obregón. The various armies of the North split and reunited along new lines. In the North, where the revolutionary troops had always lacked a clear political orientation, former comrades-in-arms now rode against one another in battle. Soldiers surrendered to an enemy force one day and, as a condition of their release, took up arms the next day to fight under a new general. Betrayal followed betrayal, and most of the principal revolutionary leaders died at the hands of assassins and traitors.

When the bloodletting came to an end in the early 1920s, the veterans returned to their villages and towns to find that there was not much left to come home to. The Mexican economy was in shambles and thousands of miles of roads, bridges, and railroad track had been blown up or torn out. The telegraph and telephone systems as well as public utilities were so seriously disrupted that they had to be completely reconstructed.[27] Mining, the most important industry in Mexico before the revolution, was now in decline.[28] Production of all staple crops, particularly beans and corn, was down to about half of the prerevolutionary yield. In 1924, for example, less corn was harvested than in any other year during the previous two centuries.[29] Cattle that had not been slaughtered on the spot to feed the troops of the revolutionary armies were often rounded up and driven across the U.S. border, where they were traded for arms and ammunition. Hacienda buildings, sugar and cotton mills, and crops had been burned to the ground, and where large estates were left more or less intact, landowners often refused to sow their fields for fear that revolutionary forces would reap the harvest. As a result of this severe dislocation in cattle raising and agriculture, food prices soared. Widespread starvation prompted food riots in cities throughout Mexico, and each day hundreds of peasants and urban poor who had survived the armed phase of the revolution now died of malnutrition.[30]

After more than a decade of fighting that intimately touched the lives of millions of people, the old order of the Díaz regime had been overturned and a series of governments—some reactionary, some conservative, some moderately progressive—had followed in rapid succession. But the great mass of Mexicans were economically no better off than before the revolution. Workers still labored long hours for pitiful wages under miserable conditions. And those who had joined the revolutionary armies to fight for land had not witnessed the fulfillment of the promise that "the land would belong to the tiller." After so many years of hardship and destruction, a comprehensive land reform program was not to be initiated in earnest until the late 1930s. Although workers and particularly peasants constituted the bulk of all revolutionary combatants and casualties, the revolution did not bring them the economic, political, and social status for which they had fought.

The "triumph of the revolution" did not alter their low status because the politically conscious peasantry and working class were not sectors that emerged victorious from the revolution. On the contrary, the gains made by peasant armies, like those led by Zapata, were undermined or neutralized by the manipulations of politicians like Carranza who represented the aspirations of landowners, industrialists, and a highly mobile and ambitious middle class. While the workers and peasants were the principal actors in the revolutionary drama and it was mostly their blood that was shed, there was no point during a decade of conflict when peasant troops or workers' battalions, fighting under peasant or working-class leadership, were able to seize and hold national power.[31] By 1920 Zapata had been treacherously assassinated. Pancho Villa had been defeated in battle, and his once powerful army of 40,000 reduced to an ineffectual force of a few thousand. In addition, as we have noted before, many of the *villista* generals (and even some of Zapata's men) who had begun the revolution as popular leaders, used the spoils of war to enrich themselves. As a result of this tendency, those peasant or working-class leaders who were not eliminated in the course of the revolution often acquired middle-class characteristics and middle-class interests and were quickly assimilated into the new ruling class.[32]

THE NEW RULING CLASS

By the end of the revolution the leadership of Mexico had fallen into the hands of Carranza and the men closest to the old general, and a new ruling coalition had formed. The coalition was composed of (a) the new elite of recently landed revolutionary generals, (b) industrialists and businessmen who had prospered during and immediately after the revolution, and (c) members of the old land-owning oligarchy who had become aware that they could pursue their prerevolutionary interests and preserve much of their prerevolutionary status by declaring their adherence to the new regime.

Not every family that had enjoyed social prestige and economic and political power before the revolution was able to hold onto its former position. Some of the old landowners lost everything in the revolution. Some died in the course of the war, and many others chose to emigrate to Europe or the United States. But a remarkable number of these families survived with their property more or less intact, and some of the most economically powerful were able to further enrich themselves under the new order.[33]

Old money was joined by new wealth amassed during the revolution and the period of physical reconstruction that followed. Reconstruction offered the growing community of capitalists a wide variety of opportunities for investment and profit.[34] Friends and relatives of the successful revolutionary generals grew rich, sometimes overnight, on highly lucrative government contracts.[35] In addition to the reconstruction of the communications network and the initiation of public works projects, a variety of industries introduced before the revolution developed rapidly in the 1920s and 1930s. Mining picked up and petroleum production soared.[36] Iron, steel, cement, paper, textiles, shoes, beer, tobacco, soap, sugar refining, and flour milling were all expanded from their prerevolutionary base, while new enterprises—among them metal goods, window glass, and foodstuffs—developed for the first time during this period of economic recovery.[37]

The emergence of a new capitalist class, or "industrial bourgeoisie," and the consolidation of this group's political power has been described by Andre Gunder Frank.

> The viable economic base of the more aristocratic upper class was destroyed by the Revolution. But many of its members and their wealth survived. Their money was invested in finance, commerce, industry and later again in agriculture; and the ex-aristocrats became the nucleus of the new bourgeoisie. Their ranks were soon supplemented by their erstwhile enemies, the individual beneficiaries of the same Revolution, many politicians and generals among them. As their economic position became consolidated, so did their political power.[38]

The interests of the new bourgeoisie differed, of course, from those of the old aristocracy. The new group possessed a modern capitalist orientation and looked to the commercialization of agriculture, industrialization, and a minimum level of government regulation in order to promote their modern financial, commercial, or industrial enterprises. It was hardly as if nothing had altered since the days when Mexico was controlled by Porfirio Díaz and his coterie. On the contrary, the social and economic changes wrought by the Mexican Revolution were extensive, and they laid the basis for a modern and industrialized Mexico. But it is important to understand that the changes that were produced by a decade of conflict were changes most appropriately summed up in the term "bourgeois revolution"—a transformation reflecting the interests of those people in a society who control capital and the means of production, and those people who share in the profits of capital. It was the Carranzas, the Obregóns, and the other representatives of the rising Mexican bourgeoisie who gave ideological character to the political order that emerged from the revolution. Although the Mexican Revolution was made by peasants and workers, it was in no way a "popular revolution" since neither the peasants nor the workers gained effective power, nor did their representatives come to control the state. As we have noted, for all their sacrifices the peasants and workers in fact derived very little immediate benefit from the revolution. The benefits they did receive came in the form of legislative guarantees.

The expressed goals of the popular forces that had participated in the revolutionary struggle were written into a new Constitution of 1917. This constitution became the one legacy provided by the revolution to the worker and peasant combatants.

THE WORKER'S LEGACY

It is one of the ironies of Mexican history that the great legislative breakthroughs for the Mexican working class were made during the period when the dominant *politico* in Mexico was General Venustiano Carranza—hardly a figure one would be tempted to describe as a great friend of the working man. The labor legislation that came out of the Mexican Revolution was, in its day, the most progressive body of labor guarantees on record anywhere in the world. Yet, ironically, the very fact that such laws were produced was due to the political and strategical needs of a conservative on his march to national power.

Although Carranza was a conservative within the revolutionary coalition of the North, the general made his first overtures to labor as early as 1914. At that point in the revolution, Carranza's forces (led by Obregón) had taken Mexico City, ousted the reactionary Huerta, and installed Carranza in the National Palace. But Carranza found himself in a very precarious military and political situation. In September 1914, Zapata had renounced Carranza because of the latter's lack of concern for land reform, while Pancho Villa, who had once figured among Carranza's outstanding divisional generals, had met secretly with Zapata and agreed with the guerrilla leader that Carranza could never be trusted with the leadership of the revolution.

Carranza countered by calling Villa and the other "Constitutionalist" leaders to Mexico City to discuss the program for the new *carrancista* regime. But Villa and his forces refused to meet in territory controlled by Carranza, and so the proceedings were moved to the northern city of Aguascalientes and the meeting became the Convention of Aguascalientes. This city rapidly filled up with Villa's troops and, against the express wishes of Carranza, the *villistas* brought Zapata's representatives into the convention hall. Among the *zapatistas* was one of the greatest orators of the period, Antonio Díaz Soto y Gama. Proclaiming Zapata as the heir of Karl Marx, St. Francis of Assisi, and Jesus Christ rolled into one, Díaz Soto y Gama explained to the delegates the basic goals of Zapata's movement.[39] Speaking with great eloquence, he persuaded the convention to accept the principles of Zapata's *Plan de Ayala,* a blueprint for radical agrarian reform that Zapata had already put into practice in the areas of Morelos State that he controlled.[40]

Carranza chose to ignore the results of the convention, dismissing the meeting as an inconsequential pack of *villistas* swayed by a bunch of hot-headed *agraristas.*[41] But Carranza was in serious political trouble. Only a month or so after his loss of face at the Convention of Aguascalientes, Zapata's forces, dressed in their loose, white peasant clothes, enormous sombreros, and heavily armed, marched on Mexico City. And when the Morelos peasants reached the capital, they were joined by Pancho Villa's Northern Division. This display of military strength forced Carranza to remove his troops to the port of Veracruz, on the Gulf of Mexico. Desperate for military support to counter the challenge of the *zapatistas* and *villistas,* Carranza turned to the working class for the military clout that he needed.

To recruit the support of workers, Carranza sent his ally, General Obregón, to negotiate an agreement with the labor unions of Mexico City. Obregón, always skillful in appealing to workers, persuaded the union leaders to send their members to the front in separate units called "red battalions." Carranza, in turn, gave union leaders his permission to proceed behind the lines, "to agitate and organize the workers in the districts reclaimed from the enemy."[42]

In return for support on the battlefield, Carranza issued his Decree of December 12, 1914. In this document Carranza openly acknowledged the insufficiency of the narrow political goals which had been the rallying cry of the liberals who unleashed the revolution in 1910.[43] Carranza had finally realized that the scope of the revolution had to be enlarged if it were to express the social and economic aspirations for which the peasants and workers were willing to fight. And, therefore, in the Decree of December 12, Carranza stated his intention "to establish a regime which will guarantee the equality of the Mexicans among themselves; . . . legislation to better the condition of the peasant, of the worker, of the miner, and in general of the working classes. . . ."[44]

With the Decree of December 12, Carranza attempted to reassure organized labor that progressive labor legislation would have top priority for any government he might head. He promised that his administration would give attention to the "just claims of the workers in any conflict arising between them and employers." Although Carranza was anything but wholehearted in these gestures toward the working class, Alvaro Obregón, Carranza's divisional general, had in fact maintained close ties with organized labor and Obregón played a key role in winning labor support at this critical time.[45] It was Obregón, for example, who expropriated the Mexico City Jockey Club and presented the building to the labor unions as a headquarters for their central organization, the *Casa del Obrero Mundial* (House of the Workers of the World). The "Casa" had been established as a training, organizational, administrative, and propaganda center for the entire Mexican labor movement. When Obregón and the other *carrancista* agents first approached labor leaders to bargain for their support, there was great dissension among the membership. Once the decision to support Carranza was taken, many workers individually deserted their union battalions to join the struggle under the leadership of Villa or Zapata.[46] But even with a substantial number of workers leaving the so-called red battalions to fight with the revolutionary forces of Villa or Zapata, Carranza's army, reinforced by the influx of workers, militarily overwhelmed both the *villistas* and the *zapatistas*.

Since the support they had given to Carranza proved important to his ultimate success, in 1916 organized labor looked to the general to make good his promise of progressive legislation for the working class. In November of that year, delegates from all over the country met in the central Mexican city of Querétaro to draft a new constitution. Once again, it was Carranza who called together the convention, and once again he tried to pack the meeting with his own people by excluding the representatives of his political enemies, Zapata and Villa. This time Carranza felt reasonably confident that his own people and his own political line would dominate the proceedings from start to finish. The delegates to the convention shared an ideological perspective that has been described as "corporate liberalism"[47] They accepted private capitalist enterprise as the system that would prevail in Mexico, and they differed fundamentally only to the degree that they supported or rejected the principle that the state should play a strong regulatory role in the process of capitalist development. This disagreement became evident in the final months of 1916 as delegates quickly grouped themselves into two opposing factions: the moderate liberals or "reformists" who supported Carranza and rejected state intervention, and the radical liberals, or "Jacobins," who identified themselves with the more progressive General Alvaro Obregón and pushed for an active regulatory role for the Mexican state.[48] Among these radical liberals were a group of revolutionary leaders who had fought with Carranza's armies, but whose deepest sympathies lay with the agrarian cause of Zapata. The *agraristas* at the convention were determined to see the principles of Zapata's *Plan de Ayala* incorporated into the constitution itself.

After several weeks of infighting and political intrigue, the radical liberal faction gradually gained the upper hand, and the more conservative *carrancistas* were forced to give way on the most crucial issues.[49] Carranza presented to the convention his own proposals for the new constitution. Carranza's draft was a conservative document, emphasizing restraints on the power of government, and sticking closely to the precepts established sixty years earlier in the old Constitution of 1857. His proposal offered no program for land reform, specified no restraints on the power of the church, and offered few specific guarantees to labor.

But the Jacobins fought back, and while the final draft of the constitution adopted six weeks later included about three-fourths of the 132 articles originally proposed by Carranza, the document that emerged was far more radical in both spirit and letter than the proposals Carranza originally had in mind.[50] The radical liberal members of the assembly were determined to extend all the existing guarantees to workers and to state them explicitly in a separate article dealing exclusively with labor. The result, Article 123 of the Mexican Constitution, was, as we have noted, the most progressive piece of labor legislation in any country of the world of 1917.

First, the article established the power of the government to intervene in labor relations in order to promote conditions favorable to the workers. It guaranteed the right to organize unions and the right to strike. These rights were to be enjoyed by workers in public service, as well as those employed by private enterprise. Article 123 established an eight-hour workday and carefully limited overtime. Well-defined limitations on child labor were set, and the principle of equal pay for equal work regardless of sex was laid down. A provision for maternity leave and limits on physical labor for pregnant women were included in the legislation. The authors of the article were careful to state explicitly that

> The minimum wage for workers shall be *sufficient to satisfy the normal material, social and cultural needs* of a head of family and provide for the compulsory education of the children. In every agricultural, commercial, manufacturing and mining enterprise, *the workers have the right to share in the profits.* . . . A social security law is considered of public utility, and shall include disability insurance, life insurance, insurance against unemployment, sickness, accidents and the like. . . .[51]

The constitution established employers' liability for work accidents, and it granted every worker at least one day of rest each week. All wages were to be paid in legal currency rather than merchandise or credit at a company store, and three months' severance pay was due any worker laid off his job. In addition, "employers must furnish workmen with comfortable and sanitary dwelling places. . . . They shall also establish schools, clinics and other services necessary to the community when factories are not located in inhabited places. . . ."

Both state and national governments were required to enact specific labor legislation in conformity with the guidelines laid down in Article 123.[52] Through these provisions and the requirement that all state labor codes conform to these constitutional principles, the radical liberal drafters meant to insure that the working class would receive the full share of the revolutionary legacy that belonged to them.

THE PEASANTS' LEGACY

The dominant radical group responsible for the progressive labor legislation was every bit as determined to provide both the constitutional principles and the mechanism through which the peasants could take possession of the land for which they had fought. Article 27 of the new constitution established the nation's ownership of all land and water resources, all forests, minerals, and other products of nature. In Article 27 the radical liberals were able to lay down the conditions for expropriations of private holdings by the state. The key passage is as follows:

> The nation shall at all times have the right to establish regulations for private property which the public interest may dictate, such as those regulating the use of natural resources for conservation purposes or ensuring a more equitable distribution of public wealth. With this end in view, the necessary measures shall be taken to break up the large estates;[53]

In addition to restricting land ownership on the part of the church and foreigners, Article 27 provided for the restoration of land to peasants who had been despoiled of their communally held properties before the revolution, and the distribution of land to "population centres that lack land and water, or do not have them in quantities sufficient for the needs of their people. . . ." These grants were to be made from the expropriation and distribution of the land holdings of "adjacent large properties."[54]

In summary, the constitution adopted in 1917 provided both the most progressive array of guarantees to labor known anywhere in the world at that time, plus the legislative basis for the widest scale land reform program in history. The radical framers of the constitution left the hall in Querétaro deeply satisfied that, within the framework of a capitalist system, they had secured for both workers and peasants the legislative foundation for the economic and social justice they had sought in the revolution.

UNFEASIBLE AND UNENFORCEABLE LEGISLATION

Unfortunately the mere stroke of pen on parchment could not transform the aspirations of peasants and workers into reality. Two very basic problems stood in the way. The first was the nature of the legislation itself. The second problem was the conflict between the goals expressed in Articles 27 and 123 and the social, economic, and political interests of the men to whom the task of enforcing that legislation would fall.

With the best of good intentions, the radical liberals at the Constitutional Convention had drawn up a set of labor laws that unfortunately did not relate to the social and economic conditions of Mexico in 1917. Deeply influenced by the advanced proposals of European and North American labor movements, the authors of Article 123 adopted as their own some of the most progressive ideas that were current in capitalist countries at that time. But Mexico was far from comparable to countries like Britain and the United States in terms of her political and economic structure, industrial base, capital reserves, and the level of political consciousness and organization of her work force. Mexico had just emerged from a war that had divided the working class and peasantry and had devastated the economy. The men who wrote Article 123 made the mistake of trying to institute laws appropriate for societies in an advanced stage of development in a country that was recovering from war and had only just embarked on the road to capitalist development.

Thus, for example, it was unfeasible to place sanctions on child labor in an economy so backward that families relied for their survival on the pitiful wages received by children. Likewise, the establishment of minimum wage was equally unrealistic in a period when there were relatively few factories and millions eager to enter the industrial work force. Progressive labor legislation is a luxury that belongs to a fairly advanced stage of development. The problem for Mexicans was how to *arrive* at the point where progressive legislation could even be considered. And yet the labor code written into the constitution presupposed that this stage had already been reached. As always, when abstract principles clash with an unfortunate reality, it is the unworkable, if admirable, principles which fall by the wayside. Thus, it is no surprise that Article 123 was not taken very seriously either by the postrevolutionary political leaders, nor the industrialists and businessmen who were to build Mexico's industrial base. Had they attempted to apply these impressive humanitarian laws to the conditions that then existed in Mexico, the capitalist development that these powerful groups desired would have been impossible to achieve.

In contrast, the constitution's agrarian legislation did not conflict with the goal of capitalist development in Mexico. On the contrary, the long-term effects of land reform generally encourage capitalist development. Land reform programs normally break down traditional structures, stimulate efficient utilization of land resources, move people from the backward agricultural sector into the cities where they provide a pool of cheap labor for the factories, and create internal markets for the goods of industry. The problem with Article 27 was not that it clashed with the long-run needs of capitalist development, but rather that it conflicted with the short-term, immediate interests of the men who came to power at the close of the revolution.

The radical liberals who dominated the Constitutional Convention were never in a position to enforce the legislation they had written. It would be General Carranza, a landowner and industrialist, who would assume the presidency in 1917, and to him fell the task of enforcing the constitution. Once Carranza was elected president, the fortunes of both peasants and workers took a turn for the worse. Carranza, who had actively sought the support of labor, now turned his back on the working class, which only three years earlier had turned the tide in his favor. The labor leaders he had once courted with promises of favorable legislation were now the victims of brutal government repression. In 1923, Carleton Beals described Carranza's administration in this way:

> ... the revolutionary elements were one by one eliminated and supplanted by politicians and unprincipled militarists. The enlightened constitutional provisions were ignored or malconstrued ... land was not distributed except in certain states where it was forcibly torn away at the first opportunity, labor not only did not receive the protection accorded it by the constitutional code, but its organizations were openly persecuted.[55]

OBSTACLES TO LAND REFORM

Carranza's relationship with the agrarian movement was one of the darker stains on his political career. At the point in the revolution when he feared the growing power of Zapata's forces in Morelos, Carranza attempted to undercut Zapata's appeal to peasants with generous overtures and concessions of his own. Thus in 1915, Carranza issued the Decree of January 6, a document that restated some of the main points of Zapata's *Plan de Ayala*. Ironically, it is Carranza's decree that is generally taken as the *formal* beginning of the great Mexican land reform. But, in fact, once Carranza felt secure in his power, he turned his back on the peasants, just as he did with the working class. He used workers' battalions to combat peasant armies, and in 1919, Carranza personally arranged for the assassination of Zapata and other radical peasant leaders.[56] Shortly before he was assassinated, Zapata himself denounced Carranza's betrayal of the peasantry in an open letter published in March 1919.

> You have betrayed the agrarian reform and taken over the *haciendas* only to give the property and its proceeds to your favorite generals . . . a group of friends are helping you enjoy the spoils of war: wealth, honours, business deals, banquets, luxurious and licentious feasts, drunken carousing, orgies of ambition, of power and of blood. . . . The hopes of the people have been turned to scorn. . . .[57]

On the basis of his previous record, the *agraristas* felt nothing but despair when Carranza was installed in the Presidential Palace. Although progressive legislation was on the books, without the support of the federal government there was little hope that a politically weak and divided peasantry could successfully petition for land grants in accordance with the procedures stipulated in Article 27. And government support would not come as long as Carranza, a landowner himself, remained in power.

And so, despite official acceptance of agrarian reform as a main tenet of the revolution, sporadic land distribution took place on only a token scale over the next twenty years. Although militant *agrarista* organizations survived in some areas of Mexico,[58] the armed opposition of landowners was usually sufficient to repress these peasant movements in their efforts to force the application of land reform legislation.

The landholders' opposition to the implementation of agrarian reform took a variety of forms. The most brutal was the use of private armies or police forces called "white guards." The white guards, conservative peasants in the pay of the landlords, specialized in the assassination of *agrarista* organizers and the destruction of crops and homes belonging to peasants bold enough to seek land grants under the agrarian law. Because the land reform law stipulated that only peasants living in "population centers" of a certain size were qualified to petition for land grants, the white guards often scattered the population of whole villages by burning houses, diverting river waters to demolish adobe huts, or by killing off so many villagers that the number required for the petitioning process would not be reached. If these methods failed, landowners blacklisted those peasants who had enrolled their names on an agrarian petition, and these unlucky peasants would have to leave the region to find work.

In their fight against land reform, the landowning class found an ally in the Catholic church. In September 1922, a peasant league in the state of Durango filed the following report with the archbishop of the state:

> Father Reyes of Gómez Palacio is so violently anti-*agrarista* that he refused

to administer the last rites to Eulalio Martínez, merely because, in life, he had been an *agrarista*.

Father Santiago Zamora of Mapimí sustains on every occasion that taking possession of idle lands is theft, and the government that authorizes it, as well as the peasants and their families who benefit from it, are bandits.

The priest of Nazas, Manuel Gallego, is an avowed protector of the *hacendados* of that region, whom he serves unreservedly, attacking Article 27 of the Constitution within and outside of the church.

Father Margarito Barraza, formerly of the Hacienda of Dolores, now of El Rodeo, has preached incessantly against agrarianism, and has publicly declared that all members of the Agrarian Committee of El Rodeo shall be without benefit of clergy even in the hour of death.

Anastasio Arellano, curate of Peñon Blanco, threatened the Secretary of the Agrarian Committee, telling him that upon all who touched the lands of Pablo Martínez del Río would fall the "curse of God." . . . Father Arellano is sold body and soul to the owners of the Hacienda de Catalina, which has resulted in his possession of an automobile and other properties which do not harmonize with the humility and poverty which Jesus preached.[59]

The effect of the church's anti-agrarian position was powerful enough in a northern state like Durango, which lacked a strong Catholic tradition. Much greater was the effect of clerical opposition in various western and southern states of Mexico, where the influence of the church over the peasantry had always been a determining factor in the social and political life of the region.

In 1926–27, Ernest Gruening studied the agrarian problem in Mexico. While traveling in the state of Guanajuato, he interviewed a priest who was attached to a large *hacienda*, and ministered to the community of peons who worked the *hacienda* lands.

"Have these workers been offered their communal lands?" I asked one of them.

"They have not, they do not want them," replied the priest.

"Why do they not want them?" I asked. "It seems strange that anyone should not want something that is given for nothing."

"They would not know how to take care of the lands if they got them," said the priest.

"Why not, aren't they working the land now?" I inquired.

"They could work the land, but they wouldn't know anything about buying and selling, and they would lose the money they had put in for seed and tools if they could ever get enough together to buy these."

A few minutes later, Gruening approached one of the peasants laboring in the fields of the *hacienda*, and the following exchange took place.

"You people haven't received any *ejidos* in this region?"

"No, señor, we haven't."

"Is it because you don't want them?"
"Yes, we want them, but—"
"But what?"
"If we got them, we wouldn't be able to take care of them."
"How is that? Aren't you working the land now? How would it be any different if you were working your own plot?"
"Oh, working the land would be the same, but we poor people wouldn't know anything about selling our product, and we would lose whatever we had paid for seed and tools."
"Who told you that?"
"The boss."
"Anyone else?"
"The padre."[60]

As Gruening's account indicates, the alliance of the priest and the landlord would not have functioned so effectively to block land reform had it not been that a great many peons had accepted and internalized a concept of themselves as inherently inferior and destined by nature to live in servitude. Linked by personal and paternalistic bonds to a powerful landlord, many peasants were reluctant to cast off the ties that bound them to the patrón and his estate. In contrast with the agricultural worker who sold his labor for a cash wage, peons who were attached to the hacienda and given a hut or a subsistence plot in return for labor enjoyed a kind of security as their reward for loyalty to the landlord.[61] The patrón might be a harsh and cruel father figure, but his paternalism was at least a familiar arrangement to the peasant, accustomed all his life to play the role of dependent.

In the minds of the labor force, the person of the hacienda owner—who mediates between them and the outside world—may also come to represent the hacienda itself: his well-being may seem a validation of their collective effort. . . . Once such a system becomes established, its functioning may become essential to the feeling of security of those who must live in terms of it. Disturbances of the system, whether due to changes in the position of the worker or of the owner, tend to be felt as threats to a way of life.[62]

Given the security provided by the known, if oppressive, condition of dependent peon, we should not be surprised that many peasants did not push harder to obtain the ejidal lands to which they were entitled under agrarian law.

Yet another barrier to the implementation of land reform was the extensive foreign ownership of land in Mexico. At the outbreak of the revolution, more than 40 percent of Mexican agricultural land was owned directly and indirectly by American citizens.[63] By 1923, the pattern of land ownership still heavily favored foreigners; approximately one-fifth of all private agricultural property belonged to foreigners. Americans owned the greatest amount (about 41 million acres), followed, in order, by Spanish, British, German, French, and a variety of other foreign landowners and landowning companies.[64] Most foreign landowners enjoyed the full support of their own governments, which were always ready to apply pressure to prevent any change in the land tenure pattern.[65] Like domestic landowners, the foreign companies built their own police forces, maintained close ties with federal forces, and at times went in for sharp diplomatic arm-twisting to protect their property from expropriation.

All of these obstacles to land reform were compounded by the lack of commitment or enforcement at the national level. Although the mandate for land distribution was clear, neither Carranza, nor Obregón, who followed him in the presidency (1920–1924), nor Plutarco Elías Calles, who followed Obregón (1924–1928), had any desire to carry the program forward. These men were or had become large landowners in the North of Mexico, and they were supported by large landowners from all parts of the republic. It was in their personal interest to leave the large landholdings intact. And these men ruled Mexico until 1934. Indeed, their hegemony over the Mexican political scene was so extended, and so complete, that they came to be known as the "northern clique" or, more solemnly, as the "northern dynasty."

THE NORTHERN DYNASTY

This group held power for nearly two decades. First came Carranza, who called himself the "First Chief of the Revolution" and exercised political power during four critical years. In May of 1920, Carranza tried to impose his own successor, but he was driven from office by a military junta led by Obregón and Plutarco Elías Calles, a *carrancista* general from the northern state of Sonora. Carranza fled from Mexico City with 50 million pesos of the national treasury, but was assassinated before he could reach asylum in the United States. The junta gave the job of "acting president" to another northerner who remained in the National Palace only six months, just long enough to stabilize the situation so that he could oversee the election of Obregón. Obregón, the general from Sonora who had labored so long in the shadow of Carranza, held office until November 1924. Then Obregón chose his friend Calles to succeed him and, in this way, the hegemony of the northern group was preserved. But when Calles's presidential term was up in 1928, Obregón's ambition led him to commit a very serious political error. Through all the years of military struggle and political infighting, Obregón was the one figure whose power and influence in revolutionary circles had grown steadily. He had tremendous staying power, and he thought he could reassert this power by returning to the presidency. Accordingly, he initiated a constitutional reform that would permit his reelection as president. Notwithstanding considerable opposition, the constitution was amended to permit Obregón's reelection. But before he could assume office, he was assassinated by a religious fanatic, enraged by the constraints that the northern leaders, Calles and Obregón, had imposed on the Catholic church. "It has been generally accepted that the attempt at reelection created a favorable climate for Obregón's murder."[66]

Calles, whose political ambitions were no more modest than Obregón's, learned an important lesson from Obregón's fight for reelection and the support it cost him. Accordingly, Calles never attempted to take advantage of the constitutional amendment permitting reelection.[67] He determined, instead, to direct Mexican politics from behind the scenes, placing in office a series of puppet presidents directly responsible to him. In addition, he created for himself the title of Lider Mámixo de la Revolución (Supreme Leader of the Revolution), and from this new position he succceeded in dominating and manipulating the incumbent presidents, while sustaining northern control over Mexican politics until 1934.

Throughout their seventeen years of political hegemony, the northern dynasty displayed considerable unity of purpose. These leaders were preoccupied with the material reconstruction of Mexico and her economic growth along capitalist lines.[68] In the field of agriculture, they were mainly concerned with the development of commercial agricultural exploitation based on large- and middle-sized properties. For one thing, they were determined to preserve their own large landholdings and those of their friends and associates. At the same time, they were interested in building an agricultural society based on the middle-sized family farm that had flourished in the United States. Neither of these interests was consistent with the mandates of the land reform legislation of 1917, which envisioned the division of large estates into small parcels and the provision of a plot for every peasant who wished to farm the land. The contradiction between the "goals of the revolution" as expressed in Article 27, and the goals of the strong-arm presidents who comprised the northern dynasty simply went unresolved during their period in power. And, of course, the land reform program itself was one of the principal casualties in the confusion over goals and priorities. Even Obregón, who had fought at the constitutional convention for the inclusion of specific agrarian legislation, was not energetic in implementing that policy once he came to power. The following is an excerpt from an interview with a peasant who headed an agrarian petitioning committee during the administration of Obregón. In this report he recounts a trip to Mexico City made by the committee in order to enlist Obregón's help in winning a land grant.

> Obregón's offered to help us, the peasants of the Laguna. But when it came to the point, he sold out to the Chamber of Agriculture, which was made up of all the landowners around here.
>
> We went to Mexico City with all the documents they asked of us as proof with which to confront the lawyers of the landlords. I, myself, carried the documents in twelve soapboxes, and guarded them in a room. In them were decisions favorable to us, handed down by the judges in Durango. On their side, the Chamber had all the big lawyers of Mexico City, as well as Joaquín Moreno, the owner of El Siglo de Torreón, the regional newspaper. We had three meetings with them and in the first it was obvious that the lawyers thought that because we were illiterate, we would not know how to defend ourselves, and they would beat us easily. They never imagined that we would present the proof we had from Durango. . . .
>
> We gave the documents to an intermediary who passed them on to the President, Álvaro Obregón. But the lawyers, seeing that they could do nothing legal to stop us, slipped some money to Obregón, and accordingly, he did not act in our favor.
>
> In the last confrontation, by way of explanation, they offered us the pretext of a law book, but when they showed it to me, I said to General Obregón, "Don't bother showing me these books of yours because I don't know how to read. I see that they have red covers, but, as for what's inside, we have never bothered much with that."
>
> Then the government offered to pay all the expenses of our stay in Mexico City and the trip back to the Laguna, whilst the lawyers continued slipping money to Obregon.[69]

THE CONSOLIDATION OF NATIONAL POWER

It is difficult to know whether Obregón failed to act on the petition of the Durango peasant committee because he had accepted a bribe, as the peasants claimed, or because the large landlords of the region were too powerful a group to take on. In either case the unofficial policy of indifference or "benign neglect" of agrarian reform continued under Obregón and his successors until 1934. The lack of official support to peasant petitions meant that fewer than 940,000 out of a rural population of almost 12 million received small land grants between 1917 and 1934.[70] During that time Carranza, Obregón, and Calles had other matters on their minds. They were concerned principally with the consolidation of national power. They were preoccupied with the struggle to establish the preeminence of national over regional or local power, i.e., the authority of the president over hundreds of local and regional strongmen who ruled whole sections of the republic like personal kingdoms. All over Mexico former "revolutionary generals" and their henchmen had established themselves as the political chiefs of various towns, states, or regions where their word became law.[71] Many of those whose power and prestige originally derived from victories in battle now exchanged the title of "zone commander" for that of "state governor." The essentially military structure of power remained intact and the generals at the top, Carranza, Obregón, and Calles, had the job of maintaining control and discipline over the lesser military men, the local bosses. The autonomy exercised by the regional bosses, or *caciques*, threatened to build into a centrifugal force capable of pulling apart the frail unity and peace established after the revolution.

Thus, during the 1920s and early 1930s the energies of the northern dynasty were directed toward building a strong central government. In addition to dealing with local and regional politicians, this meant curbing the power of the Catholic church and checking the political force of nascent labor and peasant organizations. Above all, the presidents wished to prevent the renewal of armed conflict, an eventuality which was never far below the surface of Mexican politics during these years.[72]

In the aftermath of Obregón's assassination, the need to stabilize the situation, legitimize their power, and extend and prolong the political hegemony of the northern clique was increasingly apparent to Calles. Accordingly, he gradually developed the idea of forming a political party that would provide an institutional framework for centralized rule and might solve the ever-troublesome question of presidential succession. Calles and his group could thus retain power and dictate the policy of the developing nation without running afoul of the "antireelection" principle. Calles himself introduced the idea of a new official party that would incorporate militant *agraristas*, labor leaders, military strongmen, regional bosses, industrialists, commercial landowners, merchants, and others—all the divergent groups currently vying for political power—within a single, all-inclusive party structure.[73] In his September State of the Union address, Calles announced his proposal for the National Revolutionary Party (Partido Nacional Revolucionario, or PNR). The PNR was to be a loose coalition of already existing regional and special interest parties. In March 1929, delegates were sent once more to the central Mexican city of Querétaro to participate in the founding of the new party.[74] The PNR was to have a structure flexible enough to permit the enthusiastic coexistence of the incredibly varied assortment of groups that collaborated in its formation.[75] Differences among the interest groups were to be resolved through broad policy decisions and a heavy emphasis on unity and solidarity over decisive selfishness. Personal differences among leaders were smoothed over with the signing of the Querétaro Pact of Union and Solidarity in which leaders pledged their willingness to accept the policies and candidates of the new party, submit to party discipline and eschew the use of armed force in the resolution of political conflicts.[76]

With Calles's initiative in 1929, an institutionalized structure was established to resolve the problems of policy determination and presidential succession. It is often asserted that Calles's principal motivation in founding the PNR was to perpetuate himself in power; to provide a mechanism through which he could remain "Supreme Chief of the Revolution" while appearing to have relinquished power to a successor. Whatever the designs that motivated Calles's initiative, the result spelled irrevocable political change for Mexico. The new official party not only began the process of legitimizing the revolution, but it also provided the means through which a new "revolutionary" elite would continue in power up to the present time. The structure of that party and the way it maintains and exercises its political power are the subject of chapter 2.

2

A RULING PARTY IS FORMED

Tacho Somoza, who runs Central America's most efficient dictatorship, confided to an *Excelsior* reporter last summer that he envied the official party and wished he had one of his own.

Joseph C. Goulden
December 1966

$\mathbf{F}$ew people observing the motley conglomeration of semi-independent parties, movements, interest groups, and political cliques that was the PNR in 1929 could have believed that it would develop into a unified and enormously powerful political organization. From a frail coalition held together principally by the forceful personality and political clout of President Calles, the PNR evolved gradually toward institutionalization and legitimacy. By the late 1930s, the PNR had undergone various changes in its internal structure and had been renamed the Party of the Mexican Revolution (Partido de la Revolución Mexicana, or PRM). By this time the political potpourri pulled together by Calles had emerged as the "official party," a ruling party linked directly to government institutions at local, state, and national levels.[1]

For all his long and checkered career as a military man, politician, and administrator, Calles is probably best remembered by Mexicans in his creative, unifying role as founder of the official party. But once this party was established, the man who did the most to shape its features and set its course was Lázaro Cárdenas.

CÁRDENAS COMES TO POWER

When the orange, green, and white sash of office was draped across the chest of Lázaro Cárdenas, few Mexicans realized that the inauguration of this young general from western Mexico would mark a definitive break with the past. Cárdenas had come to the presidency through the familiar route of military service and political loyalty to the northern dynasty. At sixteen he had left his native Michoacán and walked half-way across the republic to join the forces of General Calles. As a soldier he rose quickly through the ranks of the Constitutionalist Army, and by the age of twenty he held the post of lieutenant colonel; at twenty-seven, he was a general. Calles remembered him as a loyal and dutiful officer, and accordingly, after the revolution he appointed Cárdenas to serve as governor of Michoacán.[2]

It was during his term as governor (1928–1932) that Cárdenas began to distinguish himself as a progressive force within the Calles camp. He initiated a serious land reform program, distributing 350,000 acres of *hacienda* lands to 181 peasant villages. He encouraged the formation of peasant leagues throughout the state, and in so doing won for himself the vigorous support of national peasant organizations such as the National Agrarian Party (Partido Nacional Agrarista). Along with his agrarian program, Cárdenas's social reforms, especially the commitment to popular education he demonstrated with his construction of technical schools explicitly designed for Indians and for working class women, earned him the respect of most of the progressives in the PNR.[3]

In the early 1930s these progressive elements began to coalesce behind Cárdenas as a candidate for president of the republic. The politicians who rallied behind Cárdenas were those who were most frustrated by *callista* corruption, by Calles's concessions to foreign capital, and the anticlerical demagoguery and ultrarevolutionary rhetoric used by Calles to cover his regime's failure to provide concrete benefits to the peasants and working class.[4] In Cárdenas, leftists saw a man who was honest, popular, and clearly concerned with social transformation. What made Cárdenas a particularly attractive candidate was that while demonstrating his commitment to social justice, he had managed to retain his legitimacy as a loyal *callista*. Cárdenas had been one of the key military figures who stood by Calles when the chief's control over national politics was threatened by military coup in 1929. A year later, at Calles's request, Cárdenas had served briefly as head of the official party, and in 1932, as minister of war in the cabinet of Abelardo Rodríguez, Calles's puppet president. Thus support for Cárdenas's candidacy offered progressives the possibility of shifting the course of national politics to the left while avoiding a head-on clash with Calles and his conservative clique.[5]

The Clash with Calles

Calles considered Cárdenas to be an "extremist," and it is doubtful that the old revolutionary chief wanted to see Cárdenas in the presidential palace. But Calles's party was in crisis, torn by the conflict between conservative and radical forces. In effect Calles was obliged to choose Cárdenas or a man like him in order to defuse the increasingly militant demands of leftists within his own organization and to reduce the pressure from peasant and labor groups across the republic. With the unity of the party at stake, the *jefe máximo* had no choice but to support Cárdenas to avoid a direct confrontation with progressives. All Calles could do was accede to Cárdenas's candidacy and hope to control the young general once he came to office in the same fashion that Calles had manipulated the men who had served him in the presidency from 1928 to 1934.[6]

But Cárdenas was determined to be his own man, and he soon came into direct conflict with Calles. Again and again the two leaders clashed over the issue of who would be the real head of the Mexican political system, and whose policy would prevail. Cárdenas differed sharply with Calles over the issue of labor's right to organize and strike. By June of 1936, the two leaders had broken publicly over the fact that Cárdenas refused to suppress the strikes that were spreading throughout Mexico as workers, encouraged by the new president's pro-labor sympathies, demanded the full rights guaranteed to them by Article 123 of the constitution.[7] Calles complained loudly in newspapers and public statements that labor unrest was wrecking the economy and the very stability of the Mexican state was threatened. Cárdenas faced this charge directly, stating:

> If the stikes cause some uneasiness, and even temporarily injure the economy of the country, when settled reasonably, and with a spirit of equanimity and social justice, they contribute with time to making the economic situation more stable, since their rightful solution brings about better conditions for the workers. . . .[8]

On the question of land reform, Cárdenas stood firmly by the principle that the land belongs to those who work it. In the Constitution of 1917 he found the concrete mechanism through which agrarian justice could be achieved. Cárdenas clearly meant to throw the full power of his office behind a dramatic, large-scale land distribution. Accordingly, he gave encouragement and support to peasant syndicates, leagues and petitioning committees as they organized to press their demand for the immediate resolution of the "agrarian problem." If the peasants could articulate their demand for land, Cárdenas would respond with the full authority of his office.

Another area of conflict between Cárdenas and Calles was the issue of foreign investment. Of Calles's position, one observer wrote, "perhaps not since the time of Díaz had any leader made so firm a defense of foreign capital."[9] Cárdenas, on the other hand, was determined to set limitations on foreign ownership of Mexican resources and infrastructure. In the course of his first years as president, Cárdenas locked horns with Calles over this issue.

As Calles felt his power slipping away he regrouped his forces to attack the man he had set in the presidential chair. But Cárdenas outmaneuvered him by organizing the National Committee for Proletarian Defense. Cárdenas brought tens of thousands of workers and peasants into this popular militia, trained to defend his government against coup or insurrection.[10] Under this program, arms were eventually distributed to 60,000 peasants who constituted a "rural reserve," organized to defend Cárdenas and the land they would receive from him.[11] Leaders of the National Committee for Proletarian Defense openly denounced Calles, labeling him a traitor to the Mexican Revolution and as an enemy of the working class.[12] With the backing of a popular militia, Cárdenas began to feel more secure in his position. Thus, when the Calles-Cárdenas split reached its climax in 1936, Cárdenas was able to take decisive action. In the spring of 1936 he learned that Calles was orchestrating an elaborate military coup, and so Cárdenas immediately ordered the former president's expulsion from Mexico along with other prominent *callistas*.

Once rid of Calles, Cárdenas still had to cope with the old *callista* machine and its supporters throughout the republic. Calles's strength had rested to a large extent on the backing or reluctant cooperation of regional strongmen.[13] Some of these regional chiefs could be won over to the Cárdenas camp by the offer of direct and significant participation in the reform movement of the new regime. In the case of those regional chiefs who would not support Cárdenas, a clear effort was made to deprive them of their peasant following by incorporating their supporters into a unified peasant confederation sponsored by Cárdenas.[14]

The problem facing the president was more than the question of winning the cooperation of regional strongmen or ousting Calles's people and replacing them with his own. Rather, Cárdenas had to build a whole new coalition of support because the policies that he intended to push would inevitably bring down on his head the full opposition of conservative forces in Mexico.

Cardenas's Program

The policies Cárdenas hoped to pursue were not revolutionary; they were reforms aimed at improving, rather than overturning, an existing situation. On this point there was a great deal of confusion on both the right and left during the Cárdenas years. Cárdenas's speeches and those of his top ministers were full of talk of "state ownership of the means of production," "worker cooperatives," and "workers' democracy as the first step towards socialism."[15] In several addresses, Cárdenas threatened that factory owners who did not comply with the rulings of government arbitration boards would have their property expropriated and nationalized "for the good of the nation." He asserted that it was the role of government to "intervene in the class struggle on the side of labor which was the weaker party." Yet, only weeks later Cárdenas would turn around and state, "The working classes know that they cannot appropriate factories and other instruments of work because they are not, for the time being, either technically fitted for management nor in possession of the financial resources needed for the success of an undertaking of such magnitude."[16] And in February 1936, Cárdenas went on to reassure capitalists that, "The government desires the further development of industries within the nation since it depends upon their prosperity for its income through taxation."[17]

While Cárdenas's rhetorical turnabouts often confused his contemporaries, in retrospect it is clear that the policies he had in mind were inspired by the doctrines of socialism, but were in fact piecemeal reforms rather than revolutionary transformations. Cárdenas accepted the division of Mexican society along class lines. He viewed his task as one of "conciliation" among conflicting classes in the interest of "national progress." For Cárdenas, the plight of the exploited groups in Mexican society would be remedied through political and legal action on the part of the state. Social contradictions would be mediated by the government in such a manner that the state itself would act to protect the interests of peasants and workers rather than permit the masses to take justice into their own hands and eliminate their exploiters.[18]

> Evidently Cárdenas felt that while class conflict certainly existed, for the good of the country, class struggle should not be allowed to overflow into the liquidation of one of the contendors. And why for the good of the country? Simply, because class struggle without restraint was, for him, anarchy, and—this was decisive—because he considered the capitalist class to be necessary for the progress of Mexico.[19]

Thus Cárdenas was not setting out to destroy the bourgeoisie. He was, rather, attempting to shake up a social, political, and economic structure that had grown rigid since the revolution. He had to force the bourgeoisie to yield some of its power so that some desperately needed reforms could begin. Far from building socialism, Cárdenas's reforms were calculated to improve the conditions of peasants and workers enough to establish the "social peace," the climate of political stability, which would permit capitalist development to proceed in Mexico. Cárdenas was interested in fostering a particular kind of capitalist development; his plan involved heavy government intervention and control in all sectors of the economy.[20] But, notwithstanding the active role foreseen for government, Cárdenas's vision of Mexican development was essentially a capitalist one.[21] "The government's design was to develop a capitalism which was Mexican-owned, tax-paying, and beneficial to the nation."[22]

But even the moderate reform implemented by Cárdenas would meet with fierce resistance from the interest groups entrenched since the revolution. Landowners, industrialists, bankers, and foreign capitalists had thrived during the years that Carranza, Obregón, and Calles held power. These bourgeois interest monopolized power and privilege in Mexico. They were unwilling to permit even the most modest reforms (such as piecemeal land distribution or slightly improved working conditions) much less the more significant reforms (large-scale land reform and nationalization of foreign-owned petroleum and railway companies) that Cárdenas wanted to carry out.

Cárdenas was working against incredible odds. Once he took office, Mexican capitalists began investing abroad or accumulating their profits in foreign bank accounts. Foreign capitalists began withholding their funds as fear of labor militancy and possible expropriation of their holdings made investment in Mexico increasingly unattractive. The press, controlled by conservative money, vilified Cárdenas and his administration. The middle class was injured by inflation, frustrated by the feeling that they would be left out of the social transformations directed by this new administration, and profoundly frightened by what they regarded as Cárdenas's communist leanings. The president's support for the Spanish Republican cause and his policy of open immigration for Spanish Republican refugees was taken by middle class Mexicans and devout Catholics of all social classes as proof that Cárdenas meant to establish in Mexico a "godless" state modeled on the Soviet Union.[23] Finally, during these years, fascism was on the rise in Mexico as it was in Europe.[24]

Faced with this array of destabilizing forces, Cárdenas had to move decisively to build a new power coalition to back his regime. His government was threatened by the bourgeoisie, diehard partisans of Calles, organized fascist groups, and the specter of economic reprisals by the American and British governments. And he had not yet secured the solid support of socialists, communists, and organized labor groups. This predicament prompted him to make a direct appeal for the backing of workers and peasants.

A NEW POWER COALITION AND THE RESTRUCTURING OF THE OFFICIAL PARTY

To gain the necessary support, Cárdenas moved ahead with a program of liberalizing labor legislation, strengthening peasant and labor unions, and uniting each under the forceful leadership of men he trusted to support his regime. The appeal for the allegiance of the peasants and workers, in many cases an appeal made over the heads of their old guard *callista* leaders, was an essential step for Cárdenas in the formation of the supportive coalition needed to back up his reform administration.

In order to consolidate the support he was winning, Cárdenas set about reorganizing the official party in a way that would strengthen the relative position of the peasant and labor groups. A first step was to draw peasant groups out from under the domination of labor unions and establish them as a separate political force within the party. The separation of peasants from labor was consistent with Cárdenas's policy of never relying completely on the political loyalty of any one group.[25]

Cárdenas's next step was to institutionalize peasant and worker participation in his government by creating a role for the two groups within the official party. In December 1937, Cárdenas dissolved the PNR and called for the formation of a "new" revolutionary party to be named the PRM, the Party of the Mexican Revolution. The reorganized party featured a four-sector structure. Each of the party's sectors, peasant, labor, military, and the so-called popular sector, were to play an equal role in making national policy. According to Cárdenas's vision of how the new political coalition would operate, the party's candidates for public office would be drawn in fairly equal proportions from all four interest groups. Local party organizations would caucus before any local, state, or national election to determine the number of candidacies to be allotted to each of the sectors.[26] Once the nominees were selected by this process, their electoral victory would be all but assured as all four sectors would close ranks behind the party's chosen candidate.[27] With peasants and workers chosen by their sector leaders to stand for election on the official party ticket, Cárdenas anticipated that the interests of the masses would be safeguarded by members of their own class who had been elected to public office. By providing for the protection of peasants' and workers' interests and by vastly increasing their influence within the political system, Cárdenas hoped to build a base of support for the land reform program and the nationalization of railroads and petroleum that he would carry out during his administration.

In short, he hoped permanently to redefine the balance of power in Mexican politics, giving far greater weight to peasants and workers.

The sectoral organization of the official party was the keystone of Cárdenas's new power structure. For this reason it is worth examining each of these sectors more closely.

THE LABOR SECTOR

Cárdenas's initiative toward labor was not the first occasion on which union leaders had been asked to lend the support of their movement to a national political figure in return for increased influence in the formation of government policy.[28] As we saw in chapter 1, Carranza had exuberantly pledged that "labor would enjoy special benefits once hostilities ceased."[29] But far from reaping a harvest of special benefits, the workers found that even the most basic rights guaranteed to them under the Constitution of 1917 were ignored by the postrevolutionary governments. The House of the Workers of the World was shut down by government order and its membership and activities suppressed. The House was replaced by a new labor organization, the Regional Confederation of Mexican Workers (Confederación Regional de Obreros Mexicanos, or CROM) directed by men loyal to the Carranza regime. When Obregón broke with Carranza, he, in turn, called on the membership of the CROM to back him in his bid for national power.[30] In the power struggle that followed, the CROM swung its support of Obregón. And yet again, the workers had little concrete benefit to show for their intervention and participation in national politics. The Obregón regime did not provide the working class with the benefits for which it had struggled so long.

Thus when it came time for Cárdenas to make his appeal for working-class support, he had to find some way to convince labor leaders that he did not intend to repeat the old patterns of deceit and betrayal. He had to back his rhetoric with some kind of concrete action. But Cárdenas was in no position to give real power to the working class. What he did do was to give government backing to the dynamic Marxist labor organizer, Vicente Lombardo Toledano. Within a year, Lombardo Toledano was able to persuade tens of thousands of workers to organize unions, to join government-organized unions, to bring previously independent syndicates into federation with one another, and finally to affiliate with the government-sponsored Mexican Workers Confederation (Confederación de Trabajadores de México, or CTM).

The CTM was then to form the base for the labor sector of the official party. Although other labor organizations joined the party independently of the CTM,[31] the giant confederation dominated labor sector politics. With full government support, the CTM continued to expand its base until Cárdenas's administration came to an end in 1940.

"When Cárdenas left office, the CTM lost not only much of its stimulus from the presidency but also much of its ideological militancy."[32] The rhetoric of "class struggle" was abandoned in favor of an ideology that championed "national unity." The short-lived tradition of militant labor struggle gave way to a policy that stressed collaboration with government and industry to hasten the economic development of Mexico.[33] Thus, throughout the 1940s and 1950s, the CTM led the labor sector into a policy of ever increasing cooperation with government and big business. And as this process accelerated, the more militant labor unions in the confederation—the petroleum, mining, electrical, and railway workers' unions—dropped out of the organization.[34]

In the meantime, the CTM was plagued by *continuismo*, the tendency of leaders to perpetuate themselves in office. The CTM committees at national and state levels increasingly dictated the selection of leaders in affiliated unions.[35] With officers imposed from above, union rank and file found themselves powerless to remove and replace leaders guilty of bad management, dishonesty, or abuse of power. Because workers in the same industry were members of various regional federations within the CTM, horizontal contacts among them were discouraged, greatly reducing the opportunity for a successful revolt from below. And because the national leaders were not elected by direct vote but instead by a public show of hands of carefully selected delegates, opportunities for removal of incumbent leaders were further limited.[36]

The lack of internal democracy within the labor sector was exacerbated by the fact that the old-guard CTM leaders drew ever closer to management and government as they became a moneyed elite in their own right. Over the years, as the same group of labor leaders continued in office, many amassed personal fortunes so large that their interests began to coincide more with those of big business than with the working class. Eventually workers within the CTM movement began to claim that they were "exploited by their own leadership." As one observer noted:

> Critics of the CTM point to the absence of union democracy and rank-and-file control. Fidel Velázquez, Secretary General of the CTM since the 1940s, is cited as the prototype of union leadership within the Mexican labor movement—unresponsive, oligarchical, and often corrupt.[37]

And this model of union corruption has persisted into the 1980s, as another observer indicates:

> The union leadership has become a political bureaucracy headed by the old

labor bosses, some of whom have been in power for as long as forty years. The oligarchic model of union organization has permeated all levels of the labor structure from top to bottom. Corruption is said to be endemic.[38]

The tacit alliance between CTM bosses and management has led to a general decline in the number of strikes and in the militancy of the demands pressed. Furthermore, corrupt union officials frequently collaborate with management, speeding up the rate of production and quelling protests.[39] And given these links between union bureaucrats and big business and government, the official labor movement has gradually lost its independence as an autonomous interest group and the economic and political bargaining power of the workers has declined sharply.[40] Over time the role of union leaders was totally transformed. Instead of bargaining for concessions to labor, they worked to assure labor support for the government. "Many large unions have been instruments of government policy, an unfailing source of electoral support for the PRI, and an ally of management rather than a countervailing force in economic life."[41] Of course some demands on management are formulated, contracts are negotiated, strikes organized, and some benefits won by the organized working class. But, "all of these events have taken place, usually in circumstances which would not prove embarrassing to the government or to government-protected sectors of the economy."[42]

If the integration of the organized workers movement into the official party has spelled the end of any genuine independence or political autonomy for the working class, there is a curious irony in this turn of events. For some students of Mexican labor movements have argued that working-class support is not even so crucial to the ruling party as it was in the past. As the Mexican political situation stabilized and the threat of armed insurrection against the federal government diminished, the government came to depend less and less upon the potential military aid of the workers.[43] In terms of the balance of power within the official party, this new situation of increased political stability has meant that the influence of the labor sector has declined steadily since its heyday under Cárdenas.

THE PEASANT SECTOR

The second group that has suffered a steady decline in political influence is the peasantry. It is ironic as well as tragic that the major instrument that has rendered the peasants politically ineffective is the very organization designed by Cárdenas to give the peasants genuine political power.

In June 1935, Cárdenas ordered the formal organization of a peasant sector for the official party. To form the peasant sector, landless peons, sharecroppers, agricultural wage earners, the owners of small land parcels, and the recipients of government land grants were all incorporated into a single organization, the National Peasant Confederation (Confederación Nacional Campesina, or CNC).

Cárdenas's drive for unification of peasant groups was prompted by his apparently sincere belief that such an organization would come to represent a political force equal to that of any interest group or class in Mexican society. He calculated that millions of peasants, united in a single federation, would prove strong enough to stand up to the power of the landholding class. Whereas the landowning *patrón* had formerly monopolized political and economic power in the countryside, the new National Peasant Confederation was designed to alter that situation. Through the CNC, Cárdenas set out to break the political influence of the great landowners by creating an alternative network to replace or offset the patronage traditionally provided by the landowners.[44] In order to do this, Cárdenas tried to institutionalize a patron-client relationship through which government goods and services would come to the peasantry in return for the peasants' loyal adherence to his own regime.

Once this mutually supportive government-peasant relationship was established, Cárdenas anticipated that the CNC would develop into a compelling spokesman for peasant interests, capable of lobbying for the extension of land reform, agricultural credit, irrigation projects, and improvements in rural welfare such as electrification, schools, and medical facilities. Cárdenas had great confidence in the capacity of peasants to govern their own communities and to pressure effectively for their interests, just as he believed they could successfully cultivate any land grant that they would receive under his agrarian reform program. Nevertheless, he saw a key role for government in guiding and assisting the peasants in meeting the new challenges which would come with political enfranchisement and control of property. For Cárdenas, land distribution was not a unilateral measure taken by a progressive government. The president understood the importance of the political interaction between peasant demands and government response. It was not his place to "bestow" land upon the peasants. To be effective, agrarian reform had to come in answer to a clearly articulated demand on the part of peasants for land that was rightfully theirs. Hence, Cárdenas believed it crucial to create a climate in which peasants could organize politically. And so he promoted an institution which would give a voice to peasant organizations.

Unfortunately, the CNC did not develop along the lines envisioned by its founder. The peasantry never became a political force equal to any of the other major interest groups in the political arena. The men who succeeded Cárdenas in the presidency looked to groups other than the peasants and workers for their base of support. We have already noted that as the official party machine gained full control over national politics, it became increasingly unlikely that the government would ever need to call upon an armed peasant and worker militia to rescue itself from a military *coup d'état*. Accordingly, the loyalty of the peasantry became marginal to the government, although government support continued to be crucial to the peasantry. And in most regions of Mexico, the mutually supportive relationship between the peasants and their national government gradually disintegrated.

In addition to the decline in the peasants' strategic importance in the years following Cárdenas's regime, the organizational structure of both the CNC and the official party have contributed to holding the peasantry in the relatively powerless position it has occupied to the present day. The membership of the CNC is made up of a variety of different kinds of peasants. Included in its ranks are landless peasants, agricultural wage workers, sharecroppers, *minifundistas*,[45] and *colonos*.[46] The bulk of CNC members, however, are *ejidatarios*[47] who are automatically incorporated into the CNC by virtue of their membership in their own ejidal community. The mass of peasants who make up the CNC's rank and file are supposed to be represented on the local level by a local peasant union or ejidal commissariat (the governing body of the ejidal community), at the state level by the State League of Agrarian Communities and Peasant Syndicates, and at the national level by the Executive Committee, and the Secretary General of the CNC.

One basic problem for peasants affiliated with the CNC is that their organization has a rigidly hierarchical structure. The *ejidatarios* who form the main body of the CNC membership exercise direct influence in the organization only in the election of their local officers. These local officers who form the ejidal commissariat have some influence in elections at regional and state levels. However, the ballots presented at the state conventions are accepted by acclaim, while the slate itself is prepared ahead of time by state level politicians of the official party. Only at the local level are offices filled by a voting procedure, and oftentimes serious irregularities occur in these ejidal elections. Once every three years, the subtle play of forces at the top level of the organization determines the selection of the secretary general of the CNC. Most other top functionaries are ushered into office by a unanimous voice vote at the state or national conventions.[48]

Because middle- and upper-level CNC officials are appointed rather than elected, the CNC functionary owes his position of power and prestige not to the peasant constituency he, in theory, is chosen to serve, but to a group of powerful state and regional politicians, many of whom are representatives of the landowning class. Thus the responsibility of the CNC officer is to the politicians who appoint him.

When we look at the way in which CNC operations are financed, we better understand the degree of control that high level politicians are able to exercise over local and regional CNC functionaries. In most states, the regional committees depend for the larger part of their budget on subsidies from the state machine of the official party. Aside from the subsidy paid directly to the CNC by the party, various government agencies pay regular extralegal subsidies to the peasant organization and provide the all-important patronage which further ties the interests of the CNC official to the government and to the government agencies. As both recruitment and financial support in the CNC flow from the top down, the CNC rank and file has no lever of control over its officers.

The relatively brief but secure tenure of the CNC official also contributes to his irresponsibility. CNC office is inevitably a patronage plum for which the recipient has waited many long years. Once installed in his position in the hierarchy, the CNC functionary may have only three years in which to exploit the financial and personal benefits which go along with the job. But, since these rewards can be bountiful, particularly when compared to the lot of the average peasant, to many people the long wait in the patronage line is more than justified by the material opportunities for social and economic improvement available during even a brief tenure as CNC officer.[49]

Thus many of the CNC's problems spring directly from the socioeconomic structure of Mexico; specifically, the lack of alternative roads of social and economic mobility open to people of peasant origin. For peasants who have so few avenues for the expression and realization of their personal aspirations, the CNC offers an important opportunity for advancement. The men who have the tenacity to climb step by step up the CNC hierarchy are generally rewarded with social and economic status of which ordinary peasants only dream.

It might seem that under this system of leadership recruitment, the CNC members would at least have the leadership services of a group of quick-witted, dynamic individuals who have managed to push their way to the head of the patronage queue. Unfortunately, however energetic, efficient, and dedicated aspirant leaders of the CNC may be in the promotion of their own careers, overenthusiasm in the representation of the peasant constituency is self-defeating to rising CNC politicians. It is to be avoided at all costs. This is because Cárdenas's vision of a representative peasant organization has been completely distorted. Over the last forty years the orientation of the CNC has gradually altered. It has become far more involved in maintaining the status quo of land tenure than in pushing for the extension of the agrarian reform program. Over the same period, it has changed in such a way that it no longer is an organ for the expression of peasant interests. Since 1940 the CNC, like the workers' CTM, has proved to be an instrument through which the government controls the peasantry, rather than a means through which the peasants may exercise a measure of control over their government and its policies.[50]

THE MILITARY SECTOR

In addition to a labor and a peasant sector, the official party of the late 1930s featured a sector comprised entirely of military personnel. Incorporation of the military into the party was part of Cárdenas's plan to reform and reorganize the army and bring it under civilian control. Military intervention or the threat of a military coup had been a constant of postrevolutionary politics up to Cárdenas's day. Enormous political power was wielded by this top-heavy military establishment, which absorbed more than one-third of the federal budget, boasted one general for every 338 enlisted men, and had supplied every president and most of the state governors since the revolution. Cárdenas was keenly aware that the power of this conservative force would have to be reduced if his reform administration was to survive.[51]

Cárdenas's strategy to subordinate the military to civilian control involved reorganizational measures which he, a revolutionary general himself, was well equipped to undertake. He restructured the army by pushing for greater professionalism: instituting proficiency tests for commanders of all ranks, remedial training for those who failed, and competitive examinations to determine promotion. Placing a ceiling of 55,000 troops on the army and closing down marginal military installations, Cárdenas was able to cut the military's share of the federal budget from 25 percent in 1934 to 19 percent in 1938. All this he accomplished while sweetening the reorganization with pay boosts to officers and enlisted men, increased equipment and uniform allowances, and improved military housing and medical services.[52]

The other key to Cárdenas's plan to control the military was the incorporation of army men into the PRM. In December 1937 he recommended the formation of a military sector for the new official party in which the army would be represented "not as a deliberating body or as a class corporation" which would promote the interests of a "special caste," but as a group of responsible citizens.[53] On the face of it, Cárdenas was proposing to enfranchise military men and bring them into a political process to which their status had previously denied them access.[54] What he in fact accomplished with this move was to force the generals' political activities into the open and oblige them to operate in a political context in which they were constrained to share power with three other organized sectors. "We did not put the army in politics," Cárdenas explained, "it was already there. In fact it had been dominating the situation, and we did well to reduce its influence to one out of four."[55] Of course the military chiefs were not fooled by Cárdenas's maneuver, but they saw little alternative to acting out the citizenship role that had been thrust on them.

The life span of the military sector was brief. At no time did the sector participate in official party politics as fully as the other three sectors. For example, the military role was limited in that the sector did not take part in the nomination process at the national level, nor in state and local elections.[56] But even with limited participation, the formal incorporation of the army into the political process succeeded in reducing its tendency to intervene surreptitiously and illegally. In 1941, the same desire for civilian preeminence which earlier had made compulsory PRM membership for military personnel seem a good idea, now led to Cárdenas's successor to disband the sector.[57] Soon after his inauguration, Manuel Avila Camacho dissolved the military sector, and its members either left the party to join right-wing opposition movements, or were absorbed into the other sectors of the official party. And so, by the early 1940s, the official party was left with the same trisectorial structure it retains up to the present day.

THE POPULAR SECTOR

Given the heavy emphasis that Cárdenas placed on his peasant and labor support, industrialists and businessmen regarded his administration as a terrifying threat to their interests. But, as we have noted, Cárdenas was in no position to destroy the bourgeoisie. He was trying to break their monopoly on political power and bring them under government control. Thus, while carrying forward programs favorable to peasants and workers, Cárdenas maintained contact with business interests and attempted to involve organized business groups in his administration through their formal participation in the official party. As in the case of the military, it seemed a good idea to incorporate potential enemies directly into the intraparty political process rather than simply sitting back to await their attempts to sabotage or overthrow the government. For its part, the business community responded favorably to Cárdenas's initiative. Business leaders perceived the growing concentration of power in the federal government, and they opted for a strategy of maintaining links with the national administration in order to obtain the contracts, concessions, and compromises that would favor the expansion of business and industry.[58]

Thus, when Cárdenas called for the formation of a "popular sector," a large assortment of professional, trade, civic, and business associations were formally incorporated into the official party. By virtue of their membership in these organizations, industrialists, landowners, businessmen, and a variety of middle-class groups automatically became affiliated with the ruling party. Included in the "popular sector" are doctors, lawyers, teachers, and other professionals, as well as merchants, manufacturers, middle- and large-sized landowners, youth organizations, women's organizations, and a number of social associations. This sector is basically a federation of middle-class and elite interests rather than the "popular" grouping implied by its name. Nevertheless, included in the same heterogeneous conglomeration are some skilled workers' unions and the union of government employees. Thus it is probably more accurate to say that the popular sector brings together not only middle- and upper-class groups, but also people whose objective interests are much closer to those of the labor sector but who, for various reasons of social status, are not considered—or more significantly, do not consider themselves—to be laborers. Through their incorporation into the popular sector, skilled workers, white collar employees, managers, clerks, low-level government functionaries, postal workers, and even municipal street sweepers are encouraged to identify with their employers, rather than with their own class interests.

In 1943 the groups that had been drawn into the popular sector were reorganized as the National Confederation of Popular Organizations (Confederación Nacional de Organizaciones Populares, or CNOP). The CNOP, like the peasants' CNC and the workers' CTM, operates at local, regional, state, and national levels. The secretary general of the CNOP sits on the party's Central Executive Committee, as do the secretaries general of the CNC and CTM. However, unlike the CNC and CTM, the CNOP has no legally prescribed relationship with the government. No special legislation such as the labor code or the agrarian code formally binds the CNOP to the machinery of government.[59] This lack of institutionalized restraint has left the CNOP relatively free to develop along the lines most convenient to its membership. Because membership in the CNOP and the official party is more a matter of choice for popular sector people than for peasants and labor, "its members must be continually courted and cajoled into allegiance. This gives a premium to the political skills of the CNOP leadership and creates pressures for efficiency and effectiveness that often are missing in the other sectors."[60]

The popular sector enjoys other political advantages over the peasant and labor sectors. Members of the popular sector have generally received specialized education or technical training far superior to that available to either peasants or workers. Their representatives are professional bureaucrats, technicians, lawyers, and entrepreneurs, people well equipped by background and training to lobby effectively for the sector's interests. Such people also command extensive corporate or personal fortunes which provide them with the financial means to work as vigorously and efficiently as possible to defend their political and economic interests. To the extent that crucial policy decisions are fought out within the official party, the popular sector clearly has the upper hand in terms of financial, educational, technical, and personal resources. "The Popular sector is the strongest of the three divisions of the Party. This is due in great part to its ability to produce leaders from within its own ranks of middle-class members who possess the requisite political skills of manipulation and conciliation."[61]

The result is that of the three sectors, the popular sector receives by far the greatest share of government benefits.[62] Since the creation of the CNOP in 1943, this sector has dominated the legislature. In the Chamber of Deputies the proportion of popular sector representatives has climbed steadily. For example, between 1976 and 1979, the popular sector's share of deputies' seats rose from 42 to 49 percent, while labor's share dropped from 30 to 23 percent and the CNC fell from 29 to 26 percent.[63] The number of senators who belong to the CNOP has also increased over the years, while the number of peasant and labor sector representatives has declined proportionately.[64] Hence, peasants and workers are underrepresented in the national governing bodies. For example, the peasant sector has almost half of all members of the official party, but it holds only a quarter of the seats in the Chamber of Deputies.[65] They are also underrepresented throughout the official party apparatus. Popular sector members control the vast bulk of committee positions and political appointments at all levels of the party hierarchy. Through this numerical advantage on party committees and the preponderance of nominations and appointments it receives, the popular sector plays a role in the government which is disproportionate to its size, but not to its economic importance. Of the three party sectors, popular sector members have the greatest access to the president of the republic and the greatest influence over policy formation. Hence, party decisions on the allocation of scarce resources among the three sectors are generally highly favorable to this powerful sector.

POLITICAL DOMINANCE OF THE BOURGEOISIE

We know that one of Cárdenas's main purposes in organizing the various sectors of the official party was to provide the workers and peasants with some political clout to strengthen their political position with respect to the middle class and the bourgeoisie. But neither the CTM nor the CNC evolved into the vigorous representative organ that Cárdenas envisioned. To the extent that the CTM and CNC were organized to consolidate worker and peasant support for the governing party and its leaders, the two confederations have functioned with relative success. But insofar as their role is also that of representing the working class and peasantry, articulating the demands of these classes and pressuring effectively for their interests, the official party's labor and peasant sectors have been a failure. Within the official party itself, both the peasant and labor sectors have continually lost ground to the increasingly powerful popular sector. This process has accelerated since the official party was reorganized in 1946. In that year, the ruling party was renamed the Institutional Revolutionary Party (Partido Revolucionario Institucional, or PRI), and neither its name nor its basic structure has been altered since. The reorganization of the official party in 1946 did nothing to redress the imbalance among the three sectors. On the contrary, the PRI is structured in such a way that the preponderance of appointments, nominations, and patronage of all kinds continues to flow to the popular sector.

Interest Groups

While the popular sector has come to dominate intraparty politics, the old landowners, the industrialists, the businessmen, and bankers, in short, the bourgeoisie, has also strengthened and consolidated its political position outside the ruling party. The economic power of the bourgeoisie is sufficient to make it the most influential pressure group in Mexico. Although some crucial sectors of the Mexican economy are state owned or state controlled (petroleum, railroads, electricity, and, as of 1982, domestic banks), and while a variety of government credit banks play a key role in directing development, the entire public sector produces less than 10 percent of the gross national product.[66] The remaining 90.5 percent is produced by private enterprise. And among the largest enterprises, foreign-owned businesses, or those with strong foreign participation earn more than half of the total income.[67] Together, Mexican and foreign-owned enterprises wield enormous economic and political influence in the decision-making process. Immense economic empires are often controlled by foreign and domestic industrial, commercial, and finance capitalists organized in conglomerates, or "*grupos.*" Beyond the economic power commanded by the *grupos* on the basis of their holdings, the political impact of these entrepreneurs is further enhanced by the confederations, associations, chambers of commerce, and clubs which they have organized to protect their interests.[68] Giant umbrella organizations like the National Confederation of Industrial Chambers (CONCAMIN), the National Confederation of Chambers of Commerce (CONCANACO), the Confederation of Employers (COPARMEX), and the National Chamber of Consumer Goods Industries (CANACINTRA), do not operate as members of the official party, yet they exercise great influence over PRI and government policy. In these confederations, member enterprises cooperate with one another and with their foreign colleagues to work out a unified strategy for the pressure group. The organized business community has virtually unlimited financial resources at its disposal, and is able to employ the full-time services of lawyers, technicians, and experts in every field, as well as paying full salaries to the representatives elected by the organizations to speak out for business interests.

> Their financial solvency . . . makes it possible for them to sponsor special studies, formulate position papers, conduct propaganda campaigns, and communicate their attitudes openly to the bureaucratic structure. The government often (but not invariably) consults their leaders in matters perceived to touch on the interests of their members, thus giving them advance opportunity to influence the shape of legislation or executive action.[69]

In this way the entrepreneurs' organizations have developed effective techniques for influencing legislation and administration and for modifying decisions made by the president.[70] CONCAMIN and CONCANACO "can censure the economic reports sent them by the government and, with the support of the major newspapers, propose modification of the government's economic and financial policy."[71] This high degree of organization and efficiency backed by big money gives the capitalists formidable influence above and beyond their participation in formal party politics.

The Bourgeoisie and the Mexican State

Over the last decade a lively debate among scholars has focused on the question of how, or in what fashion, the bourgeoisie is linked to the Mexican government—or, as it is usually termed in these discussions, "the Mexican state." One way to address the issue is to ask whether, and to what degree, the same people occupy elite positions in both the economy and in government. This approach has its limits, but if we do find the same individuals or members of the same groups or families in both types of position, there would certainly be a strong suggestion of an identity of interests.

Another way of framing this issue would be to ask how much independence or autonomy the Mexican government has from the economic powers that be, that is, from the industrialists, financiers, large commercial landowners, and others. We need to establish whether the "Mexican state" in the persons of elected and appointed officials, civil servants, and bureaucrats simply acts on behalf of the class interests of the bourgeoisie. If political and economic elite groups are not one and the same, what evidence can we point to that indicates the independence of one from the other? Are there instances in which the Mexican state has clearly acted against the interests of the bourgeoisie—or in favor of one sector of the bourgeoisie and against the interests of another? We have already noted that the peasantry and working class have very few means by which to pressure either the party or the government to respond to their needs. Certainly members of the bourgeoisie (or bourgeoisies) possess abundant resources which give them great weight when compared with the masses of peasants and workers. But to note the relatively greater power and influence of the upper classes or even of the middle sectors is not to specify the degree of freedom they enjoy to pursue their class interests, unrestrained by the central government.

Some scholars argue that the Mexican government has a striking number of different means to control the economy, and that it exercises this control in ways that frequently place the interests of the nation as a whole ahead of the concerns of the upper classes.[72] Furthermore,

> since state ownership and control is sanctioned and encouraged by nationalist sentiments of both the regime and the population in general, the private sector can do little to challenge effectively the continuous expansion of such ownership and control without appearing to be "unpatriotic" and "unrevolutionary."[73]

As we have noted, the state owns or controls the most important industries in the country and holds large shares in many private firms. "Needless to say, the government's pricing policies in these industries as well as its decisions regarding the purchase of goods and services for them can seriously constrict the options of the private sector."[74] In addition, the state manages energy resources and much of the raw material required by private industry.[75] As we will see in greater detail in the next chapter, the government also plays a major role in credit and finance, in channeling investment, and in determining the form, shape, and direction of industrial and agricultural development. However, the fact that the state possesses and wields these powers does not necessarily mean that it does so in conflict with or in opposition to the interests of the bourgeoisie, or at least of the dominant sectors of the bourgeoisie. Purcell, for example, stresses the various mechanisms for economic control available to the Mexican state. But she also notes:

> The government, however, has not used its potential power to hurt the private sector. Instead, "beginning with the administration of Lázaro Cárdenas, and particularly since the presidency of Miguel Alemán, government and private industry have cooperated to mutual advantage in what might be termed an 'alliance for profits.' "[76]

Notwithstanding the high degree of government participation in the economy, the bourgeoisie, it seems, retains many means to press its interests. Apart from the influence of organizations like CONCAMIN and CONCANACO as pressure groups, "another way in which business might exercise power vis-à-vis the public sector is through membership of business leaders in government institutions."[77]

> Representatives of the private sector sit on the boards of development banks, regulatory agencies and commissions, fiscal boards, and some government-owned enterprises such as the railroads. They thus have an opportunity to be consulted by the government on a variety of economic decisions. This kind of consultation has become broader over the years and now extends into agencies dealing with social as well as economic issues such as the social security commission. . . . Finally, high government positions are becoming increasingly available to business leaders. The most notable is that of . . . a former official of CONCAMIN who is at present minister of industry and commerce.[78]

Does this mean that we cannot distinguish between the politicians, elected officials, appointed functionaries, and the others who run the state and the big businessmen, bankers, and industrialists who comprise the bourgeoisie? In an empirical study which traces the socioeconomic origins, education and career patterns, and class links of Mexican politicians through the twentieth century, Peter Smith finds that "the bulk of Mexico's political leadership has come from a tiny, and highly privileged, socioeconomic stratum."[79] Drawn largely from the urban middle class, the overwhelming preponderance (80–90 percent) of these political leaders are university educated. Furthermore almost all of the university graduates studied at the same institution, the National University in Mexico City (Universidad Nacional Autónoma de México, or UNAM), where most trained as lawyers or teachers.

> People from lower-class occupations, by contrast, have never formed substantial portions of the national political elite. It comes as no surprise to learn that *campesinos* and industrial workers were totally excluded from the

Díaz group. What is surprising is the fact that they have been almost as totally excluded from the revolutionary and postrevolutionary cohorts. . . . The two major groups in whose name the Mexican Revolution presumably took place, peasants and workers, have had very few agents from their own ranks in decisionmaking centers of the government.[80]

A striking finding of Smith's study is the clear distinction between what he calls "the economic" and "the political" elites.

The Revolution did not alter, in any fundamental way, the class composition of the national political elite, but it did lead to an effective reallocation of political power *within* the country's upper stata. . . . On the basis of socio-economic trends in Mexico, one might expect that rising capitalists, particularly industrialists (of either upper- or middle-class status), would be moving into positions of political power. This has not happened, . . . [because] the Revolution has brought about a separation of political and economic elites.[81]

Smith finds that the economic and political elites do not overlap. Although they share some socioeconomic characteristics, they are definitely not the same individuals. For example, while urban, middle- and upper-class backgrounds are common to both groups, the fathers of the economic elite were largely merchants and small industrialists, while the fathers of the politicians were in the professions, military or civil service, or were themselves politicians. Both elites are overwhelmingly university graduates; but while the politicians studied at the National University, the economic elite generally received technical training at either the Polytechnical Institute in Mexico City or the Technological Institute of Monterrey. A notable 44 percent of the economically powerful are foreign born or sons of immigrants in contrast to the politicians, virtually all of whom come from Mexican families. But Smith underscores that if "entrepreneurs and office holders emerged from a single class" it is from "demonstrably different segments of that class."[82] Indeed it is hard to find instances of intermarriage between the two.[83] There is little crossover between the two groups, and, generally speaking, the economic elite does not take an overt part in politics, nor do individual families branch out into both business and politics, with one son becoming a governor, for example, while another heads a large corporation.[84]

On the basis of his findings, Smith argues that there is an identifiable "state interest" which can be distinguished from the class interests of the bourgeoisie.[85]

Instead of a unified power elite, Mexico therefore appears to have a fragmented power structure that is dominated, at the uppermost levels, by two distinct and competitive elites. They have specific common interests, most notably in the continuing subordination and manipulation of the popular masses and in the promotion of capital accumulation. But aside from this tacit consensus, and the collaboration needed to maintain it, these elites are at the same time struggling for control of the country's development process—and for supremacy over each other. . . .[86]

The struggle among bourgeois elements for supremacy over competing interests is a pattern also noted by Nora Hamilton. Hamilton focuses not so much on competition between economic and political elites as on conflicts between and among those segments of the Mexican bourgeoisie whose interests are tied in with foreign capital, those elements which participate in joint ventures involving heavy government funding, and other Mexican capitalists whose interests diverge from these more powerful groups.[87] In Mexico,

. . . the linkages among the dominant state factions, foreign interests, and the dominant segment of the national bourgeoisie are varied and complex, and each may seek to maximize its specific interests with varying degrees of şuccess. But the state is limited to options available within the framework of a structure in which these groups are dominant.[88]

Based on the evidence provided by Hamilton, Smith, Lomnitz, Camp, Stevens, the Purcells, and others, it seems fair to say that the bourgeoisie comprises a complex of economic groups, which at times have conflicting interests or at least different preferences with regard to state policy. It is also clear that the bourgeoisie does not "rule" directly, that it does not control the functioning of the Mexican state in any absolute sense, and that the government is run by a political elite that is identifiably distinct from the industrialists, bankers, commercial landowners, and commercial elite who make up the bourgeoisie. However, for all the distinctions that can be drawn between the bourgeoisie as a social class, and the Mexican state as an autonomous entity, it is equally clear that the influence of the bourgeoisie over the policy makers who manage the state is more powerful than that of any other group in society, if it is not, at all times, absolutely determinant.

The Bourgeoisie and the "Revolutionary Family"

Perhaps the most significant form in which the bourgeoisie presses its interests is through the inclusion of key representatives in an informal but immensely powerful decision-making body variously referred to as the "revolutionary coalition" or the "revolutionary family," an inner circle of extremely powerful men who have the ear of the president and advise him on all key questions of policy or succession.[89] All other political organs in Mexico—the PRI itself, the Senate, the Chamber of Deputies, the federal and state government bureaucracies—are subordinate to the revolutionary family. So powerful is this small elite that it easily overrides the decisions of the official party and all the formal interest organizations that stand behind that hierarchy.

The exact membership of this inner circle is a matter of speculation. Probably only the members of the family themselves know for certain who belongs to the group and who among that number are the most influential members. But among those who have studied Mexican politics, there is general agreement that all living former presidents, the most powerful regional strongmen, the governors of the most important and richest states, the mayor of the federal district, the commander-in-chief of the army, the head of the Bank of Mexico and other important banks, the wealthiest foreign and domestic industrialists and those who control key industries, the American ambassador, key cabinet ministers, the secretaries general of the CTM, CNC, and CNOP, the president of the Senate, the rector of the National University, and a few intellectuals of international repute may all enjoy partial or full access to the deliberations and decisions of this select policy-making group. In general, the "family" consists of those men whom the president feels constrained to consult on major policy decisions.[90] The decision on who will succeed in the presidency, the choice of PRI nominees for state governors, the selection of federal senators and deputies, and the choice of party candidates for the most important political posts at national, state, and sometimes even the local level, are all decisions in which the revolutionary family may play a key role.

Not every member of this elite is consulted on every issue, nor does each member's opinion carry equal weight.[91] Indeed it might be more accurate to speak of an "immediate family" of very influential men, and a larger "extended revolutionary family" which includes all members of this elite circle. But even the term "family" itself is somewhat misleading in that it tends to conjure up an image of a close-knit group of people who sit together around a table hammering out political decisions. In fact members of the revolutionary family may never see one another. The president does not arrive at his decisions by a show of hands or by counting votes, but rather by sounding out the opinions of family members and assuring that no particular policy or decision meets with the intractable opposition of a significant number of important family members.[92] The idea of a family conclave is to build consensus among the most important representatives of the most powerful or potentially powerful elements in Mexican society.

Members of the three party sectors, particularly members of the popular sector, participate in the revolutionary family as selected advisors to the president, but not as formal representatives of their sectors. In the deliberations of the revolutionary family, as in the decision-making process in the official party, the interests of peasants and workers are underrepresented, or they are not represented at all. If and when they are consulted by the president, the secretaries general of the CNC and CTM may try to influence the selection of candidates, and particularly the choice of a presidential nominee acceptable to the peasantry and to labor.[93] However, although the president may consider the objections raised by a peasant or labor representative, in the end the preferences of these two groups are usually outweighed by the members of the revolutionary family who represent the interests of foreign capital and the national bourgeoisie.[94]

Mexican political mythology has it that the peasants and workers are the heirs of the Mexican Revolution. However, as discussed in chapter 1, the group that really emerged victorious from the revolution was the rising middle class, the industrial and agricultural bourgeoisie, and members of the prerevolutionary elite who managed to preserve their former positions of power and privilege by declaring themselves to be "with the revolution." During the six decades of relative political stability that have followed the revolution, the power relationships that emerged at the end of that struggle have been institutionalized in the official party and in the extraparty pressure groups. The popular sector enjoys an advantaged position within the governing party, and bourgeois interests are preeminent in the Mexican political system as a whole. As a result, the development policies that have been promoted in Mexico over the last forty years clearly reflect the interests of the national bourgeoisie and its foreign business partners.

3

THE MEXICAN ROAD TO DEVELOPMENT

Chapters 1 and 2 reviewed the process through which a bourgeoisie composed of industrialists, bankers, businessmen, and large landowners has consolidated its power. As we have seen, the bourgeoisie exercises enormous influence over government decision making through the interest associations it has formed and the direct access it enjoys to the president and top-ranking government officials. Logically enough, the development policy pursued by the PRI and by successive administrations from 1940 onward promoted the interests of the dominant national bourgeoisie and their foreign business partners. This policy brought about the rapid modernization and economic growth of Mexico. Indeed, Mexico's economic record throughout the 1950s and 1960s was so impressive that the country was often regarded as one of the two or three outstanding models of economic and political modernization in a nonsocialist Third World setting. Indeed, in the boom years of the 1960s it was common to hear the development process which had unfolded described as the "Mexican miracle." In this chapter we will examine the pattern of development to understand just how this phenomenal growth was produced.

THE "MEXICAN MIRACLE": 1940–1970

Although Mexico has one of the highest rates of population growth in the world (3.5 percent a year), and the total population has more than doubled from 20 million in 1940 to over 50 million in 1970, during those same years the economy grew steadily at an average annual rate of almost 6.5 percent.[1] In 1969–1970 the rate of growth reached 7.4 percent,[2] a figure so high that it was surpassed only by Japan and Finland among the nonsocialist developed nations, and a few especially advantaged countries (Libya, Korea, and Israel) in the developing world.[3] To put it another way, although the population tripled from the mid-1930s to the mid-1970s, during this same period the per capita value of all goods and services produced in Mexico nevertheless increased by more than 160 percent.[4] In 1971 production per person reached $700 per year, placing Mexico somewhere between Portugal and Spain in the economic hierarchy of nations.[5] Furthermore, Mexico's economic expansion was all the more remarkable when we consider that it was sustained for almost thirty years with relatively little interruption and that it was "balanced" in the sense that agriculture grew in line with industry.[6] By the 1970s, production of grains and legumes had grown to the point that Mexico had become a net exporter of food. It had also become self-sufficient in the production of petroleum products, steel, and most consumer goods.[7] In 1940, 65 percent of the population lived in the countryside. By the 1970s well over half of all Mexicans were living in towns and cities of more than 2,500 inhabitants. While 65 percent of the 1940 work force labored in agriculture, by 1970 less than half were agricultural workers, and the majority of working Mexicans were employed in industry, commerce, finance, transport, communication, and services.[8] Throughout this period of rapid economic growth, population growth, and demographic shifts from the countryside to the cities and from agriculture to industry and services, the Mexican peso remained relatively stable. Notwithstanding two periods of inflation and devaluation in the 1940s and 1950s, it was used by the International Monetary Fund and other international banking agencies to support shaky currencies in other countries. Roger Hansen noted in 1971 that whether we measure Mexico's growth in aggregate or per capita terms, whether we compare the Mexican statistics with those of other Latin American countries or with the industrialized, developed countries of the world, whether we look only at the period from 1935 to 1970 or compare Mexican development with that which occurred during the period of most rapid industrial growth for each country concerned, the Mexican record in the postwar period was a "singular achievement."[9]

The Mexican Strategy for Development: The "Trickle-Down" Theory

Mexico's outstanding rate of economic growth and steady expansion in the industrial sector was the result of a calculated strategy of development that has been pursued with considerable consistency from the time Cárdenas left office in 1940. This strategy is based on a "trickle-down" theory of development that focuses on the long-term aspects of economic growth.[10] The strategy presupposes that as a nation's economic output grows, some of the benefits of development ultimately reach people at all levels of society. But the distribution of the benefits of development takes place only *after* a period during which the profits of economic growth are reinvested to build an industrial base for future development.[11]

In order to sustain a rapid rate of growth, a developing nation like Mexico must raise its rate of domestic savings and investment.[12] That is, the profits that result from industrial growth must be poured back into industry. The trickle-down theory hold that if a country like Mexico is to maximize economic growth, these profits cannot be distributed to workers in the form of higher wages.

In line with this strategy, Mexican wages have risen very slowly during the post-1940 period of rapid industrialization. The slow rise in wages has not kept pace with a rapidly rising cost of living. As a result, Mexican workers have experienced a fall in real wages; that is, while their paychecks have been increased from time to time, the prices of food, clothing, housing, etc., have increased even more, and thus workers find that their peso buys less with each passing year.[13]

While workers' real wages have declined, the income of industrial entrepreneurs has climbed rapidly.[14] The government has placed almost no limits on profits nor on the expansion of industrialists' incomes. Naturally, government policy makers are aware that when a rise in entrepreneurial incomes accompanies a fall in real wages for workers, the gap between rich and poor grows wider. Indeed, in 1958 the incomes of the richest 5 percent of all Mexicans were 22 times those of the poorest 10 percent; by 1980, the gap had more than doubled and the rich enjoyed incomes 50 times greater than those of the poorest sector of the population.[15] However, the growing inequality of income distribution in Mexican society has been posed by those in power as a necessary, if unfortunate, "short-term consequence" of development.

Taxation Policy

There are strategic reasons why a government does not step in to curb the accumulation of wealth in the hands of rich industrialists. In order to assure a supply of capital for private investments in industry, the Mexican development plan has called for a policy to provide strong incentives to both domestic and foreign entrepreneurs. Part of this policy is to maintain an extremely low rate of taxation on income received by industrialists. Taxes are low both on interest earned from investments and on profits derived from production. Although taxation of high-income groups is known to be one effective way of redistributing wealth throughout a society and narrowing the gap between rich and poor, it has not been utilized by the Mexican government. Indeed, a survey of tax policy in Latin America in the 1960s revealed that Mexico imposed the lightest tax burden on her upper class of any of the eighteen countries studied.[16] And taxation on foreign-owned enterprises is so low that in foreign business circles Mexico enjoys the reputation of providing one of the most favorable investment climates in the world.[17]

Where the Mexican government has taxed the public—as in the case of the sales tax—the taxes imposed tend to be regressive. In contrast, income tax is so light that it not only fails as a redistributive method, but it raises very little revenue for government spending.[18] Tax evasion, a common practice in most countries, reaches truly impressive proportions in Mexico. One Mexican expert estimates that roughly 75 percent of the upper class manages to escape payment of the relatively light taxes levied on them.[19] They do so while those in charge of tax collection wink and look the other way. Tax reforms implemented in the mid-1970s improved the collection of income taxes from the salaried middle class but left the bourgeoisie effectively untouched. However, this and other aspects of the Mexican taxation policy are entirely consistent with the development strategy that has been applied since 1940; the government assures that entrepreneurs need not worry about heavy taxes biting into profits in the expectation that capitalists will thus be stimulated to make further investments in the industrial sector.

Opting for a low rate of taxation on high-income earners, the Mexican state has necessarily had to look elsewhere for the revenue to support the ambitious programs of infrastructural investment and other public expenditures. To raise these funds, the Mexican government has borrowed abroad from multilateral international institutions like the World Bank and the Inter-American Development Bank, from bilateral institutions such as the U.S. Agency for International Development and the Export-Import Bank of the United States, and from private foreign banks and financial conglomerates.[20] Whereas development in the immediate postwar period had been financed with revenue from taxes, profits of public enterprises, and foreign earnings from exports and tourism, by the late 1960s, "Mexico's public foreign debt . . . started to grow until it finally became the foundation of its economic growth."[21] By the 1960s, the foreign debt had reached $1.8 billion and it increased at a geometric rate through the 1970s,[22] until by 1982 the debt was a staggering $80 billion and Mexico had earned the dubious distinction of being the most indebted country in the world.

Thus, unwilling or unable to tax the rich, the Mexican government has relied on foreign borrowing to balance the budget for public expenditures—with all this implies for the loss of autonomy that results when a developing country comes to count on foreign creditors to so great an extent. In their public utterances Mexican political leaders regularly and passionately denounce the interference of foreign capitalists in domestic policy formulation as well as the pressures applied by international and American financial institutions on Mexican affairs. Justified as these denunciations are, it is also important to note that this lamentable situation results from more than the overall dynamic of dependency. The problem we see here is more than the "standard" problem of unequal exchange in which Third World countries grow more indebted as they pay rising prices for imported manufactured goods while their earnings from exports fall. In the Mexican case, the staggering dimension of the foreign debt is clearly the consequence of a general strategy of development which has doggedly favored the industrial bourgeoisie, whatever the costs to the nation as a whole. As one Mexican economist has noted,

> . . . the Mexican government continued to balance its deficits—both from its social expenditure and its investment program—with debt instead of placing greater financial responsibilities on the richest sectors of the Mexican society. The government stabilizing development strategy was designed to pamper the industrialists who not only evaded, legally and illegally, the fiscal burden but also benefited from consumption at very low prices of enormous quantities of state-produced inputs, such as electricity, transportation, communications, and oil, giving back very little.[23]

Other Incentives to Investment

Throughout the 1940s new Mexican industries were protected from foreign competition by high tariffs on imported manufactures. In the 1950s import licensing, that is, government control over goods imported into the country, became the mainstay of the protectionist policy for Mexican industry.[24] This protectionist policy was part of a drive toward "import substitution." Under an import substitution program a government attempts to encourage the establishment and growth of manufacturing firms producing goods that have previously been imported from abroad. High tariffs and import licensing were designed to give Mexican entrepreneurs and their foreign business partners a strong competitive advantage over firms producing goods abroad. At the same time the government has also used licensing to restrict the amount of internal competition with which a new producer must contend.[25]

In addition to providing protection for Mexican products, the government devised other policies calculated to encourage investment by private businessmen and to attract foreign capital. Since 1941, new enterprises have been granted tax exemptions for periods ranging up to ten years. Furthermore, duties paid by manufacturers on the machinery and materials they purchase abroad have been rebated to them.[26] The government has also provided credit to entrepreneurs at rock-bottom rates of interest. Nacional Financiera, a government bank established in 1933, provides funds to private businessmen who would otherwise encounter serious difficulties in raising capital for investment in industry. With government backing, this credit bank has expanded into international credit markets and is able to channel foreign loans into private business. In this way low-cost capital from international sources is available to Mexican entrepreneurs through loans guaranteed by Nacional Financiera.[27]

Taken as a whole, these government policies created a very favorable climate for both foreign and domestic private investors. "It is reported that profit rates in Mexico are among the highest in the world."[28] Through the postwar period of rapid growth, high returns on investment and economic stability stimulated a steady flow of foreign capital into Mexico. One of the challenges facing policy makers was how this flow of foreign funds was to be regulated.

Foreign Investment and "Mexicanization"

Since 1940, Mexican policy on foreign investment has been a compromise between two conflicting tendencies or desires. The first is a desire to reduce or eliminate foreign economic control over the Mexican economy. Indeed, as noted in chapter 1, the elimination of foreign economic influence was a primary objective of the national bourgeoisie which led the revolution and established the official party. At the turn of the century these people had found their own economic ambitions cramped by the dominance of American, British, and other foreign businessmen in virtually all key areas of the Mexican economy. Many representatives of the national bourgeoisie joined the revolution in 1910 precisely to oust the foreign businessmen who had gained such extensive control during the regime of the old dictator, Porfirio Díaz.

The sons and grandsons of the old bourgeois revolutionaries are now the people who formulate policy in Mexico, through their role in the government, the official party, or the various influential businessmen's associations. Many of them still cherish the dream of a Mexican economy completely controlled by Mexican entrepreneurs, by men like themselves. As a group, these men share a repugnance toward the notion of foreigners, particularly Americans, holding economic power in their country.[29] Therefore, when they formulate economic policies, they are moved in part by strong desires to exclude foreign investors from a controlling role in the Mexican economy.

But these desires conflict with the Mexican leadership's commitment to the goal of rapid economic development, a commitment which has prevented them from indulging their desire to go it alone with no outside financing from American or other foreign sources. Policy makers operate on the assumption that high rates of growth cannot be achieved without heavy foreign investment. Their chosen development strategy has forced them to lay aside their nationalist pride and to accept the inevitability of policies designed to attract foreign capital.

Thus Mexican policy makers have worked out a compromise between their desire for economic independence and their need for foreign capital. Their compromise is a policy that encourages foreign investment at the same time that it subjects that investment to certain nationalistic restrictions. It is a policy of so-called partnership through which foreign capital is obtained while control over its use supposedly remains in the hands of Mexican nationals. The name given to this policy is "mexicanization."

Mexicanization divides all industries into four categories. The first are fields reserved exclusively for the state. These include all key public services such as railroads, telegraph, postal service, and electricity. The oil industry and primary processing of petrochemicals all fall into this category, but concessions are granted by the government to private firms. The second category includes areas reserved for Mexican investors such as broadcasting, automotive transport, and gas. The third category covers fields in which foreign ownership is limited to 49 percent. Insurance, advertising, publishing, cinema, domestic transport, food processing and canning, soft drinks, basic chemicals, insecticide, fertilizer, mining, agriculture, and livestock all belong to this category. The fourth category covers all fields in which foreign capitalists are free to invest without restraint.[30]

The mexicanization policy requires that Mexican nationals hold majority ownership of enterprises in certain key sectors of the economy. The industries to which this restriction applies are defined by law. However, the interpretation and application of the legislation (i.e., which enterprises fall into which category) is left to the Mexican executive, and there is considerable leeway for the president to determine where and when mexicanization restrictions will be applied. It is precisely this flexibility that leaves foreign firms so much room for maneuver. The discretionary power allows the government to accept or reject foreign capitalists' contentions that they should be exempt from restrictions. The methods of persuasion used by foreign firms range from simple, straightforward payoffs, to diplomatic arm-twisting, to threats that they will withdraw their proposals for creating thousands of jobs unless they are permitted to create them on their own terms.[31] In the early 1970s, for example, Chrysler Corporation threatened to pull out of Mexico completely unless it was given leave to acquire full ownership of the failing enterprise it had previously shared with Mexican capital.[32]

As a result of the pressure they exert and the loopholes that are left open, many favored foreign industries manage to escape mexicanization limitations entirely.[33] Several of the largest firms in Mexico— General Motors, Ford, General Electric, Anderson Clayton, Monsanto, and Admiral, to name a few—are entirely owned by American interests. In some cases these U.S. firms have made their investments in sectors where Mexican partnership is not required. In other cases, their continued activity in the Mexican economy has been considered so important that the government has simply chosen to look the other way and ignore violations of the mexicanization principles.[34]

Sometimes, despite their efforts to prevent it, foreign firms are forced to mexicanize, that is, to sell majority control of an enterprise to Mexican investors. When a foreign-owned company is faced with the prospect of mexicanization, there are a number of ways in which it can comply with the law by selling a majority of its stock to Mexican citizens, and at the same time retain control of the enterprise. Thus many foreign firms have developed a variety of techniques to evade the mexicanization requirements. Some of the favorite methods include:

1. Spreading the stock among a group of Mexican investors so numerous that none of the Mexicans is able to challenge the foreign company's controlling block of stock
2. Retaining control of the company's management through a special management contract
3. Retaining control by becoming the main purchaser of the goods produced by the "mexicanized" firm (e.g., DuPont owns only 33 percent of Química Flúor, but is the major customer of the chemicals produced by Química Flúor)
4. "Selling" the Mexican stock to a trusted Mexican investor or issuing stock to the public without issuing voting rights to the public
5. Paying a Mexican businessman for the use of his name as a majority Mexican partner[35]

Circumvention of the mexicanization requirements is facilitated by the fact that there is a great deal of money to be made by Mexican businessmen who are willing to lend their names and influential connections to help foreign firms gain or retain control over enterprises in Mexico. This is a symbiotic relationship: the foreign investors need the collaboration of their Mexican "partners" and stand to realize enormous profits with the help of a Mexican "front man," while the Mexican "name-lender," (prestanombre) is normally well paid for his cooperation. However, the relationship between the Mexican front man and his American partners can be as hostile as it is mutually profitable. In Carlos Fuentes's novel *The Death of Artemio Cruz*, the protagonist is engaged in such activities and has increased an already substantial fortune by fronting for American firms that wish to circumvent the restrictions on the foreign ownership of natural resources. We come upon Cruz as he meets in his Mexico City office with two American businessmen who seek his aid (and, specifically, the use of his name) in obtaining concessions to exploit sulfur deposits along the Mexican Gulf coast:

Boiling water would be injected into the deposits, the North American explained, and would dissolve the sulfur which would be carried to the surface by compressed air. He explained the process again, while his compatriot said that they were quite satisfied with the exploration. . . . Cruz, at his desk, tapped his fingers on the glass and nodded, accustomed to the fact that when they spoke Spanish to him they believed he did not understand, not because they spoke it badly, but because he would not understand [the scientific details] in any language. . . . One North American spread the map on the desk as he removed his elbows, and the other explained that the zone was so rich that it could be exploited to the limit until well into the twenty-first century, to the limit, he repeated, until the deposits ran dry. . . .

The North American winked an eye and said that the timber cedar and mahogany was also an enormous resource and in this, he, their Mexican partner, would have one hundred per cent of the profit; they, the North Americans would not meddle, except to advise continuous reforestation. . . .

Then [Cruz], behind the desk stood and smiled, hooked his thumbs in his belt and rolled his cigar between his lips waiting for one of them to cup a burning match and hold it to him. He demanded two million dollars immediately. They question him: to what account? For although they would cheerfully admit him as their Mexican partner for an investment of only three hundred thousand, he had to understand that no one could collect a cent until the sulfur domes began to produce. . . .

[Cruz] repeated quietly, those are my conditions, and let the North Americans not suppose that they would be paying him an advance or anything of that sort: it would merely be what they owed him for trying to gain the concession for them, and indeed, without that payment, there would be no ' concession: in time they would make back the present they were going to give him now, but without him, without their front man, their figurehead— and he begged them to excuse his frank choice of words—they would not be able to obtain the concession and exploit the domes.

He touched a bell and called in his secretary who read, rapidly, a page of concise figures, and the North Americans said okay a number of times, okay, okay, okay, and Cruz smiled and offered them whiskies and told them that although they might exploit the sulfur until well into the twenty-first century, they were not going to exploit him for even one minute in the twentieth century, and everyone exchanged toasts and the North Americans smiled while muttering 'that s.o.b.' under their breath.[36]

Cruz, like real-life Mexican businessmen, is willing, for a price, to use his influence in government circles to win his American partners the concessions they desire, and to protect their investment from nationalization by the government. The *Wall Street Journal*, however, recently warned potential U.S. investors that the relationship with a Mexican *prestanombre* can be a "difficult and dangerous" affair and securing the cooperation of a reliable and willing Mexican name-lender can prove more of a challenge than a small U.S. firm is able to undertake.[37] But once the services of a well-connected Mexican front man are secured, the relationship is mutually beneficial and unquestionably part of what makes Mexico such an inviting field for foreign investors eager for both high profits and maximum stability. " 'Mexicanization' has its bright side for foreign companies: they become eligible for generous tax and import duty exemptions, are virtually assured of immunity from nationalization or expropriation, and have greatly increased opportunities for expansion."[38] Foreign businessmen have long recognized the advantages offered by Mexico as a field for investment, and foreign investment in Mexico has expanded with each passing year.[39] From 1950 to 1970, foreign investment increased more than fivefold to $2,822 million,[40] while in 1979 alone it grew by 72.6 percent.[41]

The Emphasis on Capital-Intensive Production

One consequence of the heavy flow of foreign investment into Mexico has been the importation of advanced technology along with foreign capital. The trend of government policy has been to encourage modern, highly mechanized means of production because this type of production is generally believed to result in higher rates of capital accumulation leading, in turn, to higher rates of growth. Stimulated by government loans, Mexican and foreign entrepreneurs have built modern factories outfitted with equipment imported from industrially advanced countries, particularly the United States. Indeed, 80 percent of the goods imported into Mexico are machinery, chemicals, or semiprocessed manufactures produced in the United States. Mexico has become the United States' leading customer in Latin America, and ranks sixth among all nations purchasing American-made goods. Excluding oil, the prices of the raw materials which Mexico exports to the United States have declined steadily over the last twenty years. But the cost of machines and manufactures supplied to Mexico by American firms has risen. The result of this disparity has been an increasingly unfavorable balance of trade for Mexico with respect to the United States.[42] Thus, the Mexican government has gone heavily into debt to finance the purchase of the modern machinery with which Mexico's new factories are equipped.[43] As we shall see, even the discovery of vast oil reserves did not reverse these trends, as the Mexican government spent more to import heavy capital equipment and food than it earned from oil exports.

In addition to putting Mexico heavily in debt to American and international banking agencies, the import of modern industrial equipment has had disastrous consequences on an already serious problem of unemployment. The machinery purchased abroad is designed for economies in which the cost of labor is relatively high and labor-saving devices are at a premium.[44]

In a country like Mexico, where there is a scarcity of capital and a plentiful supply of workers, it might seem logical that industrialists would search for production techniques that emphasize the use of manpower ("labor-intensive" production) rather than machines ("capital-intensive" production). But Mexican industry is so closely tied to foreign capital that Mexican factories tend to be designed as branch plants of North American, European, or Japanese firms. The same technology applied at the parent plant in Pittsburgh, Hamburg, or Osaka is applied in the Mexican plant. There has been very little experimentation in Mexico with labor-intensive forms of production. Both Mexican and foreign capitalists find it more profitable to invest in machinery than to rely on the labor of human beings. "Mexican businessmen are generally biased toward what is considered more 'modern' equipment; this implies preferring capital to the use of labor. Machinery is considered to provoke fewer conflicts than labor unions and labor legislation."[45] Foreign-owned industry is even more capital intensive than domestic Mexican plants.[46] It may be that some experimentation with labor-intensive techniques would create more jobs in Mexican industry and ultimately improve the economic and social conditions of the Mexican working class. But the welfare of the working class is not a focus of concern for either foreign or Mexican capitalists, except insofar as higher incomes for workers expand the internal market for the goods produced by modern industry. What concerns the capitalists, of course, is higher profits. And higher profits are realized with greater certainty and ease when sophisticated machinery is employed in place of people. Unfortunately, even the "mexicanization" regulations have not been utilized to channel foreign investment into forms which more adequately meet the needs of the mass of unemployed peasants and workers. Analyzing this situation, an American investment banker noted, "the principal motivation behind Mexican policies toward foreign investment has been to protect sovereignty. . . . There has been virtually no effort to promote social welfare goals through regulation of foreign investment."[47]

As we might expect, the result of a development policy that emphasizes capital- rather than labor-intensive production is that employment has not kept pace with industrial growth. As the industrial sector has expanded in Mexico, the number of laborers added to the work force each year has declined. That is, the industrial work force has grown at a slower rate than industrial output.[48]

Nowhere in the Mexican economy is this trend toward capital-intensive production more evident than in the petroleum industry. With the discovery in the mid-1970s of vast oil reserves, petroleum soon became the central focus of the national economy. But although, as we shall see later in this chapter, petroleum production earns billions annually, fewer than 200,000 workers are employed in the entire petrochemical industry.[49] The point is even more dramatically underscored when we consider the ratio of capital investment to the creation of new employment opportunities. In some phases of the recent development of the oil industry, only one new job was created for every $250,000 of capital invested.[50]

Estimates indicate that between 750,000 and 800,000 new workers enter the labor force each year.[51] But even during the boom years of rapid economic growth in the 1960s, only 300,000 new jobs were created annually.[52] Thus, the number of jobs available in industry has not grown sufficiently to absorb even the current job seekers, much less the additional agricultural workers who would have to be absorbed into industry if overpopulation and unemployment in the countryside are to be reduced. Estimates on unemployment vary, because the official statistics tend to disguise much of the problem. However, the 1980 census made clear that only half of the labor force—some 12 million Mexicans—have regular employment,[53] and most reliable sources indicate that the number of chronically unemployed or underemployed workers may even be higher than the official figures suggest.

When unemployment is high and the supply of labor overabundant, the surplus of available workers tends to depress wage levels. During the period of most rapid industrialization, wages were held so low that they surpassed their 1939 level only in 1966.[54] Lower wages, of course, mean a lower standard of living for workers and higher profits for the industrial entrepreneurs. And higher profit for industrialists, as we have noted, is a key part of the Mexican government's strategy to stimulate private investment. In countries where labor unions are militant and independent of government control, it is difficult, if not impossible, for the political elite to pursue a development program in which wage increases are held to a minimum. But when the greater part of the work force is not unionized and when workers who do belong to trade unions are mostly incorporated into a single labor federation like the CTM, which is neither militant nor independent of government control, this type of development is quite feasible.

A relatively tiny proportion of the labor force is organized into certain unions which constitute an "elite" within the working class. These few unions (petroleum workers, electricians, railroad workers) have a long tradition of militancy, and have managed to win wages that are substantially higher than those earned by any other sector of the Mexican labor force. "The labor unions are well organized in a number of sectors, and in return for labor peace, an orderly system of wage adjustments and active efforts to 'cool-out' workers in the rest of the economy, a small proportion of workers in the industrial sector are relatively well paid."[55] But the aggressive tradition of the petroleum workers', electricians', and railroad workers' unions stands out as the historic exception within the labor movement. Virtually all other workers have been forced to accept wage contracts negotiated for them by their leaders in close collaboration with the private owners of the enterprises involved. In contrast, the wage contracts of electricians, petroleum workers, and railroad workers are negotiated directly with the government, because these are the industries that are government-owned. The higher wages enjoyed by workers in the nationalized industries "appear to be the price the government is willing to pay for the loyalty and support of these groups of workers in the name of the whole working class."[56]

Government Spending

The pattern of government spending in the years since 1940 has reinforced all the advantages to private capitalists that we have noted above. If a government is determined to maximize economic growth, it must concentrate its expenditures in "bottleneck breaking" investments; that is, investments in road construction, hydraulic systems, electrification, communication lines, and so forth—investments that create the infrastructure underlying a modern industrialized economy.[57] Because private investors are generally unwilling or unable to undertake projects that yield low profits in the short run, the task of building an infrastructure usually falls to the government. Government spending on infrastructure, like other aspects of the Mexican development policy, is specifically designed to create the optimum conditions for productive private investment.[58] Large government investments are made for improvements in transportation, electric power, the distribution network of petroleum and gas products, and so forth. These public outlays are aimed at creating an environment in which industrialists find it easy to establish new firms and to build productive facilities.[59]

If a government pours revenue into the construction of a modern infrastructure, subsidies to business, and credit concessions to nascent industry, it may have very little money left over to spend on essential public welfare services. It is difficult for the state to undertake the expansion of education, medical facilities, rural electrification, and public housing when the bulk of its revenue is tied up in bottleneck-breaking investments to increase industrial output. Indeed, throughout the 1940s and 1950s while Mexico invested heavily in industrialization, less than 15 percent of the total government investment was allocated to social welfare expenditures.[60] By 1980, health and welfare expenditures had dropped to 13 percent.[61] In the last year for which figures are available, 1975, state spending on public education was only 8.4 percent, although by that period, school-age children comprised half the population. Social security has covered only one quarter to one third of the work force through the present decade.[62] Overall the figures indicate that "despite the populist tradition of Mexican politics, the level of expenditures on welfare is relatively low—benefits being effectively limited to that third of the workforce that is unionized."[63]

Policy Priorities and Dependency

There are limits on the financial resources that any government has at its disposal. Consequently, policy makers must choose among a variety of development patterns or strategies, some of which emphasize rapid economic growth, while others stress more equal income distribution and more immediate social benefits for the population. No government can spend its money in a way that *maximizes* industrial development and, at the same time, make the needs of a population of desperately poor people its top priority. A choice must be made. And in Mexico, the political leadership has consistently opted for those development policies which give highest priority to the growth of the industrial and commercial agricultural sector. Other national goals, such as full employment, higher wages, more equitable income distribution, and social welfare, have been given low priority as Mexico's ruling elite has pushed the economy toward ever higher levels of productivity.

As we have noted throughout this chapter, virtually every aspect of the Mexican strategy for development—a strategy geared to the needs and interests of the bourgeoisie—tends to further enmesh the country in a net of dependent relationships with multi-national corporations, with private American investors, with official U.S. banking institutions, and with American-dominated international bodies like the World Bank or the International Monetary Fund. The propensity to borrow abroad rather than tax Mexican industrial profits; the choice of an import substitution policy which requires technology and equipment available only in advanced industrialized economies; the decision to use import substitution to produce luxury consumer goods like autos rather than machinery to build a foundation for an autonomous industrial capacity—each of these policy choices has reinforced dependent relations with the United States, circumscribing the alternatives for future development.

Given the historic and geographic links between the two countries, the unequal distribution of resources north and south of the border, and the degree of integration of the Mexican with the U.S. economy, we would logically expect to find bilateral relations characterized by "interdependence," or even a high degree of "asymmetrical interdependence."[64] But, in fact, statistics on national income, balance of trade, foreign investment and ownership, and foreign loans provide a picture of the most skewed form of dependent relations: foreign firms dominate the most dynamic sectors of the Mexican economy. They are more capital intensive, feature higher rates of labor productivity, are housed in larger plants, and offer higher wages than Mexican industries.[65] Eighty percent of all technology employed comes from foreign sources.[66] Foreign companies produce 35 percent of the total industrial output and hold 45 percent of the share capital of the 290 largest firms.[67] And notwithstanding Mexican efforts to attract European and Japanese investors, four-fifths of all foreign-owned companies operating in Mexico in 1979 were American.[68] Among foreign capitalists, American investors predominate; 70 percent of direct foreign investment comes from the United States, and almost all credit to public or private Mexican borrowers comes from U.S. banks.[69]

The balance of trade between the two countries is probably the area in which Mexican dependence is most evident. Mexico sends 69 percent of all its exports to the American market and buys 64 percent of all its imported goods from U.S. sources.[70] However, while the United States is Mexico's main trading partner, American goods sold to the Mexicans in 1981 represented only 5 percent of total U.S. exports.[71] Even in the years of the oil boom, as we shall see, the negative balance of payments increased to $2.3 billion in 1978 and $4.2 billion in 1979 as Mexicans were forced to import food and capital equipment in ever greater quantities. By 1981, Mexico's exports to the United States had grown to an impressive $9.7 billion, but in the same year Mexicans imported $12.1 billion worth of goods from the U.S. And linked to most of these indicators of dependency is perhaps the most telling set of statistics: U.S. income and wealth per capita remains, even in the 1980s, seven times that of Mexico; one of every five Mexican workers now seeks employment at least part of the year in the United States.[72]

What we wish to underscore with these few data is that Mexican economic dependence on the United States is, in itself, a conditioning factor that shapes and delimits—if it does not totally determine—the development options available to Mexican policy makers. But beyond the grim reality of the limitations imposed by *any* dependent relationship between unequal countries, the priorities established by the elite which has directed policy since 1940 have served to consolidate American dominance over Mexican affairs at the same time that they have produced and reinforced gross inequalities between the Mexican upper classes and the popular masses.

Given the form that economic development has taken in Mexico since the Cárdenas years, what could we expect would be the result of the dramatic discovery and exploitation of vast quantities of oil along the Gulf coast of Mexico?

MEXICAN DEVELOPMENT IN THE AGE OF PETROPESOS

From the time that the extent of Mexico's oil reserves became widely known in the mid-1970s, government spokesmen asserted that Mexico would not repeat the mistakes—indeed, the tragic errors—that had occurred in other oil-rich nations. Venezuela was cited most often by Mexican leaders, as by countless North American and European analysts, as a negative example of the gross mismanagement of oil wealth which results in the exacerbation of virtually every economic and social problem existing at the moment that petrodollars start to flow into an economy. Some analysts of the Mexican situation went so far as to draw hope from comparisons between the probable course of events in Mexico and the bizarre and tragic happenings then unfolding in Iran. If comparisons with Iran or with Saudi Arabia or the Arab Emirates seemed farfetched, the parallels with Venezuela were numerous enough to lend an air of seriousness to such discussions. One key point, however, was lost, or at least obscured, in almost every analysis of Mexico's future which was couched in these comparative terms. Mexican leaders were not free to pick and choose development strategies from the counter of history, just as one chooses hot or cold sausages.[73] In developing oil production, the Mexican state was operating within the framework of a development strategy—inherited from past decades—which sharply limited the range of alternatives available in the 1970s and 1980s. The logic of the development process which we have outlined in this chapter dictated a restricted set of options for the utilization of petroleum wealth.

Oil Wealth: Promise for the 1980s

Under the luxuriant vegetation and off the steamy tropical coast of Campeche, Tabasco, Veracruz, Chiapas, and Tamaulipas lie what may well come to hundreds of billions of barrels of oil. Once the dimensions of Mexico's petroleum resources became known beyond elite Mexican government circles and the American CIA, each new estimate of certain and potential reserves was higher. By 1978–1979, Mexican resources were widely understood to run to 200 billion barrels, with only 15 percent of the country surveyed. By 1980 proven reserves had reached 60 billion barrels and many experts believed that Petroleos Mexicanos (or Pemex, the state-owned oil company) would soon uncover oil reserves to exceed those of Saudi Arabia, thus making Mexico the number one oil power in the world.[74] Although there was some reason to doubt the scientific rigor of the measurements applied, and it seemed possible that Pemex might exaggerate findings to strengthen its position vis-à-vis other state agencies or to bolster national pride and enhance Mexico's international standing,[75] by July 1981, five new giant oil fields had been uncovered off the coast of Campeche and proven deposits stood at 70 billion with potential reserves listed as 300 billion barrels.[76] The remarkable speed with which exploration progressed was surpassed only by the dimensions of the discoveries: in the Bay of Campeche seismic sounding began in 1972; sixty well-defined subterranean structures were quickly identified, and exploratory drilling was underway by 1974; proven reserves rose geometrically until it was clear that petroleum resources here would make the North Sea reserves seem skimpy. In the "Reforma" fields in Chiapas and Tabasco, one large field alone, the "Bermudez" field, held oil wealth almost equal to that of the North Slope of Alaska.[77] Thus, even in the late 1970s, CIA experts set Mexico's potential output for 1985 at 10 million barrels a day, and indeed, by 1981, 2.75 million barrels were in fact pumped daily.

Exuberance over this news of actual and potential oil reserves has been tempered from the start by some sobering considerations concerning the role of petroleum in national development. From the day in March 1938 when Lázaro Cárdenas expropriated seventeen foreign oil companies, the national oil enterprise, Pemex, has stood as a central symbol of Mexican sovereignty. The 1938 nationalization began as a labor dispute between the Oil Workers' Union and foreign managers. A

Mexican tribunal ordered wage increases and shorter hours, and when the foreign companies refused to comply, Cárdenas seized the holdings of the British, Dutch, and American oil companies[78] and "restored a great birthright to the Mexican people." Although the United States moved to retaliate with the imposition of low import quotas on Mexican petroleum and an embargo on the supply to Mexico of American investment funds, technology, and transport facilities, the onset of war in Europe made a quiet settlement of the oil companies' claims expedient if not imperative for both countries.

Poor in expertise and equipment, the Mexicans struggled to run their own petroleum industry. Although Mexico had been the world's principal oil producer from 1910 to 1921,[79] in the first years after nationalization, Pemex, "suffered from dwindling reserves, decrepit plants and equipment, grossly inadequate transport and pipeline facilities, a chronic shortage of Mexican technicians, continuing foreign pressures, intractable labor problems, low prices and the challenge of hammering the foreign firms into a single corporation at the nation's service."[80] By the 1950s Mexico's known petroleum resources were exhausted, and international oil prices were too low to justify costly exploration. Thus Mexico was forced to import oil to meet domestic demand and the country remained an oil importer through the early 1970s. Only with the news that great riches lay beneath the earth and the coastal waters of the Gulf, did it become clear that what had been strictly a symbol of dignity, national unity, and pride could now become a real source of funds for national development.

The New Development Plan: "Export-led Growth"

A plan for development, based on projected reserves and production was soon formulated. The central tenet of the program was that oil would be pumped out of the ground not in response to demand on the international market, but at a pace consistent with the slow, steady expansion of the Mexican economy. To avoid the "financial indigestion" or inflation brought on by sudden and massive accumulation of foreign currency earnings from oil, a policy of slow exploitation of petroleum wealth was announced by President José López Portillo (1976–1982). Official policy called for Pemex to draw only 1.1 million barrels per day, rather than the estimated 10 million potentially available. Furthermore Mexico was to move away from dependency on the United States by selling this oil to a diverse range of customers with no single country taking more than half the available supply. Sales to Japan and western European clients were foreseen, along with purchase on favorable credit terms by energy-poor Third World nations in Latin America and the Caribbean.

To escape what it termed the "petrolization" of the economy, that is, the creation of a lopsided economy excessively reliant on oil revenues, the López Portillo regime sought to promote slow growth of the industrial sector through "export-led development." The export-led growth policy promised to resolve the contradictions of import substitution which, as we have seen, proved unworkable in Mexico, as elsewhere in the Third World, because of the high and ever-rising cost of imported components, technology, and capital equipment. An export substitution program, in contrast, proposed gradual replacement of primary exports—in this case, crude oil—with processed and manufactured exports. Thus refined oil, petrochemical products, and manufactured goods of every description would gradually take the place of crude as Mexico's chief export. By 1990, it was projected, Mexico would earn 85 percent of all foreign exchange from the sale of industrial products and only 15 percent from crude oil.[81] The key to this transformation lay in utilizing oil revenue in the short run to establish the long-term basis for a modern, internationally competitive industrial capacity.[82]

To build such a capacity, López Portillo's "Industrial Development Plan," launched in 1979, called for the creation of new "development poles" through the decentralization of industry from Mexico City, Monterrey, and Guadalajara to neglected, peripheral regions of the country. Eleven new industrial zones were to be established in the marginal hinterland areas; four were "industrial ports" under construction at Tampico and Coatzacoalcos on the Gulf, and Salina Cruz and Ciudad Lázaro Cárdenas on the Pacific.[83] To encourage investment in these new zones, the Mexican government called on its customary repertoire of incentives to private investors: tax credits of 25 percent for new investments, an additional 20 percent tax rebate on the basis of the number of jobs created, and discounts of 30 percent on electricity, natural gas, fuel oil, and basic petrochemicals for investors in the new industrial ports.[84] It gives some sense of the rewards involved when we consider that under this system of tax credits and rebates, Mexican and foreign investors such as the largest private conglomerate of Mexican capitalists, the Monterrey-based Alfa group, paid taxes of only 17–19 percent on all corporate earnings in this period.[85]

Thus the plan for development foresaw a gradual expansion of Mexican industry with particular emphasis on steel, petrochemicals, capital goods, and machinery such as pumps, turbines, electric motors, and forged metal products—all goods which had formed the bulk of expensive inputs during the import substitution attempt. The assumption was that the internal market for Mexican products would grow as oil revenue "trickled down" to the masses, while cheap energy and cheap labor for both private- and state-owned enterprises would give Mexican producers an advantage over North American, European, and Japanese competitors in the international market. Finally, oil revenue would be directed to support a "Global Development Plan" designed to create 2.2 million new jobs in all sectors of the economy between 1980 and 1982. Thirty percent of these jobs were expected to open in industry, the rest in agriculture and the service sector. By 1990 a total of 12.6 million new jobs would be available to absorb the 800,000 annual entrants into the labor market.

To its ideators, this program seemed certain to bring prosperity— first to the industrial bourgeoisie and the financial risk takers, and eventually even to the mass of peasants and workers, as the wealth generated through exports trickled down to them. Instead, as we shall see, within the context of an international system in which Mexico was bound by strong and multiplex ties of dependency to the United States, and within the framework of the development policy which had been pursued in Mexico since the Cárdenas years, export substitution development proved no more successful than the import substitution schemes of the 1960s. Why did the export-led development strategy turn out to be so difficult to implement?

"Petrolization"

The most immediate obstacle to realizing an oil-based development scheme was, very simply, the petrodollars could not be expected to flow into Mexico unless and until petroleum flowed out. Finding and drilling the wells to produce at a rate which would earn Mexico the foreign exchange to underwrite ambitious development plans required heavy investments—as always—in technology and capital equipment. Although Pemex had been in operation since 1938, and oil had been produced in Mexico since early in the twentieth century, in 1979 three-quarters of all capital goods utilized by Pemex were still imported, almost entirely from the United States, where Texas-based oil companies like Brown & Root of Houston offered the specialized equipment and expertise geared to off-shore drilling along the Gulf coast. In the development of the rich oil fields in Campeche Sound, Brown & Root was hired as project manager to oversee engineering and construction.[86] For Pemex, such assistance has been crucial. The Chicontepec basin in Campeche Bay may turn out to contain as much as 100 billion barrels. But low porosity and permeability of the oil-bearing rock have necessitated the drilling of 16,000 separate wells—as many as Pemex had sunk in all its history.[87] In addition, the development of each new oil field has required the construction of gathering lines, roads, railroad spur lines, and other support facilities. Moreover, the blowout of the oil well "Ixtoc I" in June 1979, which spilled a total of 134 million gallons into the Bay of Campeche before it could be capped nine months later, dramatically demonstrated the need for human skills and equipment of the most sophisticated kind.

Lacking technical personnel as well as adequate research facilities, Pemex, already the largest single employer in Mexico, expanded its payroll from 80 to 120 thousand employees over the five-year period from 1976 to 1981. But still foreign specialists were required. Furthermore, balance of payments problems grew worse as Pemex was forced to import capital goods with price tags that rose about twice as fast as the value of crude oil on the international market.[88] To make matters worse, "the prices of goods Pemex imports rise faster than do those of other imported goods; as a result, the short run impact of oil development on the economy is more inflationary than the development of other sectors."[89]

Other countries peddling advanced technology tried eagerly in these years to sell their goods on the Mexican market. For example, in 1978 the Commercial Division of the Canadian Embassy advised Canadian firms:

> Pemex has an ongoing need to purchase a wide range of equipment including pipe, flanges, connections, valves, fasteners, gaskets, insulating materials, boilers, steam generators, heat exchanges, cooling towers, storage vessels, pumps, compressors, air dryers, power plants, laboratory and data acquisition equipment, . . . electrical substations, switches, transformers, electrical cable, fire control equipment, drilling equipment, well repair and maintenance equipment, etc., to be used in new projects or to maintain existing facilities.[90]

But for all the enthusiasm of Canadian, western European, and Japanese suppliers to break into this market, American companies remained the primary source of both equipment and skilled technical inputs. Thus, the hope that oil wealth would provide the lever with which Mexico could pry itself free from U.S. domination proved ill-founded as Mexico turned to the United States for the bulk of purchases necessary to build an infrastructure for oil and gas production. And as for the hope of diversifying petroleum sales, 80 percent of Mexican oil was sold to American buyers in 1978–1979,[91] and by 1980 the figure was still 77 percent.[92] Furthermore, 99.3 percent of natural gas sold went to American customers, shipped directly to the United States through a pipeline constructed for that purpose.[93]

Another hope which had been expressed in the Global Development Plan was that Mexico would escape the kind of unhealthy reliance on oil earnings which would distort the economy and the society as a whole. Yet from 16 percent in 1976, the share of hydrocarbons in Mexico's export earnings rose to 40 percent in 1979, 65 percent in 1980, and reached 75 percent in 1981.[94] By that same year, one-third of all government revenue came from the sale of petroleum. This tendency to rely more and more on petroleum revenue was the inevitable, if unfortunate consequence of the lag in the growth rate of all sectors of the Mexican economy other than oil. In the face of rising prices for manufactured imports, increasing foreign borrowing to support the free-spending government programs already in place, plus the growing need to import food—which we shall detail in the pages that follow—only oil earnings could plug the gap.

Thus by the end of the 1970s, pressure had mounted to export ever greater quantities of oil to meet the interest payments on the external debt and pay for the growing number of goods and services purchased abroad.[95] As one analyst noted, "when confronted with the choice between raising domestic taxes or increasing oil revenues to finance government programs, . . . the politically expedient choice is oil exports."[96] Given this pressure, by 1980 the López Portillo regime had abandoned its previously established limits on the extraction and sale of oil, and production rose from 2.25 to 4 million barrels a day. In 1982 the first official admission that the model of oil-spurred growth had failed was given in a report from the Mexican Institute of Petroleum which bluntly stated, "economic expansion will continue to depend for the most part on oil, for which no substitute can be foreseen before the end of the century."[97]

Social Costs of Oil Production

It is often said that, given the steady concentration of wealth they have witnessed since the Mexican Revolution, peasants and workers did not expect to see great improvements in their lives as a result of the discovery of this new "national treasure." On the other hand, it seems doubtful that they anticipated that oil would bring greater misery. Yet for many, if not most of them, it has. Among other negative consequences, the rate of inflation which accompanied the oil boom has confirmed economic planners' worse fears. Officially 30 percent in 1980, the annual rate of inflation was estimated at over 100 percent by the end of 1982. Notwithstanding the imposition of price controls and heavy state subsidies for staple foods, cost-of-living rises in the "boom" period have far outstripped the real income of the lower half of the Mexican population.

The challenge of creating jobs for the growing masses of unemployed and underemployed has certainly not been met by the oil boom, notwithstanding the optimistic projections of the Global Development

Plan. The capital-intensive nature of petroleum and petrochemical production means that thousands of dollars of capital must be invested for each position opened. A study of the Colombian petrochemical industry in the late 1960s found that an investment of $39,000 was required to create one new job. This figure was twenty times the sum needed to generate a job in clothing, footwear, textiles, glass, or metal products.[98] In Mexico a decade later, the cost of each additional position varied from one industry to the next, with estimates ranging from $6,000 to $25,000 for each new job.[99] However, as we have noted, in some phases of recent development at Pemex, an astounding $250,000 had to be invested before a job was added to the payroll. The problem indicated by this statistic is not simply that more workers do not find employment in Pemex, but that every peso invested in Pemex and other capital-intensive sectors is investment foregone in areas which feature a more favorable ratio of labor to capital. Furthermore, even the government's policy of selling petrochemicals domestically at well below the world market price, as well as the special discount rates provided to industrial firms, tend to increase employment. Randall explains, "the subsidies are a factor in cheap energy prices which make it more profitable to hire machines than people."[100] However, acceptance of ever higher rates of unemployment has become a matter of official policy:

> In March 1979 the administration announced that it would put into effect a National Industrial Development Plan, placing priority on the growth of basic industries in preference to labor-intensive industries. While the latter were regarded as a desirable means of creating employment, it was feared that they would build additional inefficiencies into the economy.[101]

If oil-fueled development does little to create jobs or directly improve the lives of poor people, nowhere has this inadequacy been felt more intensely than in the Gulf coast states which have been the scene of the exploration, drilling, and construction associated with petroleum production. "Pemex crews have spurred the flight from land- and water-related work by destroying large tracts of fertile terrain and contaminating productive rivers and estuaries."[102] As one biologist reported: "With their dredges they can make and remake rivers. . . . They have cut grooves across the entire state . . . [turning] the hydrological system upside down."[103] The hostility of peasants and peasant organizations toward Pemex is an indication of the degree to which the state oil company has wreaked havoc on the precarious rural economy of these tropical zones.[104] The destruction of rich agricultural land and coastal fishing grounds by oil seepage and the wholesale expropriation of farmland which is used for exploratory ventures and then abandoned in ruined condition have been responsible for the decline in productivity in what was once a key agricultural region. Tabasco state has been particularly hard hit. Amid the shrinking acreage of cultivable land, petroleum development has eaten away at resources, ecologically and economically destroying much of the richest farmland in Tabasco state.[105]

Particularly bitter are those peasants who raise crops that are subject to government-imposed price ceilings. These people have lived since the earliest years of the current boom, with a local rate of inflation that hovers around 300 percent.[106] Although few jobs have opened for local people, their villages and towns have quadrupled or quintupled in size with the influx of Pemex personnel, foreign technicians, equipment salesmen, their dependents, and hangers on.[107] Shantytowns have developed at the margins of new industrial ports and oil installations as hundreds of thousands of untrained men and women pour into the development zones in search of work which in the end goes to more skilled or specialized workers, or to those who can afford to pay the requisite bribes. The social infrastructure of schools, hospitals, and other services is inadequate to meet even the planned population increases, not to speak of unplanned migration. The social disintegration of the previously existing communities is all but complete as the search for oil has brought in the prostitutes and petty and major criminals characteristic of boom towns. In essence, the corruption rampant in Mexican government and society at all times has, in these last years, reached epic dimensions in the coastal zone.

At the center of the decline in public and private morality is Pemex itself. Notorious for its corrupt practices, even in a society distinguished neither for efficiency nor honesty in public administration, the Pemex bureaucracy has been charged with raking off public funds through crooked maneuvers and raising the price of imported machinery to include kickback payments of as much as 45 percent.[108] Ironically, the same oil industry which is often posed as offering a cure for Mexico's economic, social, and political ills is itself riddled with corruption, bureaucratism, and "labor problems" which consist largely of Mafia-like control over an oil workers' union run, literally, by a mob of gangsters.

> Since its foundation, the company has been characterized by a wasteful and inefficient use of resources, with administrators, technical staff and union leaders all involved in the sale of contracts to private companies, and of jobs to the vast number of people seeking them.[109]

Only 40 percent of workers employed by Pemex hold regular contracts. The rest buy their jobs each month with payments amounting to hundreds of thousands of pesos to the bosses of Sindicato de Trabajadores Petroleros de la República Mexicana, or STPRM, the oil workers' union. The union's power is based on its enormous and varied financial holdings in landed estates, supermarkets, credit unions, and other enterprises, its capacity to enforce a closed shop, and, above all, its role in the modern sector most closely related to the symbolism of the revolution. This is what enables it to secure wages for its members which are, on the average, twice those received by other industrial workers. But this power also permits union leaders to engage openly in the game of *vendeplazas*, or job selling. The *sub rosa* system of payoffs has its own graded scale: in the late 1970s a general worker's job sold for 40,000 pesos while a mechanical engineer could secure work for 150,000 pesos. The kickback required for temporary jobs was based on the length of the contract with a 2,000-peso payment needed for 28 days, 4,000 for a sixty-day job, and so on. And so closely interwoven are the private affairs of Pemex managers and oil union leaders—all of whom serve freely on the boards of directors of companies which receive Pemex contracts—that the directors of the government enterprise are hardly in a position to expose corrupt union officials.[110]

Thus the operations of the state oil company are shot through with corrupt practices at every level. Oddly enough, while Pemex corruption is a regular topic of editorial comment in several Mexican newspapers and magazines,[111] the issue of company corruption came to a head only in 1982, when a United States federal grand jury began to investigate charges that American oil equipment companies had made payments of tens of millions of dollars to secure contracts from Pemex officials. The case brought by the U.S. Department of Justice against a small Houston-based firm was the first major criminal investigation under the Foreign Corrupt Practices Act of 1977, which prohibits bribery payments to foreign government officials to obtain or retain business contracts.[112] The disclosures in Washington, D.C., resulted in the forced resignation of two top-level Pemex administrators. However, although two high-level officials have been brought to account, there is no way to redress the injury to the poor and powerless who have been the victims of this bureaucratic system built on corruption. The would-be oil workers who must trade bribes for jobs exemplify only one form of victimization. Pemex has paid generous compensation to wealthy ranchers and plantation owners for land expropriated for oil operations. However, when powerless peasants are expropriated they receive compensatory payments so low that they are effectively left with nothing with which to make a new start. But the biggest losers in this system of corruption, the real victims of government malfeasance, mismanagement, and collusion, are the Mexican people as a whole. This is because the cost of developing the petroleum-exporting potential of the country, as we have seen, has been borne in every other sector of the economy. And that cost would not have been so high had the price tags on equipment and technology not included bribes and kickbacks to Pemex administrators and union bosses.[113]

In chapter 8 we will examine the fiscal disaster which has overtaken Mexico and Mexicans—above all, middle- and lower-class Mexicans—with the oil glut of 1981, the drop in petroleum prices it prompted, and the resulting crash of the Mexican economy in the autumn of 1982. However, at this point it is sufficient to underscore the fact that the pattern that events have taken since Mexico became an "oil-rich nation" in the 1970s is a direct outgrowth of the overall model of development that has guided Mexican policy makers over the last four decades.

AGRICULTURAL POLICY

Just as the policy of the Mexican state in directing a program for industrialization or a strategy for the utilization of oil wealth has reflected the interests of the dominant Mexican bourgeoisie and of foreign capital, so too has the agricultural policy pursued in Mexico since the massive land reform initiated by Cárdenas in 1937. In the final section of this chapter we will look at that agrarian program, how it has shifted over time, and how those changes fit within the overall strategy of Mexican development.

Land Reform Under Cárdenas

As we know, land reform was one of the central goals of the Mexican Revolution. The incorporation of agrarian reform legislation into the Constitution of 1917 represented a great victory for peasants and peasant leaders, and paved the way for a series of agrarian laws promulgated during the 1920s and 1930s. We also recall, however, that agrarian reform was carried out on only a token basis during the 1920s and early 1930s, and it was not until Lázaro Cárdenas came to power in 1934 that large-scale land distribution began in earnest. During Cárdenas's administration it appeared that the Mexican peasant would finally realize the great *agrarista* dream: the day when the government would provide every peasant family with a plot of land sufficient to guarantee an income adequate to meet the family's basic needs.

Cárdenas's land reform was spectacular, not only because he distributed close to 45 million acres in five years, but also because of the type, quality, and location of the land he distributed. In the twenty years that had elapsed since the revolution, Cárdenas's predecessors had distributed less than 19 million acres of mostly marginal land. The earlier land distributions consisted almost entirely of arid, unirrigated, steep, rocky, and infertile land lying far from roads and markets. Large productive estates were not touched. The holdings of powerful landowners were left intact, and their economic and political power was not diminished by any of the halfhearted agrarian reform gestures made during the 1920s and early 1930s.

Cárdenas's approach to land reform was far more radical. Rather than handing out marginal lands that no one had ever been able to work profitably, Cárdenas expropriated and distributed highly productive, choice lands. Almost all of the land distributed by Cárdenas was already under cultivation in modern, economically efficient plantations.

The Laguna region in north-central Mexico was the setting of Cárdenas's largest and most dramatic land reform effort. It was here, in one of the most modern agricultural areas of Mexico, that well over a million acres of efficiently organized and highly profitable cotton plantations were seized by the government under the provisions of the Agrarian Code, and distributed to 38,000 peasant families. With the assistance of three hundred government engineers and agronomists, Cárdenas carried out most of the Laguna reform in just forty days. The speed of the Laguna distribution was typical of Cárdenas's approach during his administration. When attempting to effect radical change, Cárdenas favored the swift, irreversible, political act. As in the case of the expropriation of the petroleum industry, Cárdenas made up his mind to move on land reform, and then implemented his decision with such speed that he was able to expropriate hundreds of large *haciendas* before the opposition had time to rally its forces to obstruct the sweeping changes. The extraordinary rapidity with which land reform was carried out meant that the old order was swept away while the large landowners were still reeling under the shock and could offer no concerted opposition to Cárdenas's program.[114]

The Goals of Land Reform

Cárdenas understood the far-reaching implications of land reform in a society such as Mexico. Agrarian reform is an instrument through which land, as a productive resource, can be transferred from one part of society to another; generally speaking, from certain individuals in a society (a small number of large landowners), to other members of that society (a mass of landless peasants). But in addition to the transfer of land as a *productive* resource, land reform can operate to redistribute wealth, status, and political power within a society. In a traditional agricultural society, where land is the basis of most socioeconomic status and political power, the implementation of a thoroughgoing land reform has profound social and political as well as economic consequences.[115] Cárdenas understood this fact well enough. He was aware that in expropriating and redistributing large landholdings, he would do more than break up some large estates and divide these holdings among thousands of hitherto landless peasants. He understood that in so doing, he would transfer to the peasants a new economic and political power as well as a new social status. He would lay the basis for a redistribution of economic and political power within Mexican society.

Given that Cárdenas needed the political support of the peasantry, he was anxious to assure that social and political power would in fact be transferred to the landless peasants. Therefore he was determined to promote the *economic* success of the land reform he had set into motion. In order to establish a firm economic base for the ejidal program, he (1) organized the ejidal holdings into farming collectives, and (2) set up government institutions to support the land reform program and to aid the new land recipients in their struggle to break the old patterns of dependency on large landowners.[116]

Collective Agriculture

As we have already noted, most of the land distributed by Cárdenas had previously been organized into large, modern agricultural enterprises. The basic rationale for the collective *ejido* was the desire to distribute the land of the few to the many, without destroying the productive capacity of what had been highly productive estates. Therefore, some way had to be found to break up the large estates and distribute their land in the form of small holdings, and at the same time to preserve the economies of scale that go along with large-scale enterprises. The answer to this problem was the collective *ejido*. Under this system each peasant in a peasant community was given a specific piece of land on what had been a neighboring *hacienda*. Each peasant, then, had the right to farm his small plot, but agricultural machinery, wells, fertilizers, insecticides, and other equipment were owned or purchased on a collective basis. A variety of different, more and less collectivized forms evolved to meet the needs of the *ejidatarios*. In some *ejido* communities, all the individual plots were merged into a single large agricultural unit and worked on a collective basis from sowing to harvest. At harvest time the profits from the sale of the crop would be divided according to a formula that allotted each member of the *ejido* some measure of profit corresponding to his contribution to the joint effort.

On other collectivized *ejidos*, *ejidatarios* farmed only the plot they had been assigned, but shared in the use of agricultural equipment. The collectivized form of agriculture featured a number of advantages. It maximized the economic use of scarce irrigation waters. It facilitated the use of heavy, expensive agricultural equipment, as well as the harvesting and marketing of the crop. And finally, it permitted the peasants—long used to executing fairly specialized tasks on the *hacienda*—to continue to work in specialized teams. As one observer explained it, the system of collectivized agriculture helped "to smooth the transition from *hacienda* to *ejido* agriculture by maintaining the existing labor organization as far as possible."[117]

Under the land reform program of 1937, a variety of supporting institutions were established to aid the newly landed peasantry. The National Ejidal Credit Bank was set up to provide credit, technical assistance, and supervision to the collective *ejidos* and to guide the *ejidatarios* in establishing their own internal administrative structures. In addition to the bank, Cárdenas oversaw the creation of schools of agricultural technology designed to train *ejidatarios* and their sons. Furthermore, the new land recipients were encouraged by the Cárdenas administration to form their own unions, councils, and associations. These organizations were specifically designed to arbitrate disputes arising within or between *ejidal* communities, to protect and promote the interests of the *ejidatarios* in their dealing with the National Ejidal Credit Bank and other government agencies, and to consolidate the political support of the *ejidatarios* for the government that had given them land.

There is a considerable body of statistics recorded in the first few years of the collective ejidal experiment in Mexico.[118] These data indicate substantial economic progress for the *ejidatarios*. After a brief period of economic disorganization immediately following the land distribution, the *ejidos* soon began to function with an efficiency that permitted them to repay the credit loans initially extended by the National Ejidal Credit Bank and, in some cases, to realize substantial profits. For example, in one area of the Laguna region, the purchasing power of the peasants increased more than 400 percent during the first three years following the land reform.[119]

The Downfall of the Collective *Ejido*

Unfortunately, the honeymoon period of the collective *ejidos* was all too brief. Serious troubles began for the collectives as soon as the Cárdenas administration came to an end in 1940. Some of the problems that developed were inevitable, in the sense in that they arose from shortcomings built into the ejidal system at the time that the land reform was carried out. Some of the difficulties confronted by the *ejidos* grew out of the contradictions inherent in an attempt to establish an island of socialism in a sea of capitalism. Other problems which have plagued the *ejidos* over the last thirty-five years spring from limitations on their success imposed by government policies unamiable or even hostile to their development. We will look at each of these limitations in turn.[120]

Shortcomings built into the ejidal system. Many of the problems that were to plague the ejidal system in Mexico were built into the system from the beginning. In the Laguna region, where the first large-scale land reform was undertaken, many problems arose simply from the haste with which the program was carried out. For example, the engineers and agronomists who surveyed the region miscalculated the amount of irrigated land available for distribution. Much of the land originally classified as irrigable subsequently received water only in the years when the Rio Nazas, the region's principal water source, reached its maximum height. Likewise, the boundary lines established for the new *ejidos* were only vaguely determined, and often boundaries drawn between two *ejidos* or an *ejido* and a private property overlapped, creating a situation ripe for conflict. Finally, the census carried out in 1937 to determine the number of peasants eligible for land grants included not only 18,000 peasants native to the region, but about 10,000 seasonal laborers and 10,000 strikebreakers who had moved into the Laguna during a general strike that immediately preceded the reform. Thus, once the ejidal grants were distributed, the number of people to be supported by the land had more than doubled.[121]

Other problems that developed in the Laguna reform, as well as in the land reform programs which followed, grew from deficiencies in the Agrarian Code that provided the legislative basis for the program. Several provisions in the Agrarian Code created confusion and economic waste when applied to the concrete situation of a land distribution. In addition, the code was riddled with loopholes that permitted the large landowners to retain a substantial part of their old estates, and with these estates, much of the political and economic power they had monopolized in the prereform era. For example, the Agrarian Code permitted each landowner to choose the 150 hectares he would retain as a "small private property" *(pequeño propiedad)*. Naturally, he chose the part of the *hacienda* that included his house, stables, barns, warehouses, wells, irrigation canals, and the network of roads and communication lines connecting the estate with the outside world.[122]

Sometimes [the landowner] chose irregularly shaped, narrow strips, extending outward from his buildings in order to retain what he considered to be the most productive lands. . . . In other words, the heart or hub of the *hacienda* was detached, and the remaining parts were given to the *ejidatarios*. The *ejido* was thus formed from fractionated appendages detached from the central core.[123]

During the process of land reform, the unity and logic of well-organized and efficient agricultural properties were often destroyed. The agrarian law emphasized that the unity of agricultural production should not be disrupted.[124] This was the rationale for distributing land in the form of collectives rather than autonomous individual plots. But when it came time to put this theory into practice, it was the poorest land that was distributed to peasants in disjointed blocks, while the landowning class was permitted to retain the most fertile, best-irrigated land, and virtually all of the capital equipment.

Under the agrarian law, in addition to retaining 150 hectares of his own choice land, the landowner was permitted to subdivide and sell land that was not required for distribution to neighboring peasant communities. As a result, the *hacienda* was often "broken up" into 150-hectare parcels and "sold" to various members of the same family. This system of "parceling out" a huge estate which is then worked as a single *hacienda* unit is a common phenomenon in all regions of Mexico. It has come to be known as "neolatifundism," the creation of new *latifundia* (large landholdings). In addition to the "sale" of 150 hectare parcels to family members (including minors), it is not uncommon for neolatifundists to employ a lawyer or some other trusted person, who for a fee, lends his name to be used for a land title. As in the case of Mexican businessmen who front for foreign investors in order to circumvent mexicanization laws, an individual who lends his name to cover illegal land concentration is called a *prestanombre*, or name-lender.

Where a *hacienda* was located in an area of particularly dense peasant population, it would be unlikely that the old landowner would find himself in possession of land that was not required for the agrarian reform. In such cases, the old landowner would retain only the 150 hectares guaranteed him under the Agrarian Code. But even those whose property was genuinely reduced to 150 hectares enjoyed the advantages of working a capital-intensive enterprise. And in many such cases, the old landowner used his newly acquired capital resources to set himself up in a variety of agriculture-related businesses in the main cities and towns of the principal agricultural regions. In this way many of the old *hacienda* owners came to control the supply of credit, machinery, fertilizer, insecticides, and other products essential to the *ejidatarios* of the region. Hence the *hacienda* owners whose wealth had formerly been based on land ownership, entered into a powerful modern commercial class with strong ties to the industrialists. In this way many members of the old landowning class became even more completely integrated into the national bourgeoisie.

An "island of socialism." The Mexican land reform, even in its most dramatic instances, did not produce a total change in land tenure patterns. Indeed, in no region of Mexico, not even during the Cárdenas years, did the land reform program bring about a thoroughgoing transformation. Nowhere did private landholdings disappear. On the contrary, the Mexican government was quick to reassure Mexicans and foreigners alike that the right of private ownership would continue to be respected. Wherever private property, be it land or petroleum holdings, was expropriated, some form of compensation was provided.[125] In theory, the huge estate, the *hacienda*, was reduced to a number of so-called small private properties. But, in practice, the large estate continued to be a prominent feature of the rural Mexican scene.

In the regions where agrarian reform was implemented, the Mexican countryside became a crazy quilt of agricultural collectives scattered among *haciendas*. The collective *ejidos*, with their communal labor, profit sharing, cooperative credit system, and marketing system were "islands of socialism" floating in a sea of capitalism. The peasants involved in this experiment were socially isolated from the surrounding environment in which capitalism prevailed as a mode of production with a corresponding system of values. Although Cárdenas attempted to carry forward a series of reforms in rural Mexico, the country was then and remains today an economy dominated by capitalist enterprise. Thus, from the very start, the collective *ejidos* were an aberrant form, struggling for survival in a capitalist society. Obviously this situation was full of contradictions that were difficult if not impossible for the collectives to resolve.

One contradiction inherent in this situation was that the goods produced on the collective *ejidos* had to compete on the market with goods produced by capitalist enterprises. While a private commercial farmer can cut production costs by laying off workers and replacing them with machinery, the numbers of workers involved in ejidal production necessarily remains constant. The collective *ejido* cannot reduce its labor force because labor is provided by the members of the collective itself.

A second contradiction between the collective *ejidos* and the larger society quickly developed as ejidal leaders sought to increase the self-sufficiency of the collectives. The early years of the agrarian reform witnessed the birth of collective credit societies, mutual crop insurance companies, marketing co-ops, collective agricultural machine stations, and a host of other cooperative enterprises. But to the extent that these cooperative institutions were successful, they directly threatened the interests of the old landowners who had converted themselves into agricultural entrepreneurs dealing in agricultural equipment, supplying agricultural credit, and marketing cotton, wheat, and sugar. Any growth of the economic independence of the *ejidatarios* automatically conflicted with the interests of this new agribusiness sector which was dominated by the old landowners and by American capital. Therefore, it is not surprising that almost all the peasant-run projects aimed at increased economic independence for the collective *ejidos* were eventually quashed by the withdrawal of government approval or government funds.

The shift in government policy on land reform. The collective ejidal system, for all its technical problems implanted at the time of the land distribution, and for all the contradictions inherent in the establishment of an isolated collectivist experiment, might still have survived as a viable system were it not for the conservative swing in agrarian policy following the selection of Manuel Avila Camacho as official party candidate in 1940.

The international politics of the World War II period provided the rationale for the dramatic shift in agricultural policy away from the *agrarista* priorities of the Cárdenas years. During the 1940s, government support for the peasants' struggle against the large landowner was brought to a close. As the Mexican historian Jesús Silva Herzog explained, "Revolutionary language was toned down and substituted by new terminology. Very seldom did one hear of revolutionaries and reactionaries, but of the unity of all Mexicans."[126] With fascist forces gaining strength in Mexico (as occurred in several Latin American countries),[127] communist and socialist leaders as well as official party spokesmen expressed the belief that the national security of the country required all leftist elements to close ranks behind the constitutional government. Led by the socialist Lombardo Toledano, the CTM, for example, virtually prohibited its affiliated members from exercising their right to strike lest they jeopardize the national security and the allied war effort.[128] Tremendous stress was laid upon the need to increase production of raw materials to supply the allied forces. Avila Camacho and the ranking officials of his government seldom missed the opportunity to develop this theme in their public addresses:

The soldier will fight until death to preserve our national territory, but together with him we will all fight, each person in accordance with his own resources and within the range of his special activities. The worker, by producing more and sensing—during all his working hours—that our survival will depend in great part upon the number and quality of what he produces. The peasant by multiplying his effort and his crops so that in these great years of trial, the plow and the spade will prove as indispensable as the gun or airplane. . . .[129]

Not only were workers and peasants urged to defend democracy in the field or in the factory, but in the name of both national unity and the need for higher production of raw materials, the expropriation and distribution of land slowed from 2,934,856 hectares per year during the Cárdenas administration to 559,262 hectares per year under Avila Camacho.[130]

Under President Miguel Alemán (1946–1952), land distribution slowed to a trickle, and the situation of peasants grew worse. Supported by the national bourgeoisie, Alemán placed overriding priority on rapid industrialization and the emergence of Mexico as an economically stable, developed country. Unfortunately these goals were pursued only at a high price.

Rapid industrialization, an Alemán fetish, required low wages and the sacrifice of the labor force to capital accumulation. . . . Continuous protests from organized labor made no perceptible change in Alemán's philosophy or conduct. . . . For Alemán, the sacrifice of a generation of workers and peasants was a small price for making his nation materially strong, industrialized, modernized, advanced.[131]

The correlate of Alemán's emphasis on industrialization was the frankly antiagrarian character of his regime. Alemán, like Avila Camacho before him, was obliged by his position at the head of the "revolutionary" party to concern himself with the welfare of rural Mexico. He had to pay lip service to the "goals of the agrarian revolution," and he had to continue the pattern of heavy government investment in agriculture.[132] But for Alemán, government investment in agriculture meant investment in huge dams and other public works near the U.S. border; projects that increased the economic productivity of privately held lands.[133]

Alemán's very first legislative initiative, sent to Congress only two days after his inauguration, was a proposal for the revision of Article 27 of the constitution. Alemán's revision of the agrarian law redefined the amount of land classified as "nonaffectable"; it enlarged the size of estates that could be legally owned by single individuals.[134]

The changes in policy under Alemán were typical of the overall trend in agrarian policy in the post-Cárdenas years. Each new administration continued to repeat the rhetoric of the past, asserting the government's commitment to land reform as a "major goal" of the Mexican Revolution. At the same time, each of these administrations pursued specific policies which, logically enough, reflected the interests of the dominant bourgeoisie. Taken as a whole, these policies undercut peasant gains of the past, and slowed the process of land reform until the trend culminated in the 1980s, under President José López Portillo, with a virtual abandonment of the *agarista* commitment of the revolution. The shift in agrarian policy from 1940 to 1980 can be summarized as follows:

1. While *ejidatarios* had been encouraged by Cárdenas to work their land in collective form, later policy actively favored the breakup of the farming collectives and the formation of innumerable little groups within each *ejido*. In this way much of the political and economic potential of the collective *ejidos* has been reduced.[135]
2. The size of landholdings defined by agrarian law as "unaffectable" (unavailable for expropriation) has been increased.[136] At the same time, the government has ignored "neolatifundism," the illegal ownership of land in excess of the established maximum acreage. The result has been increased concentration of landholdings.
3. As a consequence of the above, the number of acres of land distributed annually to peasants under the agrarian reform program has been drastically reduced.[137] Equally important, the quality of the land that has been distributed is markedly inferior to the land distributed during the Cárdenas land reform.[138]
4. Militant peasant organizations, which under Cárdenas had received official sanction and had been encouraged to organize peasants to agitate for land distribution, have generally been discouraged or repressed since 1940.[139]
5. Perhaps the most significant policy shift has come in the area of government expenditure. Since 1940 the bulk of government spending on agriculture has been channeled into the support of private commercial agriculture at the expense of the *ejidos* and the tiny subsistence farms (*minifundios*).

The Emphasis on Commercial Agriculture: Land Reform Abandoned

The shift in government spending from the ejidal to the private commercial sector is a trend which, as we have seen, can be traced to the immediate postwar period. Through the 1940s and 1950s it was expressed chiefly in terms of massive state investment in infrastructural development which benefited large private owners. The planning of irrigation projects, for example, was typical of the bias in favor of private commercial agriculture.

Most [of Mexico's major irrigation projects] have been developed in the rather sparsely populated north and northwest, where large private holdings predominated over ejidal lands. In fact much of the land directly benefited by the new hydraulic systems is owned, directly or indirectly, by prominent Mexican politicians and their friends and relatives. . . . In contrast, little has been done to bring water to the heavily populated central mesa region where most of the land is held by *ejidatarios* and the owners of small private plots.[140]

The government policy on credit is also typical of this shift in priority. Agrarian law prohibits peasants from using their ejidal holdings as collateral for crop loans. As a result they are dependent on government loans as the only source of credit at normal interest rates.[141] "Statistics on government credit to the ejidal sector reveal just how limited the government commitment to *ejido* agriculture has been."[142] The proportion of government credit earmarked for support to the *ejidos* declined steadily after 1940. "Furthermore, even those funds available to ejidal agriculture have been channeled to the few highly productive, commercially oriented *ejidos*."[143] The cutback in credit supplied by the government bank has forced *ejidatarios* to borrow money at usurious rates from private banks and money lenders. The giant American-owned corporation Anderson-Clayton has been particularly active in the field of loans to peasant farmers. The exorbitant interest rates paid by *ejidatarios* who have been denied government loans make it extremely difficult for them to realize profits at the end of the agricultural cycle. "In many cases half or three-quarters of the crop serves to repay such loans."[144]

Government spending on agricultural research has reflected the same bias in favor of the large, commercial landholding. From 1940 to 1970, government-sponsored experiments concentrated on raising the productivity of grain and cotton cultivated on large commercial estates. Techniques developed in the so-called green revolution dramatically raised the productivity of wheat and cotton crops. But such increases are produced only with the heavy use of chemical inputs, mechanized equipment, and well-irrigated land. The vast majority of *ejidatarios* had no access to these inputs and, as such, the "dramatic discoveries" of this sort of agricultural experimentation only served to further marginalize the subsistence producer.[145] Indeed, *ejidatarios* have suffered very directly as a result of the technological innovations developed in Mexico for the large commercial farm. As green revolution technology raised the production of large commercial farmers, the market prices for these crops dropped. When market prices declined, the commercial farmer could continue to increase his profits because the new technology permitted him to increase his output. But the small peasant was unable to apply this technology to increase his production, so he had to live with lower prices for his crops. To make matters worse, through the 1960s, as the government poured funds into green revolution research, relatively little research money was granted to study methods for increasing production on small subsistence plots.

This systematic shortchanging of ejidal and smallholding peasant agriculture continued unchecked until production had declined to "sub-subsistence" levels on the plots of *ejidatarios* and *minifundista* producers. Deprived of credit and technical inputs, *ejidatarios* and *minifundistas* reached the point where their plots no longer provided food to maintain their families, let alone a surplus for sale to urban Mexicans. Meanwhile, enjoying the flexibility that ready credit provides, commercial producers, in search of higher profits, had given over ever-greater proportions of the lands to cash crops: coffee, tomatoes, strawberries, and other fruits destined for the U.S. market.[146] Commercial holdings which had been planted in edible grains and legumes were increasingly converted to sorghum to fatten beef cattle for export. By 1970 only 22 percent of the land in the irrigation districts was devoted to corn and bean production.[147] As a consequence of this shift away from basic food crops, Mexico, which a decade earlier had proudly entered the ranks of agricultural exporters, was now obliged to import 15 to 20 percent of all foodstuffs.[148] Indeed, one study estimates that perhaps half of the tortillas presently consumed by Mexicans are made from imported corn.[149] By 1980 the total bill for food purchased in the United States had reached $2 billion.[150]

Food imports became indispensable as the yearly growth rate in agriculture declined from 5 percent to 2.5 percent, a level below the rate of population increase. While one-third of the work force was employed in the agricultural sector, productivity was now so low that agricultural production contributed less than 10 percent to the gross national product.[151] Indeed, by 1980 total agricultural output was only 1 percent higher than it had been in 1975, although the population had increased 10 percent over that same five-year period.[152] In short, by the 1970s the "logical limits" of the government's agricultural policy favoring the private sector had been reached.[153]

> The dramatic growth of Mexican agriculture in the 1950–1970 period was primarily the result of infusing large amounts of capital into a previously undercapitalized agriculture. When the sectors which were able to absorb the new inputs and production methods had achieved full adoption and when the technological limits to raising yields had been approached, the growth of grain output could no longer keep pace with population growth.[154]

This decline in agricultural production, which prompted a crisis in the balance of payments in the late 1970s, also provided the stimulus for a new emphasis in research and government spending on smallholding agriculture. Financed by the World Bank and channeled through the Mexican Program for Public Investment for Rural Development (Programa de Inversiones Públicas para el Desarrollo Rural, or PIDER), a series of development plans were designed to increase crop yields on rain-fed smallholdings. Attempting to apply modern technology, new credit resources and government-sponsored "commercialization opportunities" to smallholding peasants in the central Mexican state of Puebla, the pilot program was posed as an effort to extend the "miracle of the green revolution" to subsistence peasants. Thus, in the late 1970s, "agricultural development officials, foreseeing a new role for the smallholding sector, began to maintain that, given the right ecological and institutional conditions, large increases in the production of basic foodstuffs could be obtained from 'traditional' peasants."[155]

But, in fact, the notion that small, intensively cultivated parcels can produce efficiently is not new. As early as the 1960s land-reform experts like Rodolfo Stavenhagen were demonstrating empirically that "the idea of the inefficient *ejido* is one of those myths which are propagated without scientific basis. There is no serious study of Mexican agriculture which does not show that the *ejidatario* and the private owners can make the soil produce with equal efficiency."[156] One study demonstrated that if agricultural productivity is measured in terms of all units of input *except* the owner's labor (that is, productivity per unit of capital invested, irrigation water, seed, fertilizer, etc.) the tiny private plots *(minifundia)* turn out to be the most efficient of all types of farming in Mexico. The *ejidos* are the second most productive. And measured in these same terms, the large-scale landholdings turn out to be the least efficient producers.[157] In short, the small farmers, both *ejidatarios* and *minifundistas,* do more with the few resources they have than do the large landowners. The Mexican peasant farmers take the small amount of capital available to them, the few tractors and other agricultural equipment at their disposal, the negligible amount of irrigation water that they have for their fields, and grow more with these resources than do the so-called efficient commercial farmers with similar inputs.

Although these same data were long available to government economists, until the late 1970s, agricultural policy was based on the highly questionable assumption that only the private commercial sector could produce efficiently enough to support the overall economic growth of Mexico, as population shifted from the countryside to industrialized urban centers. Counterposed to this policy and the assumptions on which it was founded, was a whole school of Mexican and foreign agricultural development experts—sometimes referred to as "agrarian populists" or as *"campesinistas"*—who asserted that peasants, as producers, have skills, strengths, and knowledge of their particular situation that have remained untapped. Essentially, these experts argued that smallholding peasant agriculture can be made more productive and thus is not necessarily fated to disappear in the process of capitalist development.[158] The experiments in Puebla state were to provide the testing ground for these concepts and hopes. "Plan Puebla" was designed to reverse the policy trend which for decades had favored commercial agriculture at the expense of small peasant farmers.

Unfortunately, preliminary results of the pilot projects carried out in Puebla were mixed. They indicated that the production goals of a program emphasizing government support to peasants can be met. But the anticipated social welfare benefits, the hoped-for increase in "social justice" are far more difficult, if not impossible, to obtain within the framework of the power relations that characterize the Mexican countryside. In his study of Plan Puebla, Edelman found that the program actually accelerated the impoverishment and marginalization of the poorest peasants because the better-off peasants managed to accumulate a modest amount of capital as the program gave them access to relatively inexpensive government credit. Furthermore, they were able to operate on a scale that allowed them to circumvent exploitative intermediaries and sell directly to the state commodities agency.[159] Meanwhile, "for the poorer peasants a process of proletarianization has been set in motion, spurred by rising rents for land, increased reliance on intermediaries, higher risk levels in crop production, and higher unit costs of production."[160]

> Thus while the early phases of the green revolution benefitted the agrarian bourgeoisie at the expense of *ejidatarios* and smallholders, the 'second green revolution' seems to have reinforced inequalities within the peasantry and resulted in the proletarianization of its poorest sectors.[161]

Notwithstanding these early indications that the new "peasant-oriented" development projects tended to drive their intended beneficiaries off the land at an accelerated rate, in March 1980, President López Portillo announced the establishment of the Mexican Food System (Sistema Alimentario Mexicano, or SAM), a comprehensive plan to raise productivity among smallholding, subsistence producers—the same rain-fed agriculture targeted by Plan Puebla.[162] Posed as an effort to raise the nutritional level of the population by stimulating the production of basic foods within the peasant economy, SAM gave strong incentives to encourage staple crop production for the national market. It did this by providing price guarantees and generous credit terms, plus discounts on all agricultural inputs to anyone producing beans, corn, rice, or wheat. With the introduction of a shared-risk concept, that is, compensation to smallholders in the case of crop failure, the government created a system of subsidies to production as well as supports for processing and consumption. Announced with great optimism, SAM was projected to bring about self-sufficiency in corn and beans by 1982, and all other staples by 1985.[163]

Unfortunately, even the early indications suggested that SAM would produce results tragically similar to those of the Puebla pilot project on which it was modeled. Favorable weather conditions and massive government spending in 1980–1981 brought about some immediate rises in productivity. But over the long run, the project appeared more likely to benefit commercial farmers, middlemen, and the better-off peasants rather than the rural poor who constitute the supposed "target group."[164] Corruption in the administration of SAM ran rampant even in the first year of operations. But even more significant and more troubling was the fact that the broader social goals of the project could not be realized given that the fundamental power structure of the countryside remained unaltered. Thus it proved impossible to translate rises in staple crop production into more protein and vitamins on the tables of either the urban or the rural poor. And when López Portillo's successor took office, SAM was officially terminated and the entire bureaucratic structure dismantled as part of the "austerity" measures imposed in 1983.

The Future of Land Reform

In evaluating the results of the Mexican land reform it is crucial to remember that any successful agrarian program necessarily requires a great deal of initial and continued input on the part of the state. Government input may take the form of investment in infrastructure (dams, irrigation canals, roads, rural electrification), provision of credit, or aid to a number of important supporting institutions (agricultural extension services, marketing facilities, agricultural schools). When these expenditures were forthcoming during the Cárdenas administration, ejidal agriculture showed great promise as an economically viable and even highly productive form of agricultural exploitation. However, when, after 1940, this crucial state input was in large part withdrawn and redirected toward the private commercial sector, the entire land reform faltered and sank into a morass from which it was never to emerge, notwithstanding occasional, sporadic attempts to resuscitate some of the more economically and politically important land-reform districts.

Until the 1980s, it was widely held by students of Mexican land reform that the agrarian reform made by Cárdenas was "irreversible and final."[165] Those who sustained this view were correct in that the land distributed to the peasants was never snatched away by the government and restored to the old *hacendados*. However, the post-1940 official attitude and legislation reversed the progress of the *ejidos* and undercut their productive potential. Thus land was never officially returned to the old landowners. But the lack of government support to the *ejidos*, and particularly the shortage of low-interest credit for *ejidatarios*, has made their existence as farmers so difficult that many sought a solution that represented a total throwback to prerevolutionary days: they secretly and illegally arrange to rent their ejidal parcel to a large commercial farmer who possesses the necessary capital to make a profit from the land. Then the *ejidatario* works for the commercial entrepreneur as a peon on the parcel that is, on paper at least, his own land.[166] By the mid-1970s, unable to afford the agricultural inputs, some 80 percent of all land reform beneficiaries had lost effective control of their parcels in just this manner.[167]

Recognition, confirmation, and consolidation of this trend came with the rural development program implemented by President José López Portillo as part of his effort to resolve the dramatic problem of declining agricultural productivity. Until López Portillo came to office, no post-1940 Mexican leader had ever taken any measure against the *ejido* as an institution,[168] and even if the real effect of their policies was to undermine the land reform sector, all modern Mexican presidents had defended the *ejido* and the *ejidatario* as the primary symbols of the revolution and its achievements. Indeed, virtually all speeches and the presentation of statistics were designed to suggest that the reform process which, in fact, had culminated under Cárdenas was still in progress and was being carried forward with ever greater enthusiasm and dedication.[169]

López Portillo, in contrast, promoted an agrarian policy that represented an undisguised move away from land distribution as a means to bring "social justice" to the peasantry. Stating bluntly that agrarian reform was a "failure," and that, in any case, there was "no more land left to distribute," López Portillo proceeded on the premise that Mexico's urgent food needs dictated a policy of "betting on the strong."

The first step in the process which promised to alter irrevocably the face of rural Mexico was the seemingly innocent—indeed, well-meaning—dedication of López Portillo to resolve all outstanding land claims during his term in office. This effort, it was asserted, would then bring to a close "the first stage" of the Mexican land reform, that of the distribution of land. However, the procedure through which land distribution was to be "concluded" was that the state governors (political appointees all) were empowered to settle all disputes within their domains, including tenure conflicts and questions concerning rights to water, forests, and pastures. Thus enormous discretionary powers came to rest in the hands of the state governors, the vast majority of whom were major *latifundistas*, as was López Portillo's minister of agrarian reform. The rationale offered for this policy which called an official halt to land distribution was that it would inspire confidence in private commercial landowners, calming their fears of expropriation, and stimulating them to reinvest their profits in agriculture.

To further encourage private investment, including foreign investment, agro-industry was promoted. To this end, transnational corporations already active in Mexico—Anderson-Clayton, Carnation, Del Monte, Nestlé, Ralston Purina, and United Brands—were urged to expand their operations so that eventually every stage of food production from cultivation to processing, distribution, and marketing would be largely in the hands of these giants.[170]

A reorganization of the land reform bureaucracy, carried out in the name of efficiency, reinforced the antiagrarian tendencies of the López Portillo program. This reorganization turned over to the Ministry of Agriculture or the Ministry of Water Resources—bureaucratic structures dedicated to serving all agricultual interests, both public and private—powers and responsibilities which previously had come under the auspices of the Agrarian Reform Ministry. Thus the government agencies explicitly designed to defend the peasants in the face of competing claims from private agricultural enterprise were either dismantled or their powers subsumed by other ministries which have no special responsibility to the ejidal sector.

However, the most serious blow to the aspirations of the landless peasantry was dealt by the López Portillo administration with the Law for Agricultural and Livestock Production, proposed by the president in his State of the Nation address, September 1980. The new legislation—a *latifundista's* dream—removed virtually all remaining restrictions on the concentration of productive land in the hands of the few. As we have seen, previous agrarian reform law had limited the amount of land which could be legally held by an individual according to a precise formula geared to the quality of the land and its potential use. Thus *latifundistas* were forced to pretend to graze cattle on prime land or they were obliged to employ the services of *prestanombres* who served as the owners of record for various portions of what was actually one individual's giant estate. With the "New Law"—as it came to be called—the need for such subterfuge was removed as the limitations previously imposed on the size of holdings were effectively lifted. Thus large landowners were free to shift from cattle ranching to cash crop cultivation without giving up any of the extra land that they had been permitted to hold on the grounds that it was too arid or mountainous to plant with crops. Now, only land defined by the secretary of agriculture as "underutilized" was subject to expropriation. With this legislation in place, we cannot wonder that López Portillo was able to proclaim that no further land was "available" for distribution to landless petitioners.

Beyond its role in bringing land distribution to a halt, this legislation undermined the already weakened ejidal system by removing the inviolable status of ejidal holdings. The New Law created "production units" in which *ejidatarios* and private landholders could join together in "free association" to produce staples, thereby qualifying jointly for subsidized credit. This alteration in agrarian law opened the *ejido* to private investment, legalizing the *de facto* arrangements which, we have noted, had prevailed for decades.[171] The overall effect of the law is to speed the takeover of ejidal lands by private commercial farmers and multinational agribusiness conglomerates. "Given the differences between [private commercial] farmers and *ejidatarios*, the relationship is a free association only in the sense that an employer-employee one is."[172] In essence "associated agricultural enterprise" means that ejidal lands are turned over to private capitalists for exploitation, effectively destroying the *ejido* as a system of common peasant production. Cynthia Hewett de Alcántara notes that this arrangement is often likened by its proponents to the collective and cooperative experiments of the Cárdenas years, in which the scattered resources of the peasantry, in cases like the Laguna and other collective ejidal zones, were grouped into more productive units to provide a higher standard of living to land recipients.

> But there is, in fact, a fundamental difference between the programme carried out during the 1930s and the present one: the balance of political forces in the earlier period permitted the exercise of considerable power by the peasantry, but that of the 1970s does not. The promotion of 'association' between landless labourers or *minifundistas* and private or public capital thus seems to imply the real risk that only those jobs would be created, and only those crops grown, which meet the financial needs of investors. Those needs, in a relatively free market economy, are not congruent with the basic livelihood requirements of most rural people.[173]

In short, the policy of pooling the resources of small peasant and ejidal sectors with large-scale capitalist enterprise serves only to accelerate the process by which peasants become a cheap labor force working their own lands for their capitalist "associates."[174]

The overall effect of these policies, the insufficient supply of land and capital for peasants, and the despair of receiving land grants have forced the growing population of landless peasants to seek work in the countryside as wage laborers. However, with the increased mechanization of commercial agriculture and of food processing, wage labor opportunities are not expanding in the rural areas at a rate sufficient to absorb those who have been pushed off the land. Indeed, as we have noted, the development strategy which has been promoted by the Mexican state since 1940 is one that has proved incapable of expanding employment opportunities to accommodate the landless peasantry or those who migrate to the cities in search of work. In chapter 4 we will focus more specifically on the indicators that reveal the human consequences of this model of development.

THE HUMAN COSTS OF MEXICAN DEVELOPMENT

The development strategy pursued since 1940 by those in power in Mexico led to a high rate of economic growth accompanied by social neglect and economic inequality. Per capita income may have reached one thousand dollars in 1976 and two thousand by 1980, but these figures are more a reflection of the enormous wealth amassed by a small group of industrialists, financiers, and commercial landowners than an improvement in the overall standard of living in Mexico. Over the last forty years the income of upper-class and upper-middle-class Mexicans has grown steadily in both relative and absolute terms. But by the 1960s income inequality was as marked as in the period leading up to the revolution in 1910.[1] The gap between rich and poor has continued to grow until today the wealthiest 10 percent of the Mexican population enjoys an income 52 times greater than the poorest 10 percent.[2] One Mexican banker recently estimated that there are presently more than 200 Mexicans holding fortunes of at least $100 million.[3] The increased affluence of these and other members of the upper class is reflected in the construction of palatial homes, private country clubs, golf courses, stables, exclusive new resort areas, condominiums by the sea, modern shopping plazas, and similarly extravagant projects. They travel abroad, shop abroad, and invest abroad.

However, at the same time that the growth of national income has produced greater luxury and ease for a small sector of Mexicans at the top of the economic ladder, the cost of living has risen steadily for all Mexicans. Official government figures showed inflation at 22 percent in 1974, 33 percent in 1980, and an estimated 100 percent by 1982. But, as inflation has driven prices up, workers and peasants have not experienced a corresponding increase in wages or income from the land they work. In terms of what their money will buy, peasants and workers find that they are poorer with each passing year. Indeed, even during the heady years of the oil boom from 1978 to 1981, notwithstanding government price controls, the consumer price index rose by 20 percent while real wages dropped by 2.4 percent.[4] And, of course, this loss of purchasing power by peasants and working-class Mexicans is reflected in virtually any figure that indicates the breakdown by social class and income of consumption of essential goods and services. For example, half the food purchased in Mexico is consumed by the top 15 percent of the population while the poorest third get only 10 percent of the food.[5]

TABLE 1
Consumer price index (1968 = 100)

Year:	1972	1973	1974	1975	1976	1977	1978
	120.3	134.8	166.8	191.8	222.1	286.7	325.5

Source: Banco de México, *Indicadores Económicos*, Vol. 6, No. 5, Abril 1978, p. 48.

Thus the data on total national income, overall production, or even gross national product per capita reveal only a part of the picture. For a more complete understanding of what "development" has meant in Mexico, we need to go beyond the aggregate figures to look at the way in which income and social benefits are distributed across the total population. At this point we need to focus on those statistics that indicate what lies behind the impressive figures on growth, and look at those data that provide a picture of the way that the great majority of Mexicans live while their country is undergoing rapid modernization.

RURAL MEXICO

As we noted in chapter 3, the problem of unemployment and underemployment slices through the economy with more than half of the work force without jobs or in precarious work situations in which they receive less than the legal minimum wage. The most dramatic evidence of this chronic problem is found in predominantly agricultural states like Chiapas, Guerrero, and Oaxaca, where 90 percent of the work force lack permanent employment. While an almost universal condition in these improverished southern states, joblessness is endemic throughout the rural zones, and two-thirds of unemployed and underemployed Mexicans are found in the countryside.[6] On any given day, in villages throughout the countryside, hundreds of thousands of able-bodied men can be found sitting in front of their houses or in the center of a dusty little plaza waiting for work. These are the people who either have no land of their own or who own a *minifundio*, a plot of land so small that it does not require the labor of all family members who might contribute their manpower. To survive, these peasants rely on work offered by large landowners in the region or by more fortunate peasants who have small plots of their own which occasionally require the labor of extra farm hands. Perhaps a truck will be sent from a neighboring estate to cart the landless peasants off for a day of work in a landowner's fields. If the truck should come, the agricultural workers are in no position to haggle over wages. More likely, no truck will come at all. On the average, agricultural day laborers find work only 135 days out of the year.[7] As a result, their income level is very low—the lowest in Mexico.[8]

In the early 1970s, the average income of all people engaged in agricultural work was $64 per month. Almost 30 percent of the people working in agriculture had a family income of less than $24 per month.[9] While these figures must be revised upward to take into account wage and price rises in the last decade, in terms of real disposable income, peasants are, if anything, worse off in the 1980s than these earlier statistics indicate. The most critical situation is that of the families of agricultural day workers, or *jornaleros*. This group includes families who have never received a parcel of land under the agrarian reform program. It includes *minifundistas* whose parcel is too small to sustain a single family. It also includes the families of younger sons of *ejidatarios* who, in accordance with agrarian reform law, have passed along their ejidal land grants intact to their oldest son. In 1970, at the close of a decade of spectacular overall growth, of the 1.5 million families headed by an agricultural wage worker, one-third earned an average of only $18 per month. Another 43 percent earned between $24 and $48 per month, while only 5 percent managed to bring home more than $80.[10] These figures refer to the combined income of all wage earners in the *jornalero* family, which, on the average is comprised of at least five potential wage earners. Although five people may be prepared to contribute their labor, the family income remains so low because the *jornaleros* are unable to find steady employment and when they get work, they often receive far less than the legal minimum wage.[11]

The mimimum wage is established by a national commission according to the type of work performed, local conditions, the cost of living index in the region, availability of work, and a series of other economic factors. As a matter of development policy, increases in the minimum wage have run well behind cost of living rises. Furthermore, in rural areas actual wages are rarely more than 60–75 percent of the legally established minimum.[12] Indeed, in the early 1970s, the president of the National Commission on Minimum Salaries acknowledged that 80 percent of the employers in some rural areas (Chiapas, Guerrero, and Oaxaca) systematically evaded payment of the minimum wage. Apparently the national commission was powerless to do anything about this situation.[13]

Social and Economic Conditions

The daily life of peasants, whether they are *ejidatarios*, agricultural wage workers, or the owners of tiny private plots *(minifundistas)* is full of hardship. In general, the income they receive from their work on the land is insufficient to sustain themselves and their families. Their land is mostly rocky, infertile, and either too arid or too wet to be cultivated profitably. The vast majority of peasants farm without the help of work animals, tractors, or machinery more sophisticated than a machete, wooden plow, or hoe.[14] In the mountains and in tropical regions where the bulk of the peasantry are *minifundistas*, the peasant is likely to leave his house at four or five in the morning to walk for hours just to reach his plot of land. The land may lie five or ten miles away from his village, and the peasant must reach his plot before the midday sun makes heavy work in the fields impossible. On this small parcel of land, the peasant is likely to raise subsistence crops for his family's consumption: corn, beans, chili peppers, and calabash. The more fortunate peasant may own a cow, a few pigs, a mule, or a donkey. If he has no work animals he may have to walk for miles carrying as much as eighty or a hundred pounds of firewood on his back.[15]

When we look at the peasant population as a whole (including *ejidatarios* as well as landless peasants and *minifundistas*) we find that peasants throughout Mexico occupy the lowest position on all the different scales used to measure standard of living. For example, there is greater illiteracy among the peasants than among any other group in Mexico. More than two-thirds of all Mexicans who can neither read nor write live in the countryside. Even among the economically active portion of the rural population, the vast majority would have to be considered functionally illiterate, as fewer than 15 percent of adult males in the poorer, largely rural states of central and southern Mexico have attended even four years of primary school. In contrast, illiteracy has been reduced to only 10 percent in Mexico City and the proportion of children who complete primary school is six times higher in the cities than in the countryside.[16]

Almost half of all rural dwellings consist of no more than one room. A 1979 report indicated that only 28 percent of rural Mexicans had access to electricity and less than half had sources of safe drinking water. These figures contrasted with those from the cities where 80 percent have electricity and 70 percent potable water.[17]

Nutrition in Mexico is poor in general and has declined steadily over the last decade. Somewhere between one half and three quarters of the population do not consume the minimum daily requirements established by the World Health Organization which is a meager 2,750 calories and 80 grams of protein each day.[18] In terms of diet, again peasants as a group are worse off than urban Mexicans: less than half the peasant population regularly eats meat, fish, milk, or eggs. Consumption levels in rural areas sometimes drop below 1,900 calories,[19] and in a number of zones the poorest peasants are reduced to eating wild plants, leaves, roots, insects, birds, and rodents.[20] The state marketing board, CONASUPO (Compañía Nacional de Subsistencias Populares) has 7,500 outlets set up to supply basic foodstuffs to the poor. But income is so low in the countryside that CONASUPO sales represent only 5 percent of Mexico's total retail food purchases indicating that "millions of impoverished Mexicans are outside the basic welfare service."[21]

Since 1910 government statisticians have broken down census figures in such a way as to reveal differences in the social condition of the population in the countryside and in the cities. Unfortunately, even in 1982, this kind of elaborated breakdown of the 1980 census was not yet available, although some preliminary indications suggest that the sharp contrast between rural and urban life will not be reduced. Still, the figures in Table 2, based on the 1970 census, show clearly enough the contrast between urban and rural standards of living, and they help us to grasp the motives of the millions of Mexicans who leave the countryside each year in the hope of improving their lot in the cities.[22]

TABLE 2
Urban and Rural Social Conditions

	Urban Population	Rural Population
	(Percentages)	
Live in dwellings of only one room	30.6	48.1
Live in homes supplied with electricity	84.5	34.5
Cannot read or write (persons over the age of six)	17.8	39
Go barefoot	1.6	12
Wear huaraches (sandals)	3.8	22
Wear shoes	94.4	65.6
Eat only tortillas (i.e., no bread)	12.8	34
Do not eat meat even once a week	11	30
Do not eat eggs even once week	15.8	30

Source: Secretaria de Industria y Comercio, Dirección General de Estadística, IX Censo General de Población, 1970, (México, D.F.: 1972), pp. 135, 273, 1081–1082.

Marginality

Taken together, these statistics can be used to construct an "index of marginality." When we analyze the data on housing, literacy, diet, and education we find that the people who do not eat meat are often the same people who do not drink milk. Those who do not drink milk are often the same people who do not wear shoes, who cannot read or write, who live in one-room dwellings, and so on.[23]

There is a close correspondence among all these factors. The population that is marginal in terms of one variable is also likely to be marginal in terms of all the others.[24] For example, because they cannot find regular employment, rural workers also fail to qualify for social security. Whereas 60 percent of urban wage workers are covered, only 11 percent of rural wage laborers and only 3 percent of *ejidatarios* qualify for social security benefits.[25] Because these different forms of deprivation and various disadvantages tend to overlap and reinforce one another, González Casanova asserts that not only are there great numbers of Mexicans who have little of anything, but "there is an immense number of Mexicans who have nothing of nothing. . . ."[26]

> Despite the fact that the percent of marginal population has decreased in the past 50 years . . . the marginal population has increased in absolute numbers, and should present trends continue, it will increase in the future. . . . And although marginality occurs in the cities in forms characteristic of slum life, it is a phenomenon which is most closely associated with rural life.[27]

Not only are the peasants the poorest sector of the population, but the gap between the rich and poor is far wider in the countryside than in the towns and cities of the republic.[28] The accumulation of wealth in the hands of a few and the poverty of the vast majority of rural people is a direct result of the governmental policies examined in chapter 3. If there remains any doubt concerning the decline and ultimate failure of the land reform program in Mexico, the persistence of economic and social inequalities in the countryside gives silent testimony to the decline of agrarian reform since 1940.

Rural Exodus

The rise in the number of marginal people in rural Mexico is due in part to the increased pressure of population on the land. To be sure, the rural population is increasing at only a third the rate of the urban, and by 1980 less than 40 percent of all Mexicans were living in the countryside. But in absolute terms the rural population has grown from 14 million in 1940 to 23 million in 1970 and an estimated 28 million in 1980.[29] At the same time, however, land resources have remained constant. Only 12 percent of the land surface of Mexico is suitable for agriculture without irrigation. Under the existing agrarian reform program, utilizing the technology presently applied in Mexico, this amount of land is insufficient to support the current rural population, not to speak of the generations to come.[30] Even if official projections on new irrigation water to be produced by future hydraulic projects are correct, the amount of farm land that could be made available with the additional irrigation waters would still be inadequate to feed and employ the rural population. Those peasants who have received ejidal grants are prohibited by law from subdividing their lands among several sons and daughters. Thus, for each peasant who inherits an ejidal plot from his father, there may be five or six brothers and sisters who take their place in the ranks of the landless peasantry. For this reason the number of landless peasants increases each year.

The bracero program. From the Second World War through the early 1960s, the pressure of overpopulation in the countryside was somewhat relieved by the opportunity for temporary immigration and employment offered by the *bracero* program in the United States. Mexican workers had always moved quietly across the Rio Grande in a continuous ebb and flow that fluctuated according to general economic conditions and the labor market on either side of the border. But now the flow was to be organized, regulated, and massive. The *bracero* program was conceived in 1942 as a way to cope with the severe wartime labor shortage in the United States. The *braceros* (hired hands, or in Spanish "arms") were workers—mostly agricultural workers—who contracted to work in the United States for a specific period of time, usually three to four months, at a wage determined in advance. During the next two decades Mexican *braceros* sweated in the fields of the southwestern United States and in the factories of the North, often under highly exploitative conditions and at wages well below those earned by American workers. In the United States the *braceros* faced both racial prejudice and the hostility of the American agricultural work force whose own wage level—low as it was—was further undercut by the *bracero* program. The Mexican migrants often worked, ate, and slept in substandard conditions while the official program inspectors, under pressure from the American employers, ignored violations of the safeguards built into the *bracero* contract. In the end, some *braceros* were cheated out of wages that were due them after months of labor in the field or factory.[31] But in spite of the often grim situation encountered by *bracero* laborers in the United States, the conditions in rural Mexico were such that each year hundreds of thousands of workers sought to enter the *bracero* program. At times northern Mexican cities witnessed the outbreak of riots as hundreds of hungry peasants were turned away from the *bracero* induction centers once the quotas were filled.[32]

In 1964, under pressure from the American labor movement, the *bracero* program was terminated by joint Mexican-U.S. agreement. But between 1942 and 1964 an estimated twelve million men had worked as *braceros*, some of them returning to the United States for a few months each year over a period of ten to fifteen years.[33] The money earned by the *braceros* in the last six years of the program alone brought an estimated one billion dollars into Mexico.[34] Once the *bracero* program ended, legal migration to the U.S. by agricultural workers was reduced to a fraction, and the Mexican government lost not only an important source of revenue, but an important safety valve for the reduction of unrest in the countryside.[35]

Migration to the United States. The steam valve provided by the *bracero* program may have been shut tight in the mid-1960s, but the flow of Mexican workers to the United States never ceased; it simply resumed its unregulated, semiclandestine character. From the late 1960s to the 1980s, roughly 50,000 Mexicans have been issued work permits each year.[36] The rest enter illegally in a variety of ways. They wade the Rio Grande and climb the chain link and barbed wire fences that guard the border, evading the searchlights of the border patrols. They march across the desert and the badlands that mark the 1,945-mile border between the two countries. They travel hidden in the holds of boats that deposit them on lonely stretches of beach along the California shore, or ride concealed in the trunks or under the floorboards of vehicles driven by "coyotes" who specialize in running the illegal migrants across the unguarded portions of the border. Or they sell or mortgage their land and their possessions to raise funds to buy forged visas and other documents. Hundreds actually lose their lives in this desperate effort—lost in the desert, suffocated in the back of a tank truck, or perhaps killed by a coyote they paid and trusted to deliver them to "the other side."

Still, hundreds of thousands, perhaps millions, do succeed in crossing the border each year. Under the circumstances, it is impossible to say with any accuracy how many "undocumented" Mexican migrants make their way to the United States every year.[37] The gross flow is thought to be roughly one million—mostly men in their twenties, but also women and dependent children—and estimates of the number of Mexicans illegally resident in the United States range from 2 to 6 million.[38] Between 1930 and 1977 more than eight times as many Mexicans were apprehended as illegal immigrants than were issued visas to live and work in the United States.[39] But the figures on apprehensions provide only a very partial idea of the total volume of poor Mexicans flowing across the border. This is because just a fraction of those who attempt the trip are actually caught, and many who are seized, after a few hours in detention and a bus ride back to Tijuana, Juarez, or Nogales, continue their efforts to cross until they succeed, sometimes only hours after their first deportation by the U.S. Immigration and Naturalization Service.[40]

In the last decade, as the movement of migrants into the U.S. economy became a major "policy issue," increasing attention has been given to determining the motives that prompt millions of poor Mexicans— two thirds of them rural people—to bear great personal risk and hardship to make their way across the border and live without legal status or protection in a strange land. For, once they make it to the American side, the migrants may be treated as "captive labor" by a work contractor, they may be grossly overcharged for wretched housing, their sub-minimum wages may be withheld at the end of a job by an unscrupulous boss, and so on. In short, they are prey to a wide assortment of abuses because those who would exploit or cheat migrants proceed more or less secure in the knowledge that undocumented Mexicans have no legal recourse and that fear of exposure as an "illegal" forces them to suffer in silence.

Given what we already know of the economic and social structure of rural Mexico, the limits on agricultural resources, and the failure of land reform as a program for the future, it comes as no surprise that studies of patterns of migration to the United States indicate that the motives are overwhelmingly economic.[41] In 1976, for example, Cornelius compared wage scales in the United States and Mexico and found a differential of 13 to 1: that is, average pay for unskilled labor was $2.50/hour north of the border, as compared with $1.53/day in Mexico. "Even when travel, coyote fees and other expenses are subtracted, the average illegal migrant . . . can usually net more income from three months or less of work in the United States than he could from an entire year in his home community."[42] Another study which confirms the finding that the motive for migration is largely economic emphasized that adverse economic conditions in Mexico have far more to do with the decision to brave the journey than the lure or promise of favorable conditions in the United States. In fact, Jenkins has found that when conditions worsen in Mexico, immigrants flow northward irrespective of what the market for unskilled labor may be in the United States in that period.[43]

Disposed to accept any kind of work, the vast majority of migrants are employed in agricultural labor: harvesting crops and performing other heavy work in the fields. Some, however, have been drawn into construction or industry. The construction boom in Houston has been fueled in part by the availability of cheap Mexican hands for unskilled jobs. Likewise, the development of a new and thriving textile and apparel industry in southern Texas is due largely to the presence of a pool of poorly paid illegal immigrants, and to the consequent inability of needle trade unionists to organize American citizens and documented Mexicans in a setting in which cheap foreign labor is in abundant supply.

Overall we can say that immigration to the United States has served as an escape from the devastating personal consequences imposed on poor Mexicans by the development pattern we have examined. It is a strategy which has turned millions of Mexicans into economic refugees, exposing them to serious hazards and indignities, and placing them in a situation in which they depress the wages of other poor people, if they do not actually take jobs from them.

The border industrialization program. Another policy that has been eagerly promoted by the Mexican government as a solution to the problem of rural unemployment and unrest is the "border industrialization program." With full support from an American government anxious to reduce the flow of Mexican migrants to the Southwest, the border industrialization program was launched in 1965 with a bilateral agreement which permitted the construction of American-owned assembly plants in twelve cities along the Mexican side of the border. Under the agreement, all duties and restrictions on imports and foreign capital are waived by the Mexican government on the condition that none of the goods produced are sold in Mexico. Special U.S. tariff regulations, Item, 807.00 and 806.30, permit "American products" assembled abroad to return, duty-free, provided that the components involved were originally produced in the United States. Under these tariff regulations, only the "value added" to the product is taxed as the goods reenter the United States.[44]

Mexican policy makers have supported the border program in the expectation that hundreds of thousands of new jobs would eventually be created in these plants. Furthermore, it was hoped that revenue pumped into the economy in the form of wages paid to factory workers would have a "multiplier effect," stimulating other economic activities and creating work in the service sector. Given these expectations, every possible inducement was given to U.S. firms to locate in northern Mexico, "twinning" their assembly operations to plants just across the border in cities like El Paso, Texas, or Nogales, Arizona. "Mexicanization" restrictions would not apply to these ventures; 100 percent foreign ownership was permitted. And to stimulate the development of these assembly plants, or *maquiladoras,* the Mexican government constructed industrial parks where low rents, cheap electricity, water, and transportation facilities were offered to attract U.S. firms.[45] Indeed, the conditions were so attractive that over the next decade, hundreds of U.S. companies leaped at the opportunity to locate in Mexico. Clothing, electronic components, auto parts, tools, toys, sports equipment, televisions, radios, cameras, and communications hardware were only the largest of the industries that responded to the offer. From the American industrialists' point of view the key advantage of the border was the unlimited supply of cheap, nonunionized, and relatively docile labor. While these same qualities had been sought and found at an even lower price in overseas assembly operations in Haiti, Taiwan, Korea, and Singapore, location in Mexico reduced transportation costs to the point that higher profits could be realized even after paying Mexican workers twice the going rate in a Taiwanese sweatshop.[46] And when American businessmen drew comparisons between their Mexican employees and unionized American workers, the Mexicans won highest praise:

> Mexican women are 40 percent more productive than their North American counterparts. Taught all their lives to submit to male authority, they rarely object to the conditions imposed upon them. A US businessman whose job is to promote the *maquiladoras* to foreign firms explained: "there's no welfare here. You can punish Mexican workers. Also there's the 48-hour week. You don't see any horsing around here, no queues for the water-fountain or the bathroom. These girls work."[47]

Given these inducements, by 1982 some 600 assembly plants had been constructed, employing a labor force almost entirely of young, unmarried women. *Maquiladora* workers currently receive a minimum wage established by the Mexican government of $1.35/hour, plus benefits which, in 1982, came to 75/cents hour. While this rate of pay is substantially higher than the wages received by the average Mexican worker, it represents a great saving to American employers, who must pay a basic hourly wage of $3.55 across the border in the United States. In some operations, the differential is even greater: "With the devaluation of the peso, a Mexican worker assembling a seat belt earns just over $1 an hour, while his American counterpart makes $12."[48]

Successful as the experiment has been from the point of view of American capitalists, it has fallen far short of even the most modest expectations of Mexican supporters. Altogether, 130,000 jobs have been created, but even these are highly vulnerable to reversals in the American economy. In the 1974 recession, for example, 55 assembly plants shut down, laying off 26,000 workers.[49] Apparel operations are particularly unstable. "Companies often were formed for the duration of a specific contractual arrangement, then dissolved, only to reappear when another production run or consignment was negotiated."[50] The American firms shift their operations back and forth among numerous domestic and foreign plants, hiring and firing at will. In general, one of the attractions of employing Mexican, rather than American labor is that, like *braceros,* the assembly plant women can be discarded at pleasure: when their labor is no longer required, or they become pregnant or too old or tired or nervous to withstand the physical wear of the minute, repetitive tasks they perform hour after hour. "Temporary" *maquiladora* workers may be dismissed without notice or severance pay, and many firms turn over their work force at a rate which guarantees that few attain permanent status.[51] It is easy for these firms to pursue such personnel practices because the supply of job seekers is virtually unlimited, and the tasks they are called upon to perform are relatively simple, if mind-numbingly tedious.

Apart from the disappointing figures on total numbers of jobs created, other bright hopes for the program have proven equally unrealistic. Since the vast majority of *maquiladora* workers are women, their employment has little impact on the rate of illegal migration because most undocumented workers are men. Indeed, the presence of the assembly plants in the border towns inflates the economy of those cities, which in turn, draws more unemployed people from southern and central Mexico into the North.[52] Only 3 percent of the new arrivals in the border cities have actually found employment in the *maquiladoras.*[53] As in the oil boom towns on the Gulf coast, the influx of hopeful job seekers who do not find work swells the ranks of the unemployed in the border region, stretching the social infrastructure to the breaking point. Although the Mexican state has spent millions on an industrial infrastructure to attract the foreign firms, its social expenditures on health and education facilities in the area have been modest. This is not surprising, however, when we consider that those who hold the real power and influence in this context—that is, the owners and managers of the assembly plants—live and seek their social services on the American side. As *Forbes* cheerfully reported:

> The Certron Corp . . . has a *maquila* in Mexicali that pays 670 employees $1.36 an hour to snap spools of audio tape into plastic cassettes. Korean workers could beat that price by nearly half; but Certron couldn't jet its managers once a week to check on a Korean plant. When American managers are needed at a *maquila* plant every day they can live 30 minutes across the border in American towns with their kids in American schools, as about 350 American managers of Juarez plants do.[54]

Finally, the expectation that the border industrialization program would stimulate the Mexican economy, creating related jobs through a multiplier effect, has not been borne out. On the contrary, the *maquiladora* plants provide a classic example of a perfect "enclave economy." With all components imported from the United States, and all finished products immediately exported, there is no possibility that the assembly process will spin off into other productive activities. The only possible stimulus for the local economy comes in the form of wages paid to local people. But, given the proximity to the border, it turns out that most of those paychecks are spent on the American side.[55] The higher quality and lower price of American consumer goods, along with the advertising that bombards the Mexicans day and night from the Spanish-language American media, lead those receiving paychecks to buy U.S.-made products. Indeed the propensity of northern Mexicans to pour their disposable income into goods and services in the American border towns has stimulated the economic development of these cities and the general expansion of commercial opportunities in the southern United States. This, in fact, is the chief argument put forward in the U.S. Congress by supporters of the *maquiladoras* who have fought repeal of the tariff regulations which facilitate the border industrialization program.[56]

Migration to the cities. Just as migration to the North has been a constant of Mexican rural life throughout the century, so, too, the exodus from the countryside to the cities, above all, to Mexico City, has constituted a steady trend from the days of the revolution onward. The shift in the relative proportion of rural to urban population since 1910 clearly reveals this pattern (see table 3).

TABLE 3
Proportion of Urban and Rural Population 1910–1980

	% urban population	% rural population
1910	28.7	71.3
1930	33.5	66.5
1950	42.6	57.4
1970	58.6	41.4
1980	65 (estimated)	35

Source: *Compendio Estadistico*

However, in the last two decades the movement has reached massive proportions as each year well over one million Mexicans pour into the cities hoping to break out of the vicious circle of poverty that life in the countryside has become. Rural migrants enter Mexico City at a rate of more than half a million each year. This means that an average of about 1,370 people arrive in the capital each *day* to seek their fortunes in the big city. And although the population of the capital is swollen by these migrants, in the 1970s Mexico City was only eighth among Mexican urban centers in its expansion, and it currently falls behind the oil boom towns and some of the border cities in its rate of population growth.[57]

The population of Mexico City is now 15 million and projections for the year 2000 vary from a highly optimistic 29 million to somewhere in the range of 34 or 35 million, depending on whether the current rate of population growth persists or can be reduced by a program of birth control.[58] Mexican policy makers came very slowly and reluctantly to a position of support for a nationwide, government-sponsored family planning scheme. Although the population growth rate of 3.5 percent that prevailed through the last decades meant that the total population doubled every twenty years,[59] until the early 1970s no official move was made. Opposition to birth control from the Catholic Right was reinforced by popular notions that linked masculinity to frequent reproduction. Furthermore, nationalistic objections were raised by sectors of the Left that claimed that mass birth control campaigns were part of an imperialist plot fostered by a U.S. government fearful of being "swamped" by a more numerous and fruitful neighbor. Only in 1973, when the economic consequences of unchecked population growth had become frighteningly apparent, was the National Population Council created and the first government-funded Family Planning Centers established. By 1980, more than five thousand of these centers had been opened, and official reports were claiming that 38 percent of all fertile women were making use of these facilities, causing the birthrate to drop from a high of 3.6 percent to under 3 percent.[60] Unfortunately, while in the long run the "responsible parenthood" program may bring about a decline in birthrate, the short-term impact will be negligible.[61] Table 4 illustrates the trends in population growth (a) when the growth rate is held constant, or (b) if the more optimistic projects of reductions in the growth rate come true.

TABLE 4
Mexican Population 1970–2000 at Constant and Declining Growth Rate
(Figures in Millions)

Year:	1970	1975	1980	1985	1990	1995	2000
a)	50.6	60.1	71.1	85.8	103.9	126	153
b)	50.6	60.1	71.1	85.8	101.9	120.5	140.7

a) population growth rate constant at 3.5 percent

b) growth rate held constant at 3.5 percent until 1980; 5 percent yearly reduction projected in the growth rate until 1990; 10 percent annual reduction in the growth rate projected for the period 1990–2000

Source: Secretaria de Recursos Hidráulicos, "Estudio de los Recursos Humanos por Cuencas de la Secretaria de Recursos Hidráulicos, Bioconservación, S.A., *Supervivencia*, Año 2, No. 5/6 enero/abril 1976, p. 17.

Thus, although estimates of the total future population vary widely, what all analysts agree upon is that the current population will double again by the year 2000 and that Mexico City will become the largest city in the world sometime within the next twenty years. And whereas today one Mexican in five lives in the capital, by the turn of the next century one third of all Mexicans will live in the metropolitan area which currently sprawls 35 to 40 miles in every direction, radiating outward from the Plaza of the Constitution. As the city spreads, it gobbles up what was once the richest farmland in the country. Government seizure of ejidal land for urban construction is a process which over the last two decades has claimed 8,926 hectares in 127 expropriations in the Federal District and 16,600 hectares in 300 separate expropriations in the State of Mexico.[62]

The loss of prime farmland is only part of the ecological disaster wrought by the growth of Mexico City, a fact obvious to any visitor to the capital from the time the city looms as a dark brown smudge on the horizon. Sitting in a ring of mountains more than 7,000 feet above sea level, with prevailing winds that carry factory emissions from the most heavily industrialized zones into the city center, the city suffers an almost permanent air inversion. Indeed, by the mid-1970s, Mexico City was two to five times more polluted than Los Angeles, depending upon which pollutant was being measured.[63] But toxic industrial emissions represent only part of the problem. Most analysts agree that 70 percent of the pollution comes from vehicular traffic. Through the 1970s, 400 automobiles were added each day to the 2½ million vehicles already circulating in the Federal District.[64] By 1981, the rate of increase in the number of cars was 3.5 times the population growth rate and, in addition to the cars there were 200,000 buses and trucks.[65] These buses move six million people a day, while 3 million daily riders commute underground on the 35 miles of subway lines. But encouraged in part by the artificially low price for gas which, as we have seen, was a key component of government energy policy, 10 million trips are made each day in private cars and taxis.[66]

Into this smog-blackened atmosphere come the rural poor in a desperate effort to improve their economic and social condition. Once in the city, however, they find that the work they had hoped to secure is unavailable in the urban areas, especially for those who lack specialized skills or experience with industrial production. As we have noted, something like 750,000 or 800,000 new people enter the Mexican work force each year. And if there are few new opportunities for people in the countryside, jobs in industry have certainly not expanded to absorb the rural surplus. Because industrial development in Mexico has moved steadily in the direction of increased reliance on advanced technology, as industry expands, the number of jobs has not increased proportionately.[67] Thus, the rural migrants make their way to the city, full of hope, only to discover that the city is already full of urban unemployed. According to the estimates provided in a study carried out by the Subcommission on Migration of the Department of the Federal District, there are presently more than 2 million unemployed and 8 million underemployed people in the capital, a figure which constitutes 60 percent of the economically active population.[68]

URBAN MEXICO

Life in the Slums

Generally unable to find the jobs they seek in the city, the rural migrants are forced to squat on the outskirts of the large urban centers. Here, on the periphery of the cities, squalid slums spring up like mushrooms as migrants construct makeshift dwellings out of mud, corrugated paper, hammered-out tin cans and scrap lumber. By 1970 there were 452 such slums or "lost cities" (ciudades perdidas) in and around Mexico City which housed 1.5 million people, 70 percent of them rural migrants. In addition to the lost cities, poor neighborhoods (vecindades or barrios) in the capital house another five to six million people. Some of the lost cities are perched at the very edge of deep ravines on the Mexico City-Toluca road, while other slum neighborhoods sit rotting in the heart of downtown Mexico City, stashed away in the streets behind the National Palace.[69] Even in exclusive, upper-class zones, small squatters' communities cluster on beds of volcanic rock, along drainage ditches, or wherever some space has been left because the terrain is too rocky, hilly, swampy, or unstable to construct architect-designed homes for the rich. The slums on the main route between downtown Mexico City and the international airport are carefully concealed from the eyes of tourists and other foreign visitors by high walls, constructed by the municipal government and decorated with slogans praising the PRI and its candidates of the day.

Hidden away behind the municipal walls, the lost cities grow and fester. In many of these communities the birthrate is even higher than in the countryside, but the infant mortality rate is also tragically high. Manuel Mejido, investigative reporter for the Mexican daily Excelsior, found that in the slum called Colonia Juan Polainas 60 percent of all babies die before their first birthday. In Juan Polainas 2,032 people live in 441 one-room dwellings. Together the 2,032 residents share 27 water taps, 51 open toilets, and 77 wash basins. Often more than one family will occupy a 10-foot square windowless room, and sometimes pigs, goats, and chickens, and other domestic animals live indoors as well.[70] El Capulín, a slum that sits precariously under a web of high tension wires, is typical of thousands of poor neighborhoods and lost cities in the capital. El Capulín lacks the most rudimentary public services. The people light their homes by pirating electric current from the heavy electric lines that run directly overhead. There are no schools or medical services, no paved roads, no drinking water, no garbage collection, and no sewage system. Drainage is so poor that one torrential rainfall can wash away hundreds of houses. In May 1972, for example, 50,000 people in Mexico City were left homeless after an unusually heavy rain and hailstorm. Even when the weather is clear, the unpaved streets run with black, brackish water that is full of human and animal wastes. Poverty is the common denominator among the residents of El Capulín. Although the general census for 1970 indicated that only 36,559 people in the capital go barefoot, in El Capulín, where 90 percent of the people have migrated from rural areas, no one wears shoes.[71]

Nativitas, a community of 2,500 people who share only 236 houses, suffers much the same conditions as Juan Polainas and El Capulín. In these and other squatter communities, *caciquillos* ("little strongmen") who have no legal title to the property, lay claim to the land beneath the squatters' huts. The *caciquillos* force the squatters to pay rents up to $15 per month for the privilege of occupying the little squares of land on which their huts sit. The slum dwellers may be forcibly thrown out at any time. Although they may have been paying rent to the self-appointed "landlord" for a period of years, the squatters have no legal recourse if they are turned out of their makeshift homes.[72] For the most part the police are conspicuously absent from the slums and lost cities, and the crime rate in these places is so high that, by 1970, Mexico had attained the sad distinction of numbering among the five countries with the highest rate of homicide in the world.[73]

When the police do appear, it is often to extort money from the owners of the tiny general stores that serve the residents of the lost cities. However, the uniformed police and the small payoff they demand seem benign in comparison with the secret police who are well known for their extortion of large sums from those whom they discover have a previous criminal record.[74] In order to produce the forty or fifty dollars demanded by the secret agents for their monthly payoff, those with past criminal records tend to fall back on the tricks of their former trade: armed robbery, mugging, and picking pockets.

One high crime area is Nezahualcóyotl, the city that has become infamous as the largest slum in the Western Hemisphere. This lost city sprawls just to the east of Mexico's modern international airport. With a population estimated at 3 million in 1981, Nezahualcóyotl is a collection of poor one-room houses, shanties, and shacks which is now larger than San Francisco, or Toronto and Vancouver combined. Nezahualcóyotl developed in the 1940s as a refuge for the poor who could not find housing of any sort inside the capital. Early promoters sketched out "streets" and cheap house plots in the vast dry bed of Lake Texcoco, an area long considered uninhabitable because it was subject to periodic dust storms and floods.[75] During the 1950s and 1960s this population center grew rapidly as hundreds of thousands of squatters joined the initial working-class settlers on the public lands they had made their home. But neither drainage, nor sewers, nor running water nor electricity was added.[76] In 1970, conditions in Nezahualcóyotl were little changed from its spontaneous, makeshift beginnings a quarter of a century earlier. Although the giant slum was now officially incorporated—thus becoming the third or fourth largest "city" in Mexico— and electric power had been extended into its main streets, municipal "improvements" never kept pace with Nezahualcóyotl's growth. In the 1970s only 2 percent of the roads were paved, and the streets still ran with putrid garbage in the rainy season and became thick with dust in the dry season. More than half the houses were one-room dwellings and 80 percent were without any kind of toilet facility. Ninety percent of the population suffered from chronic hunger, malnutrition, and parasitic infections.[77]

Lacking drinking water, sewers, or garbage collection, the overcrowded population of Nezahualcóyotl is ravaged by disease as are slum dwellers throughout the republic. The big killers are gastroenteritis and amoebic dysentery. Even in the 1980s, gastroenteritis and respiratory infections, which account for only 5 percent of fatalities among North American children, caused almost half the deaths among Mexicans under 5 years of age. The National Institute of Nutrition reported that the combination of gastroenteritis and overall malnutrition gave Mexico a mortality rate among preschool children that is 12 times higher than that of the United States.[78] Furthermore, diseases like polio, rabies, and typhoid fever still occur in Mexico with alarming frequency. In 1972, for example, Mexico suffered what the Pan American Health Organization called "the world's worst typhoid epidemic since World War II and possibly the worst of this century."[79]

Occupation and Income

The vast majority of slum dwellers, whether they have migrated from the countryside or were born in the city, are unable to find steady employment. In some of the slums and lost cities like Colonia Juan

Polainas, the proportion of adults who cannot find regular work runs as high as 97 percent. How do these people manage to survive and provide for their families?

Most of the people who cannot find steady work engage in such work as selling chewing gum, pencils, plastic toys, or national lottery tickets. Normally they have no fixed stall from which they vend their wares. Rather, they wander the streets, looking for customers for their handicrafts, candy, ice cream pops, hairpins (sold in five-pin bunches), and plaster statues. They jump on and off city buses hawking plastic combs, comic books, movie magazines, hair tonic, ball-point pens, and glossy postcards.[80] From tiny little boys to stooped old men, they bend low to shine the shoes of passersby. Some manage to live on what they earn singing on crowded buses, playing musical instruments on street corners, or improvising dances for the benefit of tourists strolling in Chapultepec Park. Youthful sword swallowers work the grassy margins of some of the principal boulevards, thrusting flaming knives down their throats as an assistant collects tips from motorists halted in traffic. Others clean windshields, wash, and "guard" cars in the hope that when the owner returns to his auto, he will reward this attention with a few pesos. The early morning edition of newspapers are often sold in the streets at 4:00 A.M. by children sometimes no older than eight or nine. To beat out their competitors, the newspaper vendors rush up to the windows of cars stopped temporarily at crowded intersections.

Some of the unemployed who live at the outskirts of the city wait at the roadside for the trucks that pass carrying produce destined for the city markets. These people gather the fruits and vegetables that fall off the back of the trucks, wash them in the polluted water of their slum community, and travel on into the city where they set up little pyramids of guavas, papayas, tomatoes, peanuts, etc., on the sidewalks of the main plazas and shopping districts. Here, unfortunately, they must compete with peasants who have left their villages in the middle of the night to make it to the city in time to set up their own little pyramids of fruit, vegetables, and nuts.

Another occupation is the age-old standby of the poor: prostitution. And thousands of women who will not or cannot sell their bodies gather up their children each day and travel downtown where they ask directly for alms or beg indirectly, pretending to have lost their busfare home. Those who ask for alms are known as *pordioseros*, from the words *por Dios*, "for God's sake" or "for love of God."[81]

Finally, there are approximately 4,000 families in Mexico City totaling more than 20,000 people, who live by scrounging the garbage dumps for saleable waste.[82] These people have a long-standing grudge against the municipal garbage collectors whom they accuse of skimming off the most desirable waste items such as paper, cartons, glass bottles, and metal cans, which represent the more highly prized merchandise on the rubbish market. The garbage truck drivers who carry 3,800 tons of waste to the municipal dump at Santa Cruz Meyehualco extract a payment from the garbage pickers for every load of trash they deliver.[83] At another major city dump, Santa Fe, 1,000 well-organized ragpickers sift through a pile of rubbish a mile and a half long and hundreds of feet high. Working this dump for the valuable recyclable items is a hereditary privilege passed on from parent to child. The garbage pickers have organized three cooperatives to protect their access to the source of their livelihood.[84] In the city of Monterrey, where there are an estimated 90,000 ownerless dogs,[85] garbage scroungers compete with dogs and rats as well as municipal garbage collectors for access to the garbage dumps.

Whatever the jobs that desperate slum dwellers create for themselves, the going is usually rough. Obviously there is no social security for those who perform the kind of work described above. In addition, these people are often victimized by policemen and other authority figures who demand kickbacks from the poor to allow them to sell whatever it is they are trying to sell. Finally, the urban sprawl of Mexico City, Guadalajara, or Monterrey is such that simply reaching his or her place of work may cost the peripheral slum dweller as much as two hours on one of the rickety old buses that crawl downtown through the city streets. Even with the construction of an ultra-modern thirty-five mile subway line, public transport in most poor neighborhoods remains woefully inadequate. In many cases the poor cannot afford the price of a subway ticket, which costs twice as much as the first-class bus and more than three times as much as the fare for the old second-class buses. Only about half of the buses registered for service are in operation at any one time. In grave need of repair, the buses lurch back and forth, belching out the heavy black diesel exhaust that contributes to making Mexico's large cities among the most dangerously polluted in the world.

By the 1980s the condition of some of the earlier settlers and early settlements had stabilized as rural people managed to create for themselves a community within the broader social fabric of the city. However, the constant stream of new migrants to the capital meant that housing and public services became more inadequate each year, and two-thirds of the metropolitan area was comprised of lost cities, slums, and squalid working-class districts.[86] Despite the efforts of the public housing agency (Instituto del Fondo Nacional de la Vivienda para los Trabajadores, or INFONAVIT) to provide workers with low-rent apartments and low-cost mortgages, demand for accommodation in Mexico City ran 10 times higher than supply,[87] and González Casanova estimated the overall housing deficit as 5 million units.[88] Between 1971 and 1975, 100,000 units were actually constructed by various government agencies, and roughly 600,000 people were actually relocated. But only a third of those needing accommodation qualify to apply for INFONAVIT houses because they are reserved for the salaried working class. An exception was made in the late 1970s when a small group of marginal families was given the chance to rent low-cost INFONAVIT apartments because the construction of new freeway exits necessitated the expropriation of land on which they held squatters' rights. It gives us some idea of their desperation when we consider that, to raise money, these marginal people generally sublet their prized apartments to other, better-off families, and moved out to new *ciudades perdidas* on the far periphery of the city.[89]

The Working Class

Urban poor people who are fortunate enough to find steady employment generally live in conditions only slightly better than those of the rural migrants and the urban subproletariat. Like their unemployed neighbors, workers find that housing and social services are in short supply. Most working-class districts suffer from inadequate schools, medical facilities, drainage, refuse collection, and other services. Indeed the line between a working-class *barrio* and a full-fledged slum is often difficult to establish.

As we have noted, the abundant supply of unskilled labor tends to depress the wages of those who are already employed, minimum wage laws are often disregarded, the basic labor guarantees provided by the Constitution of 1917 have yet to be applied, and only a minority of the working class is covered by social security. Inflation bites into the worker's paycheck, and the cost of living has risen so rapidly over the past ten years that workers are forced to labor longer and longer hours simply to maintain their families at the same standard of living. "Although the 1980s have brought a small but continuing rise in living standards for a small part of the working class (those organized in strong unions), those of most unorganized workers suffered serious deterioration."[90] After basic food and rent are paid, these people rarely have any money left to put aside as savings. As a result, an illness or an unforeseen expense normally precipitates an economic crisis for the working-class family. Even salaried workers who are somewhat better off have great difficulty accumulating savings. Salaried workers bear a particularly heavy tax burden because the unemployed have no reported income to tax, while the bourgeoisie is taxed lightly or manages to evade taxation altogether.

Naturally many workers dream of a better future for their children, if not for themselves. Accordingly, they struggle to send their children on to higher education. However, the number of working-class students attending secondary school in Mexico is disproportionately small, and we find that among all the students enrolled in the public National University, only 14.7 percent are sons or daughters of workers.[91] In fact, 43 percent of all university students come from the richest 9 percent of Mexican families, and the average university student's parents enjoy a family income 3.2 times the national average.[92]

CONCLUSION

In chapters 3 and 4 we have examined the rapid process of economic development, which those in power like to call the Mexican miracle. We have also surveyed the conditions in which the bulk of the population lives as the ruling elite struggles to push Mexico into the ranks of the advanced, modernized, industrial nations. The data presented in this chapter should give some notion of the real-life experiences that are often lumped together under such seemingly neutral terms as "foregone consumption," "the social costs of development," and "social dislocation." While Mexico has shown remarkable progress on a number of economic scales, and has joined the ranks of the "oil-rich nations," the majority of its people continue to live in a condition most accurately described as wretchedness or squalor. And most live this way with very little hope of ever escaping. For people whose social welfare has been sacrificed to the goal of capital accumulation, the term "Mexican miracle" must have a very bitter ring. One group of Mexican intellectuals described the miracle this way:

> If there is something "miraculous" in Mexico, it is that the people tolerate a situation of backwardness and dependency in which millions of Mexicans barely manage to survive, and justice and democracy are conspicuous by their absence or exist only in the rhetoric of the PRI.[93]

OPPOSITION, CO-OPTATION, AND REPRESSION

"The people want their rights respected. They want to be paid attention to and listened to."

Emiliano Zapata

Mexican peasants and workers are well aware that their country has undergone rapid economic development in recent decades. Indeed they are frequently reminded of this achievement by the government that has fostered this growth. But they are also aware that they have not shared equally in the fruits of the development process. And this realization has led to great frustration and unrest in both the countryside and the cities. Those who have been the victims rather than the beneficiaries of economic development look for some way to demand changes in government policies that condemn them to a continued life of poverty. But, as we know from our earlier discussion, the CTM and CNC, the official party sectors originally designed to give voice to workers' and peasants' demands, do not, in practice, operate as militant champions of the two groups they ostensibly represent. Even less do they pressure to see peasant and working-class interests incorporated into national policy. Despite elaborately constructed appearances to the contrary, neither the CTM nor the CNC is a popular organization in the sense in which we normally think of a peasant or labor union movement. As we have noted, the main work of these two organizations is to modify or suppress the demands of its members and to contain potential unrest among peasants and workers. It is their job to deliver peasant and worker support for the PRI (particularly at election time) and to gain popular acceptance for government policies which, in most instances, run counter to the interests of both peasants and workers.

CNC and CTM politicians often organize mass rallies at which banner-waving peasants and workers, carted to the scene by the truckful, shout and cheer for official party candidates and for government repre-

125

sentatives. But these carefully orchestrated displays should not be confused with genuine support for the PRI or its program. When peasants and workers are interviewed privately, there is a striking unanimity of disaffection and disenchantment with the official party. As one peasant told me in 1970:

> I have only two years of schooling. But you do not need to read and write to understand that the program of the PRI is made to benefit rich and powerful people like the PRI politicians themselves. For people like us, things grow worse year by year. But I go to the demonstrations and shout "vivas" along with everyone else, because they give you five, sometimes ten pesos and a meal. Besides, if you refuse to go when the truck comes to the *ejido* to pick you up, you only make enemies in the CNC and trouble for yourself.

Similar expressions of disillusionment with the organs of the PRI can be heard in private conversations in any city, town, or village in Mexico. These feelings of discontent are voiced not only by the peasants, workers, and the chronically unemployed who bear the heaviest brunt of the official development policy, but also by students, intellectuals, and a sizable sector of middle-class people who feel the bite of taxes and inflation and the stultifying effects of one-party rule. The fact that so much discontent is expressed, albeit privately, suggests that Mexicans enjoy a certain freedom to vent their dissatisfaction, so long as their criticism remains incoherent. It is when the discontented attempt to organize and act in unison to give impact to their criticism and demands for change that they run into trouble. For the official organizations linked to the PRI provide no hope for those who want to push for a reordering of the priorities of Mexican development. And the forms of political expression available to people who want to modify the Mexican system and the policies it produces are severely limited. In this chapter we will look at those limitations and at the various alternatives open to Mexicans who are unhappy with five decades of official party management.

A HEGEMONIC SYSTEM

If it is not totalitarian, Mexico's government is nonetheless a far cry from what we understand to be a liberal democracy in spite of the rhetoric and the laws on the books. The Mexican Constitution provides for the separation of power among three branches of government, legal opposition parties, independent organized interest groups—in short, most of the features characteristic of a liberal democratic system. This appearance is utterly deceptive. For in reality, the Mexican system is marked by a nearly complete centralization of power and authority in the hands of the president and his party. The president heads both the PRI and the national government and enjoys a wide range of constitutionally invested and de facto authority. Neither the judicial nor the legislative branches are independent of his control. The decisions of the Supreme Court of Justice generally follow the policy of the executive, and the preponderance of citizens who do make use of the judicial process are businessmen, large landowners, and members of the middle class seeking relief from taxation and land expropriation orders.[1] Because the process is complicated and expensive, workers and peasants who appeal to the Court constitute a small minority.[2]

Historically, the legislative branch has displayed even less independence than the judicial. The Chamber of Senators is composed entirely of members of the president's party, and both the Chamber of Deputies and the Chamber of Senators have been frankly regarded in Mexico as a rubber stamp for presidential policy. Until the recent Political Reform of the late 1970s which we detail below, bills passed to the legislature by the president were normally approved by acclaim. Those few pieces of legislation which were not passed unanimously never met with more than 5 percent opposition.[3] Furthermore, all essential legislation passed on to the Chambers of Senators and Deputies by the president was immediately approved by unanimous decision. Today the presence of a handful of left-wing deputies has created a livelier atmosphere of debate in the Chamber, but it has not altered the fundamental role of the legislature, which is to support presidential policy.

Even today, the president is rarely challenged publicly. A ban on direct criticism of the president in the Mexican press is enforced by the state monopoly on the supply of newsprint paper. Since 1935, a government agency has set the price and allotted quantities of paper to each publication based on its circulation as determined by government auditors.[4] Newspapers and magazines critical of official policy are often forced to buy paper on a black market or "borrow" from sympathetic periodicals against the day when those publications may incur the hostility of the regime. Further control of the press is exerted through the embute, or regular payoff to reporters who cover government agencies. The Christmas season is made particularly jolly for both Mexican and foreign journalists by the arrival on their doorstep of huge baskets of liquor and gourmet foods sent by government and party figures. But perhaps the most subtle form of control of the press is exercised through the use of the government's advertising budget, which constitutes the bulk of paid advertisement in many publications. For example, until government advertising was withdrawn in 1982 Proceso, a weekly news magazine which attempts to maintain a clearly independent editorial line, received $117,000 from newsstand sales and subscriptions and $53,000 from the government publicity and propaganda carried in its pages each week.[5]

OPPOSITION PARTIES

Up to the present decade, the power of the president and the PRI has not been checked by a vigorous opposition party or parties. The Mexican political system has featured a number of minor parties, the most prominent of which were the occasionally left-wing Popular Socialist Party (Partido Popular Socialista, or PPS) and the right-wing National Action Party (Partido de Acción Nacional, or PAN). But these parties never played the role normally associated with opposition parties in most democratic systems. Historically, the relationship between the PRI and its official opposition was so close that the parties were often referred to as a "kept" opposition. Indeed, in some cases opposition parties were financed by the government itself.[6] At election time the opposition parties either would throw their support to the official party candidate from the outset, or they would provisionally oppose PRI candidates as a means of bargaining with the government for patronage positions, loans, contracts, and other favors for the most prominent opposition party members.[7] Operating in this fashion, the PPS, PAN, and other lesser parties played a crucial role in maintaining the dominance of the PRI. Their presence in the political arena helped sustain the fiction that orderly democratic procedures operate in Mexico. As such they contributed to the legitimacy of one-party rule, and in so doing they reinforced the centralization of power in the hands of the president and his party.

Even today, although they occupy an established place in the political arena, Mexican opposition parties have no chance whatsoever of taking power through electoral means. Over the last sixty years the electoral process has taken root in Mexico and contests for the presidency, the Senate, the Chamber of Deputies, and other offices have all proceeded in an orderly sequence, if not without frequent outbreaks of violence, particularly at the local level.[8] But when we look at that orderly procession of electoral contests, one fact stands out: the winner is inevitably the candidate of the official party. Although many political groups have been successful in gaining registration as legally recognized parties, none has won even 20 percent of the vote in any presidential election. Ballot stealing, strong-arm pressure at the polls, and electoral fraud of every description contribute to the official party's electoral preeminence. On occasions when opposition candidates have polled a substantial majority over their PRI competition for the governorship or a seat in the Senate, the election results have been nullified by the government on one technicality or another. The corruption of the electoral process in Mexico is so well known and well documented that few people take the final statistics without a large serving of salt. But when the final votes are tallied, by whatever process they are tallied, the official party has never lost a presidential, gubernatorial, or senatorial contest, and opposition parties have never achieved more than the status of pressure groups.[9] Indeed, in the presidential election of 1976, the opposition parties did not even field a candidate to oppose the PRI's José López Portillo.

With their failure to contest the election of 1976, it became clear that the "kept" opposition had reached the point where it was not viable enough even to make a seemingly serious, if unsuccessful bid for office. Between 1961 and 1976, the proportion of abstentions in congressional and presidential elections rose from 31.5 to 38.1 percent, despite regulations which oblige Mexicans to vote.[10] And a survey carried out by the Mexican Institute of Public Opinion in 1977 showed a high level of apathy, with 90 percent of the respondents in the Federal District asserting that even symbolic participation in politics was meaningless,[11] and 67 percent declining to participate altogether.[12] Thus in 1977, a new Federal Law on Political Organizations and Electoral Processes was proposed to the legislature by López Portillo. The reform law provided structural and administrative changes which gave increased opportunities for opposition parties to mount meaningful political activities.

The Political Reform

To begin with, the registration of new opposition parties was greatly facilitated by the legislation. Any political group which is active for at least four years preceding an election and can present a declaration of principles, a program for action, and set of statutes, may seek conditional registration as a recognized political party. If the party wins at least 1.5 percent of the total vote in the next three elections, or if the party manages to enroll at least 65,000 members, its registration becomes definitive. Furthermore, the Political Reform Law gives "minority" parties the right to sit on the supervisory committees at the polls, and it makes such parties eligible to receive grants from the electoral commission toward the payment of campaign expenses. Finally, the new legislation increased the size of the Chamber of Deputies to 400 seats. Of those seats, 300 are contested in the usual (single-member

TABLE 5
Presidential Elections 1924–1982

Year	Candidate	Percentage of Vote
1924	Calles	84
	Flores	16
1928	Obregón	100
1929	Ortiz Rubio	94
	Vasconcelos	5
	Others	1
1934	Cárdenas	98
	Villaneal	1
	Tejeda ⎫	
	Laborde ⎭	1
1940	Avila Camacho	94
	Almazán	6
1946	Alemán	78
	Padilla	19
	Castro ⎫	
	Calderon ⎭	3
1952	Ruíz Cortines	74
	Henríquez	16
	González Luna	8
	Toledano	2
1958	López Mateos	90
	Alvarez	9
1964	Díaz Ordaz	89
	González Torres	11
1970	Echeverría	84
	González Morfín	14
	Others	2
1976	López Portillo	100
1982	de la Madrid Hurtado	72
	Madero	16
	Martínez Verdugo	4
	Ibarra de Piedra	2
	Others	5

Source: *Compendio Estadistico* and *Comercio Exterior*, Vol. 28, No. 8 August 1982.

district) fashion. Based on past electoral results, it is clear that the vast majority of these seats are expected to go to the PRI. But 100 of the seats are set aside to be distributed among the minor parties according to the proportion of the total vote they receive throughout the country. At the same time, the electoral preeminence of the PRI is guaranteed by clauses in the law which ensure that no particular opposition party grows too strong. Should an opposition party win a grand total of 90 seats in these two pools, it finds one half of the "minor party" seats stripped away.

Although the Political Reform safeguarded the numerical superiority of the PRI, it did open new organizational opportunities to opponents of the regime. Three parties gained conditional registration in 1977, and definitive registration two years later after winning more than the requisite 1.5 percent of the votes cast in the 1979 elections. These three were the Mexican Communist Party (Partido Comunista Mexicano, or PCM), the misleadingly named Mexican Democratic Party (Partido Democratico Mexicano, or PDM), a grouping well to the right of the PRI, and the moderately leftist Socialist Workers' Party (Partido Socialista de Trabajadores, or PST). In addition to these parties which succeeded in gaining official political status, the reform legislation had the effect of stimulating the development, or reinforcing the previously precarious existence of a bewildering array of formations on the left: the Party of the Mexican People (Partido del Pueblo Mexicano, or PPM), the Revolutionary Socialist Party (Partido Socialista Revolucionario, or PSR), the Mexican Workers' Party (Partido Mexicano de Trabajadores, or PMT), the Revolutionary Workers' Party (Partido Revolucionario de Trabajadores, or PRT), the Movement for Socialist Action and Unity (Movimiento de Acción y Unidad Socialista, or MAUS), and the Communist Left Group (Unidad de la Izquierda Comunista, or UIC). By 1980 over a dozen small groups, movements, and tendencies on the left were attempting to qualify for legal recognition. And registration of the Trotskyist PRT had opened the way to the selection of the first female candidate for the presidency, Rosario Ibarra de Piedra, a human rights activist who came to prominence in the 1970s as the leader of mothers of *desaparecidos*, political activists who had "disappeared" while in police custody.[13] However, the most important development generated by the reform has probably been the rejuvenation and reemergence of the Mexican Communist party as a significant political actor.

The Mexican Communist Party

Established in 1919, the first Communist party in Latin America, the PCM reached its apex of influence under the Cárdenas administration. In the cold war atmosphere that followed World War II, the Communists were denied legal registration. The party persisted, nonetheless, existing from 1945 to 1979 in a twilight zone of official exclusion from electoral politics. Drawing repressive fire from time to time, the PCM was only intermittently perceived as a threat to the system because its small size, largely middle-class intellectual composition, and lack of organic links to the working class meant that it posed no effective challenge to the predominance of the PRI. By 1974, its membership had dropped to an estimated 1,400.[14] Through the years when it did not contest elections the PCM survived, all the same: it maintained contact with its small base—mostly railroad workers and teachers, and ousted the more Stalinist elements in 1963. After 1968 the PCM gradually evolved along the lines of a western European "eurocommunist" party by rejecting the motion of a single road to socialism, developing a more specific analysis of the Mexican political reality, establishing a healthy distance between itself and Moscow, and denouncing the Soviet invasion of Czechoslovakia in 1968 and of Afghanistan in 1979.[15]

In 1977, with the possibility of pursuing open, legal political activity, the Communist leadership and its small core of members went all-out, gathering more than 75,000 signatures to gain official registration in time to present a full slate of candidates for the 1979 elections. The party also democratized its internal structures and struggled to overcome its image as dogmatic and sectarian. Losing no opportunity to find common ground with other groups on the left, it formed an electoral coalition with the PPM, PSR, and MAUS in 1979, and in 1981 "submerged" itself in the Unified Mexican Socialist Party (Partido Socialista Unificado Mexicano, or PSUM), a grouping of leftist parties and movements, with the secretary of the PCM, Arnoldo Martínez Verdugo, as its presidential candidate. With an official 5 percent of the vote in the 1979 congressional elections and almost 8 percent in 1982, the PCM was securely established as a parliamentary leftist opposition and with 18 seats in the Chamber of Deputies, had become second only to the PAN among minority parties.[16] Stimulated by these electoral successes, party membership grew to 16,000 by 1980[17] and by 1982, the PCM had registered two significant, if precarious, victories at the local level: it won municipal elections in Guerrero state in 1979, and in 1980, together with its electoral ally, the left-reformist Coalition of Isthmus Workers, Peasants, and Students (Coalición de Obreros, Campesinos, y Estudiantes del Istmo, or COCEI), it took the local elections in Oaxaca's second largest city, Juchitán. However, the victory in this Oaxacan city of 80,000 points to the fundamental weakness of the Political Reform as a method to introduce and promote real democratic competition within the dominant-party system. The newly elected mayor of Juchitán has been the target of two assassination attempts; his house has been riddled with bullets, and a member of his town council was tortured and murdered. Furthermore, the PRI-controlled government of the state of Oaxaca voided the results of the 1980 election, and only with a second victory for the Communist/COCEI alliance in 1981 did the governor reluctantly accept the results. However, the state government has refused to release the funds budgeted for the municipality of Juchitán, crippling the leftist coalition's efforts to carry forward promised reforms. The state government has also intervened to conduct the first audit of the municipal books since 1910, claiming that public funds were being channeled to Central American guerrilla forces.[18]

Evaluations of the Reform

Does the Political Reform and the activity of the plethora of small parties it has stimulated mean that genuine, as distinct from "kept" opposition groups currently present an alternative to PRI rule? Or does the participation of the left-wing opponents of the PRI serve merely as elaborate window dressing for democracy? Critics of the reform underscore the tokenism implied in budgeting $20 million and a few hours of free broadcast time to be shared among all opposition parties, when the PRI spent an estimated $200–300 million on the last presidential campaign, and the candidate moved about in a fleet of jets and helicopters accompanied by an entourage that included 150 members of the press.[19] Skeptics point to the persecution suffered by the PCM in Juchitán and to the electoral irregularities that still occur with discouraging regularity as in the days before the Political Reform.

> In general the leftist opposition continues to be excluded from gaining control of important elective offices at the state and municipal levels. Voting boxes are stolen, votes are purposely miscounted or lost, representatives of the opposition parties are expelled from the voting places during the counting of the ballots, election results are nullified on false grounds, and official recognition is denied to elected candidates of the opposition parties on one or another pretext.[20]

Whether they view this as a positive or negative development, virtually all analysts agree that the Reform "contributed substantially to the established regime's political legitimacy, by incorporating the bulk of the opposition into the existing party system according to the regime's own rules."[21] A Mexican observer agreed with this assessment but noted, critically, that the Reform was intended to guarantee "that the organizations which participate do not acquire excessive strength at the level of popular struggle . . . and that they continue to confine their participation to the terrain of elections and legislative reform.[22]

Another group on the left maintained, "The Political Reform is preventative"; it is an attempt to control left-wing opposition "by capturing them" so that "to the degree they are weak, compromises are extracted and independence is eroded."[23] In general the objections raised to the reforms by spokesmen on the Mexican left were well summarized by Harris and Barkin, who explain:

They were intended to strengthen the existing regime and give it a more convincing democratic facade. . . . These reforms have not resulted in any substantial change in the structure of political representation. By permitting leftist political organizations an opportunity to participate legally in the electoral process and be represented in the legislature, the regime hopes to restrict the action of dissident elements to this arena, which continues to be dominated by the PRI.[24]

However, left-wing Mexicans who have chosen to participate in the electoral system—particularly those whose parties have accepted the small campaign subsidy, the monthly allotment of media exposure, and the other benefits offered by the government—defend their participation in terms of the opportunity it affords to communicate their message. Rafael Fernandez Tomás of the PST asserts:

We realize this is a two edged sword. The dominant class wants to institutionalize the opposition and therefore control it more effectively. But the reform also gives us the opportunity of working openly and freely to build up our base.[25]

For Pablo González Casanova the 1977 law is "a first step, still incomplete, toward a true political reform."[26] He asserts that, at this point in Mexican political history, the formation of opposition parties and the pursuit of electoral goals serves to heighten the consciousness and independent organization of the working class. "As these parties play their new role, the electoral and political system expands its channels of communication and becomes more flexible and vital."[27] González Casanova argues that for leftist parties this is a crucial "first step" in that it lays the basis for the transition to socialism with the construction of an "advanced, multiparty bourgeois democracy."[28]

Other leftists, enthusiastic about the possibilities opened by the reform process, point, above all, to the opportunities that have developed at the local level. "At the municipal level, the political possibilities have multiplied with the legalization of opposition participation. This is not because repressive tendencies diminish, but because the political cost of repression rises."[29] They are also heartened by the expectation that the presence of even a small delegation of Communists and other leftists in the Chamber of Deputies will shift the entire debate on Mexican development in a more progressive direction, raising issues that touch squarely on antiimperialist and social welfare concerns.[30]

In the short run it seems clear that the new opposition parties, like the largely discredited ones of the past, have reinforced the legitimacy of one-party rule. It may be that in the longer run they will be successful in carrying forward the task of popular mobilization in order to pose an effective opposition to the PRI. This possibility turns on their capacity to avoid being drawn into the center of gravity occupied by the PRI. For the Political Reform opens meaningful opportunities for opposition to official party hegemony only insofar as the new parties can resist the pull that historically has been exerted by the party and the state acting in combination. This is likely to prove very difficult because the system has traditionally drawn in and neutralized its opponents through a system of elaborate mechanisms that function to defuse dissidence, protest, and nonconformity of every kind. In the past the concentration of power and authority in the hands of the ruling party has been so complete that a range of political activity outside the PRI was tolerated simply because the political groups involved had no chance whatsoever of success. In short, the PRI system tended to absorb all opposition: organized and unorganized, institutional and spontaneous, urban and rural, individuals as well as groups. For the most part the PRI has managed to neutralize potential opposition and retain political control because of its success in *co-opting* all serious rivals for power. When those methods have failed, as we shall see, brutal repression has been employed. It is essential that we look carefully at the way this system of co-optation has functioned in the past if we hope to understand the prospects for the emergence of a genuine opposition in the future.

THE CO-OPTATION PROCESS

Co-optation is a term used to describe the process by which individuals or groups independent enough to threaten the ongoing domination of a single group or party (in this case, the PRI) are traded small concessions or favors in exchange for moderating their demands and reducing their challenge to the dominant group's control over the system.[31] This process takes place to some extent in almost every political system. But in Mexico, the process has been refined by the PRI to the point that it has paralyzed almost all potential opposition.

The key to the co-optation process lies in the centralization of power in the hands of a very few people who sit in Mexico City. There is only one way to get things done in Mexico. Whether one is a functionary of the PRI, a government bureaucrat, or the leader of an "independent" peasant or labor union, one is forced to go to the center, to the government offices in Mexico City to get action. There is no alternative source of authority. Bureaucratic institutions exist at the local, regional, and state levels, but decision making of all kinds takes place in Mexico City and nearly all policy directives emanate from the government offices in the capital. In many cases politicians find they must go directly to the president himself for the favors or governmental decisions they seek. Peasant leaders, for example, note that they spend as much as one-third of the year in government offices in Mexico City because, although these government agencies all have branch offices at the regional or state level, it is more efficient to travel a thousand kilometers to Mexico City than labor long hours in the state capital to win a favorable decision from, say, the regional secretary of water resources, only to have that decision overturned in Mexico City.[32]

With all decision making in the hands of the president, his close advisors, and his party, how can would-be independent peasant or labor unions win the concessions they need to retain the support of their membership? How can they win these concessions without compromising too much, without being absorbed by the centralized system they are attempting to challenge or change? As we shall see, in most cases they do not retain their independence. In most cases they are co-opted or bought off. They receive policy concessions for their followers only in return for moderating their militancy.

Most would-be independent popular movements in Mexico are sooner or later absorbed into the system they originally set out to change. Co-optation of this sort occurs because cooperation or collaboration with the PRI is one of the few avenues of social and economic mobility open to many people in Mexico. More important, it is practically the only way organizations can win the concessions from government that they need to fulfill their role as peasants' or workers' representatives.

CO-OPTATION FOR PERSONAL MOBILITY

Intellectuals

There are some fortunate individuals who manage to achieve prestige, power, or wealth without scrambling for a prominent position in the PRI-government structure. In some cases a person is so rich that the wealth and status available through politics will not substantially enhance his position. Another obvious category of people who do not need to play at PRI politics are Catholic priests, who have their own hierarchy of prestige and whose participation in politics, in any event, is strictly prohibited by the Mexican Constitution. Finally, people who are talented enough to gain an international reputation need not depend on the place they might make for themselves in the official party or government bureaucracies. Some opposition scholars and intellectuals, for example, retain their sense of political independence and personal integrity by finding work with an international organization like the United Nations, by taking positions as visiting professors at European and North American universities, by publishing abroad, or by working in Mexico in institutions largely funded by foreign foundations. But when and if these appointments come to an end, even the most independent intellectual comes face to face with a sad fact: private universities in Mexico tend to be traditional, conservative, and, for the most part, Catholic.[33] Technical institutes, which in the last decade have expanded at an accelerated rate, are under direct federal government authority. And among public institutions, only the National University, UNAM, with an enrollment of 250,000 students, has any claim to independence from direct government control. Indeed, one scholar found that while "no public university is completely independent of government control, . . . UNAM seems to enjoy considerable self-rule [when viewed] in cross-national perspective."[34] In the formulation of academic policy, student admissions, faculty selection, fiscal and administrative decision making, and even, to some degree, in the appointment of the rector, or head of the university, UNAM exercises substantial independence from government interference—although the level of autonomy has varied notably from one period to another.[35] All the same, even Levy, who stresses the amount of discretion available to the administrators of UNAM, acknowledges that historically the president of the republic can, and has, forced rectors out of office when policy pursued at the university seriously discomfited the regime in power.[36]

The heavy hand of government meddling in the appointment or resignation of university officials, however, is not the most serious limitation that weighs on academic freedom. Rather, the principal constraint on the independence of UNAM administrators and professors, as on intellectuals in all sectors of Mexican life, is the "interpenetration" of the governmental and intellectual elite:

> The single greatest danger to autonomy at the professorial and director levels stems from very substantial personnel overlap with the public sector. . . . Sycophancy is a real danger as universitarios at all levels may aspire to government jobs via the venerable Mexican co-optation process.[37]

This threat to academic independence is particularly serious in a university system like the Mexican one, in which few faculty members hold full-time appointments and most are "established practitioners." This means that the bulk of the faculty are technicians, professionals, or public officials who give a few hours of class each week for the prestige value of a university affiliation, while focusing most of their energies on their nonacademic careers. Given their contact with the university, government officials, doubling as university professors, identify talented students for public office.[38] "Clerks, administrators, and technocrats are recruited by officials who supplement their jobs in ministries or federal agencies with part-time teaching positions at the university. This is not considered 'moonlighting'—on the contrary, such officials are highly valued as linking the university with the public sector to which it ultimately belongs."[39] The overlap between political and administrative posts in government and key positions in academia has been noted in every systematic analysis of "elite recruitment," that is, every study that focuses on how top- and middle-level Mexican *politicos* make their way into positions of power and authority.[40] For example, in his study of the political elite, Smith notes the disproportionate number of high-level politicians and bureaucrats—in some administrations, close to 70 percent—who are drawn from UNAM. According to Smith, the National University "has operated as a kind of gateway into politics for children of the bourgeoisie," which is due to the centrality of "the institution's geographic and political location."[41]

Thus for intellectuals who choose to live in Mexico, some direct or indirect association with the government is virtually impossible to avoid, whether they are employed at the university, in a government-funded research center, or carry out intellectual work within the government or party itself. Obviously, not every intellectual in Mexico can earn a living on the staff of the handful of opposition publishing houses and periodicals. Sooner or later all intellectuals who are not independently wealthy must deal with this dilemma: how to earn a living in Mexico and still retain political independence. One Mexican economist, Miguel Wionczek, framed the problem in these terms:

> One of the things that the capitalist and socialist countries have in common is that both (for different reasons) offer the scientist and technician a margin of liberty for research and a decent standard of living. In Mexico, on the other hand, until very recently this group has faced the humiliating alternative of living a life of sacrifice and self-denial, or accepting unconditionally the rules of the political game.[42]

Once an intellectual is on the government payroll, he normally finds it difficult to change the system from within. For example, most leftists who enter the government or the PRI with the hope of "burrowing from within" are deeply frustrated after a relatively brief association with the inner workings of the government and party. Some leftists find themselves undergoing a rapid change in attitudes and even in vocabulary.

One left-wing economist described the process to the author in this way:

> When I returned to Mexico from my studies abroad, the only job offering open to me was on a special commission on agrarian problems in the Ministry of the Presidency. I reluctantly took the job, because by that time I had a wife and two children to support and could not afford to fool around launching left wing study groups and magazines. Naturally, I promised myself that I would do everything in my power to remain consistent with my ideals, and to work for change from my position within the government.
>
> But very soon, I found that I was changing. Even my vocabulary and my way of expressing myself was altered. Rather than call the president "Díaz Ordaz," I soon picked up the exaggeratedly respectful "El Señor Presidente" that all my colleagues used. My vocabulary soon filled with classic PRI rhetoric, with talk of "the ideals of the Mexican Revolution" and "devoted service and self-sacrifice for the fatherland." I had the greatest difficulty in dropping this language even when I came home at night.
>
> I believe that nothing I was able to accomplish in two years at the Ministry of the Presidency changed government policy in any way at all. To pretend otherwise would be sheer self-deception.

Although the experience can be deeply frustrating, a large proportion of self-defined leftists end up working either in the government or in the PRI bureaucracy. A graphic illustration of this tendency is provided by the story of one group of young graduates from the National University.

In the early 1960s the graduating class of the School of Political Science of the National University was comprised of a majority of leftist students. It is the custom for each graduating class to choose some person to stand as their *padrino de graduación*, a godfather for the graduating class. Normally a relatively rich and influential person is chosen because the honor carries with it certain obligations. The *padrino* generally provides a banquet for the graduating group and presents each student with a class ring.

In this case, the left-wing students prevailed over their more conservative classmates, and rather than choose a rich businessman or a PRI *politico* to serve as the class's *padrino*, a left-wing publisher was honored. Instead of receiving class rings, each student received a book from their godfather's publishing house, and a set of volumes was raffled off to provide funds for a banquet. The students were proud and happy to have honored someone whose political views they respected, and the graduating banquet turned out to be a most festive occasion.

Two years later, according to custom, the group was to meet with their *padrino* for a class reunion. Only a handful of students showed up. Everyone else in this once largely left-wing group of young political scientists was employed by either the PRI or the government. Of the few who were not, two had become housewives and two were unemployed. Only one member of the class had managed to find a job outside the government or party.

We can infer from this and other tales that recruitment of university graduates directly into government or official party jobs is a direct and often irresistible process even for students with a history of left-wing politics. Indeed, one of the best ways for a student to assure himself an attractive job offer after graduation is to build himself a reputation as a militant leftist student leader. Many of the choicest plums in the government and party hierarchy are reserved for buying off the most articulate, charismatic, and hence, politically dangerous leftist students. The routine co-optation of militant student leadership has become so institutionalized in Mexico that personally ambitious students have been known to form radical student movements and initiate student strikes specifically to draw the government's attention to themselves so that they might reap the rewards which accrue to a co-opted militant.

Not only are political leaders recruited directly from militant student groups; so, too, are the technocrats:

> Able students in science, engineering, medicine, architecture, etc. are spotted by instructors who become their tutors or thesis advisors. Networks based on personal loyalty to a tutor eventually become the backbone of research institutions, state corporations, and technical task forces in the ministries and agencies. . . . As a result, an increasing proportion of university graduates in the technical fields and in the liberal professions find employment in the Public Sector.[43]

In a study of the Mexican political elite, Camp has noted the unusual degree to which Mexican intellectuals make their way into government service. "The most distinctive characteristic of the Mexican intellectual's relationship to the state is the simple fact that the majority of the leading intellectuals since 1920 have served the government or followed government careers."[44] The intellectuals themselves generally attribute this trend to the absence of other alternatives, or the low demand for writing, art, music, and other cultural production in a poor country with a huge population of only semi-literate people. However, Camp points to data that indicate that those intellectual figures who have been drawn into state service share a common background and an educational formation with the politicians they eventually join in government. In terms of their urban origin, socioeconomic background, social and kinship ties, upbringing, and education in Mexico City, the overwhelming majority of the intellectuals turn out to have been in contact from childhood or adolescence with the men who eventually come to direct the Mexican state. Thus recruitment of intellectuals into the party and government is a natural outgrowth of old school and family ties. It is these links, according to Camp, which give the intellectual his "self-definition" and which determine whether he will—to put the best possible face on it—decide to "give shape" to his ideas by serving the state, rather than play the role of critic which is common to intellectuals in other societies.[45]

Notwithstanding these assorted influences and pressures, as we shall see, there are students and intellectuals who are totally committed to challenging the government and the PRI. To maintain their integrity and independence from government control, they move within the small, constricted range of job alternatives open to educated people who do not wish to work directly or indirectly for the PRI. These people are fortunate because this range of possibilities, though narrowly limited, does exist. But what, we might ask, happens to peasants and workers whose educational preparation is such that these options are unavailable to them?

Peasant Leaders

In chapter 2, we noted that official party politics is one of the few avenues of upward mobility open to people of peasant origin. Working with the CNC, a peasant who is ambitious and anxious to raise his socioeconomic status may overcome his disadvantaged background and rise through the ranks to occupy positions that provide considerable power and wealth.

Peasants who rise through their affiliation with the CNC normally begin their career as the representative of their own *ejido's* administration. The job carries with it a daily salary equal to the minimum wage in the countryside and the opportunity for frequent interaction with men influentially placed in the regional CNC hierarchy. If he displays the proper mixture of deference and assertiveness, the ejidal representative will eventually be recognized and placed in one of the CNC's lower-level patronage positions.

The peasant who wins such a position generally improves his economic situation because service as the CNC representative to a government agency normally carries with it a salary that is substantial by rural Mexican standards.[46] For example, in the Laguna region in 1968 some of the posts offered to peasant representatives by the government were (1) twelve representatives to the Ejidal Bank at a salary of $7.20 (U.S.) per week; (2) ten representatives to the Medical Services Committee at a salary of $7.20 per week; and (3) twelve representatives to the Government Insurance Bank at weekly salaries ranging from $7.20 to $20.00 per week.

If we bear in mind that the 1965 mean yearly income for *ejidatarios* in the Laguna region was between $112.00 and $128.00, while the smallest yearly income received by men serving in the official party as peasant representatives was $336.00, it is easy to understand the economic value of these patronage positions.[47]

Once a peasant's "loyalty" to the CNC and the party is recognized and rewarded in this way, tighter bonds of "mutual aid and trust" may develop between him and stronger figures in the CNC-PRI machine. One of the advantages of admission to the circle of low-level patronage recipients is precisely this opportunity to interact and develop political alliances with key men in the CNC structure at the regional or even the state level. The quick and ambitious peasant should be able to trade his current post for ever more prestigious and lucrative positions in the CNC hierarchy. With every step up the CNC ladder, the salary grows and so do the opportunities for kickbacks, payoffs, and other illicit gains. Some particularly adept peasants have parlayed their positions as professional peasant representatives into sizable personal fortunes. Some have even acquired enough money and land to take their place in the ranks of large landowners.

Because the CNC provides stepping-stones for socioeconomic advancement on an individual basis, some peasants are drawn into the official peasant organization precisely because it offers opportunities for the extraction of wealth and prestige that are otherwise absent in the world of an uneducated or poorly educated rural Mexican. For peasants who refuse either to join the CNC or to cooperate with the government and the official party, life is very difficult indeed. Obviously, then, the temptation to work within the system is very great for potential peasant leaders.

Labor Leaders

The same temptations that lure peasant leaders into the official party machine also draw many potential labor leaders into the CTM. Affiliation with the CTM opens to an ambitious worker a wide range of patronage positions and sinecures at salaries well above a laborer's pay. The top leaders of the CTM are regularly assigned seats in the federal legislature, and, at lower levels, salaried positions in local and state government, on regional committees, as labor representatives to government agencies, arbitration boards, and the like are available to the tried and true CTM man.

At the heart of the system lies corruption backed by force. Progovernment leaders use union funds and live lavishly at the expense of the rank and file. A select few receive high political posts in Congress, state governments, or the government bureaucracy. The CTM garners the majority of these sine-cures; the party distributes the rest among friendly non-CTM labor groups.[48]

Furthermore, because jobs in industry are relatively well paid and hard to obtain, union officials are able to wield great influence and rake off large amounts of money by apportioning these positions to workers who are able to scrape together the funds to buy a job.[49]

If we compare the opportunities for upward mobility that exist in Mexican society for ordinary peasants and workers with the range of economic and social possibilities that open to peasants and workers who are co-opted into the official party family, we must wonder not that so many people are co-opted, but rather that many peasants and workers actually choose the rough, rocky course of independent polit-ical action.

THE CO-OPTATION OF ORGANIZATIONS

Thus far we have looked primarily at the process of co-optation on the personal level. What stands out is the nearly irresistible pull of the PRI as the major avenue to personal material success for peasants, workers, and even for intellectuals. But, part of this same process, and even more significant than the co-optation of individuals, is the co-optation of whole organizations.[50]

There is a wide range of Mexican peasant and labor organizations that are not affiliated with either the CNC or CTM. Most of them have developed in response to specific dissatisfaction with the two PRI sec-tors in terms of their performance as representative organs. Some of these peasant and labor unions are locally or regionally based, while some, at least nominally, blanket the entire republic. Some are affiliated with the Mexican Communist Party; some are independent of affiliation with any political party. But all face a common dilemma.

Generally speaking, the leadership of independent organizations is not imposed from above as with CTM and CNC officials. Independent leaders need popular support to stay in office. Indeed, they need popu-lar support if the organizations themselves are to survive. Obviously the leaders of independent organizations cannot maintain the loyalty of their membership if they cannot effectively represent these members' interests. Peasants and workers who choose to affiliate with an inde-pendent organization have normally taken a bold step. In most cases the easy road is to register with the appropriate affiliate of the PRI. Opting for membership in an independent union is often a very committed act. But regardless of how committed a peasant or worker may be to certain ideals, he still needs to be represented by an organization that can effectively advance his interests; an organization that can win labor contracts, represent him before an arbitration board, petition the Ejidal Bank in his behalf, or market his cotton crop at a decent price. Peasant and labor unions that cannot provide these services for their members have great difficulty in surviving as viable organizations. Unfortunately, independent labor and peasant unions operate at a serious disadvantage. The bureaucracy that administers the land reform program, for example, is complex, enormous, and totally in the hands of official party politicians. A variety of federal banks, agencies, ministries, and departments exercise a determining control over land distribution, agricultural production, sales, and the rural economy as a whole. Together these federal banks and agencies decide which and how much land will be distributed to landless petitioners, which peasants (and which private owners) will receive irrigation water from national hydraulic projects, and how much technical aid, agricultural equipment, fertilizer, and insecticide will be made available to peasant landholders. In addition, they determine when and where new lands will be opened to cultivation, when credit will be supplied for crop diversification, and when processing plants such as cotton gins and cane mills may be set up by peasants in the countryside. The Department of Agrarian Affairs (after 1971 the Ministry for Agrarian Reform), for example, investigates the cases of lands held in violation of the limits set by agrarian law or maximum holdings. This same agency determines when and if these lands should be expropriated, and which peasants will become the beneficiaries of the distribution. In many cases independent peasant groups struggle for years to draw official attention to illegal holdings only to find that when the land is expropriated, it is distributed to CNC-affiliated peasants.[51] In other cases, independent peasant groups have lobbied vigorously for crop diversification or large-scale irrigation projects. But when the project becomes a reality, the independent peasant organization members are excluded from the program.

In short, the administrative bureaucracy that directs almost every aspect of the agricultural economy is firmly controlled by the ruling party. As a result, the more militant the peasant organizations are, or the more serious the challenge they present to PRI control, the greater are the difficulties they face in winning concessions for their members or in consolidating the concessions they have won in the past. As a study of independent peasant movements in the Northwest of Mexico indicated, these organizations were unable to sustain their non-revolutionary left *agrarismo* for the same reasons that others had failed before them: they were totally excluded from the system of rewards available through the regime, while their leaders were being offered lucrative and prestigious inducements to prostrate themselves before the government.[52]

Independent labor organizations are likewise in a disadvantaged position with respect to the government bureaucracies with which they deal. In many cases they are denied legal recognition from the Ministry of Labor. If they are not formally registered as labor representatives, the leaders of such independent unions cannot enter arbitration proceedings on behalf of their members, nor negotiate labor contracts, nor hold positions on the government commissions on wages. About the only thing these unions can do is call a wildcat strike that is not authorized by the CTM. So restricted is the role independent labor federations can legally play that most workers who join these organizations are forced to hold dual union membership; they retain their CTM union cards so that they will be included in the collective work contracts negotiated by the CTM, and, at the same time, they attend union meetings at the independent federation and bring their grievances to the attention of the independent labor leaders. For their part, all that the independent union leaders can do is to make extralegal representations to the Ministry of Labor or to the owners of the factory involved in the grievance. Yet, often even this extralegal representation yields more satisfactory results for the worker than he gets when he brings his complaint to his CTM representative, who is likely to be in the pay of the factory owner and who, in any event, has nothing to gain from stirring up trouble for the factory owner.

Independent labor unions typically grow directly from workers' dissatisfaction with the CTM. As the leader of one such organization explained to the author in 1972:

In 1954 a group of us could stand it no longer. The *charros*[53] of the CTM were accepting money from the owners. When the CTM leaders started signing labor agreements behind the back of the workers, we began to meet as a group to see what we could do. It was then that we formed the Sindicato Independiente de ___ ___ ___, but we had to fight another three years to win registration from the Ministry of the Interior. Even today the CTM controls all the Juntas de Conciliación y Arbitraje and we have no representation on those committees. We have great difficulty getting work contracts for our members. But the men stay with our Union because we are the only ones who fight. And the owners are afraid of us because they know we are the only ones who fight, who make demands for the working man.

With so many factors working to the disadvantage of independent organizations, the pressure is great to conform, to assume a conciliatory position toward the government, and even to bring the organization into alliance with the CTM or CNC. Careful study of those independent peasant and labor organizations that have survived for a decade or more generally shows a trend away from militant, oppositionist positions in favor of conformity, collaboration, and cooperation with the government.

THE POLITICS OF TAMALES: A CASE STUDY[54]

One way to study the process of co-optation and the trend away from opposition politics is to look at the political evolution of a specific opposition organization. An interesting organization to study is the Central Union,[55] a Communist-led peasant union that has played an important role in the politics of the Laguna region for more than four decades. In the preceding chapters we have made frequent reference to the cotton growing Laguna region of north-central Mexico. This area is interesting not only because it was the site of the first truly large-scale land reform effort in all Latin America, but also because, historically, it has been the major, and at times the only, area of Communist party strength in the Mexican countryside.

The Central Union: The Early Years of Political and Economic Strength

The original leadership of the Central Union was drawn from the ranks of the militant *agraristas* who led the fight for agrarian reform in the years before Cárdenas carried out his land distribution in the region. Some of the older Central Union leaders had histories of radical agrarianism dating back to the revolution. But the bulk of the leadership received political training in the Communist youth organizations active in the Laguna region throughout the 1920s and early 1930s. These youth cadres, encouraged by the Cárdenas administration's benign attitude toward the Mexican Communist Party, brought together young peasants and workers, and sped the formation of political consciousness and political ties between industrial workers in Torreón and the surrounding population of landless, agricultural day laborers.

During the most active period of agrarian conflict (1934–1937), the young men who were later to become Central Union officers gained valuable experience and region-wide contacts organizing their families, friends, and neighbors in support of the *agrarista* cause. Most of the

Central Union officers played leading roles in the great general strike that paralyzed the Laguna from August to October 1936, the strike used by Cárdenas to justify a massive land distribution in the region. Thus, in the years following the land reform, the original strike leaders, many of them formally affiliated with the PCM, enjoyed widespread prestige among the new *ejidatarios*. Many of the strike leaders were elected by their fellow *ejidatarios* to fill positions requiring some leadership experience, a good general knowledge of the region, and contacts with emerging peasant leaders in neighboring *ejidos*.

In 1939 a "Central Union" of representatives of the newly created *ejidos* was founded by peasants and given legal recognition by the Cárdenas administration. It was authorized by the government to carry out banking operations, administer warehouses, dams, and wells, and to establish commercial and industrial enterprises on behalf of the *ejidatarios* in the Laguna region. Most important, the Central Union was authorized to represent peasants in their dealings with local, state, and national governments and their agencies.[56] Given the early influence of the Communist party organizers in the Laguna region, and the role of Communist-affiliated peasants in organizing and sustaining the general strike of 1936, it is not surprising that the leadership of the newly established Central Union was supplied in great part by peasants formally affiliated with the Communist Party.

As long as Cárdenas was in power, the Communist peasant leaders pursued a policy of amicable cooperation with the government. This policy reflected the affinity of the Communist peasant leaders for the government responsible for the agrarian reform, and at the same time corresponded to the formal policy adopted by the Communist International of fostering a popular front with all "progressive forces" on the political scene.

During the late 1930s the Central Union fared well under its Communist leadership. It expanded its membership and activities and by 1940 was directing the operation of collective, peasant-owned cotton gins, electric power stations, mule-drawn railways, warehouses, Russian-style machine stations, and a mutual crop insurance company. The union was also in the process of launching a program of cooperative health services, educational and cultural centers, cooperative ejidal food stores, and agricultural experimentation and demonstration centers—all run by and for peasant members. Perhaps the most important activity of the Central Union during this period was its effort to gain complete peasant control over the selection, packing, marketing, and processing of the ejidal crop, as well as control over the distribution of credit funds to *ejidatarios*.

At this point in its development, the Central Union was the most powerful peasant organization in the Laguna region, more influential even than the regional committees of the CNC. The union's membership of some 30,000 highly politicized peasants formed the basis of its political strength. The Central Union also enjoyed significant economic power because the financial success of its economic enterprises gave the organization increasing independence from government support or control. Cooperative enterprises further provided Central Union members a certain measure of independence from the commercial network of money lenders, cotton merchants, and agricultural equipment suppliers, all controlled by the old landholding class and by foreign capital. Accordingly, as the growing strength of the peasants organized in the Central Union gradually came to threaten the advantages of the bourgeoisie and other vested interests, strenuous efforts were made to curb this peasant organization.

Political Repression

When the conservative Manuel Avila Camacho succeeded Cárdenas in the presidency, a series of new policies drastically altered the political climate that had permitted a peasant organization like the Central Union to thrive and accumulate political and economic clout. The inauguration of Avila Camacho ushered in a new period of anticommunism in Mexico, which was immediately expressed in a governmental effort to remove from office all Communist party members holding important positions in peasant and labor organizations. This policy forced upon Central Union leaders the difficult choice of aligning themselves with the official party, turning over their posts to CNC delegated peasants, or accepting a drastic reduction in the activities their organization would be allowed to pursue.

The Central Union officers chose to fight it out and to remain at the head of their organization. They neither joined the official party nor renounced their Communist party membership. The government responded to this decision with an effort to break the power of the Central Union. Almost all of the cooperative enterprises directed by the Central Union were taken out of the control of this organization and placed under the administration of the Ejidal Bank and other government agencies.

This attack on the Central Union was effective inasmuch as it deprived the Communist-led union of its economic power base, at the same time forcing it to curtail much of its political activity. Without the financial resources to move about rapidly and extensively in the region, much less between the Laguna and Mexico City, it became increasingly difficult for the Central Union to attend effectively to the problems of its members, or to act as a spokesman for peasant interests.

Over the next twenty-five years the Communist-led union survived in an atmosphere of official hostility which gave way at times to outright political repression. During the 1940s, Central Union officers were imprisoned, members were physically ousted from their desks at the State Agrarian Leagues, and Central Union meetings, rallies, and demonstrations were broken up by police or paid provocateurs. Central Union members lost their seats as peasant representatives on Ejidal Bank, water resource, and other committees, and were replaced in these positions by faithful CNC peasant appointees. Economic blackmail was used to force Central Union members to affiliate with the CNC on pain of losing their credit payments from the Ejidal Bank. In 1947, a rival "Central Union" (CNC-affiliated) was established by the Alemán administration to channel off what remained of the official responsibilities originally delegated to the Communist-led Central Union.

Central Union Achievements

Largely as a result of these efforts at political sabotage, Central Union membership declined from 30,000 in 1940 to roughly 3,500 members in the late 1960s. Notwithstanding the decline in membership, the Central Union survived as a significant political force in the Laguna region. Not only did it survive, but it realized some substantial political and economic achievements. Without renouncing its Communist affiliation or joining the official party family, it managed to establish a relatively permanent place for itself in the agrarian politics of the region, and it was recognized by successive regimes as the most articulate spokesman for peasant interests in the Laguna.

The Central Union's achievements would hardly be described as "revolutionary victories." Rather, those peasants who stuck with the Central Union were rewarded for their loyalty by a number of concrete economic benefits. For example, the Communist peasant leaders won the right to bargain and to sell their members' cotton with no intervention on the part of the Ejidal Bank.[57] Along the same lines, the Central Union trained or hired technicians to provide members with expert advice, so that they would not have to depend on the unreliable and sometimes corrupt technical services of the Ejidal Bank. These concessions, won after years of politicking by Central Union leaders at both the regional and national levels, meant a few more pesos in the pockets of Central Union members. The 1 percent commission on the sale of members' produce also provided the organization with a substantial part of its operating budget. But, obviously, these achievements were not radical in any sense of the word. These efforts in no way altered the basic social, political, or even the economic structure of the Laguna region.

Somewhat more significant in terms of its implications for socioeconomic change were the efforts of the Central Union to win credit concessions for the diversification of ejidal agriculture. By moving away from cotton to a variety of new agricultural activities (dairy farming, cultivation of grapes, walnuts, alfalfa, wheat), Central Union leaders hoped to break the vicious circle of region-wide dependency on a single crop with a declining price on the world market. The Central Union expended years of effort, thousands of pesos, called meeting after meeting, issued report after report in its efforts to persuade not only Union members but peasants throughout the Laguna of the need to switch from monoculture to a variety of crops. And once the demonstration experiments and educational program mounted by the organization had effectively persuaded most peasants that their increasingly precarious economic situation was intimately linked to dependency on cotton, great effort was still needed to convince the government to make funds available for crop diversification in the Laguna.

Thus most of the Central Union's political battles after 1940 did not involve efforts to transform the economic system, much less to overthrow the existing form of government. Rather, the Communist-led peasant union struggled simply to salvage the ejidal system as it was originally created in the Laguna region. As we have noted, the economic viability of the ejidal system has not enjoyed a very high priority in the development plans of those who have held power in Mexico since 1940. Since that time, investment funds that might have been made available for credit, research, hydraulic projects, and other benefits to the ejidal sector have instead been channeled into private commercial agriculture. However, the Laguna ejidal community represents a partial exception to this overall trend. The government poured more money and attention into the Laguna *ejidos* than almost any other region in the country (with the significant exception of the large, commercially oriented *ejidos* of the Northwest). And if the Laguna *ejidos* received a slightly bigger slice of the investment pie, this was largely due to the steady agitation of the Central Union. Both in the region and in Mexico City, Central Union leaders were the most active, militant, and vocal advocates of a better deal for the Laguna.

Even during the 1940s and 1950s, a period marked by increasing governmental neglect of land reform and hostility toward agrarian movements and demands, the Central Union regularly mounted mass demonstrations, brought pressure to bear on the Department of Agrarian Affairs, and sent a steady stream of delegates to Mexico City to demand audiences with incumbent presidents. The union ran candidates for public office who had no chance of electoral victory, simply to use the campaign to raise important issues. On several occasions huge "caravans" made up of hundreds of men, women, and children were organized by the Central Union and sent more than a thousand kilometers to Mexico City to march through the streets of the capital, dramatizing the economic difficulties of the Laguna *ejidatarios*, capturing the attention of the press and the government, and forcing the latter to give way, at least in part, to some of the demands of the *Laguneros*.

The agitation of the Central Union was always conspicuous in contrast to the inaction and quiescence of the Laguna CNC. The Central Union fight against corruption in the administration of the Ejidal Bank and other government agencies was untiring. The union was the only organization to effectively organize to defend ejidal land and water rights from encroachment by the large landowners, and served as the main spokesman in the fight for improved medical, educational, technical, and credit facilities for all peasants in the region. Finally, this Communist-led peasant union was directly responsible for bringing to the Laguna an agricultural rehabilitation plan which doubled the surface of irrigated land in the region.

Obviously these achievements, if not revolutionary, were at least substantial and indicate a good deal more political capacity than is normally displayed by CNC-affiliated peasant organizations. We might ask how it was possible for a group in no way connected with the official party to accomplish so much. In part the Central Union's accomplishments were the result of the sense of clear purpose and the solidity provided by an historical tradition of militant activity and a unifying ideology. In part they were due to the pragmatism and flexibility of a leadership willing to play by the rules of the Mexican political game. Let us look at each of these features in turn to gauge their impact on the effectiveness of this independent peasant union.

The militant tradition. To understand the exceptional longevity and resilience of the Central Union and to account for the tradition of militant independent peasant organization in the Laguna, we must bear in mind some of the unique features of the original mobilization of peasants in the region. The fact that the state implemented land reforms in *response* to a clearly articulated demand is an historical characteristic which distinguishes the Laguna from other regions and, indeed, from other land reform districts of Mexico. The strike leaders emerged from the peasantry in the course of intense class struggle in which they had the opportunity to elaborate an ideology and acquire a variety of organizational skills while building a base of support among their fellow peasants. The general strike had incorporated almost every peasant in the Laguna, and eventually succeeded even in gaining the support of the 10,000 strike-breakers, virtually all of whom chose to remain in the region to become *ejidatarios*. As we have noted, the outcome of the strike depended to a large extent on links forged with the urban working class (based largely on personal ties between a number of militant urban workers and the peasants they had politicized), and the ultimate success of the strike naturally reinforced these worker-peasant bonds. The connection of the strike leadership with the Mexican Communist Party enabled the peasant leaders to build upon the ideological and organizational foundation provided by the international Communist movement, even as the victory of the strikers strengthened the PCM nationally and gave it its most important base in the countryside.[58]

Therefore, when Cárdenas sent Lombardo Toledano and other labor organizers into the Laguna—as he did in all key areas of the republic—they found an organizational structure on which to build. Militant labor and peasant unions were already active and, to a large extent, unified. Cárdenas' agents had only to bring these groups under the president's political control. While mobilized peasants were eager to join a coalition of support for the reformist Cárdenas regime, these peasant organizations had experienced a period of political independence from official party control, and they had reference to ideological cues other than the official *agrarista* line. These factors proved crucial in the post-Cárdenas years when the agrarian policy of successive regimes and the ideological line of the official peasant organization, the CNC, turned sharply to the right. Thus the peculiar experience of a general strike gave rise in the Laguna to a tradition of independent peasant mobilization by groups that willingly entered government-sponsored organizations when this course promised to serve their goals but were organizationally capable of sustaining themselves outside of the CNC/official party apparatus.

The role of ideology. Apart from the tradition of militance, the Central Union was served in its efforts to sustain group cohesion by an ideology that fostered unity and abiding loyalty among the reduced core of peasants who retained membership in the organization. Indeed, it seems clear that the organization's survival over a period of four decades was due in large part to the high level of ideological commitment required of and given by its supporters.

The ideology of the Central Union has changed over time. In the late 1930s, led by avowed Marxists, the movement was openly committed to the class struggle, peasant-worker alliance and, above all, to the total transformation of the countryside by a complete land reform which would leave no individual holding more than fifty acres of land. Gradually, the expressed goals shifted from radical change in land tenure pattern to achieving compliance with existing legislation, and eventually to improving support systems to raise productivity in the ejidal sector, and increasing economic opportunities in general for the peasantry. But from the 1930s until the 1970s, one element of the common belief system which remained constant was the emphasis on solidarity, the pursuit of social goals, collective achievement, shared responsibility, and socialist morality. These shared beliefs inhibited the growth of selfish individualism, corruption in office, alcoholism, and centrifugal factionalism which plagued other peasant movements.

Extensive interviews among long-time Central Union adherents indicate that members always believed their leaders to be totally honest and committed to group rather than personal goals. The accountability of the directorate to the membership and the democratic organizational structures that enhanced the members' sense of participation corresponded to the shared ideology and clearly reinforced the loyalty of the *ejidatarios* affiliated with the Central Union. The experience of the union indicates that the greater the commitment of the organization's members to a set of shared beliefs, the more forebearance they are likely to show when goods and services sought on their behalf by their leaders are not forthcoming. Thousands of Laguna *ejidatarios* remained loyal to the organization's principal leader, Arturo Orona, and to the Central Union during the periods of repression and overall hard times suffered in the 1940s and 1950s. Throughout the difficult years when the cooperative enterprises developed by the Central Union in the early agrarian reform years were taken from peasant control and placed under the administration of government agencies, when Central Union members lost their places as peasant representatives on official boards, when their rallies and demonstrations were broken up, and their leaders harassed or imprisoned, a substantial portion of the original membership (three to four thousand peasant families) nonetheless remained steadfast. This is not to deny the significance of the important concessions the Central Union leadership—in spite of the setbacks noted above—was able to win for its constituents. Central Union members were not, after all, middle-class intellectuals who could afford to flirt with radical ideologies with no concern for their basic survival needs. However, the ideological commitment of these peasants meant that they were prepared to support their organization through difficult times rather than abandon it at the first materially disappointing signs, as is frequently the case with members of independent peasant organizations based strictly on personal loyalty to a single charismatic leader.[59]

In theory "clientelist" politics are nonideological by definition. That is, personalistic, clientelist attachments are generally viewed as the functional opposite of ideologically based political commitment.[60] And yet, in real political life we often find ideological commitment in interplay with personal loyalty and often we cannot separate ideological from personal appeal. This is very much the case for Arturo Orona and the membership of the Central Union. Where followers are drawn to a charismatic political leader because he is perceived as "recto," i.e., clean, honest, and decent, and where that leader finds the source of his personal rectitude in his attachment to a set of ideals ("socialist man" or "the true communist"), then it becomes difficult to separate the personal attributes that have attracted a popular following from the ideologically determined model.[61] Orona's reputation as a reliable person—clever, even crafty, but honorable—not only helped him win political influence among Laguna peasants, but served him in his brokerage activities among key political and business contacts in Mexico City. Thus we can also understand ideology to play a role in determining leadership qualities which in turn effect the ultimate political success of a peasant organization.

Playing by the rules of the game. The Central Union's achievements were also due to its willingness to play within the rules of the Mexican power game. Success in this game calls for special skills and, above all, flexibility and a superb sense of balance. It requires that opposition leaders know when to strike hard and when to ease off on political pressure; when to make militant, threatening gestures, and when to give in; when to hold out, and when to accept considerably less than the concessions demanded.

To play this game successfully, politicians who work outside the PRI must build a reputation for strength, flexing their political muscles often enough to remind the government that they represent a political force to be reckoned with. This is what the business of mass demonstrations, caravans, and running electoral candidates is all about. They all serve to remind those in power that a particular opposition group is strong, well organized, and can, if ignored too long, threaten the control of the ruling party in a given region. When a peasant organization like the Central Union loads five hundred *ejidatarios* onto trucks and sends them off to Mexico City to march through the streets or to make a nuisance of themselves sitting in the antechambers of the National Palace, the leadership is effectively telling the government: "These five hundred peasants are only a fraction of the people whose loyalty we command. If we can send this group to Mexico City, we have the organizational skills to bring together the discontented and transport them anywhere in the republic. We are a political group of significance, an organization to be taken seriously. Our demands must be met at least in part if we are not to create serious trouble for those in power."

Díaz seized power in 1876 by military coup and ruled Mexico as a dictator for more than thirty years. *Courtesy of* or

he pretext of gathering to play music, peasants would meet on the weekends to drink *pulque* and secretly discuss scontent with the porfirian regime (ca. 1907). *Courtesy of* Excelsior

Under the banner of "Effective Suffrage and No Reele Francisco I. Madero, a politically progressive lan from northern Mexico, touched off the struggle to ove the porfirian dictatorship and went on to become th lution's first president. *Courtesy of* Excelsior

Venustiano Carranza, the most conservative of the p revolutionary leaders of the North, emerged by 1914 dominant force among the armies of the Revolution. *Cou* Excelsior

In 1915, a *soldadera*, Ana María Fernández, posed for the camera with an unidentified comrade-in-arms. *Courtesy of* Excelsior

eral Francisco "Pancho" Villa, the bandit-turned-lutionary, was a Robin Hood figure who led the fa-s Division del Norte, an army composed of boys, miners, gamblers, bandits, and drifters. *Cour-* *of* Excelsior

ir homes destroyed, their lives uprooted, women joined the lutionary armies as combatants as well as camp followers. woman is Valentina Ramírez, a *soldadera* who took part in seige of Culiacán. *Courtesy of* Excelsior

The *zapatistas* enter Mexico City under the banner of the Virgin of Guadalupe. *Courtesy of Excel*

The *zapatistas* and *villistas* marched on Mexico City and took the capital. The two leaders celebrated their alliance in National Palace, but neither felt prepared for national leadership. *Courtesy of* Excelsior

e various armies of the North split and reunited along
v lines. Soldiers surrendered to an enemy force one day
l, as a condition of their release, took up arms the next
to fight under a new general. *Courtesy of* Excelsior

uertista soldier and his sweetheart say farewell. *Courtesy of*
elsior

oughout the years of struggle, Emiliano Zapata was able to
nt upon the adhesion and collaboration of a group of urban
rural radical intellectuals as well as the intense loyalty of
peasant troops. *Courtesy of* Excelsior

April 1926. President Alvaro Obregón *(fourth from left)* with [his] protégé, Plutarco Elías Calles *(fifth from left)* and the incr[eas]ingly powerful labor boss, Luis Morones *(next to Calles)*. C[our]tesy of Excelsior

President Plutarco Elías Calles (1924–1928) oversaw the p[ost]revolutionary period of physical reconstruction and industrial [and] commercial expansion at the same time that he consolidated [na]tional power through the formation of an official party. Here [he] steps from the first commercial Mexican aircraft, as he inaugur[ated] the national airline. *Courtesy of* Excelsior

The candidacy of Lázaro Cárdenas was supported by prog[res]sives in 1933 because the Governor of Michoacán had bui[lt a] reputation as an honest and popular leader who had prome[sed] land reform and other social transformations in his home st[ate.] *Courtesy of* Excelsior

his electoral campaign and throughout his administration (1934–1940), Lázaro Cádenas expressed his concern for ustice by traveling to remote corners of the Republic to meet face to face with his peasant and working-class ters. *Courtesy of* Excelsior

l Avila Camacho was the president whose ad-ation (1940–1946) marked the shift away e populist priorities of Cárdenas *(right).* Here ho *(center)* plays host to Mexico's wartime 'ranklin Delano Roosevelt, and first lady r Roosevelt. *Courtesy of* Excelsior

Aexican presidents *(left to right)* Luís Echeverría 1976), Emilio Portes Gil (1928–1929), Miguel n (1946–1952), and Gustavo Díaz Ordaz (1964– leave the Chamber of Deputies after attending a e to President Adolfo Ruíz Cortines (1952–1958). sy *of* Excelsior

The cover of *Siempre* takes a jibe at the expectations raised by the ca promises made by incoming President Adolfo López Mateos (1958 *Courtesy of* Excelsior

Although his victory was assured from the time he was named party candidate in 1969, Echeverría traveled 350,000 miles and more than 900 villages, towns, and cities in a seven-month t signed to build popular support for his regime. *Courtesy of Exce*

Carrying over his campaign techniques to his adminstration, Echeverría became the most visible and accessible pr since Lázaro Cárdenas. *Courtesy of* Excelsior

...idential candidate José López Portillo receives the ...ial support of CTM and CNOP affiliated unions. ...rtesy *of* Excelsior

... only are peasants the poorest sector of the population, ... the gap between the rich and poor is wider in the coun- ...ide than in the towns and cities of Mexico. *Courtesy of* ...elsior

...pite the modernization of agriculture in key regions ...Mexico, technology remains backward in many mar- ...al areas of the country. *Courtesy of* Excelsior

The backward technology of the [...] agricultural regions contrasts with [...] area like the Laguna in northern M[...]ico. Here the cultivation of an im[...]tant commercial crop and the exist[...] of highly politicized and well [...]nized peasant unions has given p[...]ants a means to pressure the nati[...] government to provide credit for [...] purchase of tractors and other sop[...]ticated agricultural equipment. C[...] tesy of Excelsior

Throughout Mexico, landless peasants have aband[...] the countryside to migrate to the cities in hope of [...] proving their lot. But jobs in the cities have no[...] creased at a rate adequate to absorb this rural sur[...] Courtesy of Excelsior

On the periphery of the cities, squalid slums sp[...] up like mushrooms as migrants construct makes[...] dwellings out of mud, corrugated paper, hamme[...] out tin cans, and scrap lumber. Courtesy of Excel[...]

...uatters build wherever they find space: in deep ..., under electric power lines, along the railroad ...-way. In some "lost cities" unemployment runs ... as 95 percent. *Courtesy of* Excelsior

...dent movement of 1968 expressed young Mexicans' ...t the hunger and misery produced by the distorted ...es of Mexican development. *Courtesy of* Excelsior

...vernment's response to the student movement ...rutal, sweeping repression in which hundreds of ...ns were killed and wounded and hundreds more ...oned. *Courtesy of* Excelsior

Despite widespread discontent with P[...]
this political machine is still cap[...]
mobilizing support as in this demon[...]
in the Constitutional Plaza, March 2[...]
Courtesy of Excelsior

A poster of Zapata carried by stud[...]
testors in the Corpus Christi day [...]
stration, June 1971, read, "You[...]
have you done to defend the a[...]
ments for which we gave our [...]
Courtesy of Excelsior

ly, the official party, PRI, comprised four sec-
asants (CNC), workers (CTM), middle-class or-
ons (CNOP), and the military. Here a student,
, worker, and military policeman line the
route along Avenida Juarez, waiting patiently
sident Lopez Portillo to drive by. *Canapress*
ervice

de la Madrid Hurtado (1982–1988) waves from the
v of his campaign bus. The PRI spent an estimated
00 million on de la Madrid's 1981 campaign tour,
he officially registered opposition parties shared
million among six parties. *Canapress Photo Ser-*

areas peasant women, who generally partici-
no other aspect of political life, line up to cast
tes for the official party. However, since the
n Communist Party and other leftist coalitions
legal status with the political reforms of the late
the Communists have captured support not
ong the urban working and middle classes, but
poorest rural zones of Oaxaca and Guerrero
Canapress Photo Service

In 1941, wartime manpower shortages prompted the Ne— New Haven, and Hartford Railroad to bring these *bracer*— ers north to lay and repair track. Whenever North A— agriculture or industry has required extra "hands," M— labor has been eagerly sought. In times of economic re— however, these same workers are hunted down and exp— unwanted "illegals." *Canapress Photo Service*

U.S. border patrolmen herd a group of Mexican youths — waiting for the trip to the Chula Vista border station, whe— will be deported. Between 1930 and 1977, eight times a— Mexicans were apprehended as illegal immigrants as were— visas to live and work in the United States. Still, each year — of poor Mexicans manage to slip across the border und— *Canapress Photo Service*

Hopes for jobs in the new border assembly plants or for a— to cross the border have brought hundreds of thousand— grants to northern cities like Tijuana. But the plants h— ployed only 130,000 at their peak, and the border cities,— oil-boom towns, lack the social infrastructure to absorb— grants, who end up squatting on mountainsides. *Ca*— *Photo Service*

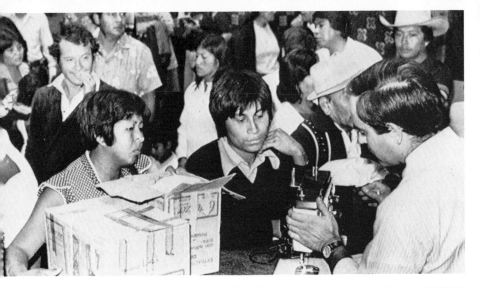

series of devaluations and the nationalization of the banks in Sep-
)er 1982 left middle- and lower-class Mexicans desperately short of
. Here thousands line up at the government pawn shop, Monte de
ad, to pawn goods like this sewing machine, purchased in better
s. *Canapress Photo Service*

visible "Americanization" of the cities worries many Mexicans as
ntucky Fried Pollo" and "Burgerboy" become household words for the
dle class. However, far more serious are the dietary consequences for
malnourished poor, whose nutritional deficiencies grow worse as they
easingly substitute refined wheat products, promoted by transnational
conglomerates, for the traditional corn *tortilla*. *Canapress Photo Ser-*

ico has both potential and proven oil reserves which may well
e it the world's leading producer. These installations at the Ber-
ez oil fields in Tabasco sit atop a supply of petroleum which most
y exceeds the North Sea reserves. *Canapress Photo Service*

In some of the "lost cities" of the Capital, as he Iztacalco, squatters have been mobilized by oppos coalitions which strive to coordinate the protest struggles of workers, peasants, and students with demands of slum dwellers. The late seventies an eighties have witnessed an upsurge of popular m ments which resist "capture" by the official p *Canapress Photo Service*

Today half of all Mexi are children under fi years of age. The futu children like this turns on whether nati resources like oil be only the few, or are aged to meet the n of the broad masse the population. *Cana Photo Service*

The Central Union traditionally enjoyed the leadership of individuals astute and flexible enough to understand these rules and to play the game with great skill. These leaders were able to read the direction of the political winds and respond quickly to changes in the political climate. For example, in the early 1940s, every meeting of the Central Union opened with a demand for the expropriation of all holdings in excess of fifty acres. However, in response to a new era of intense anticommunism and antiagrarianism, these demands were dropped in favor of appeals for compliance with existing agrarian legislation; demands that the peasants receive the land and water that they already had coming to them under the Agrarian Code. Central Union pressure for total peasant control over all the economic affairs of the *ejidos* was reduced to calls for the recognition of the Union as a bargaining agent for *ejidatarios* in a number of key transactions. When interviewed in 1968, Central Union leaders explained that these reduced demands were "more realistic, given the difficult conditions faced by peasant and labor organizatons in that period."

Again in the 1950s, Central Union leaders responded to a new set of political conditions. When Adolfo Ruíz Cortines assumed the presidency in 1952, the prestige of the government and the official party was at one of its lowest ebbs. The antiagrarian and antilabor policies of Ruíz Cortines's predecessor, Alemán, had alienated peasants and workers, while the flagrantly corrupt activities of *alemanistas* at all levels of government had become distressing to even the least idealistic of Mexicans.[62] Disaffection was so great that Ruíz Cortines came into office with the smallest majority of the vote ever recorded by an official party candidate for the presidency.[63]

Accordingly, the new president at once began the fence-mending process. In addition to a large scale "cleanup of corruption," this administration sought reconciliation with those who had suffered most severely the effects of Alemán's program of rapid industrialization. In virtually all his public addresses, Ruíz Cortines indicated that he would try to mollify peasant groups throughout Mexico. Central Union leaders seized on this evidence to sharpen their pressure and demands on the government. Indeed, the Ruíz Cortines years were a relatively successful period for the Central Union which, among other substantial concessions, received a 200 million peso credit to launch its long-ignored plan for crop diversification.

Ruíz Cortines's successor, Adolfo López Mateos, likewise projected his regime as a period of "renovation" in the countryside. Central Union leaders once more stepped up their activities and pressure, and once again received some significant economic concessions for their members.

During the 1950s and 1960s the Central Union seemed to be more "successful" in its dealings with each new regime: opposing the government less, but winning more in the way of economic benefits for its constituency. This process culminated under the administration of Gustavo Díaz Ordaz, who came to power in 1964.

As early as 1947 a special political friendship developed between Díaz Ordaz and Arturo Orona. Díaz Ordaz, then a senator and an official party regular, came to the Laguna to attend the regional congress of the CNC. During the day, Díaz Ordaz met with PRI and CNC regulars and denounced the Communist-led Central Union at an assembly of CNC delegates saying, ". . . for the CNC there exists no group of enemy peasants except those who provoke disunity to satisfy personal appetites, and those who live off the sweat of the peasants. . . ."[64] But that night he accepted an invitation for dinner at the home of Orona, where, over a plate of *tamales*, the two men established a relationship that would subsequently prove very valuable to both of them.

On successive visits to Mexico City, above all in moments of crisis for the Central Union, Orona could count on the support of Díaz Ordaz, among other key politicians, for the help he needed to keep his organization alive. Not all members of the directorate of the Central Union agreed with this approach to the problem of political survival, but, in general, cultivation of some important politicians on the national level, combined with displays of political strength on the local level, helped to keep the Central Union alive during the bleak years.

Once Díaz Ordaz came to power in 1964, the political and economic fortunes of the Central Union improved markedly. When Díaz Ordaz made his much heralded official visit to the Laguna in 1966, the Chief Executive openly snubbed the entire range of local, regional, and state CNC representatives when, stepping from his helicopter, he walked directly over to Orona, embraced the old Communist warmly and, taking his arm, led him into the presidential touring bus. During the Díaz Ordaz years, Orona could count on a sympathetic hearing and prompt action from the president whenever the Central Union was unable to resolve problems through ordinary government channels.

However, the political friendship between Orona and Díaz Ordaz placed the Central Union in a very awkward position when the Díaz Ordaz regime was rocked by the student movement of 1968. The student crisis brought into the open a deep internal conflict within the peasant union. The dominant faction, led by Orona, insisted that the organization declare its support for Díaz Ordaz, even in the face of the atrocities committed by his government. The minority faction, composed in general of younger, more militant peasants, came out in favor of an antigovernment demonstration. Orona's view prevailed, and in mid-October of 1968, the union took an advertisement in the regional daily, *La Opinión,* proclaiming the Central Union's support for the Díaz Ordaz regime.[65] This gesture of solidarity with the regime in its weakest hour bore very tangible fruit in the form of a 3.5 million peso credit given to the Central Union for the purchase of walnut seedlings and the development of a dairy industry. And in November of that same year Orona received the following letter from the president of the republic:

Los Pinos
México, D.F.
November 5, 1968

Sr. Arturo Orona
Torreón, Coahuila

Esteemed friend,

Sr. Norberto Aguirre [Secretary of the Department of Agrarian Affairs] was kind enough to transmit your message to me. Your thoughts moved me deeply, and when I said as much to Sr. Aguirre, he told me that you, too, had expressed them with great emotion.

Your words of profound human warmth and encouragement in such difficult hours of injustice and misunderstanding constituted one of the best offerings I could have received.

I also received the *tamales* that you so kindly sent me, and we ate them at home with complete confidence and pleasure. They were very delicious.

Thanking you for your courtesy, I salute you affectionately,

Gustavo Díaz Ordaz

In January of 1972, Arturo Orona was expelled from the Mexican Communist Party in which he had sat as a member of the Central Committee off and on for many years.[66] At the same time he was dropped from the ranks of the Independent Peasant Central and other Communist affiliates that had once been proud to associate his name with their organization. Orona had gone too far in his policy of collaborating with the government in return for concrete economic gains. In the eyes of many of his comrades, Orona's policy of playing along with the government in exchange for benefits to constituents had gradually become outright opportunism. In their opinion Orona had sold out; he had become thoroughly co-opted, and he had brought his organization right along with him. They reasoned that the Central Union had traded its independence and integrity in return for economic concessions, and that the long-term welfare of the peasants had been forgotten or sacrificed in the rush for short-term, bread and butter gains.

It is our intention to analyze these political developments rather than to judge them. Therefore it is important to note that Central Union leaders started out in the 1930s as Marxists committed to the struggle for a thoroughgoing transformation in the countryside, a complete land reform that would have left no individual with more than fifty acres. The realities of the political world in which they found themselves forced them to accept much less. It forced them to struggle with all their energy simply to win what amounted to compliance with long-existing legislation, with agrarian goals that were already well articulated back in 1917. They were like men on a treadmill, obliged to run at full speed simply to remain in the same place. In time they found it more useful to collaborate with what they liked to call the "progressive elements" within the government "rather than permit the administration to come under the domination of reactionary forces."[67]

The experience of the Central Union illustrates that opposition movements can and do wrest concessions from the government. However, they do so, generally speaking, only at the cost of altering, if not totally subverting, the original goals of their movement. The case of the peasant mobilization in the Laguna, furthermore, illustrates another highly sophisticated co-optive technique frequently employed by the Mexican state to defuse a threat to its control over peasants or other potentially discontented sectors of society. This technique is the establishment of competing, parallel organizations designed to absorb and transform not only the peasant supporters themselves, but selected aspects of the ideology they have long professed. The creation of new, imitative peasant centrals, outside the hierarchy of the CNC, but controlled at the national level by the government, is a development of the past decade which has contributed to the marked ideological confusion of peasant politics, as state-sponsored peasant organizations adopt the style and rhetoric of militant opposition groups. Indeed, throughout Mexico, in the 1970s, the level of political confusion among peasants rose dramatically as the regime of Luis Echeverría Alvarez (1970–1976) promoted the creation of a number of peasant unions and peasant centrals which were headed by men passionately loyal to the Echeverría administration, but which carried names of *existing* militant peasant organizations. Thus a peasant from Sonora state who had struggled side by side with the heroic Jacinto López in the land invasions led in 1956–1957 by the independent peasant organization, the General Union of Workers and Peasants of Mexico (UGOCM), might make his way to Mexico City to seek some help from the *compañeros* in the national headquarters of that organization. However, once in the capital he would discover that there were now two UGOCMs: one, the "UGOCM-Jacinto López," was in fact a new organization, sponsored by Echeverría, linked to the PRI and incorporating some malcontent veterans of the earlier organization; the second was the plain old "UGOCM," the original militant independent peasant union, which managed to signal that it was the "real UGOCM" only by the presence in its leadership group of Jacinto López's widow, Evangelina O. de López.[68] Apart from the creation of new peasant unions, the 1970s marked a second area of rapid expansion of the role of the state in key ejidal districts like the Laguna.[69] The bureaucratic presence of government in the Laguna extended to the point that by the end of the decade there were 15,000 bureaucrats to manage the affairs of 45,000 *ejidatarios*.[70] Thus the government employed a three-pronged strategy. First it undercut the tradition of independent peasant mobilization wherever that proved possible by buying off militant peasant organizations with material concessions and adopting a modified or distorted version of these organizations' ideology. Second, it created new peasant unions, independent of the CNC, but tied to the official party all the same. Finally, it attempted to displace altogether the peasant union as a fixture on the political scene by renovating existing institutions and creating new, supposedly streamlined bureaucratic structures, the efficiency and fairness of which were meant to make peasant leaders "unnecessary." The logic of this drive was explained to the author in 1977 by one of the newly appointed, young and idealistic bureaucrats.

> The so-called peasant leaders are an unnecessary evil and even the honest ones cost the peasant a lot of money in the end. *Ejidatarios* shouldn't need anyone to intervene for them in the process of dealing with their own government. The day when every peasant knows he can get what he needs from the government agencies, will spell the end of these self-styled "peasant leaders."

This functionary, along with most others interviewed in 1976 and 1977, seemed to have no concept that a "peasant leader" could be—or might ever have been—a political leader of a social class in struggle. They tended instead to see this figure exclusively in terms of his role as power broker.

SOME GUIDELINES FOR POLITICAL SURVIVAL

The gradual moderation or co-optation of the Central Union is best understood in light of what we know about the hegemonic nature of the Mexican political system. As we noted earlier, independent organizations, however pure or true to their goals they may wish to remain, exist within a one-party system. If such organizations refuse to compromise or make some kind of accommodation with the government, they may find it impossible to survive, and they certainly will find it impossible to win for their members the concessions which give the organization reason to exist in the first place. To win concessions for their political supporters, many, if not most, opposition organizations eventually accept certain limitations or restrictions on their political activities and tacitly agree to play politics within certain guidelines.

To grasp the rules of the game, it is essential to understand the central role of the president of the republic as a symbol of the legitimacy of the Mexican political system. As head of the revolutionary family, the government, and the official party, he enjoys a kind of immunity from criticism that borders on sacrosanctity. Regardless of the nature of his pre-presidential career, despite the fact that everyone knows his "popular election" has been engineered by his party, once in the presidential palace he becomes the principal representative and symbol of the Mexican nation. Thus, a direct public attack on the president constitutes an attack on the legitimacy of the political system and even on the nation as a whole. Such an attack on the president is widely acknowledged to be politically dangerous if not suicidal. The most notable instance when the ban on criticism of the president was ignored occurred during the student strike in 1968. At that time President Gustavo Díaz Ordaz was attacked directly by the student movement in slogans chanted in the streets ("Díaz Ordaz, Incapaz!"), in epithets painted on streetcars, buses, and public buildings ("Díaz Ordaz, Asesino!"), and in posters that superimposed the profile of the president over that of a gorilla. But movement participants paid heavily for their break with tradition when, on the night of October 2, 1968, hundreds of demonstrators, disbanding after a peaceful rally, were gunned down by federal troops in the now infamous Plaza of the Three Cultures in Mexico City. If it was unprecedented in modern Mexican history that the army be ordered to turn its guns on great masses of urban population, it was also unprecedented that any identifiable group of people walk through the streets bearing placards that insult the president of the republic. The ruling party has manipulated political symbols so that an insult to the president becomes an insult to the Mexican nation.

Even when a group's interests are severely injured by presidential policies, group spokesmen normally continue to maintain that the president is a man of goodwill and generous spirit—a "great Mexican" and a true friend of the group in question, be it the *ejidatarios* of the Laguna, the electricians of Puebla, or the small merchants of Ciudad Juárez. The president himself is publicly portrayed as sincerely committed to promoting the interests of people like *ejidatarios* or electricians or small merchants. The fault, it is said, lies with others. Foreign capitalists are fair game. So are vaguely defined "reactionaries who attempt to undo the achievements of the Mexican Revolution."[71] Very frequently the blame falls on "insidious" individuals who surround the president and who, in their capacities as ministers, secretaries, and agency heads, misinform, misdirect, and misadvise the president. Policy injurious to the interests of a group can then be attributed to the nefarious machinations of unnamed advisors who have taken it upon themselves to reinterpret or ignore directives given by the president in good faith. But damaging policy must not be attributed directly to the president.

There are other rules. It is safe enough to talk vaguely about the "nefarious machinations of people who have somehow gained the ear of the president," but it is a very bad idea to directly name or attack an individual who is very close to the president—unless, of course, that individual's power is on the wane. Along this line, it may be necessary for opposition organizations to do some careful investigation to determine who in fact is close to the president at any given moment. They must determine who enjoys the president's confidence and who has fallen into disfavor. Because the real lines of power in the PRI or the government may bear very little correspondence to the formal hierarchy of power in those institutions, it requires alert observation simply to know who is "in" and who is "out" in official circles. These relationships often shift frequently and dramatically. And the benefits of reading them correctly—or the costs of misreading them—may also be quite dramatic.

Another requirement for opposition groups who mean to play by the rules is that they claim that everything they demand and all their political activities are "well within the traditions of the Mexican Revolution." A favorite smear tactic used against leftist organizations is the assertion that the PRI is "the party of the Mexican Revolution," while the activities of left-wing opposition groups represent an effort to foist the Russian or Chinese revolutions on the Mexican people who already have their own proud tradition of revolution. Hence, groups must struggle to steer clear of any close association with the Russian, Chinese, or Cuban revolution, or, by extension, association with any foreign models. The safest thing for opposition groups is to identify themselves with some of the major heroes of the Mexican Revolution. For example, peasant organizations generally claim to be inspired by the militant tradition of Emiliano Zapata,[72] while opposition labor groups look to revolutionary heroes like the anarcho-syndicalist brothers, Enrique and Ricardo Flores Magón, who gave radical intellectual inspiration to the Mexican Revolution.

It is clear that rules such as these were observed by Central Union leaders. We might well ask if the union's leadership had to compromise as much or as often as they did. We might also question whether the benefits won for the union's constituency were worth the loss of political independence. But questions like these are almost impossible to answer. For one thing, it is difficult for outsiders to measure the importance to peasant members of the economic benefits won for them by their organization. Second, it is very difficult for any organization to find that middle ground between a principled, independent stance and co-optation. Most organizations are unable to establish themselves on that middle ground, and the best they can do is to play the political game skillfully and hope they can build a strong enough power base to give them some space in which to maneuver.

The political history of the Central Union illustrates the point that co-optation is not a black-and-white process. We cannot readily identify specific moments in time when an organization is "militant" or "principled" and then mark another moment when it "sells out." Rather, we are looking at a subtle, complex process in which, according to the political climate and the amount of opposition activity a given regime will tolerate, organizations move back and forth between positions of close collaboration with the government and positions of greater independence. Furthermore, not only are some regimes more tolerant of political dissent than others, but there are periods during each six-year administration when the government is more willing to deal with opposition. Generally, the first year or two of each new administration is a time of greater openness, during which the new chief executive seeks reconciliation with the groups most severely damaged by the policies of his predecessor. A brief period of "self-criticism" and "reassessment of achievements" at the beginning of a new regime signals a moment in which moderate opposition is safe. At times a new president finds it convenient to shake up or throw out a hierarchy of bureaucrats and politicians he finds already entrenched at the time he takes office. To hasten this process he may, for example, make substantial concessions to an independent organization like the Central Union in order to find in the political resurgence of that organization an excuse to "renovate" the CNC.

Naturally not all opposition organizations succumb to the pressure to collaborate with the government. And among those organizations that we might identify as having been co-opted, not all have been compromised to the same degree. The line between partial and total co-optation is hazy, but, roughly speaking, we could say that those individuals or organizations that give up an independent political identity to affiliate directly with the official party or consistently support official party candidates in electoral contests, have been completely co-opted. Those people and organizations who remain outside the PRI but cooperate off and on with the government, occasionally supporting PRI candidates at election time and playing the political game for concessions according to the established rules, could be called partially co-opted.

CO-OPTATION VS. REPRESSION

When oppositionists refuse to modify their demands or to accommodate themselves or their organization to the system, they are repressed. Repression, like co-optation, differs in degree. Like co-optation, it may be more or less complete.

One form of repression is constant harassment. Meetings and demonstrations are broken up, printing presses are destroyed by hired thugs, armed provocateurs are sent in to menace students in their classrooms, and so forth. Individuals may be followed by police agents, and they or their families may be implicitly or explicitly threatened with violence. One particularly chilling example of harrassment is the case of a student leader from Nuevo León who was seized by secret police agents, blindfolded, and tied to an unused railroad track immediately adjacent to a track carrying heavy rail traffic. The crucial point about all these forms of harassment is that they are likely to make it difficult, if not impossible, for an organization or an individual to act politically. In such cases so much energy must be devoted to self-defense—and, in the case of organizations, to internal security—that the harassed person or organization may become politically paralyzed.

An even more serious stage of repression is reached when movement leaders are summarily arrested and clapped into prison, frequently at the most crucial moment in the development of their political struggle. The leaders may be held for a year or longer, with or without a trial. But even if their imprisonment is relatively short-term, they may find upon their release that their movement has lost a momentum that is nearly impossible to recover. Some organizations have been repeatedly subjected to the short-term imprisonment of their leadership, a tactic of repression both intimidating and politically debilitating.

Further along the scale of repression is the long-term imprisonment of a movement's key leaders. During long-term imprisonment the health and at times even the spirit of leaders may be broken while, without its leadership, the movement may lose momentum and, in the long run, disintegrate completely. After their lengthy term behind bars, the leaders may be released only to find that they have neither the physical strength nor the remaining political support to resume their activities or rebuild their movement.

Lastly, the most serious and final form of repression is the assassination of principal leaders and slaying of supporters. The cases in which the activists of an opposition organization are wiped out together with the leadership occur, generally speaking, in the countryside. Sometimes the army or the police forces play a direct role in the slaughter, while at other times, "private armies" of thugs hired by landowners whose interests are threatened will carry out the massacre of peasant families involved in the struggle. It is difficult to know how often either the state or landlords have recourse to this extreme measure, but if we consider only the well-known, well-documented incidents of assassination, we must conclude that it is not infrequently employed. The names of some of the leaders who were killed because they would not compromise are well known. Peasant leaders like Rubén Jaramillo, Jénaro Vázquez, and Lucio Cabañas or radical labor organizers like Efraín Calderón Lara are some that come immediately to mind.[73] But in most cases we will never know the names or numbers of people who refused to moderate their political behavior, because these people were eliminated before they reached national or international prominence. Rural people are most often killed in their local areas and word seldom gets beyond the region, while urban oppositionists "disappear" in a variety of mysterious ways, one being the practice of dropping people out of airplanes into the Gulf of Mexico. For this reason we cannot make an accurate count of these people.[74] However, extensive interviews in the countryside and cities together with a careful between-the-lines reading of the "agrarian affairs" page of almost any daily newspaper suggest that they are numerous. The Mexico City dailies, as well as local newspapers, carry frequent accounts of violent conflict in the countryside. However, what is reported as a "shoot out between rival peasant factions," "simple homicide," or a "gun battle between police and a bandit gang" often turns out, upon careful investigation, to be an instance of armed repression of an opposition movement or leader by hired assassins. In the late 1970s, a Mexican anthropologist, Alcántara Ferrer, attempted to quantify reports of rural violence in the press:

> Between January 1977 and April 1978 there were reports of 302 "assassinations" of peasants by soldiers, police, and *pistoleros* . . . whereas in 1976, an average of seven peasants were reported killed a month, there were 20 reported killings a month in 1977.[75]

Indeed, it would be no exaggeration to say that probably every day in some part of Mexico, a dissident peasant, a radical labor leader, or a militant student is killed either by the army, the police, or by political opponents on the local scene. A study carried out by an investigative team sponsored by the International League of Human Rights and the International Federation for the Rights of Man concluded:

> The great majority of Mexicans are not affected by human rights violations. . . . But repression against specific targets, members of political opposition groups, appears to be as severe as in countries where the United States has formally condemned governments for their human rights violations.[76]

Thus, while we have some idea how many organizations make an accommodation with the government, we can only guess at the number of people and groups that refuse to be co-opted. Accordingly, we can only speculate whether as many people resist co-optation (and are eliminated from the political scene as a result) as choose the path of collaboration with their government.

It is difficult to give specific examples of opposition groups that fall into these different categories, because a group that is harassed today may be more severely repressed tomorrow, while another organization that presently has a shaky hold on its political independence may be partially co-opted in the near future. However, we could say that the Mexican Communist Party is an organization which was subject to constant harassment before it was legalized in the late 1970s, and to sporadic harassment in rural zones since that time. The Communist-affiliated Independent Peasant Central (Central Campesino Independiente, or CCI) whose leaders have been in and out of prison numerous times in the last twenty years, provides an example of an organization repressed by frequent short-term imprisonment of leaders. The railroad workers' movement, broken in 1958 by severe physical repression and the jailing of its two principal leaders, Demetrio Vallejo (twelve years in prison) and Valentín Campa (eleven years), exemplifies a militant movement suppressed by long-term imprisonment.[77]

Finally, the list of opposition movements destroyed by the assassination of leaders would have to include not only the movements of militants like Jaramillo and Vázquez, but also a group of moderates who represented the left wing of the PRI. Led by an ambitious lawyer, Carlos A. Madrazo, who had served as head of the official party from 1964 to 1965, this group was pushing for structural reforms within the PRI and greater popular participation in the nomination process. In the spring of 1969, Madrazo, together with a group of his most influential supporters, was killed in a suspicious plane crash near the city of Monterrey.

Table 6 shows the range of possibilities between total co-optation and political annihilation.

TABLE 6
Forms of Control in the Mexican Political System

	(CO-OPTATION)			(REPRESSION)		
Total Sell Out	Partial Sell Out	Middle Ground	Constant Harassment	Short-Term Imprisonment (1–2 yrs.)	Long-Term Imprisonment (more than 2 yrs.)	Elimination
(a) Dissident individuals accept positions in the PRI or in certain government jobs. (b) Opposition organizations affiliate with the PRI.	(a) Dissident individuals preserve some of their personal political integrity. Take jobs in the government, but in special areas of government (typically in newly created committees, agencies, etc.; in special task forces, in new clean-up campaigns and in semi-autonomous agencies, research institutes, etc.)	Varies in size according to the political climate; the amount of opposition activity a regime will tolerate.	Political Paralysis (a) Individuals spend so much time dealing with the threat to themselves and their families that their political energy is sapped and they are rendered ineffective.	(a) Leaders snatched from their organization at a crucial moment in the development of a political action. (b) Organization unable to carry through on a crucial political initiative because leadership has been imprisoned.	(a) Leaders will and health broken, political following may be dispersed. (b) Organization may disintegrate due to long absence of leadership.	(a) Leaders are assassinated. (b) Organizations completely wiped out either by "decapitation" (i.e., they are left without leadership when all their leaders have been assassinated) or the membership itself is wiped out by police, army action, or landowners' private forces.

(b) Organizations maintain their name, do not affiliate with the PRI, make shows of independence but "play the game" strictly by the rules, expressing loyalty to the government, never attacking the president directly, moderating their opposition in return for concrete concessions for their membership.

THE GUERRILLA "ALTERNATIVE"

Guerrilla movements in Mexico have been subject to the same forms of control used by the government to suppress other types of opposition movements. As in other Latin American countries, the success of Fidel Castro's guerrilla forces in Cuba inspired many dissident Mexicans to try the route of armed struggle. And, as in other parts of Latin America, the Mexican government developed increasingly sophisticated techniques designed to combat the threat of guerrilla insurgence. Throughout the 1960s, small guerrilla bands appeared in the Mexican countryside but were usually repressed before they could gain a foothold. In the mountainous state of Chihuahua, for example, a small guerrilla troop composed of young students, teachers, and doctors was wiped out in its very first action, an attack on a military garrison in Madera City.[78] Three years later, a student group calling itself the 23rd of September Movement launched a new guerrilla front in Chihuahua. This movement, too, was quickly eradicated.[79] In the South of Mexico, where extreme poverty and an untracked, mountainous jungle terrain create more favorable conditions for guerrilla struggle, a series of armed movements were launched. The National Revolutionary Civic Association, led by Jénaro Vázquez in Guerrero, the Mexican Insurgent Army in Campeche, Tabasco, Veracruz, and Chiapas, and the Partido de los Pobres, led by Lucio Cabañas in Guerrero, were some of the better-known movements active in the late 1960s and early 1970s. The most recent guerrilla activities, such as those actions carried out by the 23rd of September League, have centered in Oaxaca. The Oaxacan guerrilla forces were still active in the 1980s despite the death of their leader, Florencio Medrano, in 1979.

To eliminate guerrilla movements, the Mexican government has drawn upon its standard repertory of control techniques. Generally speaking, those people who have chosen the path of armed struggle are not susceptible to co-optation. Nonetheless, the co-optive approach is tried from time to time, even when dealing with committed guerrilla leaders. For example, shortly before Jenaro Vázquez was killed in 1972, high government officials offered to be "kidnapped" by the Vázquez force so that they might "engage the guerrilla leader in a dialogue." But Vázquez would have none of it. He ignored the government's overtures and was killed a short time later.

Since co-optation is generally ineffective in the case of guerrilla movements, the government normally applies repressive measures. To repress armed struggle, the government uses its standard tactic of imprisonment and assassination of leaders, but also can count on an arsenal of counterinsurgency techniques developed in the United States.

The United States used Vietnam as a testing ground to improve counterinsurgency methods designed for application in dense forest or jungle.[80] Special arms, radio equipment, and highly acute sensor devices have all been used with American assistance in the suppression of armed struggle all over Latin America. When the "guerrilla threat" developed in Mexico, the United States was anxious to share this technology with the Mexican government. Between 1950 and 1968, U.S. military assistance expenditures in Mexico amounted to $1.7 million[81] Under this American-funded program, 546 Mexicans were trained in counterinsurgency methods at Fort Benning, Georgia.[82] In addition to military training, the United States sent Mexico $745,000 in police assistance between 1961 and 1969 to cover "in-country training" by U.S. Public Safety Advisors and materials including radios, small arms, gas, and riot equipment.[83]

When compared with U.S. military assistance elsewhere in Latin America, American military aid to Mexico has constituted a very modest program.[84] However, what is significant about the training and equipment funneled into Mexico by the Pentagon is that a variety of other forms of American aid received by other Latin American countries (Food for Peace, the Peace Corps, the United States Agency for International Development, and others) have been firmly rejected by the Mexican government. This official rejection of other types of American aid grows in part from Mexican nationalist sentiment, and in part from the fear that the introduction of aid programs would establish sources of funds, power, and prestige outside of the PRI-controlled system. Thus it is noteworthy that when it comes to the suppression of guerrilla insurgency, the Mexican government has been willing to set aside its usual policy and has accepted both American arms and American advisors.

Well supplied with U.S. training, advisors, and equipment, the Mexicans concentrate the thrust of their counterinsurgency effort on isolating the guerrillas in a small area and preventing them from expanding their operations beyond this restricted zone. The army takes severe repressive measures against the peasants who live in the area to discourage their support of the guerrilla forces. Peasants are tortured to reveal the location of guerrilla camps, and those who have cooperated with the insurgents are executed as an example to their neighbors. Terms such as "strategic hamlet" and "pacification program," made familiar by the war in Vietnam, have become part of the working vocabulary of the Mexican soldier.

Up to the present time, the Mexican government has been largely successful in wiping out those who have attempted to overturn the system by armed force. The government has been able to respond quickly and effectively because the methods involved—while techno-logically more sophisticated—operate on the same principle as those used to neutralize unarmed political opposition. The leaders are elimi-nated—either imprisoned or killed—and the movement is left without direction.

CONCLUSION

In this chapter we have examined the way that the government and the official party manage to monopolize political power by neutralizing potential opposition. The pattern of control is clear enough: some groups are co-opted by the government, while those that refuse to coop-erate are harassed, repressed, or "decapitated" through the imprison-ment or assassination of their leaders. And so the party that came to power in the 1920s, emerging from a decade of revolutionary struggle, continues to perpetuate itself in power. It is not that opposition move-ments do not develop to challenge the dominance of the ruling party. It is rather that such movements are demobilized by the PRI before they can grow powerful enough to make their impact felt, because the very monolithic qualities of the PRI prevent potential opposition from de-veloping the requisite strength to wrest power from the ruling party.

Among those who have studied the Mexican political system there is substantial agreement that what sets Mexico apart from other Latin American nations and from most other countries in a similar stage of development is the efficiency and effectiveness with which the state is able to impose social control over a population of peasants and workers who have every reason to be discontented and rebellious. Virtually all observers concede that some measure of repression is involved in the maintenance of "social peace," although many insist that force is a tool of control which is used infrequently and only as a last resort.[85]

Our task has been to understand the interplay between persuasive and repressive forms of control. When coercion is relegated to a minor role or seen as a technique of last resort, it is difficult, if not impossible, to account for the docility of the masses. This is especially so when we consider that even the most casual conversation with a group of Mexi-can peasants or workers (as well as every systematic survey ever carried out) reveals both their sense of relative deprivation and their disaffec-tion from a system that shares out so little to them.[86] And those analysts of Mexican politics who point to the apparent willingness, if not en-thusiasm, with which the popular classes participate in state-sponsored mobilizations often fail to appreciate that the implicit or explicit threat of force plays a key role in drawing the masses into the political "process" orchestrated by the official party. Peasants know that they are, as they put it, "looking for trouble" if they refuse to hop on board the truck which has come to the *ejido* to carry them to a rally to shout "*vivas*" for the PRI's candidate of the day. Workers realize that if they do not show up in the designated quadrant of the Zócalo, the Plaza of the Constitution, to be checked off by a union official before the president steps out on the balcony of the National Palace, they run risks of reprisals that may include direct physical as well as indirect economic measures.

Looking at the fate of militants within the trade unions, Spalding observes, "Force, probably used more often then is commonly acknowledged, is yet another weapon in the government's arsenal. . . . All nonconformists run the risk of personal injury at the hands of union thugs."[87] Examining this same process in the rural zones, Arturo Warman, a Mexican anthropologist has written:

> Repression has always been an active factor in the Mexican countryside. Its magnitude, degree of violence and illegality vary greatly, from the simple threat of individual persecution and imprisonment, to outright slaughter and destruction of settlements. The agents of repression also vary: *pistoleros* (hired guns), "white guards," local police, special police forces, or federal institutions. Repression is used to suppress what the system cannot absorb and the people it cannot co-opt. In contrast with forms of control applied to other groups in society, in the rural areas repression is not the exception. It is a constant, surrounded by a wall of silence and indifference, concealed under the ambiguous and degrading term, "common crime." Due to its general extent and frequency, repression constitutes a complement to negotiation, absorption, and concession.[88]

The crucial point, then, is not that repression is more important than persuasion in the maintenance of order, but that both have a role to play. There is every indication that those in power greatly prefer to co-opt a student or labor leader or to buy off a group of troublesome peasants with a grant of marginal land, than to mow down dissidents in a hail of bullets—especially if the dissidents present themselves in ·a plaza in Mexico City rather than on a lonely mountainside in Guerrero State. However, while recognizing the ruling class's preference for nonviolent forms of control, its manifest willingness to employ force when it deems it necessary increases the persuasive power of its co-optive techniques. Thus, rewards and sanctions in the Mexican system are best understood as interlinked. The power of the bourgeoisie which has dominated Mexican politics and society for roughly sixty years is built upon the skillful manipulation of both. Therefore, coercion should not be seen as a mere adjunct to a system of persuasive controls. Rather, persuasion and coercion should be understood as two integral elements in a highly efficient system of class domination. In this process the stick does not appear *only* when the carrot has been refused. It is the ever-present threat of the stick which helps to make the carrot look so juicy and tempting.

THE STUDENT MOVEMENT OF 1968
A Case Study

The student movement was only the drop
of water that made the glass overflow.

Miguel Eduardo del Valle Espinosa,
Lecumberi Prison, September 1970

We have focused thus far on co-optation and repression and the role of these interrelated mechanisms in the maintenance of political stability. In modern Mexican history these techniques have been employed by the ruling party in a consistent fashion. For the most part they have proved effective in curtailing opposition and suppressing dissent. However, to round out our discussion of political control, we must also look at an important instance when these devices proved inadequate. We must consider what occurs when those in power are threatened by a large militant movement that they can neither buy off nor decapitate.

The student movement of 1968 is the outstanding example of an occasion when the standard techniques of co-optation and repression were not equal to the task. The movement began late in uly of 1968 when students from two rival secondary schools clashed in a brief encounter in the center of Mexico City. The police intervened, arresting several students and injuring a good many others. Weeks of violence followed as riot police and plainclothes shock troops moved against the students wherever they gathered to discuss their grievances against the police and the government. From late July through August the police repeatedly attacked student gatherings and invaded secondary schools, on one occasion using a bazooka to blow down the seventeenth-century carved doors of a school. Secondary students from both the vocational (technical) and preparatory (liberal arts) schools as well as university students from the National University (UNAM) and the National Poly-

173

technical Institute (IPN) organized daily demonstrations to protest these acts of brutality, in particular the army and police occupation and academic facilities.[1]

Participants in these rallies were repeatedly ambushed and beaten by riot police, and the first student deaths were registered. The force used to repress the movement became heavier every day: paratroop riflemen, military police armed with bayonetted rifles, and high-caliber machine guns backed by tanks, helicopters, and armored cars were brought into play. By the end of July, hundreds of students had been killed, hospitalized, or arrested and imprisoned, while many others simply "disappeared," never to be heard from again.

A NEW KIND OF MOVEMENT

The experience of Mexican students with the techniques of mass mobilization was limited. Until 1968 the Mexican universities differed from campuses in other Latin American countries where the presence of "youth sectors" of major political parties often turned universities into centers of intense political conflict that reflected political cleavages on the national level. In Mexico, the predominant student organization was the official student federation of the PRI, a highly bureaucratized organization serving chiefly as a training ground for future PRI politicians. Apart from this federation, "there existed only a multiplicity of small political organizations, mostly concerned with internal squabbling."[2] Historically, the Mexican universities were peripheral to the Revolution of 1917 and to the other important events in the political development of the country. The two major student strikes that shook the university in 1929 and 1966 both concerned internal academic issues related to conditions of admission, study, and examinations.[3]

In the summer of 1968, the escalating brutality directed against the students provided them with a cause, with a sense of group identity, and with a clearly defined enemy: the riot police acting as the agents of the government and the official party. The violence unified students and brought them into the center of the political stage. As repressive measures grew, many who were initially apathetic or unmoved by the events left their classrooms and joined the movement with firm conviction that the time had come for all students to present a united front. The students began to prepare themselves to stand up to the repression. They commandeered buses and built barricades. They occupied school buildings and laid in supplies of food, medical equipment, rags, bottles, and gasoline. They began to set up communications networks to contact the parents and friends of students who were taken prisoner or to military hospitals.

Finally, as the feeling grew that 1968 would be a decisive moment of confrontation with the government, steps were taken to give some organized form to the protest. Normally hostile political organizations and tendencies of the Left began to cooperate within the framework of the new movement.[4] The wide diversity of groups was further unified when students from the UNAM and the IPN laid aside traditional differences to unite their movements, and vocational and preparatory students quickly followed suit.[5] In August a general student strike was called, and a National Strike Council was formed. Comprised of 250 representatives from 128 schools, the National Strike Council included both private and public universities and secondary schools. In each school *comités de lucha* (struggle committees) organized the local protest demonstrations and directed the activities of political brigades. The brigades, each composed of roughly ten students, carried out a variety of tasks. Publicity brigades handled the distribution of leaflets, the design and printing of posters, and the painting of walls, buses, and other likely spots for political slogans, communicating to the public through all these means and by simple street-corner speeches, the grievances, demands, and goals of the movement. Medical brigades made up of students from the faculties of medicine and dentistry were responsible for medical supplies and first aid to movement participants. Supply brigades provided food, water, and matériel. A variety of other brigades carried out a series of political chores, including the collection of funds for the movement on street corners, buses, and trams. These brigades would appear in the streets for quick, spontaneous meetings and demonstrations and then disappear just as fast, before the police could pinpoint their meeting place.

The structure of the movement reflected the students' concern for the principles of direct democracy as well as their rejection of the hierarchical and bureaucratized student organizations of the past. The struggle committees operated with virtual autonomy under the loose coordination of the National Strike Council.[6] The emphasis was on direct personal participation in collective political activities. There was a corresponding rejection of complex forms of organization, particularly those involving the delegation of power and the establishment of intermediary authorities.[7] The position of the movement was hammered out in daily seminars, meetings, permanent assemblies, teach-ins, and rallies. Here principles of free speech and participatory democracy were observed despite the awkwardness of such forms in a movement that brings together people of so many political tendencies.[8]

The most significant fact about the organization of the student movement was that the National Strike Council, which coordinated the activities of these various political units and at the same time formulated the strategy for the movement, was headed by a *rotating directorate* of representatives from the 128 participating schools. Strictly speaking, the movement had no identifiable "student leaders," but rather a rotating committee of representatives, whose composition changed weekly. In this respect the Mexican movement was similar to other contemporary student movements, because the participants made a concerted effort to move away from "personalities" and the identification of the struggle with specific leaders toward more democratic forms emphasizing shared responsibilities and power.[9]

Thus in 1968 the Mexican state faced a peculiar situation that defied the standard, well-tried techniques of repression. All government methods of control had been based on the assumption that a radical opposition movement must have leaders. By definition, leaders are only human beings, and human beings are susceptible. They can be put out of action: co-opted, imprisoned, or killed.

But the students also understood this fundamental weakness of radical movements; the frailty of human beings in their role as leaders. They knew that most serious movements in the past had disintegrated when the leadership was bought off or eliminated. So, fully conscious of this problem, they determined to build an organization in which the leadership would rotate so frequently among so many different people that the government could not eliminate a handful of organizers and, in so doing, decapitate the movement. They designed their National Strike Council so that a rotating directorate would take responsibility for organizational and political activities. In this way the government would be unable to identify a few "troublemakers" and earmark them for co-optation or destruction, and the students could build a reservoir of leaders to replace those who might be lost in the process of struggle.

Throughout the summer the government continued to arrest and torture individuals it identified as the principal agitators. In some cases police intelligence was accurate enough to pinpoint and seize people who had histories of radical political leadership and who were, in fact, playing leading roles in the movement. In many other cases, however, individuals with no history of political involvement were caught in the wide-flung net and paraded before news cameras as "apprehended student leaders." For a time the government made a weak effort to portray the "disturbances" as the work of foreign agitators, mostly veterans of the May revolution in France. To that end, several young foreign tourists were snatched by the police as they walked through the streets, Mexicans with foreign-sounding last names were featured prominently in press releases on the arrests, and the police went so far as to record

Mexican names like Emilio, Antonio, or Maria Antonieta as Emile, Antoine, and Marie Antoinette, with duly gallicized last names. Later the "foreign devil" tactic was dropped when the government realized that the question of responsibility for the "disturbances" could be used to destroy the credibility of a wide variety of domestic opposition figures. Under torture a number of "confessions" were extracted from imprisoned students and a bewildering assortment of opposition figures was named as the source of arms, aid, and directives to the student movement. In addition, the Mexican Community Party, the United States CIA, the Cubans, and—most significantly—political enemies of Díaz Ordaz within the official party itself were all accused at one point or another of employing politically naïve students to do their destructive work.[10]

But in spite of these smear tactics and the large number of students arrested, bribed, tortured, and killed, the movement persisted and grew. It persisted because its survival was not contingent upon the survival of a few identifiable leaders. And it grew because the movement demands had struck a responsive chord among other sectors of the population who shared the students' intense feelings of discontent with the status quo.[11]

THE MOVEMENT GROWS

When the National University was invaded by the army, moderate professors and university administrators were drawn into the movement.[12] Led by the rector of the National University and a group of prominent professors, some 80,000 students and teachers marched solemnly through downtown Mexico City in what was to be the first of several extremely well organized and effective mass demonstrations. By mid-August the National School of Agriculture, the teachers' colleges, and several other educational institutions had voted to join the strike. On August 13 the Teachers Coalition for Democratic Freedom massed 200,000-strong in front of the National Palace.

The strike spread to schools, colleges, and universities throughout the republic as teachers and students in the provinces undertook political activities in solidarity with the Mexico City movement. Each day brought fresh arrests, yet the movement grew as more and more people saw in the student protests the long-awaited opportunity to give voice to their own discontent.

The well-publicized "official" position of peasants and workers toward the movement was conveyed by a CTM statement. "The discontent of some disoriented students has been exploited by subversive agents of the left and right in order to sow discontent and create an atmosphere of chaos in the country.[13] But while the official sectors of the PRI pursued this line, the independent railroad workers and electricians unions and the Independent Peasant Central expressed their support. In addition, a number of CTM affiliated locals, acting in defiance of their own leadership, published statements of solidarity with the students.[14]

Although the students had great faith in the mass demonstration as a means of awakening consciousness, it was the brigades that carried out the work of building links with other sectors of the Mexican population. Political brigades sought direct contact with workers in the factory. Law and medical students established legal and medical clinics to serve the poor. *Radio Universidad* broadcast the message of the movement. By the end of August, the students were able to mobilize a crowd of half a million to march through the center of the capital to the Plaza of the Constitution. In addition to the students and large delegations of their parents and relatives, the demonstrators at this August 27 rally included contingents of railroad and factory workers, electricians, taxi drivers, and pushcart peddlers, as well as small groups of peasants from outlying regions of Mexico. Middle-class people, shop workers, small merchants, professionals, and clerks left their offices and stores to cheer the demonstrators as they marched by, or to fall in behind the students who called out to them, *unite pueblo!* (people unite!)[15]

The movement did not grow simply in numbers, it also began to gain a measure of ideological cohesion. Initially the stance assumed by the participants was a defensive one. The students and their allies were intent on denying the charge that they were organized by outside agitators and inspired by foreign ideologies. As a matter of policy, portraits of Mexican heroes—Emiliano Zapata, Pancho Villa, Benito Juárez—were carried in preference to those of Che, Mao, or Ho Chi Minh. The march organizers wished to make clear that these were not demonstrations inspired by "foreign revolutionary doctrine," but a call for the fulfillment of the promises of Mexico's own revolution. Clearly expressing the position of the movement was the slogan, "We are not the agitators. Hunger and misery are the agitators."

Gradually movement participants began to exchange this defensive posture for a more assertive stance. The forthcoming celebration of the Olympic Games, scheduled to open in Mexico City in October 1968, and the repressive measures applied by the Mexican government to assure that the games would be staged without disruption provided immediate focus for the movement. The movement's symbols and slogans centered on the Olympiad and highlighted the irony of claiming 1968 as the "Year of Peace" in Mexico. The placards they carried expressed the students' deeply felt disgust at the expenditure of millions of pesos on sports arenas, publicity, and apartments for foreign athletes by a government that could not find the resources to provide housing, medical services, and primary education for a vast sector of its population. The signs underscored the brutality of the regime that was playing host to the world's athletes: "Mexico will win the gold medal for repression"—"Welcome to Mexico, site of the Olympic Butchery, 1968." Others depicted the Olympic dove of peace with a knife in its breast, the five-ring Olympic symbol as five smoking grenades, and a riot policeman racing along with his club held aloft like a flaming Olympic torch.

THE STUDENT DEMANDS

The demands that were formulated by the National Strike Council reflected both the fluid nature of that body and its fear of provoking ideological confrontation among the various political groups involved in the movement.[16] The demands necessarily dealt with government abuses so flagrant that every movement participant could support the points of protest as justified grievances. Thus, the demands focused on the agents and mechanisms of repression employed by those who hold power in Mexico, and they called for relief for the victims of this repressive process. Perhaps the most sweeping was the demand for the release of all political prisoners, both those arrested during the summer of 1968, and those serving long terms for radical activities in the past. The popular Demitrio Vallejo and Valentín Campa, radical railroad union leaders, had been held in prison since the government smashed their movement ten years earlier in 1958. Although the official line held that no Mexicans were ever jailed because of their political beliefs, Vallejo and Campa, together with other radical leaders, were clearly the victims of political persecution. Accordingly, the movement called not only for the release of these political victims, but for the repeal of Articles 145 and 145^b of the Penal Code, the wide-ranging sedition acts under which they were held.[17]

Another demand called for the abolition of the special riot police (granaderos) and the resignation of their chief, General Frías. The students pointed out that the very existence of such a squad was illegal because the constitution provides only for the maintenance of police forces under the jurisdiction of the Judicial Department, while the granaderos were independent of such control. The role played by the granaderos since 1944 (strike-breaking, suppression of demonstrations, etc.) made the riot police a particularly conspicuous agent of repression and an object of widespread popular antipathy.[18]

Along the same lines, the students also demanded the resignation of the chief of police, General Luis Cueto, and his deputy, General Mendiola. By focusing on these two men and demanding their dismissal, the students hoped to force the government to acknowledge publicly its responsibility for the repressive acts of the various police agencies. At the same time the students called for a full public investigation to determine the responsibility for police and army vandalism and brutality. For example, late in July, in broad daylight, close to one hundred men in plain clothes, face masks, and unmarked cars machine-gunned the façade of Vocational School Number Five in the Plaza of the Three Cultures. Later that night they returned with doubled strength to enter the school and beat the students they found within the building. These terrorists were members of a government-sponsored, paramilitary shock troop receiving training, salaries, and orders from the Department of the Federal District, the governing body of Mexico City. The students insisted that the president explain the existence of government-trained shock troops operating with no publicly acknowledged authorization.[19]

Finally, the students demanded that the military occupation of all schools be lifted and that the government compensate the students wounded in conflicts with the police and army, as well as the families of those students who had been killed.

These demands were neither radical nor revolutionary. We should note that the students were still directing their grievances to the government, and that the very nature of their demands underlined the authority of that government. The student movement was essentially calling for the recognition of constitutional guarantees and the protection of civil liberties provided by the constitution. When interviewed in 1968, the National Strike Council representatives who had drawn up the list of demands explained that they had settled upon these particular grievances because they dealt with highly visible, well-known government abuses of power. It was felt at the time that the unity of the movement could be sustained and a widespread base of support could be built only if the students set as their goals a series of moderate, reformist objectives with which a majority of middle-class people, peasants, and workers could identify. They reasoned that the people they hoped to draw into their movement were not sufficiently politicized at that time to participate in a movement that questioned and challenged the fundamental institutions of the nation.[20]

THE UNDERLYING CAUSES

But underlying these fairly moderate demands were grievances far more serious. Although the spark that ignited the conflict of 1968 was a series of brutal police interventions, participation in the movement was an expression of political feelings far more complex and long-term. Behind the students' involvement lay a sense of outrage so profound that no slogan or demand could give it full expression. The students were angry at the distorted priorities that had been set for Mexico by its ruling elite. The expenditure of millions of pesos on the Olympic Games was only symptomatic of what the students regarded as a criminal mismanagement of the nation's resources by those in power. To the students, the Olympics and the years of excited preparation that preceded the staging of the spectacle were nothing more than an orgy of self-indulgence on the part of a national bourgeoisie that was determined to prove to the world (and to itself) that Mexico, where so many millions were living in conditions of extreme poverty, was in fact a progressive, democratic, and modern nation. In short, the students were disgusted by the farce played out by those in power. They were tired of the speeches about "progress" and "development" and wished to put an end to the demagogical rhetoric used to camouflage the greed and corruption of the ruling elite. The movement, therefore, was born of a desire to strip away the mask and destroy forever the myth of the "institutionalized revolution," the "democratically elected president," and his "revolutionary party."

The students were also angered by the inflexibility of the system and the lack of alternative avenues for upward mobility. They understood how the co-optation process worked, and were profoundly disheartened to realize that young Mexicans like themselves have little chance of holding a job or advancing economically or socially without seriously compromising their principles and accepting the rules of the PRI. It was difficult for these young people to accept that they would be obliged to demean themselves, compromise their integrity, and run around back-slapping and hand-pumping in the corridors of the official party if they hoped to get or keep a well-paying job.

Finally, the students were outraged by the repressive nature of the system. They could no longer bear to see the most principled and courageous of their countrymen cut down by government assassins. They chose to take a stand rather than quietly watch the betrayal and assassination of Zapata played out again and again in their own time.

The sentiments that propelled students out of their classrooms and into the streets had begun to move other sectors of the population. Over the course of four months, the 1968 student movement evolved into the most articulate and threatening outburst of public disaffection that a modern Mexican government had ever faced. Not only had the standard techniques of control, co-optation, and repression failed to break the movement, but the students' courage and commitment had begun to inspire other Mexicans. The government was particularly worried that worker and peasant support for the student movement, which up to this point, was only limited and inarticulate, might strengthen and spread to other parts of the republic. Furthermore, the government was pressured to act quickly because the Olympic Games were slated to begin on October 12. And so, the government conceived a "final solution" to the problem it faced: a crushing blow calculated to obliterate the student movement.

THE "FINAL SOLUTION": TLATELOLCO

Late on the afternoon of October 2, about 6,000 people gathered for a demonstration in the Plaza of the Three Cultures at the center of a modern Mexico City housing development in an area called Tlatelolco.[21] Throughout the summer, the plaza had been the scene of some of the most violent clashes between students and police. Here students had repeatedly asked and received the moral and material support of the working-class and middle-class residents of the surrounding neighborhood. From the wall-to-wall windows of their apartments, the people of Tlatelolco had rained down streams of eggs, tomatoes, shoes, clods of dirt, and even boiling water on the soldiers who seemed almost continually to be milling about in the streets below. They provided the students with food, bottles, rags, and gasoline, or with a hiding place, according to the strategic needs of the moment. Because the Italian film "Battle of Algiers" was showing in local theaters that summer, people had begun to speak of Tlatelolco as "the Mexican Kasbah," although two urban centers could hardly be less similar than the narrow, twisting alleys of the Algerian "native quarter" and the glass and steel buildings of Tlatelolco, each one set apart from its neighbor by a broad, flat esplanade. There was, however, this similarity: both neighborhoods were quickly identified by the government as a focal point of agitation, and both were made to pay for the resistance they had mounted.

The original plan called for a mass march from the plaza to the National Polytechnic Institute. But word had come that the parade route was blocked by armored cars and troop transports. So, rather than create a situation where a clash with the armed forces was inevitable, the National Strike Council decided that the demonstrators should stay put, hear a number of speakers, and then disperse quietly.

Around five o'clock in the evening, demonstrators began to converge on the plaza. For roughly one hour they stood in a light rain listening to a series of speeches. At six, the plaza was suddenly surrounded by a force of 10,000 soldiers armed with high-caliber weapons and expansion bullets. Before the demonstrators could react, the soldiers assumed prone firing positions and trained their rifles and machine guns into the crowd. Overhead an army helicopter circled. At exactly 6:10, the helicopter dropped two green flares into the crowd, giving the signal to attack. As the soldiers opened fire, secret police who had infiltrated the crowd moved toward the speakers' platform. The infiltrators were known to one another by the white handkerchiefs tied around their right hands. Students who had identified themselves as leaders by addressing the meeting were picked off in the first round, even as they counseled the crowd to leave quickly and quietly. Machine guns strafed the speakers' platform and a number of journalists, as well as National Strike Council members, were hit.[22] Those National Strike Council members who were taken alive were stripped naked and herded into an archeological excavation near the Aztec ruins, converted for the evening into a makeshift dungeon. Several were put against the wall and shot.[23]

The remaining casualties included disproportionate numbers of children and old people who had been unable to flee the plaza, and people shot in their own living rooms as they rushed to take cover when the armored cars turned from the plaza to train their cannons on the glass façades of the high-rise buildings. Probably as many as 50 people were killed outright in the plaza and another 500 wounded (many critically), while some 1,500 others were arrested.[24] Many of those wounded later perished because doctors in the emergency wards of the city hospitals were not allowed to attend these victims until they had been placed under guard and interrogated. Eight soldiers caught in the crossfire of their own troops also died that night.[25]

THE AFTERMATH

Where more subtle techniques of co-optation and selective repression had failed, the indiscriminate use of brute force worked. The level of violence used by the government at Tlatelolco terrorized the general public and staggered the student movement. The ruling elite had been unable to pinpoint the leaders of the movement. Therefore it struck at the movement as a whole, calculating that when a sufficiently large mass of people had been arrested or killed, somewhere amid that huge number, the effective leaders of the movement would have been taken. In this way, by randomly seizing masses of active students, the leadership of the movement was captured and silenced and the movement participants were terrorized. No one knew who would be seized next, and the very lack of rational pattern to the arrests increased the fear among the students. New leaders did not step forward to replace those who had been killed or imprisoned, because they were justifiably afraid that they would share the same fate as their martyred comrades. The National Strike Council was in disarray and seemed to have lost its capacity to take initiatives or give direction to the movement. Rival factions began to emerge within the Strike Council, some favoring an end to the student strike, while others pushed for the escalation of demands. Its inability to reformulate a clear position and strategy for the movement became evident when, on November 19, the National Strike Council announced that the strike would continue until all political prisoners had been freed, and then, only days later, gave the official call for students to return to classes, though none of the six demands had been fulfilled.

In the months that followed, the student movement lost momentum and largely disintegrated. Those activities that were pursued in the next two years were organized around the demand for the release of movement activists held in federal and state prisons across the country. Protests were also registered against the countless abuses to which the political prisoners were subjected.[26] And when October 2 rolled around each year, there were small demonstrations to mark the anniversary of the Tlatelolco massacre. But what remained of the 1968 movement was a *reactive* rather than an active movement, responding to moves by the government rather than initiating its own line of activity. There was little agreement among the students as to what the next step should be.[27] There was a good deal of talk about building a genuinely *national* student federation, but the unity and consensus that would have made such a federation viable were lacking, particularly because the very idea of a national student federation was quickly taken up and pushed by the new president, Luís Echeverría, and, as such, the idea lost its appeal for genuinely radical students.

Even after the prisoners began to be released in small groups in 1971, they found it difficult to reunify the movement and push ahead with new political initiatives. A number of serious obstacles prevented a resurgence of the spirit of 1968. On the one hand much ill feeling remained between the former prisoners and those who they felt had done a poor job of maintaining the struggle in their absence. On the other side, the ex-prisoners came in for a good deal of suspicion and criticism: some for the "admissions of guilt" they had made as a precondition to the release, and others for accepting the "friendly" overtures of Echeverría. These feelings of bitterness and distrust exacerbated the differences between the old National Strike Council members and the new leadership, mostly members of the Communist Party youth sector, who had gradually emerged in 1970–1971 at the head of the new coordinating Committees of the student movement. Perhaps the most serious problem was the difficulty the students had in formulating a new strategy for action. The problem, as one student explained, "was that people were only able to think in terms of mounting larger and larger street demonstrations. Everyone wanted to do something; something dramatic. But no one was sure how best to express our feelings of unrest. Thus, there was a tendency to fall back on the old formulas: rallies and mass marches—even though 1968 had demonstrated the weakness of those forms."

Finally, it was extremely difficult to rebuild the student movement because, from 1968 on, the schools and universities were heavily infiltrated by armed provocateurs. Some of these terrorists were trained, equipped, and paid by powerful men within the government and the official party. Other bands of infiltrators were in the pay of political groups of the extreme Right. Chapter 7 will look more closely at the actions and effect of these provocateurs. At this point it is sufficient to say that the presence in the schools of armed thugs disguised as students contributed to the political confusion and distrust that has made effective student action so difficult since 1968. In a sense the paramilitary terrorists, or *porras*,[28] are the current answer to the old problem of suppression of opposition movements.

CONCLUSION

The events of 1968 indicated to the government that the old techniques of co-optation, repression, and "decapitation" were no longer entirely satisfactory. The ruling elite could not rely on these methods alone to control and suppress the development of opposition movements. And what made the situation all the more explosive and dangerous to those in power was that none of the problems that gave birth to the 1968 movement had been resolved. Indeed the problems were all the more obvious. The discontent of young people with the distorted priorities of Mexican development, their disenchantment with the rhetoric of the PRI, their disgust with the rigidity of the system, and their outrage at the repressive measures taken against them in 1968—none of these feelings had diminished in any way. At the same time, the number of landless peasants had grown. Unemployment was up. The cost of living in the cities continued to rise faster than the wages of working people. And the urban slums continued to grow and fester while the small sector of privileged Mexicans followed their normal pattern of conspicuous consumption. The influence of foreign capital was in no way reduced. The resolution of these problems clearly called for radical measures. But when the new president took office in 1970 his talk of "open dialogue," "renovation of the PRI," and "new economic reforms" was received, to say the least, skeptically. All over Mexico people wondered if the new policies proposed by Echeverría would come to grips with the economic, social, and political crisis and if the initiatives of this new regime could resolve the most serious contradictions of Mexican development. It seemed clear that if this new administration could not find ways to deal with these problems, it was going to have to devise ever more imaginative and sophisticated ways to repress unrest.

7

THE
ECHEVERRÍA
REGIME
The Limits of
Reform

When Luís Eche-
verría Alvarez assumed the presidency in 1970 he appeared to be well
aware that the political situation in Mexico had reached a crisis point.
This awareness was reflected in the vigor with which he conducted his
political campaign. Although his victory was assured from the time he
was named official party candidate in 1969, Echeverría traveled 35,000
miles and visited more than nine hundred villages, towns, and cities
during a seven-month tour designed to build popular support for his
administration. During this exceptionally strenuous and carefully
choreographed campaign, Echeverría barnstormed the republic, kissing
babies, ceremoniously accepting an estimated 5,000 petitions from the
poor, parading arm in arm with women colorfully dressed in regional
costumes, and proclaiming that the work of the revolution was indeed
incomplete, and that the improved welfare of peasants and workers
would be his first priority in office.

Notwithstanding Echeverría's efforts to convince Mexicans that his
administration would open a new epoch in Mexican history—a period
in which the inequalities and imbalances of Mexican development
would be redressed—most Mexicans seemed to doubt that the
Echeverría regime would do other than to continue the policies pursued by his predecessors since 1940. Thus, at election time in 1970,
most observers of the Mexican scene anticipated six more years of
official party rule featuring the same emphasis on high rates of industrial growth, heavy investment in the private commercial sector, fat
concessions to foreign capital, and continued concentration of land,
wealth, and power in the hands of the national bourgeoisie and foreign
investors.

There was little in Echeverría's background to suggest otherwise, In
1945 at the age of twenty-three Luís Echeverría married the daughter of

Guadalupe Zuno Hernández, a powerful political boss from Jalisco state, and the young lawyer's career was launched. Echeverría rose fairly rapidly through the ranks of the PRI, serving in the Ministry of Education where in 1956 he helped to arrange the army occupation of the National Polytechnic Institute. Serving in the Ministry of the Interior, he played an active role in the suppression of the 1958 railroad workers' strike and gathered intelligence on Castroist left-wing movements.[1] In 1963, when Díaz Ordaz, then minister of the interior, moved up to the presidency, Echeverría was named head of the Interior Ministry, a key position for political control. In this role, Echeverría became responsible for engineering PRI victories at the local, state, and national levels, and he won a certain notoriety for himself for his tireless pursuit and persecution of communist organizations, the destruction of several left-wing publications, the imposition of an official script in TV and radio newscasts, and the reversal of electoral results in two contests lost by the PRI.[2] Finally, with the exception of Díaz Ordaz himself, Echeverría was the nonmilitary national official most closely associated in the public mind with the policy of student repression in 1968. Indeed Echeverría was widely *believed* to have taken—in the face of an indecisive Díaz Ordaz—the fatal decision to move on the unarmed crowd at the Plaza of the Three Cultures and to put a rapid end to the movement with a public bloodbath of unprecedented proportions.

In light of his background, political record, his close association with Díaz Ordaz, and his overall reputation as a "hard liner," Echeverría's promises of "new and unprecedented democratic overtures" were greeted with a good deal of suspicion. There was, of course, an anticipation that the first two years of the new president's term would bring a general reduction in the most repressive aspects of the political control unleashed by Díaz Ordaz, a slight easing off in the persecution of left-wing organizations, and some token attempt at rapprochement with dissident students. For this kind of moderation was part of the standard pattern of a president's six-year term. It is expected that each new president will attempt to mend fences and restore some measure of the political prestige of the PRI and the government if they have been badly damaged by his predecessor.[3] And certainly Echeverría was acknowledged to be intelligent and skillful enough to play this conciliatory role. Indeed many Mexicans who expected to see no meaningful change in the political climate under Echeverría nevertheless hoped that the fence-mending process alone would lead him to extend a mass amnesty to the political prisoners arrested in 1968, and they were greatly dismayed when this did not occur.

SOME CHANGES IN THE POLITICAL CLIMATE

Although Echeverría's conciliatory overtures were initially dismissed on many sides as electoral rhetoric, tokenism, or unabashed demagoguery, by 1971 Echeverría had succeeded in cultivating a new style in national government, and he had begun to give substance to some of his promises.

Carrying over his campaign techniques to his administration, Echeverría became the most visible and accessible president since Lázaro Cárdenas. Virtually every other weekend he made a surprise tour of some region of Mexico, visiting the most socially and economically isolated parts of the country in order to talk with peasants and local leaders and get a first-hand view of their problems.

In contrast to the rhythm of work in previous administrations, the new president labored long hours and expected his ministers and aides to do likewise. Government officials were in their offices at 9 A.M., took quick lunches at their desks, and continued working until late into the evening.

In place of the self-congratulatory rhetoric of his predecessor, Echeverría seemed most at ease when elaborating on the shortcomings of the revolution and attacking what he called "the tragic complacency" of previous regimes. He was sharply critical of past government policy for agricultural and industrial growth, and he was more than ready to acknowledge that the "Mexican miracle" had been produced at the expense of the peasantry, working class, and subproletariat. Throughout his first year in office, the new president continually called for critics of government policy to come forward and express themselves. According to his own spokesmen:

> [Echeverría was working] to dispel the persistent myth developed over many years of the so-called "Mexican Miracle," and not because he is unaware of the real achievements which have been made, but rather because he feels that the persistence of such a myth, in the final analysis, can only favor those sectors that have obtained the greatest benefits from this growth.
>
> Those who have followed attentively the policy which has developed during the change in attitude of the last 18 months, cannot deny that something important has happened in our system. . . . Complacency has given way to self criticism. . . . An atmosphere has grown in which no one is afraid to denounce errors or to point to unsatisfied demands. . . . The ritualistic exaltation of the achievements of the government is being replaced by a more rigorous analysis of the functoning of institutions.[4]

Beyond this new accessibility and frankness, Echeverría inspired some of his former detractors when he began to attack the laziness, incompetence, and corruption of government bureaucrats in terms far more pointed than had been used by a Mexican official in two decades. He named names; he stressed the fact that corruption could not exist at the bottom of the bureaucratic chain if it did not exist at the top; and he declared himself dedicated to altering the very concept of public office, which he asserted "is regarded by many so called public servants as booty."[5]

Echeverría's attack on corruption in government was unusually strong and direct, but by no means unprecedented. What was unprecedented—or at least had not been heard since Cárdenas's days—was the attack he launched against the private industrial sector, which he scored as greedy, selfish, unpatriotic, and ultimately "un-Mexican."[6] This charge of "un-Mexican" behavior was a scathing one because since 1940 the term had been reserved for opposition of the left and, very occasionally, for clear-cut neofascist groups. To characterize the most powerful members of the national bourgeoisie in this way was a dramatic and unexpected step for the new president.

Nor was this criticism of the men "who only pursue personal wealth and enrichment"[7] expressed simply in abstract terms. When, for example, Echeverría traveled to the northern state of Chihuahua to preside over the expropriation and distribution of several thousand acres of commercial forests to a group of petitioning peasants, he seized the occasion to publicly humiliate the former owners of these lands, taking them to task for having exploited the forest lands to bring maximum short-term profit at the expense of long-term conservation. In front of a large crowd of peasants and representatives of the press, he addressed the former owners by name, saying:

> We must educate the new generation [of entrepreneurs] so that they comply with their social responsibility. Mexico needs modern entrepreneurs who do not think only in terms of personal profit, but in terms of the general progress of the country and the duty they have to serve society. . . . You must abandon the old entrepreneurial mentality which seeks personal enrichment as an ultimate end. . . . Today we must demand that industrialists do not carry on raping the land as you have done in the past.[8]

The sense that a new political atmosphere now prevailed in Mexico was heightened by the gradual release of the political prisoners of the 1968 movement. While the mass amnesty many hoped for was never granted, men and women originally sentenced to serve 35 or 40 years were freed one at a time or in small groups until more than 100 had been released. Those who, fearing further persecution, had sought exile abroad were encouraged to return to Mexico when the minister of the interior, Moya Palencia, broadly hinted, "There is no Mexican who is forced to live outside his country. There are only those who choose to live abroad."[9]

It seems that Echeverría managed to convey to many intellectuals a feeling that greater critical expression would be tolerated. As the novelist and essayist, Carlos Fuentes, wrote in August of 1971, "Echeverría lifted the veil of fear thrown over the body of Mexico by Díaz Ordaz. Many Mexicans felt free to criticize, to express themselves, to organize without fear of repression.[10] The Magna Carta of the new intellectual freedom was Echeverría's oft repeated assertion that "there is no such thing as ideas which are exotic or alien to the Revolution." This statement struck directly at Díaz Ordaz, who throughout his presidency attempted to touch xenophobic chords by characterizing the ideas of those who disagreed with him as "deriving from foreign philosophies," "exotic," and "alien to the principles of the Mexican Revolution."

A perceptible loosening of government censorship of newspapers and magazines became part of this new period of greater intellectual openness. While far from enjoying complete freedom of the press, journalists felt themselves at greater liberty to write what they saw, to muckrake, and in particular to write serial exposés on neolatifundism and government corruption and mismanagement.[11]

THE ECHEVERRÍA REFORMS

In the first year of his administration Echeverría came forward with 160 legislative initiatives. As one progressive piece of legislation followed another, it became apparent that the new president was operating on the assumption that his regime was the PRI's last chance to reform itself from within.[12]

Social Spending

In a sense the least controversial reforms were those which tackled the country's obvious and grave social welfare problems. Raising government expenditure on health, housing, and education, the Echeverría administration expanded the social security system to cover another 10 million Mexicans, so that by the end of this sexenio more than one-third of the population was reached by these services.[13] As we noted in chapter 4, a National Workers Housing Fund, financed in part by a special levy on employers, was set up and 100,000 units were constructed.[14] The Ministry of Education budget quintupled and greater emphasis was placed on technical education; technical institutes increased in number from 281 to 1,301 during this six-year period.[15]

If the desirability of increased welfare services had few *outspoken* opponents, the method of financing these benefits drew heavy fire. For in order to increase the revenues available to the government for social expenditures, an extensive "fiscal reform" creating a new tax structure was proposed. The fiscal reform, in turn, was only one component of a comprehensive new economic program which was central to Echeverría's reformist project. This program was billed as a move away from the development priorities of the past thirty years. Income redistribution would be emphasized, even at the cost of slowing the rate of growth of the gross national product. There would be a shift from further industrialization of the urban centers in favor of industrial decentralization and a new emphasis on agricultural development. The new government committed itself to increasing the purchasing power of the poor by creating job opportunities in industry for the large mass of unemployed and underemployed.[16] Greater concentration of wealth in the hands of the national bourgeoisie would be halted by raising both personal income taxes and corporate tax, although special incentives for reinvestment would continue. A new capital gains tax and a 10 percent tax on luxury goods would be imposed to reduce speculation and the flow of capital out of the country. Those Mexicans earning more than $24,000 a year would be taxed at 42 percent rather than the 35 percent of the past. In addition, the government would raise the rate of taxation on fixed incomes from bonds and securities.[17] Furthermore, the fiscal reform imposed a consumption tax charged at restaurants, hotels, and nightclubs, it raised real estate taxes, especially on undeveloped property, and it established new taxes on imports and exports.[18]

Rural Development

The new initiatives to promote economic development of rural Mexico focused on raising productivity while reinforcing and improving the social and economic condition of both the *ejidatarios* and *minifundistas*. Indeed, it was these years that witnessed the proliferation of the programs which we examined in chapter 3, such as Plan Puebla, designed to increase production on rain-fed smallholdings. Emphasizing subsistence agriculture, a series of comprehensive programs was launched to improve marketing and credit facilities, provide discounts on agricultural inputs, guarantee price supports, insure subsistence crops against failure, construct small irrigation and other infrastructural projects—all while extending basic social services to the rural poor. Furthermore, this complex of projects was supported by a vastly expanded bureaucracy. This bureaucracy, in turn, was overseen by a new "intersectoral unit," the Program for Integrated Rural Development which eventually came to coordinate the activities of thirty-eight federal agencies.[19]

Under Echeverría, government initiatives were designed above all to break the hold of intermediaries over the peasantry. New storage and marketing facilities, sources of credit and the rest were meant to liberate the subsistence producer from the obligation to borrow on usurious terms, or depend on a variety of local middlemen and *caciques* who buy and transport the harvest, and siphon off any marginal profit the peasant might anticipate.[20] The attack on local exploiters was further reinforced with the formulation of a new Agrarian Code. The code strengthened the internal structure of the *ejido* by requiring secret ballots for the election of ejidal officers, a measure that struck at the power of local officials who customarily perpetuate themselves in office for personal gain. Significantly, the new code took ultimate responsibility for ejidal affairs out of the hands of the state governors and their political henchmen, and placed it in the presidency itself.[21] As Grindle observed,

> the Echeverría administration can be credited with a significant "rediscovery" of Mexico's peasantry. Prior to this, of course, a number of ongoing programs had been directed toward the rural poor. . . . Under Echeverría, however, the poor rural areas ceased to be considered residual in terms of national development, to be attended by various welfare programs or marginal land redistribution efforts. In the 1970s, the traditional agricultural sector was rediscovered as a priority area, and the rural poor as a group crucial to the future development of the economy because of the role they played in the production of basic crops.[22]

Industrial Policy

Early in his administration, Echeverría began to give notice to Mexican industrialists that the rules of the game had substantially altered. He asserted that the industrial bourgeoisie was going to have to change its notion that the best way to conduct business was by turning quick, high profits from over-priced, poor-quality goods produced for a limited market behind high protectionist walls. The age of "import substitution" and protectionist policy was over. Import duties originally imposed to protect domestic industries from foreign competition would be reduced in order to force Mexican manufacturers to improve the quality of their goods and increase the productivity of their factories. Subsidies and tax waivers formerly given as a matter of course to expanding Mexican industries would be phased out. Only those Mexican industries producing low-priced goods for a popular market would receive help in expanding their productive capacity.[23]

Businessmen were told that they could no longer regard government loans as outright grants. They would have to meet payments on these debts or face takeover by Somex (the Mexican Society for Industrial Credit), a government finance agency. Even the management of the state-run petroleum and electrical industries were told to shape up. These enterprises would have to become self-sustaining, even if it meant raising rates to their industrial consumers. In light of what Echeverría scored as the inefficiency of the private marketing sector, the role of CONASUPO, the state-run market board would be expanded.[24] The budget for CONASUPO nearly quadrupled from 1971 to 1975, while the number of subsidiary companies managed by the agency grew from five to sixteen.[25]

An integral part of Echeverría's economic policy was a new attitude toward foreign investment and mexicanization. Echeverría's program called for a tightening of controls on foreign investors. Foreign-owned industry would have to generate export earnings equal to the profits they take out of the country. Loopholes in the mexicanization legislation would be closed, and Mexican prestanombres would be identified and exposed. Controls would be imposed on the import of foreign technology under the new Law to Regulate Transfer of Technology. To prevent further abuses, American firms long accustomed to charging their Mexican subsidiaries outrageously inflated sums for patent rights, trademarks, and know-how would be restrained by the obligation to register all contracts involving the sale of technology with the Ministry of Trade and Industry.[26] A 1973 Law to Regulate Foreign Investment formalized and reinforced all previous restrictions on foreign capital and went on to provide that all new companies must have majority Mexican ownership. The law also established a National Commission on Foreign Investment to approve or reject all new investment proposals according to seventeen stringent criteria.[27] Thus foreign investment was officially encouraged, but would be more closely subject to Mexican needs. Foreign investors would have to locate their factories in new underindustrialized regions. They would be encouraged to make their investments in fields where they would not come into competition with Mexican-owned enterprises. Investors, both foreign and domestic, would be pressured through fiscal reforms to put their money into industries that create jobs rather than those featuring higher rates of profit. Additional legislation would push industrialists to produce goods for export so that more foreign exchange would enter the country. To further improve Mexico's balance of trade, stricter controls would be imposed on imports and restrictions placed on foreign borrowing.[28]

Economic Nationalism

Echeverría's policy of "economic nationalism" was expressed in his commitment to reduce dependency on U.S. investment and trade with the U.S. market[29] by forging new trade relations with Canada, Japan, China,[30] the Soviet Union, and other markets in both Western and Eastern Europe. Not only would Mexico seek new markets for her raw materials in advanced industrialized countries, but the minister of trade and industry was dispatched to Latin America to expand Mexico's role as a supplier of manufactured goods to relatively less developed countries in Central and South America. The president himself circled the globe in search of new trade partners.[31] In all, Echeverría traveled to thirty-six countries, held talks with sixty-four heads of government, and concluded 160 international agreements.[32] During the administration of this "activist" president, sixty-two new countries—mostly Asian, African, and Middle Eastern—were added to the list of sixty-five with which Mexico already maintained formal diplomatic ties. New trade relations were sought in all quarters.[33]

Attempting to deemphasize the "special relationship" with the United States, Echeverría focused on creating a leading presence for Mexico in an assortment of Third World groupings: "multilateral frameworks representing developing and dependent states (UNCTAD, FAO, Third World Forums, and regional Latin American arenas)."[34] The president sought to strengthen ties not only with Cuba, but with the Caribbean basin as a whole; not only with Peru, but with the Andean Pact as a multinational body.[35] A central effort in Echeverría's projection of himself and his country onto the international stage, was Mexico's sponsorship of the Charter of the Economic Rights and Duties of States. This document, presented to UNCTAD, was based in large measure on principles embedded in the Mexican constitution and in domestic Mexican legislation controlling foreign investment and transfer of technology.[36] With the charter Echeverría proposed to codify the broad concepts underlying the then current efforts to build a "new international economic order."[37] In short, through Echeverría's personal international activity, the president's commitment to winning greater autonomy for Mexico in its relationship with the United States was recast in terms of Mexican leadership of the struggle of Third World nations for more just and balanced relations between industrialized and dependent countries.[38]

These varied programs, reforms, and initiatives, proclaimed by Echeverría as a basic reorientation of Mexican development policy, eventually found their way into domestic law or, even, international compacts. It was not difficult for the president to draft legislation to effect his economic program and have it ratified by a Senate and Chamber of Deputies controlled by his party. But the frustrations he suffered when he attempted to implement his reform program indicate some of the parameters of his power. As we noted in chapter 2, the Mexican state is probably best characterized as only "relatively autonomous" from the bourgeoisie. Thus, although the Mexican president may enjoy the awesome status of a national symbol, and while he may possess a certain immunity from direct personal attack, his power is not unlimited. He is, logically enough, subject to pressures from both the right and the left. As we have seen, pressure from the left can be controlled or reduced by the co-optation or the repression of left-wing dissidents. But pressure from the right is exerted by economic interests which are far more costly to buy off and are normally too powerful to successfully harass or threaten with violence. As subsequent events have shown, Echeverría's power and political maneuverability were severely limited by right-wing opposition to his reform program. During his regime, conservative members of the bourgeoisie, acting both inside and outside of the PRI, succeeded in blocking the implementation of the policy changes designed by Echeverría to modify the course of Mexican development.

THE RIGHT STRIKES BACK

Taken as a whole, Echeverría's reform package did not add up to anything like a fundamental transformation of the economic political or social system. Echeverría was not embarking on a new "Mexican road to socialism." Rather, he was trying to modernize and rationalize Mexican capitalism. He was concerned with spreading the fruits of development more widely and fostering a slightly more open, democratic political atmosphere. His goal was to create the climate of social and political stability that would permit further development along capitalist lines. If there is any parallel to be drawn between Luis Echeverría and Lázaro Cárdenas—and the two men were frequently compared at the beginning of Echeverría's regime—it is that Cárdenas's reforms promoted the social peace that formed the underpinning of the rapid economic development of the 1940s and 1950s, while Echeverría was working to reestablish that social peace, battered and torn as it was by the sharpening economic inequalities and social and political conflicts of the 1960s.

Echeverría's efforts to safeguard the long-term future of Mexican capitalism and his efforts to save the national bourgeoisie from its own shortsighted greed were not perceived as such by the most influential and conservative elements of that class. On the contrary, the most powerful Mexican financiers, industrialists, and landowners—particularly the traditionally conservative group centered in the city of Monterrey—profoundly distrusted Echeverría and responded with fear to his pronouncements. They believed that if this new president were to have his way, the interests of their class would no longer dictate the social, economic, and political policies of Mexico as they had in the past. They were troubled by his political reforms. They were distressed by his attempts to give educators and students more influence over the educational system, curbing their own power over the state universities. They did not like his tampering with an agrarian status quo from which they profited, nor checking the power of local rural bosses dependent on them. Echeverría's efforts to build a broad popular base of support for his regime alarmed them. His surprise visits to the countryside, his talk of "democratic overtures," and his bureaucratic cleanup campaign made them intensely uneasy. Above all, Echeverría's economic nationalism and his determination to gain greater state control over industrial development was frightening to Mexican enterpreneurs whose economic fortunes were closely interwoven with foreign capital. The new president's reforms and his populist appeals were perceived by conservative members of the national bourgeoisie as threatening their privilege and their control over national policy. And so this small but powerful group determined to harass and weaken Echeverría to render him incapable of carrying forward his program for moderate reform.

Economic Maneuvers

Conservative Mexican capitalists—the group Echeverría disdainfully referred to as "emissaries of the past"—struck back at the reformist regime in essentially two ways. They exchanged their pesos for dollars and shipped the lot to banks in the United States and unnumbered accounts in Switzerland. The exact figures on capital flight during the full six-year period will never be known. But, in 1976, when rumors of devaluation reached a high pitch, the Bank of Mexico reported net dollar sales of $885.3 million in March and April, and $600 million in August alone.[39] One Mexican economist estimates that altogether in 1976 somewhere between 4 and 6 billion dollars was shipped abroad.[40]

The other weapon capitalists used to parry the reformist thrust of the Echeverría regime was withdrawal of investment funds. During the first two years of the new administration, investment by domestic capitalists dropped sharply and the economy went into a serious recession.

The annual rate of growth of the gross national product declined from 7.1 to 4.5 percent. Per capita income fell in 1971 for the first time since World War II. Growth in agricultural production dropped to 3 percent per annum, growth in industry to 2.8 percent, and the service sector dropped to 3.3 percent. Confidence in the Mexican economy was severely shaken at home and abroad.

This reluctance of conservative capital to reinvest in the national economy set off a cycle of serious economic repercussions. As industry did not expand at its normal rate, the crisis of unemployment heightened. In addition, a spiraling inflation—the worst in twenty years—began to grip the economy. Exacerbated by food shortages brought on by droughts and floods, plus the impact of a worldwide inflationary trend, the rate of inflation in Mexico climbed. By 1974 the official statistic had reached 25 percent and the real figure was probably much higher. Prices of popular staples like beans and tortillas rose by as much as 50 percent. Such price increases completely outstripped wage hikes won by the working class. Businessmen resisted government pressure to hold the price of their products steady. Therefore, notwithstanding substantial increases of 18 to 20 percent in the minimum wage under the new administration, the domestic market for manufactured goods did not expand as Echeverría had projected, because the purchasing power of peasants and workers was even weaker than it had been during Díaz Ordaz's regime.

Despite the economic reforms designed to redistribute wealth in Mexico, the trend toward higher profits for entrepreneurs and concentration of wealth in the hands of a few continued unchecked under Echeverría.[41] The president's efforts to reverse this trend by levying heavier taxes on the rich failed for the same reason so many of his other economic reforms could not be implemented. Lacking an honest and efficient bureaucracy to collect personal income, luxury, and corporate profit taxes, the government had to continue to rely for its revenue on indirect taxation, which hits the poor harder than any other class and does nothing at all to redistribute wealth.

The same lack of an efficient, honest administrative apparatus hampered Echeverría's efforts to enforce his proposed controls on private industry and to close the loopholes in the mexicanization legislation. *Prestanombres*, for the most part, were not sought out and exposed. Foreign investors were not effectively subjected to closer supervision and restrictions. Economic relations with the United States continued as they had before, only Mexico's economic dependence on the United States was heightened as her trade deficit with respect to the United States grew worse.[42] Mexico's unfavorable balance of trade with the United States was exacerbated by the 10 percent surcharge attached to imports in that year by President Richard Nixon. This unilaterally imposed surcharge is estimated to have cost Mexico as much as $200 million in foreign exchange in 1971 alone.[43] Notwithstanding Echeverría's pledge to reduce American control over key Mexican industries, in 1972 Chrysler Corporation bought out Automex after this corporation reported losses of $12 million. Meanwhile, Longoría, the Mexican cotton trading house, was revealed to owe $80 million to foreign banks and was forced to borrow another $12 million just to pay off its back taxes. In addition, the drive to find new foreign markets for the products of Mexican light industry proved largely unsuccessful as these goods could not compete in quality and price with goods produced in Europe, North America, and Japan.

Under attack from a threatened landholding class, Echeverría's plans for agricultural renovation fared little better than his program to increase employment, control prices, collect taxes, or control foreign investment. While he pursued illegal landholders with more vigor and probably with more sincerity than had his predecessor, the neolatifundists were mostly successful in blocking his attempts to seize and redistribute their land. According to the Department of Agrarian Affairs, by 1974 the courts had granted 1,700 injunctions restraining the government from expropriating 5 million hectares of illegally held land. Where the Echeverría administration succeeded in expropriating and distributing illegal land holdings, as in the much publicized case of the Obregón family holdings in Sonora, the land seized was mostly of poor quality and the distribution benefited relatively few landless peasants. Nevertheless, the land distributions, skimpy as they may have been, had the effect of stimulating a rash of land invasions and occupations of uncultivated holdings in those rural areas where land-hungry peasants were well organized.[44] When he responded to these pressures for land with another expropriation of 10,000 acres in the Yaqui Valley of Sonora, Echeverría was confronted with the organized opposition of the northern agricultural bourgeoisie. These large-scale commercial farmers withdrew from the PRI-sponsored Federation of Landowners. Then, in December 1975, they retaliated even more directly with a production halt which forced the regime to import huge quantities of wheat and corn to make up the shortfall in grain.[45] Again, in the final days of his administration, Echeverría attempted to make good his agrarian pledges with a mass expropriation of 193,000 acres of irrigated and 120,000 acres of pasture lands. But his final *agrarista* gesture was frustrated by the commercial landowners who won injunctions to halt the expropriations, and the Monterrey industrialists who called a "sympathy strike," that is, a production halt in solidarity with the northwestern *latifundistas*.[46]

Although Echeverría had focused his agrarian program on providing more economic aid to *ejidatarios* and small holders in order to enable them to raise their productivity, the results, as we noted in chapter 3, were not encouraging. Despite substantial hikes in government funding to agriculture in general and to *ejidatarios* and small holders in particular, the rate of agricultural growth declined. Furthermore the small increases in income realized by peasant families were wiped out by inflation, and the structure of power remained unchanged in the countryside.

Another factor contributing to the economic instability and to the overall vulnerability of the Echeverría regime was that the aggressive policy of reform required a wide variety of new government initiatives which led inevitably to a rapid expansion in the role of the state.[47] As private investment declined, the state increased its participation in every sector of the economy. A "vast galaxy of state corporations (ranging from steel mills and oil refineries to hotels and shops), research institutions, development funds . . . and welfare agencies" provided the framework for a whole new range of government activities.[48] State enterprises increased in number during the Echeverría years from 84 in 1970 to 845 in 1976. The "fiscal crisis" which carried Mexico to the brink of economic ruin in 1976 was brought about in part by the imbalance between this expansion of state activity and the capacity of the government to find the financial resources to cover costs. Increasingly, "the Mexican state was driven abroad to cover the public sector borrowing requirement."[49]

> In order to meet the targets of what the Echeverría administration considered distributive justice and at the same time expand the productive capacity of the economy, the public sector's expenditures had to increase. Unfortunately, neither the revenue base nor the administrative capacity of the public sector inherited by the new administration was adequate to these tasks.[50]

Thus the fiscal reform failed not only in terms of its goal—as noted above—of equalizing incomes between the rich and poor, but also in terms of raising revenue to cover new areas of public spending.

> To be consistent with its goals of equity and social justice, the government should have restructured the tax system to curtail the consumption of upper-income groups. But this was not done. The major deficiency of the government's economic strategy was its neglect of an obvious necessity; i.e. in order to implement its rather revolutionary institutional and investment decisions, which entailed a steep increase in public expenditures, it required an equally major effort to raise . . . the necessary domestic revenues.[51]

Furthermore, as we have seen in the case of tax collection and supervision of foreign capital, the bureaucratic apparatus inherited by Echeverría in 1970 was unequal to the job assigned to it. "From an administrative standpoint, machinery was not established to monitor expenditures in order to keep them in line with allocations," and thus budget overruns were common in nearly all areas of government.[52] On many occasions government agencies proceeded to fund new programs for which the requisite monies had neither been authorized nor released.[53]

Obviously, not all of Echeverría's economic strategy was blocked by the opposition of conservative capitalists or the overextension of an unreliable administrative structure. Factors external to Mexico also contributed to the frustration of Echeverría's plans to modify the course of Mexican development. Examining this period with hindsight, we see that the entire international economy had, in fact, entered a stage of crisis marked by food and energy shortages, worldwide inflation and recession, declining prices for raw materials on the international market, a slowdown in the American economy, and a breakdown in the Bretton Woods agreement for an international monetary system based on a stable U.S. dollar.

In particular, the end of the boom cycle in the United States had immediate and grave economic consequences for Mexico. A fall in U.S. trade with Mexico, a decline in tourism, the imposition of the 10 percent import surcharge, and increased surveillance of the border against illegal Mexican entry were all factors which account in great measure for the economic problems which eventually halted Echeverría's reform efforts.[54] Still, the powerful conservative sector of the national bourgeoisie was unrelenting in the economic pressure it exerted, and this group played a determining role in frustrating Echeverría's program. For, when economic pressure alone proved insufficient to thwart the Echeverría reforms, his enemies on the right brought to bear all the political weapons available in their arsenal.

Political Maneuvers

It was dangerous for opposition on the right to strike directly at Echeverría. Even the most economically powerful hesitated to face off directly against "el Señor Presidente de la República." Instead, his enemies within the national bourgeoisie employed a variety of political techniques designed to undermine his power, and they enlisted a wide range of allies in their effort to oust the president or render him helpless. These allies included conservatives within the official party, politicians whose careers and political fortunes were inextricably linked to Díaz Ordaz and his now discredited policies, the old guard of the CTM whose interests were more closely tied to business and industry than to labor, the government bureaucrats who found the drive for honesty in administration to be a hair-raising prospect, regional and local political strongmen, and others whose power would be undercut by Echeverría's proposed reforms.

The political strategy of the right was simple and unoriginal. The plan was to exploit the discontent of peasants, workers, students, and other dissidents in order to create a climate of political and social unrest. In so doing they hoped at the very least, to embarrass Echeverría and weaken his hand. Beyond that lay the prospect that continued civil violence might lead to a right-wing military coup of the kind that subsequently did occur in Chile.

To foment the desired atmosphere of chronic violence, the conservative bourgeoisie provided money to recruit, arm, and train paramilitary shock troops. They funded the infiltration of provocateurs into the universities. And they sponsored pseudo-guerrilla groups to carry out terrorist activities in the name of leftist causes. Right-wing gangsterism of this sort had been a factor in Mexican politics long before Echeverría took office. *Porristas* (paid provocateurs posing as students) had played a part in university politics from the time the universities became mass institutions in the early 1940s. And paramilitary thugs acting under secret orders from conservative politicians within the Department of the Federal District played a key role in provoking violence and army intervention during the 1968 movement.[55] However, when Echeverría began to unfold his reform program in 1970, the activities of armed provocateurs stepped up noticeably. It seems reasonable to assume that these gangs were sponsored by political elements well to the right of the president (both inside and outside of his party), because the activities of the *porristas* were geared both to repressing left-wing movements and to undercutting the prestige and authority of Echeverría's regime.

From the time the new administration took office, ever-greater numbers of provocateurs were infiltrated by the Right into the National University in Mexico City and into the state universities in Puebla, Nuevo León, Sonora, Jalisco, Guerrero, and other educational centers. These hired thugs carried out assassinations and provoked riots and pitched battles that cost the lives of hundreds of students and professors bringing these institutions to a standstill for months at a time. While *porristas* became virtually a permanent fixture in university life in the 1970s, the clearest case of the right's use of shock troops for the complementary purposes of repressing the Left and discrediting a reformist government occurred with an event in 1971, which has become known as the "Corpus Christi massacre."

On Corpus Christi day, June 10, 1971, more than 10,000 students left the Polytechnic Institute in a well-organized march to the Monument of the Revolution in downtown Mexico City. The stated object of the demonstration was to dramatize the students' demand for the release of political prisoners held since 1968. However, the underlying motive for calling a mass march at this time seems to have been the desire to reorganize and revitalize the student movement, which had remained in disarray since the slaughter in the Plaza of the Three Cultures in October 1968. The students, led by the remnants of the political organizations that guided the 1968 movement, saw this march as a first step toward rebuilding their movement and testing its force in the political arena.

There is considerable evidence that Echeverría viewed the march as an opportunity to demonstrate his willingness to engage in open dialogue with dissidents. It seems that he hoped the march would bring the students to the Plaza of the Constitution, where he planned to emerge on the balcony of the National Palace to greet the demonstrators and invite them to air their grievances and exchange ideas with him.

For its part, the right (both conservative capitalists and Echeverría's enemies within his own party) saw the occasion as an ideal opportunity to politically harass and embarrass the president. Accordingly, the *halcones* ("falcons"), a paramilitary troop sponsored by Monterrey capitalists and equipped and trained by the Department of the Federal District under the authority of a political enemy of Echeverría, Alfonso Martínez Domínguez[56] were dispatched to the scene.

As the march made its way toward the center of the city, roughly 1,000 *halcones* assembled and waited to intercept the students. Outfitted with knives, pistols, machine guns, and cattle prods, the *halcones* passed freely through the lines of uniformed police stationed along the parade route. While 900 special service police sealed off the area and the riot police heightened the confusion by launching tear gas bombs into the crowd, the *halcones* attacked the unarmed demonstrators, killing approximately thirty students and bystanders outright and pursuing the others as they fled through the streets. The *halcones* then rooted students out of the shops, cinemas, and churches where they sought refuge, and proceeded to invade the hospitals where the wounded had been taken, attacking injured students as they lay on the operating tables and in the wards.[57] The toll was high. An estimated fifty students were killed, another fifty "disappeared," and hundreds more were wounded.[58]

Notwithstanding initial attempts by official government spokesmen to portray the events as a "riot" or "clash" between "rival student factions," the truth was hard to conceal—particularly given that many

Mexican and foreign newsmen had witnessed both the unprovoked attack and the complicity of the uniformed police squads.[59] Weapons, vehicles, and radio equipment used by the *halcones* were readily traced to the Department of the Federal District. Official investigations of the massacre were launched and some attempt was made to establish responsibility for the affair. Eventually the investigation was dropped, although Martínez Domínguez and other conservatives closely linked to him and to former president Díaz Ordaz were forced to resign. Yet, despite the resignations of a few key conservatives within the government, it was clear that the right had carried the day. For one thing, the students were forced to abandon mass public demonstrations as a political tactic. For another, Echeverría suffered great political humiliation. He had not been able to turn the demonstration to his own political advantage as he had originally hoped. He was made to appear too weak to maintain civil order in his own capital city. It was apparent that the police took their orders from authorities other than the president of the republic. So obvious was the role of the right in provoking disorder that Echeverría was forced to openly acknowledge that the attack had been arranged by reactionaries determined to undermine his power.[60] In an oblique reference to the Monterrey capitalists, Echeverría warned students that they "must not allow themselves to be used as instruments of those who operate in the shade, risking neither their persons nor their economic well-being . . .," nor should the students "for lack of reflection, lend themselves to the designs of foreign interests and reactionaries."[61] Yet the very fact that Echeverría (and it would seem, just about everyone else in Mexico) was able to identify those who organized and directed the *halcones*, underscored his weak position: he was manifestly powerless to move against these groups, to halt the activities of the provocateurs and their sponsors, much less bring any of these people to justice.

OPPOSITION FROM THE RIGHT AND LEFT

The Corpus Christi massacre provides a clear example of the interaction between opposition of the right and left. In this case leftist opponents of the regime inadvertently played into the hands of the most reactionary elements in Mexico. It is obvious that the right's capacity to make use of the left operated to weaken Echeverría and limit his ability to carry out his moderate reforms.

This dynamic continued to operate for the duration of Echeverría's administration. While Echeverría enjoyed some early success in winning over moderate left-wing dissidents, probably most leftists were never won over, and some who initially supported the president later lost their enthusiasm as it became apparent that the changes Echeverría was working to bring about were very limited indeed.[62] For the most part, leftists remained unimpressed with Echeverría's reform package, which they viewed as nothing more than palliatives. They felt that none of his policies held out any real possibility of fundamentally altering the conditions of social injustice and economic inequality that afflicted Mexico. They granted that adjustments had been made, but asserted that these were adjustments geared to preserving the system, adjustments that operated on the principle that the system must be made more flexible if it is to remain essentially unchanged. They noted that Echeverría had appointed large numbers of talented young technocrats to study the economic problem of redistribution of wealth in Mexico. But three years later, these technocrats were still producing reports, pilot projects, and long studies indicating the need for further studies. Echeverría's opponents on the left saw that he lacked the political strength to turn studies into policy. And they felt, in any case, that his policies never came to the root of the problem in Mexico, which was not a question of more or less credit to agriculture or more or less labor intensivity in industry, but rather the fundamental contradictions of capitalist development in a country like Mexico.

In the late 1930s, Cárdenas had managed to carry out some basic structural changes in the political and economic system. But to do so he had to mobilize the masses, arm peasants and workers, and risk bringing the country to the brink of civil war. In contrast, Echeverría, for all his populist utterings, was either unwilling or unable to take the steps necessary to organize a mass base of support for his reformist regimes. Lacking this kind of popular support, Echeverría had no choice but to bow to the intensifying pressure from conservatives.

Beset by opposition from both the right and the left, Echeverría began to retreat from his initial progressive stand. Since he would not or could not do more to placate, co-opt, or appeal to the left, he began to move to the right. By the end of his third year in office, it seemed that in order to hang onto power, he felt constrained to abandon his "populist" program in all but rhetoric and to adopt policies catering to conservative interests.

Echeverría's steady movement to the right became evident in a number of different areas. The same man who in 1970 had given a small measure of freedom to the press, who in 1971 had ordered the release of several journalists imprisoned for their writings, by 1974 had imposed new government controls over television programming, had clamped down on the press, and had shut down the left-wing weekly, ¿Porqué, and arrested its publishers.

In his last months in office, Echeverría definitively tarnished his record in this area with a squalid set of maneuvers, resulting in the ousting of Julio Scherer as editor of *Excelsior*. International outcry greeted Scherer's removal because the editor, and a number of colleagues forced to resign with him, had raised the Mexico City daily to the highest standards of journalism known up to that time in Mexico.[63] Echeverría's initial efforts to introduce new, young, and progressive blood into the PRI were likewise dropped as party stability and disciplined organization began to take priority over party reform.[64] Of the seven gubernatorial candidates selected by Echeverría in his first three years in power, six were under the age of forty, and all were closely associated with his reform program. In contrast, the average age of the twelve gubernatorial candidates selected by the president in 1974 was sixty, and all of these men were PRI stalwarts, old *politicos* with a power base in conservative state politics.[65]

A number of economic decisions made in 1973 and 1974 can be viewed as concessions to the right designed to reassure the most conservative sector of the national bourgeoisie. For example, in November 1973, Echeverría announced that several companies which had been taken over by the government investment corporation, Nacional Financiera, when they were on the verge of bankruptcy, would be sold to private interests now that government funding had set them back on their feet. Furthermore, private capitalists were pleased to learn in December 1973 that public funds were to be spent to search for new oil deposits and other sources of energy for industry. Clearly this news that the practice of heavy government participation in bottleneck-breaking investments would continue was music to the ears of private capital. In addition, Echeverría made a bid for greater support from Mexican financiers when he publicly promised that he would not move to nationalize the banks, as had been rumored, and capped off this gesture by refusing to let bank employees organize their own union.

This same trend toward concessions to the right was evident in Echeverría's treatment of the conservative labor boss, Fidel Velázquez. Politicians both inside and outside the CTM who were challenging Velázquez's thirty-three year reign over the labor confederation initially enjoyed the support of the president.[66] However, when Echeverría realized that Velázquez was so firmly entrenched that the union leader was likely to win in any showdown between the two, the president quickly revised his policy and provided Velázquez with the concessions he needed to consolidate his control. Given Echeverría's desperate need to curb inflation, he found he was dependent on the labor boss to hold down wage demands. Only a man who enjoyed the iron grip that Veláquez exercised over organized labor could be relied upon to hold popular pressure in check in the face of the soaring cost of living for the working class.[67] To assure his collaboration in this effort, Echeverría effectively increased Velázquez's share of the take by giving him control over a 3.5 million peso fund earmarked for the construction of 100,000 low-cost housing units for workers. Furthermore, to strengthen the labor boss's hand in his struggle against the independent labor organizations that had developed as a response to Velázquez's corrupt and authoritarian regime, Echeverría proposed legislation modifying the "right to strike" provision of Article 123 of the constitution. This modification gave firmer control over strikes to both the government and the CTM central executive by imposing a mandatory conciliation period which effectively outlawed the kind of wildcat strikes which had been undermining Velázquez's power.

Echeverría's attempts to curry favor among conservatives, or at least reduce their hostility, was reflected in his policy toward Chile. In September 1973 the president outraged the Mexican Right by denouncing the fascist coup in Chile, calling for three days of national mourning for Salvador Allende, and offering political asylum to his widow and to thousands of other Chilean refugees. However, by May of 1974, Echeverría was citing the Mexican tradition of maintaining relations with all "sister republics" and quietly dispatched his foreign minister to Santiago to pursue trade relations with the government of General Pinochet.

With the Chilean coup fresh in everyone's mind, Echeverría apparently perceived his own situation to be so insecure that he felt constrained to court actively the support of the armed forces. In light of the historical transition in Mexico from military to civilian rule, and in view of the efforts since 1937 to reduce the overt role of the army in political affairs, Echeverría's attempt to bring the army into the limelight, his sudden celebration of the "patriotism," "professionalism," and "popular roots" of the armed forces constituted a significant break in the process of the demilitarization of politics. This suggests that the threat of a military coup weighed on the president's mind.[68] In October 1973, the army received a 15 percent pay hike. Furthermore, the ambitions of middle-ranking army officers, long frustrated by the preeminence of a group of generals in control of the armed forces since they won their spurs in the revolution of 1917, were at last realized when the president retired 486 of the elderly generals and promoted the middle-aged officers to the top ranks.[69] Assuming he might well need their support, Echeverría continued to heap praise upon these "professional patriots," and the army came to enjoy a period of official prestige it had not known in almost forty years.

Perhaps the most significant of the conservative trends emerging in the course of Echeverría's term was the increasing tendency to repress the left in order to pick up support from the right. To placate the conservatives and guarantee its own security, the government took ever harsher measures to halt and silence the student Left, while peasant and labor dissidents were met with the same show or use of force. In May 1973, for example, a rally called by students in the capital to protest police brutality directed against May Day demonstrators in Puebla was met by a force of 10,000 heavily armed riot police and soldiers. In August of 1974, another student demonstration in solidarity with a peasant protest caravan and with striking workers was over before it had begun because the march was banned, and thousands of riot police were deployed to enforce that prohibition. After the ill-fated Corpus Christi day march in June 1971, every subsequent effort at organizing public marches and rallies fell victim to the same overkill tactic: the massive threat or application of police and army force.

In light of this trend, the announcement in June 1974 of the arrival of sixty-three officers from the Higher School of War of Brazil appeared to many observers as a logical event marking an overall tendency toward militarization. These men were brought to Mexico "to exchange experiences with the Mexican army."[70] In the atmosphere of polarized violence that had come to prevail in Mexico by 1973–1974, the invitation to these specialists in urban and rural counterinsurgency and electrified torture only underscored the insecurity of Echeverría's position.

Notwithstanding these attempts to reassure the Right, the atmosphere of crisis deepened. By the middle of Echeverría's term there was open speculation as to whether he would manage to complete his six years in office. Conservatives, unimpressed with the president's gestures of conciliation toward them and unmoved by his efforts to guard their economic interests, continued to cast Echeverría as a man too weak—politically and morally—to maintain even a minimal level of law and order in Mexico. Factory owners threatened to arm their own workers in order to protect private property. The conservative national bourgeoisie constantly linked Echeverría's name with that of Salvador Allende, asserting "either we are with the Allendist line of Echeverría, or we are for Mexico and freedom."[71] The implications of this comparison were lost on no one, Allende having been assassinated only two months earlier. Laying aside the tradition of presidential immunity to direct criticism, conservatives began to blast the president for his failure to control "the rising tide of violence," and when Eugenio Garza Sada, a leading member of the Monterrey group was killed during a kidnap attempt, the Monterrey industrialists used the funeral oration to attack Echeverría, even as he stood at the graveside, for creating a climate in which "crime and terror can thrive."[72] At the same time that the right assaulted Echeverría in these terms, it continued to instigate violence through the use of *porristas* and pseudo-guerrillas. The conservatives' strategy of employing provocateurs to increase the level of civil violence was reenforced by the increasing activity of authentic leftist rural and urban guerrillas. These two factors combined to exacerbate the atmosphere of crisis. Echeverría seemed to be caught squarely between these forces of opposition and his program of reform was bankrupt.[73]

THE FISCAL CRISIS

The entire process of political and economic conflict which we have examined culminated in 1976 with an economic crisis of proportions never witnessed before in postwar Mexico. As we have seen, political pressures confronting Echeverría when he assumed office forced him to move forward rapidly and dramatically with a program of reforms geared to improving the conditions of the masses, while simultaneously constraining domestic and foreign capitalists. As we have noted, the outrage of the bourgeoisie at the imposition of curbs and restraints on the accumulation of wealth, and the uncertainty aroused by Echeverría's anti-business rhetoric, led these men to withhold their investment and ship capital abroad. Furthermore, the reform program was extensive and costly; it required massive public investment and the expansion of the whole state apparatus. As a consequence, the public deficit grew from 4.8 billion pesos in 1970 to 42 billion in 1976 as the government borrowed abroad to finance its expenditures and to support the peso—then pegged at 12.5 to the U.S. dollar.[74]

Echeverría's insistence upon maintaining a stable exchange rate with the dollar, whatever the cost, meant that the peso came to be regarded as overvalued in international money markets. The artificially high value of the peso, in turn, made Mexican manufactured goods more costly for prospective buyers when compared with goods produced elsewhere. Since Mexican products were now far less competitive in the world market, sales fell and this decline in export revenues increased Mexico's negative balance of trade.

Because production of basic manufactured goods had declined with the withdrawal of foreign and domestic investment funds, and food production was now running well below demand, Mexico was forced to import both food and manufactured products. This situation led, logically enough, to a further deterioration in the balance of trade. By 1975, the external debt was reaching critical levels, and confidence in the ability of the regime to manage the economy was gone. This loss of confidence created a mood of panic among those holding substantial amounts of pesos. Moreover, given the relatively open border with the United States, it was impractical for the government to impose currency export controls. As pesos were freely and rapidly converted to dollars by nervous capitalists both large and small, the state turned abroad to borrow more to support the peso at the old rate of 12.5 to the dollar. But the effort was futile. Foreign borrowing to sustain the peso only resulted in raising the domestic rate of inflation. The inflationary spiral, naturally, brought about a decline in the real standard of living of the majority of Mexicans as prices of basic goods rose day by day. Furthermore, the fruitless effort to maintain the peso against an unavoidable devaluation heightened the mood of uncertainty. This generalized sense of insecurity gave rise to the usual desperate pattern which characterizes such historical moments: further capital flight, hoarding of goods, speculation, blackmarket sales of currency and, of course, the inevitable rumors of coup, military takeover, and American invasion. At last, in late 1976, pressure to devalue the peso became overriding. After 22 years of stability, the Bank of Mexico floated the currency to permit market forces to determine its true value. Immediately it dropped by 39 percent and a month later it declined in value by over half.[75] A process of devaluation had begun which—as we shall see— would not be concluded even six years later at the close of the succeeding president's term. Thus, Echeverría left office without achieving anything like the reconstruction or rejuvenation of the socioeconomic and political system that he had proposed. Moreover, his sexenio ended with the collapse of the economy—a collapse so complete that only the announcement that Mexico was awash in oil would, in the next few years, revive confidence and temporarily halt the crisis cycle.[76]

SOME FUNDAMENTAL CONTRADICTIONS

Echeverría's attempts at reform failed because the problems he tackled were not incidental to the economic system, but rather were the logical and inevitable results of capitalist development in a country like Mexico. As we noted earlier, the development policy that has been pursued in Mexico since 1940 has been based on the "trickle-down" theory. Government economic policy has been intentionally arranged so that enormous profits would accrue to the private industrial sector in the hope that these capitalists would reinvest the accumulated capital in ways that would further the growth of the national economy. Tax exemptions, a regressive tax structure, protectionist legislation, government spending on infrastructure, strict curbs on wage hikes, an agrarian policy favoring the large commercial private agricultural sector were all policies geared toward increasing the income of the national bourgeoisie so that, it was argued, the rate of domestic saving and reinvestment would rise. Over a period of three decades, this policy resulted not only in the "social dislocations," the human suffering detailed in chapter 4, but, at the same time, operated to enhance at every turn the economic and political power enjoyed by the national bourgeoisie. As became evident in the course of the Echeverría administration, the economic strength of the national bourgeoisie has increased over the years to the point where this group can exercise an effective veto power over any public policy perceived as threatening its own interests. By withholding investment funds and encouraging its foreign business partners to do likewise, the national bourgeoisie underscored its position of power and expressed its discontent with Echeverría's policies as it set off or contributed to a series of serious economic problems.

Just as the economic power of the national bourgeoisie has increased over the last years, the political influence wielded by this class has grown apace. As we have seen, the national bourgeoisie can shape policy through its influence in the popular sector of the official party, through its control over the appointments of senators, deputies, state governors, university rectors, and its representation at every level of government bureaucracy. It can further effect political decisions through its powerful pressure group organizations like the National Confederation of Industrial Chambers and the National Confederation of Chambers of Commerce, and through its ownership of financial institutions and mass media. If pressure exerted through these various channels is insufficient to obtain desired policy, the Mexican bourgeoisie can count on the coooperation of American partners to pressure Washington for overt and covert U.S. policy designed to push the Mexican president along lines more satisfactory to foreign and domestic capital. Furthermore, in addition to the influence members of the national bourgeoisie have over the police and military apparatus in various Mexican states, we have already seen that important sectors of this class are prepared to organize and equip private armies and paramilitary shock troops to obtain through violent means what cannot be won through political maneuver.

With a national bourgeoisie wielding this degree of power, Echeverría's program for income redistribution was probably doomed from the start. Certainly there are countries where piecemeal, social democratic reform measures have worked to reduce economic inequality and mitigate social injustice within a capitalist system. Northern Europe is a case in point. But the social democratic reforms which have been carried out in northern Europe are set in industrially advanced and economically developed societies. Unlike the Mexican workers, the working classes of northern Europe are well organized, fully literate, homogeneous, and highly productive. The reformist benefits they enjoy were implemented by social democratic parties brought to power by the workers themselves through their own highly articulate labor union movements. The northern European bourgeoisie also contrast sharply with their Mexican counterparts in that they are able to take the longer view on reforms and adjustment to the capitalist system, and are not obsessed with short-term profit maximization. Furthermore, no social democratic reformist regime in Europe has to cope with problems of a largely agrarian peasant society. Perhaps most significant, no European social democratic regime shares a border and a long history of dependent relations with the United States.

Given the structures and traditions in Mexico, had Echeverría wanted to do more than paste bandages over wounds, he would have needed to carry out a mass mobilization to provide the support for a face-off with the national bourgeoisie. But to the degree that peasants and workers are already organized in the CNC and CTM, such a mobilization would have implied either the creation of parallel political institutions or the total reconstitution of the CNC and CTM under new leadership. As it was, Echeverría was unsuccessful in his attempt to oust or even limit the power of CTM secretary general, Velázquez. And Bonfil, the progressive secretary general Echeverría implanted into the CNC to shake up that organization, was mysteriously killed in an air crash before his more militantly *agrarista* leadership could have any measurable effect. Had Echeverría attempted to stimulate the creation of new mass organizations under militant peasant and labor leadership, he would have incurred the hostility not only of the national bourgeoisie, but of his own PRI machine, and of CNC and CTM regulars from the level of ejidal delegate and shop steward right up to the top. It is one thing to give occasional presidential encouragement to a locally based independent peasant movement like the Laguna's Central Union as a means of chastising the regional committee of the CNC for exceeding the normally acceptable limits of sloth and corruption. It is quite another matter to attempt a systematic replacement of CNC and CTM functionaries throughout the republic with more militant peasant and labor leaders capable of organizing a political confrontation on a mass scale with the national bourgeoisie.

But how likely is it that Echeverría actually envisioned a systematic restructuring of the bases of power of the PRI and, by extension, of the bases of Mexican development? All the evidence suggests that his aim was to streamline, not to restructure the Mexican economic and political system. The populist appeal he worked so hard to cultivate was geared more toward building a level of support sufficient to provide greater leverage and maneuverability vis-à-vis conservative capitalists, old guard *diazordistas*, the armed forces, and other encrusted interests. His goal was not to mobilize the masses to break the power of the national bourgeoisie, but only to win enough popular support to provide him with great confidence and leverage in his role as a reformer operating within the logic of the Mexican system.

THE STABILITY OF THE SYSTEM

As Echeverría's term in office drew to a close, Mexicans of virtually every political coloration began to be almost entirely taken up with the choice of the presidential successor. This preoccupation demonstrated the staying power of the PRI and the one-party system. For, in so many respects, the Echeverría years had been difficult and disappointing ones for Mexico. During this administration the indicators of economic growth on which the myth of the "Mexican miracle" were based had begun to slip. The rate of production in both industry and agriculture had slowed, the inflation was the worst Mexicans had known in twenty years, and the country's trade deficit was widening at an increasing rate. The confidence of foreign investors had been shaken both by the poor showing of various economic indicators and by the political violence that appeared to be sweeping the country. The world economic crisis accentuated these trends, and for all the rhetoric that had flown back and forth in 1970 and 1971, the well-being of peasants, workers, and the unemployed continued its steady decline in the face of rising costs of living. Economic inequalities and social injustice were as glaring as ever. But although the Echeverría regime came at the time when the economic and political tensions brewing since the 1940s were finally coming to a head, in 1974 and 1975 the focus of attention and concern even of many left-wing opposition groups turned to the question of the presidential succession. The final two years of Echeverría's administration marked a period of furious politicking in which each political group maneuvered to obtain the presidential nominee who promised to be most compatible with its interests. At this point, opposition movements thought less about changing the system and more about obtaining greater influence over the choice of the successor. Opposition peasant leaders and CNC stalwarts alike carefully examined the agrarian record of the men discussed as presidential material. Labor leaders, from both independent unions and the CTM, studied the labor relations records of the various *presidenciables*. Meanwhile, conservative groups rallied to exert pressure for a nominee who would safeguard their interests. As opposition leaders got caught up in the process, they demonstrated the hold that the PRI has over Mexicans, left, right, and center.

The radical student left was perhaps the only major opposition group, apart from the Communist Party, which stood outside this process. The students' analysis of the political situation generally persuaded them that the choice of the PRI successor would make very little difference to their future or the future of Mexico. The students' cynicism was easy to understand. Nonetheless, the concern with the succession on the part of popularly based opposition organization was neither irrational nor out of place. If one has the task of representing bus drivers or *ejidatarios*, and what one is trying to extract from the system is a higher wage for public transportation workers or more credit from the Ejidal Bank, the line of the nominee on public transport or agricultural credit funding is necessarily a crucial question. For whatever the shortcomings of the official party system, it delivers some payoffs. And it also controls people's lives through the wages it sets, the funds it allocates to social welfare, the amount of money it chooses to channel into ejidal agriculture, the number of jobs it opens in the public sector and so forth.

As Echeverría entered the lame duck period of his administration and loyal *priistas* scrambled for prominent seats on the bandwagon of his chosen successor, Finance Minister José López Portillo, political discussion in Mexico continued to focus on Echeverría's policies. The debate centered on the president's capacity to bind his successor to the program of reforms begun during his own term in office. Indeed, there was even serious speculation about Echeverría's ambitions to perpetuate his power after leaving office, by manipulating López Portillo from behind the scenes. In the heat of such discussion, it was all too easy to overlook the fact that Echeverría's reforms had been inadequate to meet the needs of the Mexican people in the early 1970s and were likely to prove even less sufficient for the future. Echeverría's urgent desire to commit his successor "to expand and continue" his program suggests that he had a coherent and viable reform policy, but lacked the time to carry it out. It was not, however, for lack of time that the reforms failed. The reforms did not work because they could not work, given the structure of power, the impotence of peasant and workers' organizations, the intransigence of the conservative bourgeoisie, the opposition of foreign capital, and the general alignment of political forces in Mexico.

The combination of radical rhetoric and half-measures that had been the hallmark of Echeverría's administration had not curbed the power of the bourgeoisie. It had, however, frightened them sufficiently to produce a fall in investments, a massive outflow of capital, a highly unstable economic situation, and ultimately—as always—greater suffering for Mexican peasants and workers caught in the inflationary spiral. The confusion of Echeverría's last months in office—marked by the devaluation of the peso, fiscal panic, rumors of military takeover, and a massive land distribution that was violently opposed by the landholders—provided a fitting, if not a happy, end to this contradiction-ridden administration.

8

THE
CRISIS OF
THE
EIGHTIES

When Echeverría's six-year term came to a close in 1976, a sigh of relief ran through Mexican and international business circles that could be heard from Monterrey to New York and back. To Echeverría's successor, José López Portillo, fell the task of restoring the confidence of domestic and foreign capitalists and getting the Mexican economy "back on track." The new president was, in fact, an immediate hit with the international business press who praised his "realism" and awarded him its highest accolade: it referred to him as a "pragmatist."[1] *The Economist*, having described Echeverría as "a man whose economic ambitions far outran his economics and whose populism outran his popularity," had nothing but praise for López Portillo, who was portrayed as short on rhetoric and long on competence and good sense.[2] When Echeverría actually held office, his programs for reform were discussed in the financial press with great solemnity, if not without hostility. In particular, his apparently sincere efforts to clean up corruption and increase bureaucratic efficiency won him approval from the business journals.[3] But once out of office, Echeverría was lambasted for the corrupt and wasteful practices that had characterized his own administration. The former president was now pictured as self-serving and demagogic. In neat contrast, López Portillo's sobriety was credited with bringing Mexico out of the economic crisis, for even the first indications of great oil wealth were not enough to fully restore confidence after the "excesses" of the Echeverría years. As *Fortune* reported:

> Oil was obviously a very important factor in the dramatic turnaround. . . . But oil couldn't produce recovery by itself, as the experience of other developing countries has demonstrated. . . . Much of the credit has to go to President José López Portillo. . . . Many financial experts in the U.S. and Mexico are so impressed by the way he has restored confidence that they believe Mexico could have come out of the 1976 crisis even without oil, though the climb would have been slower and more halting.[4]

López Portillo was praised for imposing "tough, conservative" economic policies, and filling his ministries with "pragmatic, highly qualified technocrats." "'There is a simple reason why everyone wants to put money into Mexico,' says a prominent New York investment banker. 'It has the most competent government in North America.' "[5]

Economic recovery under López Portillo was signaled when the International Monetary Fund (IMF) removed the severe restrictions it had imposed on Mexico in 1975. Now the IMF was prepared to help Mexico out with $600 million and the promise of more than $1 billion over three years on the condition that Mexico follow a "stabilization" program. This austerity policy called for limits on external borrowing, curbs on "nonproductive expenditures," that is, welfare spending, and a monetary policy which would float the peso until it reached its own stable rate of exchange with world currencies. Central to the new regime's efforts to bring Mexico out of the 1976 crisis were López Portillo's promised cuts in public spending of all kinds, a scaling down of development projects, and a commitment to freeze wage increases at a level below the rate of inflation.

If foreign banks were reassured by Mexico's new agreements with the IMF, domestic capitalists were encouraged by the policy of "alliance for profits" which López Portillo posed as his major corrective measure to the ill-conceived and ill-fated economic reformism of Echeverría. In contrast with his predecessor, the government of López Portillo offered virtually every guarantee that private capitalists could have required to induce private Mexican investors to bring their capital back into the country and to invest it once more in Mexican industry and agribusiness.[6] Indeed, recovery under López Portillo was rapid. By 1978 it was estimated that most of the capital that had fled the country had returned, the balance of payments deficits inherited from Echeverría had shrunk, and American, European, and Japanese investors were elbowing one another aside in their keen desire to secure prime investment opportunities in the oil-rich economy.

ECONOMIC COLLAPSE

In chapter 3 we examined the elaborate programs the López Portillo regime attempted to implement in order to utilize the new sources of investment capital to spur growth in both agriculture and industry. The Global Development Plan consisted of a series of policies designed to raise productivity in both sectors while guaranteeing that Mexico would avoid the pitfalls of "petrolization," the inflationary course of overly rapid growth based on rising petroleum exports. As we noted in that earlier discussion, within the framework of the model of capitalist development which was in place, and under the pressure of the international economic forces at play through the late 1970s, it proved impossible for López Portillo to control or reduce the inflationary pressures within the economy. Nor was he able—given the alignment of political and economic forces in Mexico—to check the tendency to pump oil at an ever greater rate to meet the rising costs of imported goods and the rising expectations of Mexicans themselves.

Of course, the perils of spiraling inflation, an overvalued currency, unrestrained expansion of state activities, and profligate spending on imports were clear to the López Portillo administration from the start. The 1976 devaluation crisis had made these dangers painfully obvious, and economic policy under López Portillo represented an explicit recognition of these tendencies and a determination to counter them. But, while public policy called for restraint, the actions of both the economic and the political elites bespoke a get-rich-quick, smash-and-grab mentality. In ways that overlapped and reinforced each other, the private economic choices of the bourgeoisie and middle classes and the programs sponsored by the state both worked to undermine the overall plan for slow, measured growth.

Some analysts identify unlimited public spending as the central cause of the inflation which increasingly destabilized the Mexican economy. "The biggest culprit in precipitating inflation has been the government itself. . . . [M]inisters, governors and heads of quasi-independent agencies have been unable to resist spending large amounts of oil revenues."[7] Notwithstanding promises of austerity, efficiency, and the restructuring of the state sector along more modest lines, the almost weekly announcements of the new and ever-greater oil reserves created a spendthrift spirit in government that made limitations impossible to impose. "Measured expansion of operations" appeared to each government bureaucrat to be a policy directive for some other agency to follow. Quite apart from its corruption and waste of public resources, the unrestrained spending of Pemex alone worked to discourage frugality on the part of other government sectors. To be sure, government expenditures shifted away from the social welfare emphasis which had characterized the Echeverría years.[8] But, far from cutting back state spending, the expansion of Pemex, the construction of the new industrial centers and ports, the complex of projects designed to launch export-led growth, and the public revenue poured into rural infrastructure and agricultural production under SAM, the Mexican Food System, together carried a price tag that greatly exceeded the revenues from oil exports.

If government spending could not be restrained or suppressed in the face of expansionary pressures of promised oil riches, how then could the regime cover the costs of its own lavish spending? This was the crux of the problem. Oil revenue was insufficient to underwrite expansion because Pemex, at this point, was investing more than it earned. The import of costly technology and capital equipment, as well as the staggering bill for basic food imports, required more foreign exchange than exports could generate. To make matters worse, commodity prices for Mexico's agricultural exports were declining throughout this period. Moreover, the López Portillo government could not hope to redress the balance of payments deficits with increased sales of manufactured exports for two reasons: first, the newly rich middle sectors were consuming almost all of the nation's domestic manufactures and, second, what remained for export was uncompetitive on the international market because, despite the devaluation of 1976, the peso had once again become overvalued. Even tourism, always a key earner of foreign exchange for Mexico, was on the downswing because the overvalued peso made Mexican cities and resorts relatively expensive as vacation destinations.

Where, then, would the López Portillo regime turn to find the funds to cover its public expenditures? Ironically, the new administration resorted to the same measures that had brought Echeverría to grief. The government continued to expand the supply of money to finance the deficit, and the regime continued to borrow abroad, quickly exceeding all the limits it had established on foreign indebtedness. In 1981, for example, López Portillo set a ceiling of $5 billion on loans from foreign banks, but using future oil revenues as collateral, he ended up borrowing three times that amount. Overall, the foreign debt increased eightfold during the years of López Portillo.[9] In large measure this occurred because foreign banks were so keen to raise their stake in what they considered to be a "good risk": a boom economy in a Third World country which featured high rates of return and a long history of political stability. Smaller private investors grew bold as the major banking institutions led the way. Thus, the intense eagerness of foreign investors to get in on the action was a key factor in stimulating the overextension of Mexican spending as credit was readily available to the Mexican state—and to private Mexican corporations—for virtually any project they might propose.

Fiscal Policy and Capital Flight

As we noted in chapter 7, the decision of the Echeverría regime to allow the peso to float until it found a more realistic level of exchange on world money markets led, within a few months, to a devaluation of roughly 50 percent. To prevent a repetition of that kind of shock to the economy and the society as a whole, upon assuming office López Portillo committed himself to a policy of gradual readjustments of the value of the national currency. In adopting such a policy it was hoped that the peso would never again become grossly overvalued, with all the problems an overvalued currency brings. But two factors made gradual downward adjustments almost impossible to implement. The strong desire of foreign banks to put their investment funds into Mexico meant that the banks were virtually flinging money at the Mexican government. In addition, the state's need to subsidize basic consumer goods, especially food, made the government reluctant to allow the peso to sink when so much of that food had to be purchased abroad. Thus the central bank, the Bank of Mexico, supported the peso at what became an increasingly overvalued rate. Under these circumstances, anyone holding overvalued pesos found it relatively advantageous to convert pesos to dollars. Suspecting that the overvalued peso would eventually have to fall, Mexicans who were in a position to do so— specifically, the middle and upper classes with accumulated savings— changed billions of pesos into dollars. It was easy enough for Mexicans to convert their pesos to dollars because there were no limits on the free exchange of pesos for foreign currencies, and the open border with the United States made it impractical to impose restrictions as millions of Mexicans regularly move to and fro across the frontier.

Under these circumstances, two broad patterns of economic behavior emerged which functioned to undermine the national economy while enriching individuals. Middle-class Mexicans, sensing that the boom years would not last, tended to spend their newfound wealth in immediate and often frenetic consumption. As a hedge against spiraling inflation, they poured a large proportion of their disposable income into durable consumer goods: the houses, cars, televisions, home appliances, and other items that transformed the character of middle-class Mexican life in these years. The other key aspect of the economic behavior of the middle class is that they began to spend their over-valued pesos abroad, not only to import foreign luxury goods, but on foreign travel, particularly to the United States. Given the increased exposure of middle-class Mexicans to North American media,[10] the family trip to Disneyland or the annual shopping spree in Houston, Miami, or Los Angeles now emerged as a fixed event in the middle-class calendar. Understandably, what the middle class—generally speaking—did not do with its new wealth was to save or productively invest the money in Mexico.

What really undermined the Mexican economy, however, was not the middle class's propensity to consume, but rather the response of the wealthy to the overvalued peso. The basic strategy of the bourgeoisie was to convert pesos to dollars and get them out of Mexico and into either a Swiss bank account or a piece of real estate likely to retain or increase its value. Real estate purchases by upper-class Mexicans concentrated in the American sun-belt states, although luxurious European villas, chalets, and chateaus, as well as resort properties the world over were rapidly snatched up by rich Mexicans. The estimates of total wealth transferred abroad by the *sacadólares*, or "dollar looters," as López Portillo would eventually label these people, are staggering. Figures issued by the Federal Reserve Bank of Dallas indicated that Mexican investment in Texas alone tripled between 1975 and 1981, including $8 billion in real estate and $16.4 billion in cash deposits in Texan banks.[11] According to conservative estimates, $14 billion was deposited in Eurobanks, $12 billion in foreign currency accounts in Mexico, and at least another $25 billion in real estate purchases in the United States.[12] It was impossible to stem this outflow because until the private banks were nationalized in September 1982, there was nothing illegal—even if there was much that was unpatriotic—about these currency exchanges and transfers. Moreover, these self-serving practices—so dangerous to the economy, if profitable for the individual—were engaged in by men in the highest reaches of government: the mayor of Mexico City, state governors, senators, deputies, and members of the president's inner circle and family, if not the president himself.[13] Thus, although the president talked a great deal about the husbanding of resources and collective limitations on expectations, nowhere in government, nor indeed, in the society as a whole, were there any models of restraint either private or public. López Portillo did not differ from previous Mexican executives in using his office to assure for himself an extremely comfortable, even luxurious, retirement. But the degree of visibility of his provisions for retirement—that is, his construction of a compound of houses for himself and his family on a large and valuable piece of land visible from the main highway leading west from Mexico City—distinguished López Portillo from most of his predecessors who were more circumspect, if no more modest, in their measures to reward themselves for their years of public service.[14]

Devaluation

Since the pesos spent abroad were not demanded by foreigners for purchases in Mexico, the fixed exchange rate meant the government, through the Bank of Mexico, was forced to rebuy all these pesos with its dollar reserves. These, of course, were the same reserves that had been obtained by borrowing abroad. And they were the same reserves that were needed by Pemex for expansion of production, and by the government for the purchase of foreign foodstuffs. With currency fleeing the country, the pressure to devalue or impose exchange controls became overwhelming. Exchange controls would be hard to implement effectively. Thus, the pressure for devaluation grew, since a devalued peso would make Mexican manufactured imports more competitive and tourism more attractive and would dampen Mexican demand for foreign goods and travel. Moreover, as we have seen in the case of the 1976 crisis, fears of devaluation generally become self-fulfilling prophecies, as those holding pesos rush to turn them into dollars. Thus in February 1982, after the kind of emphatic denials characteristic of governments facing imminent currency devaluation, the central bank withdrew its support of the peso and the peso immediately lost 30 percent of its value.

While the devaluation in early 1982 resolved some of the economic dilemmas associated with an overvalued currency, it gave rise to or exacerbated a whole range of other problems. The most immediate effect was felt as soaring inflation; the price of basics such as bread and tortillas doubled, literally, overnight. The government attempted to impose price controls on a total of five thousand items, and hundreds of retail stores were closed by official order when they violated the stipulated price freezes. However, to maintain orderly food distribution, after a few days the stores were reopened and the inflationary spiral continued its climb as organized workers demanded and received wage increases[15] and manufacturers raised their prices as the cost of their imported components rose.

Now that roughly 40 pesos were required to buy one dollar, any individual or institution with dollar debts to pay found it more costly to meet these obligations. This was particularly true for small Mexican businessmen who relied on supplier credits and imported goods for their operations. Indeed, hundreds of small firms filed for bankruptcy in this period and manufacturing activity fell by 50 percent, laying off thousands of workers. Large-scale enterprises also experienced great difficulty in meeting their outstanding debts to foreign creditors. While the multinational corporations with foreign assets and liabilities were able to handle the effects of devaluation, among the Mexican giants, there were some major business failures like the Alfa group, which was forced to sell half its assets and lay off 20 percent of its workforce. Most of all, the fall of the peso with respect to the dollar spelled grave trouble for the Mexican state, which as we know, had continued to spend beyond the revenues provided by oil, borrowing abroad to make up the difference. After devaluation, the total foreign debt expressed in terms of pesos had almost doubled overnight. Thus the annual cost of servicing the external debt, that is, paying the principal and interest owned on foreign loans, rose as a result of the devaluation; Mexico owed 234 billion pesos at the 1981 rate, but 405 billion at the 1982 rate of exchange.[16]

While some superfluous government programs might be cut back, the state could not reduce its imports of basic foods for which the price tag had risen proportionately. Furthermore, the government had to finance the wage increases it had granted if it was to maintain its base of support among organized workers. And as the state was facing the problem of meeting these increased expenses, the price of oil on the world market was dropping as reduced demand and overproduction moved OPEC to cut its price. Mexico, although not a member of the cartel, was forced to follow suit in order to remain competitive. By April 1982, the Bank of Mexico revealed that oil revenues would come to less than half the amount projected for the year. Although talk flew back and forth about emergency budget restrictions, in fact the López Portillo regime was able to pare only 3 percent from its public spending. Under the circumstances, it is not surprising that the state continued to look abroad for foreign loans to cover its deficits. And foreign banks, having overextended credit based on miscalculations about Mexico's future oil revenues,[17] continued to renew loans. They were motivated by fear that the country would default on its immense debts.

At this point, however, new loans to Mexico were curtailed. Certainly the banks were prepared to lend enough to bail the country out of its immediate difficulties, enabling Mexico to service its old loans and buy the essential imports to forestall social unrest and political instability. But bankers were not keen on throwing good money after bad. Thus government and private borrowing continued, but on less favorable terms. By the summer of 1982, foreign indebtedness had reached a staggering $80 billion, of which $60 billion represented loans to the public sector. By mid-August it was clear that Mexico would be unable to meet the payments on this debt.

In the next few weeks, as Jesús Silva Herzog, the minister of finance, rushed about from Washington to New York to the other financial capitals seeking the funds to refinance the Mexican public debt, it became clear that money would be found to bail Mexico out, for the same reason that the international financial community had earlier chosen to refinance Mexico's loans; they could not afford to do otherwise, so overextended were key financial institutions in what had once appeared a sure and secure investment. Two-thirds of the $80 billion was owed to private banks and about 30 percent of that was owed to U.S. banks. Bank of America, having loaned almost $3 billion, Citibank, $2.5 billion, and Chase Manhattan, $1.75 billion stood to lose the most,[18] highlighting the truth of John Maynard Keynes's adage that if you owe your bank manager a thousand pounds you are at his mercy and if you owe him a million pounds he is at your mercy. Given the danger to these interests, the international financial community, composed of private banks, central banks organized through the Bank of International Settlements (BIS) in Switzerland, and the IMF began to move to plug the credit gap with billions of dollars drawn from sources around the world.[19] The IMF alone came up with almost $4 billion in credit. In return for crucial support in this period, the Mexican government undertook to deliver to the United States the vast bulk of its future oil and gas, all at extremely "favorable" prices.

NATONALIZATION OF THE BANKS

By this time, the most sweeping emergency measures seemed modest proposals in light of the dimensions of the economic crisis. The value of the peso had declined by 76 percent between February and August of 1982. The rate of economic growth had slowed from 8–9 percent during the oil boom to zero in 1982 and threatened to become negative as more and more Mexican manufacturers, unable to buy foreign inputs, closed down or cut back their operations and laid off their work force. Inflation reached 100 percent and continued to climb. Drastic measures seemed inevitable and by mid-August they began.

First the government froze all foreign currency accounts to prevent further capital flight. Then exchange operations were suspended indefinitely. Finally, on September 1 in his final State of the Nation address, López Portillo announced the nationalization of all private Mexican banks, placing on these institutions and the speculators they served the blame for the collapse of the economy.

> A group of Mexicans, led, counseled, and aided by the private banks, has taken more money out of the country than all the empires that have exploited us since the beginning of our history. . . . We cannot, with dignity, do anything else. We cannot stand with our arms crossed while they tear out our entrails.[20]

For the first time in Mexican history, strict exchange controls were imposed. The nationalization decree also provided for the establishment of two exchange rates: (1) a preferential rate, fixed at 50 pesos to the dollar, applied to all payments on imported goods authorized by the Ministry of Trade, and (2) an ordinary rate, fixed at 70 pesos to the dollar, which applied to other currency transactions in the economy.[21]

Over the next few months, these rates, in fact, proved impossible to maintain. Too few dollars were available at the preferential rate or even the ordinary rates. Thus, Mexicans requiring dollars turned to the black market where pesos were trading at 110 to the dollar, or they traveled to the U.S. border where they paid 123 pesos to buy the dollars they needed to meet business expenses.[22] Eventually, as we shall see, exchange controls were liberalized and the two-tier system of exchange was scrapped by the succeeding administration in favor of a "floating rate" (150:1) determined by the free market and a "controlled parity" (98.1) set and maintained by the Bank of Mexico to supply dollars to Mexicans importing raw materials or meeting foreign interest payments.[23]

The key to the bank nationalization, however, was not be found in the specific provisions for controls of currency exchange or checks on foreign transactions. The significance of the nationalization lay in the opportunity it might afford the Mexican executive to regain control and to reshape the whole economy, eliminating unproductive, over-protected, subsidized sectors of industry and reasserting state control over the movement of private capital.[24]

Beyond these economic goals, the importance of the nationalization lay in its political symbolism, the emotional appeal it made to the deeply felt patriotism of lower-class Mexicans. Striking chords of national pride and anger, López Portillo attempted to frame the move in such a way as to evoke memories and sentiments similar to those which attach to Cárdenas and the nationalization of petroleum. More than 100,000 people were brought to the Zócalo in a massive—if not a spontaneous—demonstration of enthusiasm and support for the new policy. In a staged replay of the popular response to Cárdenas's oil expropriation, during the next days López Portillo was photographed accepting hundreds of donations, large and small, from "ordinary" Mexicans who were either moved by patriotism or pressured by their superiors in government offices and unions into pledging one day's pay to defray the cost of the bank expropriation. With this gesture, it seems that the president hoped to counter the rising tide of criticism that asserted that through corruption and ineptitude he had managed to fritter away the oil wealth which was the birthright of all Mexicans. Neither the rhetoric nor the manipulation of symbols, however, was sufficient to mask what was essentially an attempt by López Portillo to cloak in the mantle of nationalism an administration that was disfigured by malfeasance and gross mismanagement. Nor could the appeal to nationalist feeling long distract attention from the precipitous decline in real wages suffered by the working class as a consequence of the devaluation.

Implications of the Crisis

To understand the longer-term implications of the crisis, it is important to underscore certain key points. López Portillo had come to office dedicated to using petroleum wealth to generate autonomous development. He expected that oil wealth could be utilized to provide Mexico with a margin of economic independence so that future development would not turn on the price of oil or the rate of interest prevailing at any given moment in the world economy. In fact, as we have seen, the years of his administration marked a steady, inexorable move toward greater reliance on oil revenue. As a result, the fall in world oil prices after June 1981—a consequence of economic forces completely beyond Mexican influence or control—constituted a crushing blow to an economy in which oil had in fact come to supply three-fourths of all export earnings and a third of government revenues. Indeed, only with the oil glut did the degree of Mexico's petrolization become fully apparent. At this stage, only by borrowing abroad could the regime maintain even the illusion of independent policy formation. In the end, however, the full dimensions of Mexico's lack of autonomy in the face of world economic forces became clear.

The irony of the situation which prevailed as López Portillo turned office over to his successor was that López Portillo had been no more successful than Echeverría in shaping economic policy to meet the development priorities he had established for his regime. To be sure, he had dispensed with many of the freespending "populist gestures," the services to the poor which had been the hallmark of Echeverría's administration. But political pressures from the mass of the population undermined López Portillo's determination to cut more completely in this area. The total Mexican population had of course grown, if at a slightly decreased rate. Furthermore, pressure from a well-organized labor movement heightened during López Portillo's *sexenio.* Thus the social benefit programs established by Echeverría could not be entirely dismantled because the desperate needs that had prompted their creation persisted into the 1980s. Most of what Echeverría had constructed as a welfare apparatus was, in fact, a direct response to the need to defuse unrest through selective distribution of government goods and services. To keep the lid on political unrest, López Portillo soon found that he had to do much the same even if he fired Echeverría's personnel and created "new" projects and called them by new names. His only alternative to this form of co-optation, as we have seen, would have been application of repressive measures against increasingly militant and mobilized opposition from the peasants and workers whose condition had deteriorated so markedly from the time Mexico had "struck it rich."

Thus the record of the López Portillo administration provides another indication of the parameters of the Mexican political system. The Echeverría administration had demonstrated the limits of reform. It indicated that a basic reorientation of the course of Mexican development in the direction of greater "distributive justice" could not be carried out because of the intransigence of bourgeois interests. The López Portillo years, on the other hand, demonstrated the limits of a system of co-optation based on ad hoc "handouts" to groups mobilized to press their demands. These constraints became clear in the course of six years as the financial resources necessary to buy off the most militant demands of the better-organized sectors of the society dried up with the decline of an oil-based economy. A period of profound political crisis was reached as López Portillo's term drew to a close because the capacity of the regime to satisfy material demands had diminished, but there had been no corresponding reduction in the need of those who were genuinely needy, nor in the expectations of any sector of Mexican society.

As a consequence of this fundamental contradiction, López Portillo left to his successor, the secretary of planning and the budget Miguel de la Madrid Hurtado, a complex of problems that were remarkably similar to the ones he himself faced upon taking office. By 1982, however, these problems were far more grave in degree. Every indicator of economic crisis was proportionately worse than in 1976, and de la Madrid did not have the promise of oil wealth to manipulate in a manner that would restore confidence. He could not rescue the economy with an influx of petrodollars, and the pattern established by Mexican capitalists in the previous *sexenio* gave little cause for optimism regarding the role of the private sector in any effort to turn the situation around.

Thus de la Madrid took office as the country tottered on the brink of what was generally regarded by Mexican analysts as "the most profound economic and political crisis of the last fifty years."[25] Within the government, there prevailed a mood of tension, disorganization, confusion, atomization, and lack of control over events. Conspiratorial behavior reached a level which far exceeded the norm, even for a period of presidential succession and transition. And, for once, the reality was even more alarming than the rumors in circulation.[26]

The New Administration

As the new administration of Miguel de la Madrid Hurtado came to power on 1 December 1982, Mexicans braced themselves for the shake-up and "clean sweep" that customarily mark the inauguration of a new regime. Only this time the cries of "moral renovation" and "austerity" had a more serious ring as they were sounded in an atmosphere of genuine economic emergency.

Like López Portillo, de la Madrid came to power proclaiming his intention to rid Mexico of the corruption that permeates every area of society and which had reached grotesque proportions during the "fat years" of the oil boom. Responding in this way to the public mood of frustration at the economic humiliation Mexico was suffering, de la Madrid concentrated on the malfeasance of the previous administration as a means to personalize and focus the anger of Mexicans on a relatively limited target. Accordingly, he launched his "moral renovation campaign" with the creation of a cabinet-level government accounting office empowered to audit the books of any public agency. The new president also took a firm public stand against fraudulent practices in public office and promised prosecution of police, petty officials, and other recipients of bribes, kickbacks, and payoffs. Even the press—deeply enmeshed in the system of corruption—would lose their *embutes*, the regular payments they customarily received from public officials either to write articles advancing the careers or interests of politicians, or to withhold potentially damaging material from publication.

While no Mexican in or out of government could doubt that the country was in desperate need of moral renovation, few believed that de la Madrid would be able to press forward with a serious attack on corruption in high places. Indeed, early in his regime, de la Madrid began to back off and soon he made it clear that prosecution of former officials would take place in response to public denunciations rather than as a consequence of active investigation by his administration. Thus some lower-level figures—bank administrators, one state governor, and the Pemex officials who were named as bribe takers in the U.S. Justice Department's case against a Texas oil company—were caught in the very loosely woven net. But no systematic investigations of "unexplained wealth" were actually undertaken. To no one's great surprise, even the most highly visible offenders from the López Portillo regime went free. However, the campaign served a short-term purpose of deflecting attention from the more profound questions that needed to be publicly addressed in this period of crisis.

Perhaps the most crucial of those questions concerned the direction that economic policy would take after the nationalization of the banks. De la Madrid had been informed but not consulted by López Portillo when the latter decided to nationalize the private Mexican banks. The new president, long a proponent of an "open economy," did not share his predecessor's enthusiasm to see the banks brought under state control. In fact, after the nationalization was announced, de la Madrid remained absolutely silent for three long weeks, refusing to give his approval to a policy he had not participated in formulating nor could reverse once in power.[27] The expropriation of the private Mexican banks in September had set Mexico on a course toward greater state direction of the economy. Indeed, in taking possession of the banks, the

Mexican state—seemingly to the surprise of its own executive—found it had also acquired controlling shares in a wide range of private companies in every sector of the economy. Thus, the state now controlled far more of the economy than ever before, and de la Madrid would have to take concerted action to undo this situation by selling off these shares to private capital if he was determined to pursue the open economy model he preferred.

In fact, when the new administration took office, an immediate shuffle of personnel signaled de la Madrid's intentions to reverse the nationalist directions of these policies insofar as possible.[28] The director of the Bank of Mexico and others associated with the nationalization were removed and replaced with figures known to have opposed the expropriation of the banks. It soon became clear that while de la Madrid could not "denationalize" the banks, he could and would move to "reprivatize" what had become state holdings by selling shares in the banks and the industries they control to private stockholders. By 1983 the president announced plans to sell 34 percent of the bank's shares to federal, state, and municipal agencies, bank workers, and bank users.

De la Madrid's preference for free-market economics found expression in other ways. Upon assuming office, he moved to liberalize foreign exchange controls and relax all restrictions on the movement of currency in and out of the country. The two-tier system established by the Bank of Mexico under López Portillo was abandoned in favor of a rate established on the open market. And in line with his other efforts to reduce state involvement in the economy, de la Madrid decontrolled 4,700 "nonessential" items on which López Portillo had set price controls after the devaluation of February 1982.[29]

The Politics of Austerity

When de la Madrid came to the presidency the most optimistic projections he was prepared to make suggested that economic recovery would take at least three years. Since, by 1983, Mexico could barely pay the interest on the $80 billion owed to foreign banks, the need for austerity, for real sacrifices from all classes and sectors of the population was posed by the new administration as Mexico's only means to cope, in the short run, with the economic emergency. In any event, the terms of the $4 billion IMF loan explicitly required cutbacks in every area of government spending as well as fiscal reform to raise $10 billion from new taxes. These new revenues would include a value added tax of 15 percent on essential and 20 percent on luxury goods, and a 10 percent income tax surcharge. Also, government officials, for the first time, would pay income taxes ranging from 30 to 50 percent.

The austerity program posed a real threat to the interests of many small Mexican capitalists. The sector of the national bourgeoisie which was not tied in with foreign capital and multinational enterprises had carried on, since the 1940s, at low levels of productivity. The small domestic industrialists had been able to operate because they were protected by tariffs from foreign competition and they were propped up by an assortment of government subsidies. Now in their hour of greatest financial need, these aids would be reduced or withdrawn altogether and it was clear that austerity would bring about the financial collapse and disappearance of the least productive sectors of Mexican industry.

De la Madrid's predecessor had whipped up nationalism as a prelude to the sacrifices the Mexican poor were going to be called upon to bear, and by the time the new president took office, peasants and workers were feeling the effects of what would become a steady decline in their already inadequate standard of living. Real per capita income fell in 1982 for the first time in decades. An estimated 800,000 jobs in industry disappeared in that year and, overall, one million Mexicans lost their jobs. Increased unemployment was posed by the government as "unavoidable" as businesses closed, most construction was suspended, and sectors of both agribusiness and industry ground to a halt for lack of capital equipment and other imported inputs.

Generally, the CTM was far more preoccupied by job losses than by the need for wage increases. Although inflation was now running over 100 percent, the government was able to hold organized labor to wage raises of only 25 percent (effective 1 January 1983) with another 12.5 percent increase promised for midyear. The state's capacity to impose this level of austerity on the working class is striking in view of the severe decline in the standard of living which had already been felt in 1982. As we have indicated, most of the five thousand items on which López Portillo had imposed price controls were now decontrolled, and the prices of the remaining three hundred "essential items" (goods like tortillas, beans, milk, eggs, coffee, sugar, cooking oil, and soap) were permitted to rise by 25 percent. Steep hikes in all government services made electricity, telephones, and railroad travel far more expensive. Gas prices doubled, and the cost of a bus or subway ride was projected to increase over the course of the year.

Peasants suffered grievously as drought hit some of the most fertile zones with a loss of 40 percent of the corn harvest. In many cases, what nature did not destroy was wiped out by the sudden withdrawal of all government credit, subsidies, and assistance. The food program, SAM, which for all its defects, had raised productivity and improved the material condition of at least some sectors of the peasantry, was canceled outright. And in line with the imposition of austerity, at this writing, no comprehensive state policy directed to rural development had been designed or set in motion to replace SAM. The only attempt to relieve the abject misery of rural Mexicans took the form of a series of public works—largely road building and repair of railroad lines—projected to provide the rural unemployed with 350,000 jobs, to be distributed through the official party patronage system.

What is likely to be the popular response to the decline in living standards in these years of emergency? Given its impact on peasants, workers, the middle class, and sectors of the national bourgeoisie, what will de la Madrid's program of austerity mean in terms of the equilibrium of the political system? Even at this early stage in his administration some of the political implications of the crisis confronting de la Madrid and the Mexican state can be outlined.

The "Crisis of Legitimacy"

Assertions that the Mexican political system is facing a "crisis of legitimacy" have been heard since the days in which President Díaz Ordaz lost control of events during the student movement of 1968 and Luis Echeverría came to power with the lowest measure of prestige and public regard ever accorded a Mexican executive. Indeed, notwithstanding his "apertura democrática" and his program for distributive justice, the crisis of legitimacy persisted as Echeverría left office, his program in shreds and the economy a shambles. Popular disaffection from the political system was underscored by the massive abstentions in the election of 1976 which brought López Portillo to power. It was this same legitimacy gap that López Portillo hoped to bridge with his reforms of the party and the electoral system. But the popular perception of him as having failed to manage the oil riches in the interests of the nation seems to have neutralized the gains he made as the president who liberalized the political system by providing some room for meaningful participation by the opposition in politics.[30]

Although it is not the first time that the issue of legitimacy has been raised, the present crisis of legitimacy is more severe than that confronting the official party, its leaders, and the state in 1968. The current crisis is aggravated because it is broader. Today not only are students awakened to the injustices of the system, but peasants are increasingly proletarianized, the working class is better organized and more militant than in 1968, the middle class is larger and has much better reason to feel frustrated than during the economic expansionist years of the late 1960s, and small Mexican entrepreneurs' interests have been severely damaged by the austerity policies.

In the face of this broad-based discontent, what are the resources that de la Madrid can muster? The new president has never previously held an elective post and hence has come to office with no grass-roots support. Always a bureaucrat, he was never schooled in official party politics; he has no links to the masses of the population through even the imperfect mechanisms of CNC or CTM organizational networks. De la Madrid is an uninspiring speaker, lacking the faintest glimmer of charisma. Moreover, his lack of any natural instinct for politics was evidenced in his top political appointments. Effectively his cabinet is filled with men almost identical to the president himself in experience, career progress, and outlook. De la Madrid did not utilize the opportunity of choosing his cabinet to spread high government posts around among figures representing various factions, tendencies, interests, or power bases within the PRI or the "revolutionary family."

As long as the country continues to reel under the shock of the economic collapse of 1981–1982, and the peasantry and working class continue to accept the need for emergency measures in a crisis situation, the broad mass of the population will give its loyalty to the Mexican state out of sheer patriotism, whatever the personal limitations of the chief executive may be. However, once the period of real austerity and shared sacrifice passes and the economy begins to pick up, these same popular sectors will expect some reasonable and concrete benefits to compensate for their forbearance of the past. Thus in the mid-term years in this present *sexenio* (1985–1986), it is quite possible that we will see the lack of popular support for the regime in power crystalize as a crisis of legitimacy for the system as a whole.

KEYS TO THE FUTURE

The collapse of the Mexican economy in the 1980s has indicated the degree to which the future of the Mexican political system is tied to forces and events external to the country. The unity or demise of OPEC, the output of other oil producers, energy use, and conservation in the industrialized countries, and the discovery of new oil reserves or alternative sources of energy are all factors which together will determine the price of oil on the world market and ultimately, the foreign exchange Mexico will earn in the years ahead. Similarly, the overall health of the U.S. economy—inflation, recession, production and employment levels, hydrocarbon purchases, trade, and the demand for unskilled Mexican labor on either side of the border—will markedly affect Mexico in ways which are predictable, based on the patterns of the past, but over which Mexico has almost no control.

Apart, however, from these and other external factors that spring from shifts in the international economy, there are a number of internal, domestic forces that we can identify as likely to shape Mexican politics and society through the 1980s. Let us look now at some of the elements that provide keys to understanding the future of Mexico.

Politics of the Right

Staggered by the shock of the economic collapse, the Mexican right has yet to regroup into any kind of new bloc of forces capable of taking concerted action on behalf of conservative interests. In this short-run period of adjustment to devaluation and nationalization, the individuals who comprise the political right have largely been preoccupied with their own immediate economic concerns: shifting currency back and forth, covering business debts, unloading foreign property in the search for liquidity, and so on. However, when we view the activities of the right as part of a longer-term historical process, particularly when we survey the economic and political behavior of conservative interests over the last decade, it is striking to note how consistent their strategy has been. And it is this pattern of defense that provides some clues to the future.

Generally speaking, shifts in the economic climate have prompted the industrial and financial bourgeoisie to invest or disinvest, to ship currency abroad or bring it home to Mexico, according to their perception of the degree of freedom they enjoy to pursue profits, unhampered by government restrictions. The rate of taxation, the level of government spending on industrial infrastructure, and the subsidies, discounts, and guarantees to business that the state has historically been willing to offer, have been crucial factors determining the movement of capital in and out of the Mexican economy. These financial moves have constituted the capitalist class's principal defense of its economic interests.

The means by which the bourgeoisie presses its political demands remain essentially unchanged and consist largely of pressure exerted through the formal interest organizations and the informal network of contacts between the economic and political elites based on their overlapping interests. Since 1976, there has been little reason for the right to resort to the widespread use of private armies of "white guards" or paramilitary shock troops, the systematic destabilization of the universities, or the other extreme tactics which were brought to bear during the years of Echeverría's reformism. But the threat of violence, as we have noted, is never absent from Mexican politics. Lockouts of workers and assaults on mobilized peasants, as well as insistent rumors of military coups and unexplained troop movements in the more conservative regions of the republic, have all occurred with regularity in the last decade. These forms of actual or potential violence have been utilized to shift the course of events whenever key sectors of the bourgeoisie— like the powerful Monterrey group—have felt themselves pressed too hard by the policies of the state as it operates to reconcile interests, redistribute wealth, and otherwise act to maintain "social peace."

The military. One element, then, which has become more significant in the complex of forces that shape Mexican politics has been the threat of military coup. Over the last years of extreme economic instability, this threat has come to seem far more credible as the Mexican domestic situation has begun to resemble that of countries like Brazil and Argentina, where runaway inflation preceded military takeovers. In the past it has been difficult even to pose the question of what form a military coup might take in Mexico because the history of "demilitarization" of Mexican politics long discouraged serious analysis or even speculative discussion along these lines. Studies of direct military intervention in Latin American politics typically begin by excluding Mexico from consideration.[31] And those which have weighed the probability of a military coup have dismissed it as unlikely or impossible. Mexican sociologist Pablo González Casanova wrote as late as 1972, "It is an incontestable fact that Mexico has controlled and overcome the stage of militarism. Militarism no longer represents a permanent and organized threat of a political force imposing its own conditions by coercion. . . ."[32] To support the hypothesis of declining military influence, González Casanova and others have cited the decrease in federal spending on the armed forces, the relatively small proportion of the national budget allotted to the military, the stability of the army at a relatively small size, the reduction in the ratio of soldiers to the labor force, and the fact that the last military man to serve as president was Avila Camacho, whose term ended in 1946.[33]

While this argument is persuasive, the recent history of military takeover in virtually every South American republic, including Chile and Uruguay—both countries long believed to have armies "too professional" to become directly involved in politics—suggests that no Latin American country is entirely immune to this phenomenon. Examining the likelihood of such a shift in Mexico, one analyst wrote in 1977:

> The military's subservience to civilian elites, however, has depended on the latter's ability to govern. Until now, the armed forces have had a definite stake in the current political system, which has treated them well and has relied heavily on them for information and cooperation in putting down antisystem groups or keeping them under control. But increased political alienation on the part of major groups, elite fragmentation, and high levels of

uncontrolled mobilization could persuade the armed forces to replace the 'dysfunctional' civilian elites with military men.[34]

Certainly the importance of the military in Mexican politics has diminished as the official party system gained control and brought different classes, interest groups, military and regional strongmen into its fold through a system of co-optive rewards and concessions. Yet Ronfeldt has pointed out the significant "residual" political roles played by the military within the Mexican political system.[35] In contemporary times, troops have been called in to suppress student movements, squelch guerrilla insurgency, repress peasant demonstrations, break up rural hunger marches, dislodge land invaders, smash strikes, pursue urban guerrillas, maintain order during contested elections, and prop up official party functionaries who face challenges from rival groups at the local and state level. Apart from these overt repressive activities, army chiefs play a key role in the collection of intelligence data: pinpointing subversive activities within their command zones, identifying issues and areas of unrest overlooked by civilian politicians, and helping the government "to secure control over isolated, unruly rural areas."[36]

Over the last several decades these military activities seem mainly to have been directed toward bolstering the PRI in the face of popular pressure for change. It appears likely that, in the short run, army men will continue to perform these functions under civilian orders. However, over time the army has extracted an ever higher price as compensation for its contribution to propping up this system. While the Mexican budget for military expenditure is exceedingly low by Latin American standards, and Mexico's army is the smallest and most modestly equipped of any nation its size, between 1979 and 1982 the army grew by 25 percent to 120,000 troops. The proportion of the national budget devoted to military spending more than doubled from 1.1 percent in 1980 to 2.5 percent in 1981. During his term in office, Echeverría built a modern military academy and López Portillo followed up, using oil revenue to purchase a dozen F5 jet fighters, forty anti-tank vehicles, and sixty light defense aircraft.[37] Furthermore, to clear the way for the promotion of younger officers, senior personnel were pensioned off at up to three times the salary they had received while on active duty.

Notwithstanding this outpouring of attention and funds on the armed forces, Mexico's military remains a small force, mostly equipped with antiquated weapons. Indeed, only in the last few years has the cavalry shifted from horses to motorized military vehicles. But these gestures toward the generals and the colonels clearly reflect the fear of the regimes in power. And this fear is that the right may successfully appeal to the military to seize power to oust a civilian government that has responded to assorted demands of various social classes and interests rather than shaping policy to meet the short-term needs of the bourgeoisie.

The strength of the PAN. The other feature of right-wing politics which has become more significant in the late 1970s is the role of the National Action Party (PAN) as a voice of opposition from the right. For more than four decades this conservative party remained hemmed in within the small area of political space. permitted it in the one-party dominant system. Since the political reform of the late 1970s made seats in the Chamber of Deputies easier for minority parties to win, the PAN has experienced an upsurge of support. In 1982 the party polled 16.4 percent of the presidential and 17.4 percent of the senatorial votes, and it is likely, of course, that the vote for PAN, as for other minority parties, was actually higher than the figures recorded. Altogether almost 4 million Mexicans gave their vote to this right-wing party and the PAN seems especially to have made gains among the urban middle class. In the largely middle-class Naucalpan electoral district, in the State of Mexico, the PAN candidate for deputy registered an absolute majority, and overall, the party won four of the 300 contested seats and thirty-nine of those shared among minority parties.[38]

In the most recent elections, the PAN's presidential candidate, Pablo Emilio Madero, spoke for reduced government involvement in the economy and against the leftist direction of Mexican foreign policy, particularly Mexican support for guerrilla movements in Central America. It is difficult to interpret voting statistics as patterns of preference in a situation in which the data are so unreliable. However, in the past, votes for the PAN were generally regarded as gestures of protest against the PRI and the one-party system, rather than indications of preferences for right-wing positions. Today the rise of voter support for the PAN is increasingly interpreted as an indication of a shift to the right. This is because the existence of contending parties to the left of the PRI offers those wishing merely to express disapproval of the official party a range of different ways to cast a protest vote.[39]

Politics of the Left

In contrast to the right, the Mexican left has changed markedly over the last decade in its analysis of society and in strategy, tactics, and composition. Probably it has also grown in size. To be sure, many of the divisive conflicts that have weakened the revolutionary left in the past persist. But a new set of possibilities and prospects have opened to the left with the current crisis of legitimacy of the regime. The key question, then, that we must examine concerns the capacity of the varied elements which comprise the Mexican left to act with sufficiently clear direction, determination, and unity to meet the mobilizational challenge posed by the systemic crisis.

The myth of revolution. The most enduring obstacle to the consolidation of a revolutionary Left in Mexico has been the fact that the Mexicans have already experienced a great historical upheaval called "The Revolution." That is, a major barrier to radical revolution in Mexico has been the existence of a bourgeois revolutionary tradition. While there are few people alive today who fought in the Revolution of 1917, there are many who directly felt its effects or who lived through the turbulent years from 1917 to 1928 that were its aftermath. Succeeding generations of Mexicans have been brought up on the myth of the revolution. They have heard countless promises made in the name of the revolution, and they have seen very few of them fulfilled. They have witnessed the assumption of the revolutionary mantle by political leaders who were representatives of the national bourgeoisie. They have watched these men appropriate the title "revolutionary" for themselves and use that label to manipulate Mexican policy to serve their own class interests. "For more than forty years," Stevens writes, the ruling party has maintained itself in power "by preempting and institutionalizing the revolutionary myth."[40] Even the mass media have selected portions of the revolutionary heritage and have utilized what were once genuinely popular symbols (*charros, mariachis, adelitas,* and the rest) as "an extension of the conservative ideology of Mexico's dominant economic interests."[41]

Mexicans of the popular classes have grown very weary of hearing about revolution. The very words "revolution" and "revolutionary" have lost their meaning. This sense of cynicism and distrust is clearly expressed in the popular folk song, "Juan Sin Tierra" (landless Juan), the tale of a peasant who gave his all in the revolution of 1917 but had nothing to show for his courageous effort.

> I will sing you the song
> Of a man who went to war,
> Who was wounded in the mountains
> Who just fought to win some land.
>
> Our General told us,
> "Fight on with great valor
> We are going to give you land,

As soon as we make the Reform."
Emiliano Zapata said:
"I want Land and Liberty,"
And the government laughed
When they went to bury him.

If they come looking for me
To make another Revolution
I'll tell them, "Sorry, I'm busy
Planting the fields of the landlord."

Under the circumstances, it has been very difficult for the revolutionary Left to present a program of struggle to people who have had this experience of "revolution." While the suffering of peasants and workers is very great, so too is their skepticism about the sincerity and efficacy of self-styled revolutionary leaders of whatever political tendency. Their hopes have been betrayed too many times for them to lend themselves readily to the plans of those who would lead them in struggle in the name of "revolution."

Committed Marxist revolutionaries in Mexico have long understood this disaffection. They have also understood that the construction of a popular base for revolution would necessarily be a long-term and complex process. They realize that they first face the task of demystifying the Mexican Revolution. They know that the hope of some day receiving a piece of land has held the landless peasantry in a quiescent state for a very long time. Even when that hope dies, it does not necessarily bring in its wake the desire to fight, but, rather may be replaced by a passive mood of resignation. Similarly, the demonstration effect of the great wealth and comfort achieved by a small urban elite likewise serves to hold the urban masses in a quiet state of expectation that, at least through individual achievement, they may one day receive their share of the pie. The frustration of these kinds of hopes does not necessarily radicalize the urban poor. Often such aspirations are replaced by apathetic despair. It has long been clear that a great deal of political work would have to go into raising the consciousness of such people and organizing them before their frustrations could be channeled into political action. Furthermore, the revolutionary Left is well aware that all serious previous efforts to build mass political movements have been countered and defeated by the twin control mechanisms of cooptation and repression.

For this reason, in the years following the destruction of the 1968 student movement, revolutionaries increasingly turned to clandestine forms of organization and activity. The late 1960s and 1970s in fact witnessed a steady rise in rural and urban guerrilla activities.

The guerrilla campaigns. As early as 1964, as we have noted, Jénaro Vázquez opened a guerrilla *foco* in the mountains of Guerrero state. His death in February 1972 did not put an end to armed struggle in that region of Mexico. As sporadic guerrilla strikes continued in Guerrero and a new *foco* was established under the leadership of another rural schoolteacher, Lucio Cabañas, other guerrilla bands were in the process of formation and training in various cities and rural areas throughout the republic. From 1969 through the early 1970s, terrorist attacks were registered against banks, government offices, right-wing newspapers, and other sites identified by guerrillas as symbols of the apparatus of repression and reaction. During these years, wealthy Mexican businessmen, politicians, and foreign diplomats became targets of a spate of kidnappings in which the hostages were generally held for a cash ransom, the promise of the release of political prisoners, and occasionally, the publication or broadcast of the guerrilla group's manifesto. These guerrillas were pursued and sometimes captured by the army and secret police, but for each arrest made, evidence of new activities by newly formed groups quickly emerged.

In analyzing the significance of these guerrilla activities, many leftists, both Mexican and foreign, found cause for optimism in what they viewed as the phoenix-like capacity of the guerrilla movement to rise again out of the ashes of earlier movements that had been suppressed. They pointed out that 20,000 infantrymen and two airborne companies had to be thrown into the effort to isolate and destroy Cabañas's guerrilla group before the Mexican government could claim to have "pacified" the state of Guerrero. This reading of the "success" of armed struggle is understandable in light of the frustration necessarily felt by leftists when they weighed the possibility of open political mobilization in the context of the co-optive/repressive system that exists in Mexico. Yet we should bear in mind that Guerrero, the principal setting for guerrilla activities, has a long history of endemic violence, both revolutionary, and more frequently, nonrevolutionary. While it would be inaccurate to characterize Lucio Cabañas's Party of the Poor as little more than the classic social bandit gang that typically flourishes in inaccessible, impoverished mountain redoubts like Guerrero's Sierra Madre del Sur,[42] neither would it be correct to see this guerrilla band as an incipient national liberation front, and Cabañas as another Ho Chi Minh.[43] Lucio Cabañas, like Jénaro Vázquez before him, succeeded in capturing the imagination and respect of dissident Mexicans. But their actions consisted of assaulting or kidnapping *symbols* of Mexico's power structure. In no case can it be said that the activities of the guerrillas genuinely undermined that power structure. Thus, although there was widespread identification with the heroism of these guerrilla fighters, and this identification gave their movements considerable impact beyond the borders of Guerrero, neither leader managed to build a mass movement. Indeed, no guerrilla group has managed thus far to formulate a coherent political program around which large-scale support of peasants, workers, and discontented intellectuals might coalesce.[44]

The experience of the Latin American guerrilla struggles of the 1960s showed that where such movements lack mass support, they were isolated and ultimately destroyed by the counterinsurgency force of the government, supported by American aid, advisers, and equipment. If any revolutionary movement is to come to power in Mexico, whether the seizure of power involves guerrilla activities in the mountains or the actions of political activists in the cities, its successful consolidation of control would ultimately depend on the existence of broad-based and durable organizations of peasants and workers, along with at least some middle-class support. The problem of mobilizing this kind of mass support in a system so effectively dominated by a hegemonic party is the central dilemma for which Mexicans of the left are currently struggling to pose new solutions.

New Labor Militance

Hopes for the construction of a broad-based mass movement in Mexico were strongly stimulated through the 1970s by the outbreak of successive waves of workers' militancy. Particularly in the capital-intensive, technologically advanced industrial sectors (automaking, steel, metallurgy, electrical products, machine tool manufacturing, and nuclear energy), various forms of militant activity developed.[45] In this period, tens of thousands of workers were politicized and mobilized in new, independent unions that refused to affiliate with the CTM. Previously nonunionized categories of the labor force—university professors and staff, doctors, researchers, technicians, and bank workers—were organized and struggled to win official recognition for their unions. In a number of highly visible cases, efforts were made to democratize the existing union structure and make it more responsive to the base. Even workers in small, relatively isolated enterprises organized initially around wage demands but quickly moved to demands for greater trade union democracy. In the course of the decade, hundreds of thousands of workers participated in strikes and mass demonstrations to protest their deteriorating economic condition and the oppressive control of the labor movement by the state.[46]

The upsurge of labor activity was stimulated in large measure by Echeverría's commitment, in the early years of his administration, to *apertura democrática.* In regard to the labor movement, this broad, vague program for democratization of the political system took the form of subtle encouragement (or, at least not active discouragement) of independent union mobilization.

As we have seen, such mobilization promised to provide a means to undermine the absolute authority of the CTM's Fidel Velázquez and dislodge him as head of the official labor sector, where the entrenched bureaucracy had become an obstacle to Echeverría's plans for renovation.

The outbreak of militant activity was also prompted by a rate of inflation which, by the mid-1970s, had reached a level never known in postwar Mexico. Inflation made it far more difficult for the official labor movement to play its customary role of holding down wage demands. Furthermore, as we have noted, the official party system suppresses, but it also controls through the delivery of at least some measure of the goods and services demanded by the base. The economic reversals of the 1970s meant that the leadership of the official labor movement had greater difficulty in meeting this crucial obligation. Thus the way was opened for more militant leadership to channel the discontent of the ever-growing number of workers dissatisfied with the rewards available through official networks.

Revolt from below. Since 1940, labor militance in Mexico has generally been expressed as a revolt from below. In one characteristic pattern, rank-and-file workers mobilize to remove their organization's *charro* leadership, that is, the corrupt union bosses who are imposed on the trade unions by the state. From the massive railroad strike of 1958 to the present, dissident workers have regularly emerged from the ranks to challenge the entrenched leadership of state-controlled organizations by presenting themselves as candidates for union office. Often these attempts to democratize the union and transform it into a genuinely combative instrument of workers' struggle have won broad support among the membership, and the *charros* have been turned out of office. Frequently, though, when an insurgent workers' movement of this kind has taken power in an open electoral contest, the government has countered by denying official recognition to the new democratic leadership. Confirmation of the electoral results by the Ministry of Labor is required for the union and its leaders to gain registration. Without this registration, negotiations cannot be conducted and contracts are not binding on management. Generally, then, the state has helped the official labor movement defeat the challenge of insurgency. Where militant grass-roots leaders have managed to take control of local and regional branches, the national organization may refuse to recognize the elections. And when the popularity of the militant local leaders is so strong that the national leadership is unable to withhold recognition, generally the impact of the movement for democracy in the union has been blunted by the lack of horizontal contacts among local branches in the hierarchically structured organization.

Typical of the fight for democracy through the renovation of an existing union structure is the process through which telephone workers have struggled to build a responsive and combative union. In 1976, the *telefonistas* organized wildcat strikes in forty cities across Mexico to press the government to force the *charro* leadership to allow free elections for the union executive. When open elections were held, 16,000 telephone workers voted overwhelmingly—86 percent—to replace the incumbents with a new and militant leadership group.[47]

In other state sectors, such as Pemex, the railroads, and the public schools, "democratic currents" emerged during the 1970s to challenge the policies of the union executive, or the legitimacy of the leadership itself. Insurgent oil workers demanded union recognition of the seniority rights of "temporary laborers," some of whom had fifteen years of service.[48] In twenty-four of thirty-six sections of the official railroad workers' union, insurgent groups occupied local headquarters and were dislodged only when the army took the union halls by force.[49] The struggle for democracy among teachers, who were organized—half a million strong—in the largest union in the country, was expressed in the formation of the Revolutionary Movement of Teachers. This renovating force managed to organize local wildcat strikes against López Portillo's austerity program, going beyond strict wage issues to challenge the cutbacks in education, and the closure of education facilities that austerity threatened to bring about. Finally, the concentration of miners and metal workers in only a few zones and the organization of these men by workplace rather than job category created conditions favorable to the growth of democratic currents at the local level in the Miners' and Metalworkers' Union. Major strikes at the Altos Hornos and Las Truchas steel works in 1975 and 1977 were indicative of the rise of a more militant leadership within this sector as well.[50]

New unions. A second pattern characteristic of these years of insurgency has been the formation of new unions among previously unorganized sectors of the workforce. Probably the most significant development of this kind was the unionization of university workers throughout the country in organizations that maintain their independence from the CTM and the official labor sector. The movement to organize university teachers, administrative staff, and manual laborers in a single unified body began at the National University in Mexico City. From 1973, manual workers and staff on the UNAM campus, most of whom had been politicized by their contact with the student movement, struck to win recognition for the union they had formed. By 1975 "academic personnel" had gained recognition for their new *sindicato* and by 1977 the two organizations had merged in the Union of Workers of the National University. Manual and intellectual workers now demanded recognition for this organization as the sole bargaining agent for all categories of university employees. The concept of a single unit for all university personnel spread to state universities throughout Mexico, and eventually developed into a struggle to win recognition for the National Union of University Workers—a prospect so threatening to the regime that López Portillo granted university workers virtually all the concessions they demanded in 1980 but denied official registration to their national organization.

The "Democratic Tendency." The third pattern that labor insurgency has typically taken is that of a jurisdictional dispute between or among several unions for the right to represent the workers in their industry. The classic example of a struggle for union democracy which has been played out in these terms is provided by the rivalry between the *oficialista* electricians' union, which is affiliated with the CTM and works in complete cooperation with the Federal Electricity Commission, and the militant Electrical Workers' Union of the Mexican Republic (Sindicato de Trabajadores Electricistas de la República Mexicana, or STERM), mobilized under leftist leadership with a program for combative defense of workers' interests. From its development in the 1960s, this radical union has stood at the forefront of labor struggle, articulating a clear "class position"; it argued that the state could pay its workers more if it spent less to provide cheap energy to private industry, thereby subsidizing foreign and domestic capitalists.

In the early 1970s, in the most optimistic and open period of Echeverría's *apertura democrática*, the renovating, democratizing forces among the electricians flourished in the atmosphere of benign neglect maintained by the new regime. A formal unity pact between the rival unions was promoted by the Federal Electricity Commission which brought the small left-wing STERM and the larger official union into a single organization (the Sindicato Unico de Trabajadores Electricistas de la República Mexicana, or SUTERM). However, when the government-sponsored merger broke down and the leftists were hounded from office by their conservative rivals, they signaled their determination to resist marginalization from the center of workers' strength and influence in their industry by refusing to form a new union. Instead, they underlined their claim to legitimate power within the SUTERM by calling themselves the Tendencia Democrática, that is, the "Democratic Tendency" of the SUTERM.[51] The electricians' formation of a democratic tendency was perhaps the most important development in the ongoing struggle for an autonomous labor movement. From 1972 to 1978, the *electricistas'* democratic current functioned as the vanguard of the insurgent union movement as the leaders of the Democratic Tendency gathered support from a broad coalition of unionists in their fight for reinstatement in the executive of SUTERM. But the significance of the Democratic Tendency activities is to be found not only in the massive demonstrations it mobilized,[52] the strikes it organized, or even the coalition it formally established in 1973, the Revolutionary Union Movement, an alliance of democratic university workers, teachers, telephonists, textile, steel, oil, railroad, and brewery workers. The greatest impact of the tendency was registered in the insurgency it stimulated in other unions and the genuinely radical program of change that it articulated. For in 1975, the electricians' Democratic Tendency met with other insurgent unionists to formulate a program, the Guadalajara Declaration, which made a variety of demands ranging from bread-and-butter, reformist demands to others that would require a total restructuring of the Mexican economic and political system. The declaration called for:

1. union independence and democracy
2. a general reorganization of the union movement
3. unionization of all salaried workers
4. across-the-board increases in salaries
5. automatic cost-of-living raises
6. defense and promotion of the social security system
7. popular and revolutionary education
8. housing, rent freezes, improved public transportation and municipal services for all workers
9. collectivization of agriculture, an end to latifundism, nationalization of agricultural credit and machinery
10. expropriation of imperialist companies
11. state control over foreign trade
12. international alliances of primary producers
13. workers' participation in the reorganization and planning of the state sector of the economy[53]

In the end, the Democratic Tendency was defeated when the Echeverría regime, under pressure from the right, began to crack down on labor activities. The leaders of the movement were fired from their jobs in the state industry and hundreds of members who had openly supported the Tendency were sacked as well. In reviewing this period, Antonio Gershenson, radical leader of the Nuclear Energy Workers, summarized the experience and pinpointed the dilemma confronting the workers' movement and the left in general: "Because there is no workers' party, the *Democratic Tendency* was forced to assume political tasks that should be the tasks of a political party and not of a trade union."[54] In fact the union insurgency of the 1970s developed almost entirely without contact or stimulation from the organized forces of the Mexican left.[55] Now that the parties of the left have been legalized and invigorated by the political reform, the way is opened for a much more concerted effort to democratize and transform the labor movement and the political system as a whole. Thus the need for a genuine mass party of the working class or for a new kind of relationship between the political parties and forces of the Left and the organized workers' movement is the conclusion most generally drawn from the experience of the Democratic Tendency.

New Options, New Tasks, and New Prospects for the Left

It can be argued that, despite the absence of labor representatives in de la Madrid's cabinet, the organized working class today enjoys greater influence than in any historical moment since Cárdenas left office in 1940. This new weight grows in part from the recent history of economic change and labor militance. It is also a result of the instability of the Mexican system produced by the economic crisis. The urgent need of the current regime to count upon the stabilizing role of organized labor and the containment of wage demands by labor leaders has enlarged the function of the unions in the political process. The unions, in turn, are well aware of their crucial importance in the implementation of the austerity program deemed necessary for the economic recovery of the country, and they have raised the price for their cooperation and participation in the system. The increase in pressure from the workers' organizations is understandable when we consider that labor accepted wage controls in the 1976–1977 crisis but never benefited from the rewards of the boom years. Now labor is demanding more than cost-of-living hikes to keep pace with inflation or government intervention to save jobs. Voices are currently raised within the labor movement, indeed even within the state-controlled, official party labor sector, calling for a fundamental restructuring of the economic system. In the midst of the present crisis, the more progressive elements within the CTM have adopted many of the demands that have long been posed by the left: demands for greater state control over the economy, closer regulation of prices, tax reform to redistribute wealth, retention by the state of all bank shares in strategic sectors of the economy, and overall, a more nationalist policy vis-à-vis foreign capital. The "class position" articulated in the 1960s and 1970s by the militant electricians' union—that the government could guarantee a living wage to workers if it did less to subsidize the capitalist class—has now been taken up not only by other workers in the state sector, but by unions representing workers in private industry as well. This, then, is a period of heightened consciousness and more militant expression of workers' interests in which even the CTM has begun to support positions once defined as radical.

The shift to the left in the official Mexican labor sector has been expressed in more than the adoption of the militant rhetoric of "class struggle." Under the challenge of insurgency, many of the old *charro* leaders have become more responsive to pressures from the base. Furthermore, the legalization of the Communist Party and the emergence of new parties of the left which claim to represent the authentic voice of the working class has prompted Fidel Velázquez, at the head of the CTM, to push the PRI toward positions more supportive of labor, insisting that the official party is, or "must once more become," the party of the workers.[56] And still another factor likely to move the official labor sector toward a more militant stance is the competition for leadership currently unfolding within the CTM. Velázquez has long surprised those who, for decades, have confidently predicted his imminent demise. But, at this writing, Velázquez is well into his eighties and it is certain that he will not exercise the leadership of the official labor sector much longer. Nor will he continue to perform the key role he has played for over forty years, mediating between the state and the organized working class. When he goes, the official labor movement will inevitably radicalize—at least in the short run—as rival political figures attempt to build a power base from which to launch their campaigns for CTM leadership, each pressing his claim to be the most effective and militant representative of labor interests.

Thus, for a variety of reasons the labor movement, as a whole, has been radicalized. However the shift to the left still leaves unresolved the problem we noted earlier, when considering the decline of the electricians' Democratic Tendency. A movement within organized labor, however successfully it may raise and pressure for a more democratic and responsive trade union, is not a political party and cannot carry out the mobilization effort ideally performed by a mass working-class party. A union movement cannot, in and of itself, broaden the base of support for change or even consolidate protest and struggles which arise in other, nonworking-class sectors. Furthermore the trade union struggles of the 1970s were limited to unions representing workers in the most advanced sectors of the economy. The better organized and better paid workers who enjoy greater job and social security were the groups which were conceded a measure of freedom to organize. This latitude was not permitted workers in the more backward sectors of the economy, not to speak of that part of the working class that remains nonunionized.[57] Thus, the further development of the workers' movement requires that some form of organization be constructed which is capable of carrying the struggle for democracy beyond the relatively privileged sector of the labor force to the popular masses as a whole.

The unions and the parties of the left. Perhaps the central question of this period is how, or in what manner the new organizational energies of the left which were released by the Political Reform will interact with the democratic currents within the labor movement. To the degree that the parties of the left can use their newfound legality to protect themselves from repression, they now enjoy wider opportunities to communicate, to mobilize, to organize the discontented and to coordinate their activities with forces within the insurgent union movement. In short, the Political Reform has stimulated the growth of parties of the left and virtually all of these new and rejuvenated organizations are dedicated, in one way or another, to establishing ties with the working class through the structure of organized trade unions. The Communist Party, in particular, has always had some links to the unions, and the revival and expansion of the party since the Reform and its alliance with other leftist groups within the framework of the PSUM, has provided the occasion to forge new links.

Thus the classic question of how to develop organic unity between the working class and the parties of the left has been reopened in a more urgent way. To be sure, the critical need for a "worker-peasant-student alliance" has always been regarded as an imperative by virtually every formation on the left in Mexico as elsewhere in the world. The difference is that now that imperative is being addressed with new ideas, new perspectives, and within the framework of a crisis. The flowering of Marxist thought in the last decade in Mexican universities and research centers has been part of this effort to pose the problems of popular mobilization in fresh terms. Some impetus has been provided as well by exiled Latin American intellectuals and activists who live and work in Mexico, having found refuge there from countries dominated by military dictatorships and other repressive regimes. Their presence has raised the level of debate and enabled the Mexican left to address the theoretical and practical tasks it faces stimulated by the reflections of the Brazilians, Argentines, Chileans, and others with concrete experience of peasant and labor mobilization.[58]

The overall issue, then, concerns the means available to the Mexican left to build the necessary links with the democratizing currents within the labor movement, and to mobilize the mass of workers and peasants who remain unorganized. This general problem can be framed in terms of a series of specific questions:

(1) Can the organized working class be won away from the official party system and the rewards it offers? By the 1980s the resources available to spread around for co-optive purposes are scanty. Thus, for the first time since the formation of the official party system, the capacity of the state to maintain its hold on the working class seems genuinely in doubt. And if the system cannot offer the best organized sectors of the working class the material benefits which in the past served to mollify labor demands, then some nonmaterial satisfactions—real union democracy, or greater participation and influence in the shaping of state policy—may have to be offered instead. The only other alternative would be massive repression.

(2) Has the experience with independent unionism been sufficiently broad, or will it become broad enough to provide the working class with an organized response should repression be applied as co-optive techniques break down? The state cannot put down *simultaneous* strikes and labor revolts in all critical sectors of the economy with the relative ease with which it once put down the railroad workers' movement. Given the small number of troops and their antiquated equipment, were a genuinely massive, unified, well-coordinated movement of militant unionists under independent leadership to develop, the repressive apparatus of the Mexican state would not be adequate to suppress such an outbreak, in view of the absolute size and complexity of the country. Thus far, none of the insurgent movements has succeeded in coordinating more than solidarity gestures for other unionists on strike, and even the most militant organizations seem a long way from carrying out a general strike. But the likelihood of mobilization on this scale clearly increases as the resources available to the state to satisfy labor demands dry up as a consequence of the fiscal crisis.

(3) Will the parties of the Left develop ways to reach and mobilize the growing number of Mexicans who are neither unionized workers nor *ejidatarios* organized by the CNC? The majority of Mexicans still remain outside any scheme of political mobilization, be it the official party system or independent, opposition formations. This mass includes the *minifundista* who toils on his tiny plot of land, living under the direct domination of local *caciques* whose power even the combined efforts of the state and official party have been inadequate to break. This mass also includes the younger sons and daughters of *ejidatarios* who historically have had no rights to land and no organiza-

tions which effectively articulate their interests, either within or outside of the official party system. Agricultural wage workers and the millions of Mexicans who migrate back and forth across the border with the United States likewise remain unrepresented by any political force, right, left, or center. Finally, the pattern of politics among urban slum dwellers indicates that their movements are readily "captured" by the PRI within the logic of a system of co-optation which rewards their most militantly pressed demands with limited benefits: transportation lines, electrification, potable water, sewerage lines, etc.[59] But the fall in oil revenues will make continued ad hoc handouts of this sort impossible to sustain. Thus the urban masses will more likely be ignored in the coming years by an official party system unable to meet even their limited, narrow demands for state services. Hence this sector, too, will grow increasingly restive and, as such, potentially open to organization by the left. In summary, then, the future democratization of the political system depends on whether the forces on the left will find ways to reach, organize, and give political voice and power to these marginalized masses. Realistically speaking, there is no single program or set of policies which would address so wide an assortment of social groups and their needs. But at least a sizable portion of these people will have to be drawn into a mass political organization of the left if the power of the PRI is to be challenged effectively. Democratization will also depend on whether it will prove possible to coordinate the organizational activities undertaken in various sectors and geographical regions of Mexico.

Some political activities of recent years give cause for optimism in this respect. The successes of the Communist Party and its noncommunist allies in mobilizing peasants in Guerrero, Oaxaca, and Chiapas provide a model of the kind of coordination that can be carried out even in the poorest, most isolated regions of the country where the power of local caciques is great. The presence, in these cases, of a clearly articulated ideological position has enabled rural organizations to escape the clientelistic/personalistic logic of "independent" peasant movements that are tied to charismatic individuals and which collapse when those leaders are co-opted or killed. In the case of groups recently mobilized by the PCM and its allies, the rural masses have the possibility of sustaining their militancy through commitment to a set of radical goals rather than individual leaders. The goals are linked to positions articulated by a coalition of parties of the left, and this coalition is sustained by the structure of a nationwide organization.

Recent years have also witnessed the emergence or reinforcement of a number of organizations dedicated specifically to the coordination of struggles on the left, including both workers' movements, peasant movements, and mobilizations among urban slum dwellers.[60] These "*coordinadoras*" have multiplied and have begun to provide the framework for at least a defensive response to repression by the state. The tendency to ally in this fashion has culminated, in the face of the economic crisis, with the formation of a *Frente contra la Austeridad*, the broadest based type of coalition which is attempting to act with some unity to protest the imposition of austerity on the masses. But the left faces a staggering challenge. Coalitions and coordinating bodies formed to oppose an austerity scheme or protest repression organize opposition in a purely negative sense. To mobilize for positive change will require a capacity to define an alternative path of development which holds out realistic promises to at least a significant proportion of those Mexicans who have suffered the costs and borne the burdens of capitalist development in Mexico. Defining a program for change is a task formidable enough in a country where oppositional political forces have long enjoyed full freedom to design and articulate alternative models. In a system like the Mexican, which is only just beginning to allow opposition forces a limited political role, the job of framing a program for genuine transformation is far more difficult. But if the parties of the left manage to formulate a project for change and build and sustain a sufficient degree of unity to press effectively for that model, the Mexican political and economic system will emerge totally reshaped from the current period of severe crisis.

ABBREVIATIONS

CANACINTRA	National Chamber of Consumer Goods Industries
CCI	Independent Peasant Central
CNC	National Peasant Confederation
CNOP	National Confederation of Popular Organizations
CNPA	National Coordinator of "Plan de Ayala"
CNTE	National Coordinator of Educational Workers
COCEI	Coalition of Isthmus Workers, Peasants, and Students
CONAMUP	National Coordinator of the Popular Urban Movement
CONASUPO	National Staple Products Company
CONCAMIN	National Confederation of Industrial Chambers
CONCANACO	National Confederation of Chambers of Commerce
COPARMEX	Confederation of Employers
COSINA	National Union Coordinator
CROM	Regional Confederation of Mexican Workers
CTM	Mexican Workers' Confederation
FNCR	National Front against Repression
INFONAVIT	Institute of the National Fund for Workers' Housing
IPN	National Polytechnic Institute
MAUS	Movement for Socialist Action and Unity
PAN	National Action Party
PCM	Mexican Communist Party
PDM	Mexican Democratic Party
PIDER	Program for Public Investment for Rural Development

PMT	Mexican Workers' Party
PNA	National Agrarian Party
PNR	National Revolutionary Party
PP	Party of the Poor
PPM	Party of the Mexican People
PPS	Popular Socialist Party
PRI	Institutional Revolutionary Party
PRM	Party of the Mexican Revolution
PRT	Revolutionary Workers' Party
PSR	Revolutionary Socialist Party
PST	Socialist Workers' Party
PSUM	Unified Mexican Socialist Party
SAM	Mexican Food System
STERM	Union of Electrical Workers of the Mexican Republic
STPRM	Union of Petroleum Workers of the Mexican Republic
SUTERM	Unified Union of Electrical Workers of the Mexican Republic
UGOCM	General Union of Workers and Peasants of Mexico
UIC	Communist Left Group
UNAM	National Autonomous University of Mexico
UNCTAD	United Nations Conference on Trade and Development

NOTES

PREFACE

1. See Robert E. Scott, *Mexican Government in Transition* (Urbana: University of Illinois Press, 1964); Robert E. Scott, "Mexico: The Established Revolution," in *Political Culture and Political Development*, edited by Lucian W. Pye and Sidney Verba (Princeton: Princeton University Press, 1965); and Samuel P. Huntington, *Political Order in Changing Societies* (New Haven: Yale University Press, 1968). By 1980 Scott had revised his analysis to deal with authoritarianism as a feature of the Mexican system. See Scott, "Politics in Mexico," in *Comparative Politics Today: A World View*, edited by Gabriel Almond and G. Bingham Powell (Boston: Little, Brown, 1980).

CHAPTER 1

1. José E. Iturriaga, *La Estructura Social y Cultural de México* (México, D. F.: Fondo de Cultura Económica, 1951), p. 33.

2. Charles C. Cumberland, *Mexico: The Struggle for Modernity* (New York: Oxford University Press, 1968), p. 233.

3. Clark W. Reynolds, *The Mexican Economy* (New Haven: Yale University Press, 1970), p. 24; Walter Goldfrank, "World System, State Structure, and the Onset of the Mexican Revolution," *Politics and Society* 5, no. 4, (1975), 431.

4. Raymond Vernon, *The Dilemma of Mexico's Development* (Cambridge: Harvard University Press, 1963), pp. 39, 42–43. "Attracted by opportunities in Mexico, United States investments rose from 200 million United States dollars in 1897 to about 1,100 million by 1911. The British increased their investments from $164 million in 1880 to over $300 million in 1911. . . ." See also Goldfrank, "World System," 430–431.

5. Barry Carr, "The Peculiarities of the Mexican North, 1880–1928: An Essay in Interpretation." Institute of Latin American Studies, University of Glasgow. Occasional Paper. No. 4, (1971), pp. 5–6.

6. Richard Roman, "Ideology and Class in the Mexican Revolution: A Study of the Convention and the Constitutional Congress." Ph.D. diss., University of California, Berkeley, 1973. p. 14.

7. Roger D. Hansen, *The Politics of Mexican Development* (Baltimore: The Johns Hopkins Press, 1971), p. 151.

8. Friedrich Katz, "Labor Conditions on Haciendas in Porfirian Mexico: Some Trends and Tendencies," *Hispanic American Historical Review* 54, no. 1 (February 1974), pp. 34–35. See also Katz, "Peasants in the Mexican Revolution of 1910," In *Forging Nations: A Comparative View of Rural Ferment and Re-*

volt, edited by Joseph Spielberg and Scott Whiteford (East Lansing, Michigan: State University Press, 1976).

9. Eric R. Wolf, *Peasant Wars of the Twentieth Century* (New York: Harper and Row, 1969), p. 31. "Among their leaders were women as well as men, *coronelas* as well as coronels."

10. Oscar Lewis, *Pedro Martínez* (New York: Vintage, 1967), pp. 89, 90, 108.

11. Wolf, *Peasant Wars,* pp. 37–38.

12. Ibid., p. 39.

13. Ibid.

14. Henry Bamford Parkes, *A History of Mexico* (London: Shenval Press, 1962), p. 290.

15. John Reed, *Insurgent Mexico* (New York: D. Appleton, 1914), p. 118. Reed later traveled to Russia, where his coverage of the Bolshevik Revolution won him international fame as the author of *Ten Days that Shook the World.*

16. Robert Quirk, *The Mexican Revolution 1914–1915* (Bloomington: University of Indiana Press, 1960), p. 224.

17. Reed, *Insurgent Mexico,* p. 127.

18. John Womack, Jr., *Zapata and the Mexican Revolution* (New York: Vintage, 1970), pp. 192–193.

19. Wolf, *Peasant Wars,* p. 36; Katz, "Agrarian Changes in Northern Mexico in the Period of *Villista* Rule, 1913–1915," in *Contemporary Mexico,* edited by James W. Wilke et al (Berkeley: University of California Press, 1976), pp. 270–271; Richard Tardanico, "Revolutionary Nationalism and State Building in Mexico, 1917–1924," *Politics and Society* 10, no. 1 (1980) 66–67.

20. Parkes, *History of Mexico,* p. 278.

21. Roman, "Ideology and Class," p. 20.

22. Parkes, *History of Mexico,* p. 280; Katz, *The Secret War in Mexico: Europe, The United States and The Mexican Revolution* (Chicago: University of Chicago Press, 1981), details the complexity and impact of foreign meddling in Mexican revolutionary politics by both private foreign interests and the government agents of Britain, Germany, and the United States. In this work Katz assesses "the influence of external pressures on the programs and policies of Mexico's revolution" (p. xi). Likewise, W. Dirk Raat, *Revoltosos: Mexico's Rebels in the United States, 1903–1923* (College Station: Texas A & M University Press, 1981), provides an analysis of the deradicalizing influence on the overall ideological direction of the revolution of active American collaboration with Mexican central authorities. The U.S. government cooperated first with Díaz and later Huerta and Carranza in the repression and physical elimination of the political and social radical elements—like the Flores Magon brothers—who had sought refuge in the United States. Raat argues that a system of suppression based on private detective agents and public forces changed the course of the revolution as the more radical groups were ruthlessly hunted on both sides of the border. See also Peter Calvert, *The Mexican Revolution, 1910–1914: The Diplomacy of Anglo-American Conflict* (Cambridge: Cambridge University Press, 1968).

23. Parks, *History of Mexico*, p. 281.

24. Ibid., p. 284.

25. In his revisionist study of Huerta, Meyer argues that the general was probably not a drug addict or an alcoholic, as he has generally been portrayed by historians, and that he may not have ordered the assassination of Madero and his vice president. But that he was viciously repressive there seems little doubt. See Michael C. Meyer, *Huerta: A Political Portrait* (Lincoln: University of Nebraska Press, 1972).

26. It is possible that only the war in Europe saved the Mexicans from a full-scale military intervention by U.S. troops. During the entire course of his incumbency, Woodrow Wilson was under heavy pressure from big businessmen with interests in Mexico. Railroad and oil interests, the great cattle barons like William Randolph Hearst, and scores of others immensely powerful men used all the influence they could muster to persuade Wilson to intervene in the revolution. But common sense prevailed, and even after the troops returned from Europe, Wilson preferred to pursue a policy that permitted him to maneuver from behind the scenes, pulling strings and imposing and lifting arms embargoes. Only toward the end of the revolution did Wilson give in and send General Pershing on a punitive expedition into northern Mexico.

27. Daniel Cosio Villegas, "The Mexican Left," in *The Politics of Change* edited by Joseph Maier and Richard W. Weatherhead (New York: Praeger, 1964), p. 127.

28. Cumberland, *Mexico: The Struggle*, pp. 250–253.

29. Ibid., p. 247.

30. Ibid., p. 248.

31. See Andre Gunder Frank, "Mexico: The Janus Faces of Twentieth Century Bourgeois Revolution," *Monthly Review* 14 no. 7 (November 1962), p. 374.

32. A very useful summary of the changing interpretations of historians on the class nature of the Mexican Revolution is provided in Gilbert M. Joseph, "Mexico's Popular Revolution: Mobilization and Myth in Yucatan, 1910–1940," *Latin American Perspectives* 6, no. 3 (Summer 1979), 46–50. In Spanish, perhaps the two most influential works in the recent analysis and reinterpretation of the revolution are Arnaldo Córdova, *La Ideologia de la Revolución Mexicana: La Formación del Nuevo Régimen* (México, D. F: Ediciones ERA, 1973) and Roger Bartra, *Estructura Agraria y Clases Sociales en México* (México, D. F.: Ediciones ERA, 1974).

33. The Mexican novelist Carlos Fuentes has vividly described both the decline and the economic, political, and social resurgence of the prerevolutionary aristocracy in his novel *Where the Air is Clear* (New York: Noonday Press, 1971). Both this novel and his later book *The Death of Artemio Cruz* (New York: Noonday Press, 1971) deal with the rise of a new industrial elite and ruling class whose wealth and power grew directly out of the revolution.

34. Jorge Carrión, "Retablo de la Política 'a la Mexicana'," in *El Milagro Mexicano*, edited by Fernando Carmona et al (Mexico City: Editorial Nestro Tiempo, 1970), pp. 174–175.

35. Hansen, *Politics of Development*, p. 37.

36. Reynolds, *The Mexican Economy*, p. 27.

37. William P. Glade, Jr., and Charles W. Anderson, *The Political Economy of Mexico* (Madison: University of Wisconsin Press, 1968), p. 87.

38. Frank, "Mexico: Janus Faces," pp. 383–384. On the emergence of the new bourgeoisie, see also Berta Lerner Sigal et al., *México: Realidad Política de Sus Partidos* (México, D. F.: Instituto Mexicano de Estudios Políticos, 1970), pp. 48–50; and Jorge Graciarena, *Poder y Clases Sociales en el Desarrollo de América Latina* (Buenos Aires: Editorial Paidos, 1967), pp. 161–163.

39. Parkes, *History of Mexico*, p. 296.

40. Gerrit Huizer, "Emiliano Zapata and the Peasant Guerrillas," in *Agrarian Problems and Peasant Movements in Latin America*, edited by Rodolfo Stavenhagen (Garden City: Doubleday, 1970), p. 385.

41. An *agrarista* is a person who sympathizes with or fights for the "agrarian cause," for the expropriation of large estates and the distribution of these properties among the landless peasantry.

42. Frank Tannenbaum, *The Mexican Agrarian Revolution* (New York: Macmillan, 1929), pp. 168–170.

43. Marjorie Ruth Clark, *Organized Labor in Mexico* (Chapel Hill: University of North Carolina Press, 1934), p. 27.

44. *Codificación de los Decretos del C. Venustiano Carranza* (México, D. F., 1915), p. 136.

45. Alvaro Obregón was so popular with certain sectors of the working class that when the general lost an arm in battle, the arm was brought in from the field, preserved in formaldehyde, and carried all over Mexico in a large glass container to be displayed as a kind of relic at union meetings.

46. For more information on the House of the Workers of the World, see Clark, *Organized Labor*, pp. 22–35; and Luís Araiza, *Historia de la Casa del Obrero Mundial* (México, D. F.: 1963).

47. Roman, "Ideology and Class," p. 42. Another thorough analysis of the convention delegates, debates, and resulting legislation is provided in E. V. Niemeyer, Jr., *Revolution at Querétaro: the Mexican Constitutional Convention of 1916–1917* (Austin: University of Texas Press, 1974).

48. Ibid., pp. 41–42.

49. Cumberland, *Mexico: The Struggle*, pp. 260–261.

50. Ibid., pp. 263–268.

51. Italics added. Article 123 of the Constitution of 1917. For translated excerpts of the constitution see Paul E. Sigmund, *Models of Political Change in Latin America* (New York: Praeger, 1970), pp. 11–15; Emilio Portes Gil, *Autobiografía de la Revolución Mexicana* (México, D. F.: Instituto Mexicana de Cultura, 1964), pp. 204–207.

52. Cumberland, *Mexico: The Struggle*; p. 268.

53. Italics added. Article 27 of the Constitution of 1917. See Sigmund, *Models of Change*, pp. 12–13.

54. See Victor Manzanilla Schaffer, *Reforma Agraria Mexicana* (Colima: Universidad de Colima, 1966), pp. 53–57; and Portes Gil, *Autobiografía,* pp. 201–204.

55. Carleton Beals, *Mexico: An Interpretation* (New York, 1923), p. 57.

56. Huizer, *Emiliano Zapata,* p. 394.

57. Emiliano Zapata, "Open Letter to Citizen Carranza," March 17, 1919, Morelos, Mexico; quoted in Rene Dumont, "Mexico: The 'Sabotage' of the Agrarian Reform," *New Left Review,* no. 17 (Winter 1962), 51. See also John Womack, Jr., *Zapata and the Revolution,* p. 319.

58. Notably in the states of Veracruz, Tamaulipas, Michoacán, Durango, México, and Yucatán. See Heather Fowler Salamini, *Agrarian Radicalism in Veracruz, 1920–1938* (Lincoln: University of Nebraska Press, 1978); Paul Friedrich, *Agrarian Revolt in a Mexican Village* (Englewood-Cliffs, N. J.: Prentice Hall, 1970); Frans J. Schryer, *The Rancheros of Pisaflores: The History of a Peasant Bourgeoisie in Twentieth-Century Mexico* (Toronto: University of Toronto Press, 1980); and Gilbert M. Joseph, "Revolution from Without: The Mexican Revolution in Yucatan, 1910–1940," in *Yucatan: A World Apart,* edited by Edward H. Moseley and Edward D. Terry (Tuscaloosa: University of Alabama Press, 1980).

59. Memorial addressed to His Grace the Archbishop of Durango by the Sindicato de Campesinos del Estado de Durango, September 1922. Quoted in Ernest Gruening, *Mexico and Its Heritage* (New York: The Century Company, 1928), pp. 217–218.

60. Ibid., pp. 218–219.

61. Katz, "Labor Conditions," p. 30. "There are also indications that the majority of *acasillados* [resident peons] never joined the Revolution. . . . [Among other reasons] the relative security which the *acasillados* enjoyed as well as the paternalism of the *hacendado* may have enhanced their sense of superiority, reinforcing their ties to the *hacienda.*"

62. Eric R. Wolf and Sidney W. Mintz, "Haciendas and Plantations in Middle America and the Antilles," *Social and Economic Studies,* 6, no. 3 (1957), 392–393.

63. Edmundo Flores, *Tratado de Economia Agrícola* (México, D. F.: Fondo de Cultura Económica, 1968), p. 338. In 1920 an estimated 54 million acres of land was held by North American individuals and companies in specific violation of prohibitions on foreign ownership set out in the Constitution of 1917.

64. Ibid., p. 338.

65. Salomón Eckstein, *El Ejido Colectivo en México* (México, D. F.: Fondo de Cultura Económica, 1967), p. 132.

66. Cosio Villegas, "The Mexican Left," pp. 128–129.

67. Ibid., p. 129.

68. For more detailed discussion of the values and goals of the northern dynasty, see Howard F. Cline, *The United States and Mexico* (New York: Atheneum, 1965), pp. 193–194.

69. Interview with Sr. J. Cruz Chacón, reported in Sergio Alcántara Ferrer, *La Organización Colectivista Ejidal en la Comarca Lagunera* (México, D. F.: Centro de Investigaciones Agrarias, 1967), pp. 20–25.

70. Manzanilla Schaffer, *Reforma Agraria Mexicana*.

71. Lerner Sigal, *México: Realidad Política*, pp. 52–53.

72. Obregón's middle-class background and personal qualities of flexibility which, we noted earlier, were central to his success as a military leader in the armed phase of the revolution, continued to count heavily in his efforts to consolidate political power in the postrevolutionary period. Tardanico, asserts,

Obregón and his Sonoran clique were well suited to the task of revolutionary state making. While oriented toward the values of private property and free enterprise, they were, above all, political opportunists, who flexibly adapted their power-claiming strategies to changing circumstances. Such pragmatism reflected the Sonorans' backgrounds as upward-striving members of the middle stratum in what Barry Carr describes as the incessant mobility and absence of tradition of Mexico's northwestern frontier society. Moreover, frontier conditions, as Carr observes, were responsible for the Sonorans' mass-mobilizing skills. For these reasons, Obregón and his partners had proved quite successful in organizing and leading the revolutionary armed forces; gaining control of the nascent state apparatus was simply the next step in their quest for wealth, status, and power (*Revolutionary Nationalism*, p. 77). See also Carr, *Pecularities of the North*.

73. L. Vincent Padgett, *The Mexican Political System* (Boston: Houghton Mifflin Company, 1966), p. 48.

74. Ibid., p. 49.

75. The most important parties and political movements into the PNR at this time were the Liberal Constitutional Party, the National Cooperativist Party, the Mexican Labor Party, The Mexican Communist Party, the Mexican Agrarian Party, the Socialist Party of the Southeast (centered in Yúcatán), and the Frontier Socialist Party (centered in Tamaulipas). Lerner Sigal, op. cit., p. 53n.

76. Padgett, *The Mexican Political System*, p. 49.

CHAPTER 2

1. Robert E. Scott, *Mexican Government in Transition* (Urbana: University of Illinois Press, 1964), pp. 116–117.

2. William Cameron Townsend, *Lázaro Cárdenas, Mexican Democrat* (Ann Arbor: George Wahr, 1952), pp. 56–58.

3. Anatol Shulgovsky, *México en la Encrucijada de su Historia* (México, D. F.: Fondo de Cultura Popular, 1968), p. 78.

4. Shulgovsky, *México en la Encrucijada*, p. 78. Calles's failure to formulate policy designed to cope with the needs of lower-class Mexicans was particularly problematic given the disastrous impact of the Depression of 1929 on peasants and workers. Statistics outlining the effect of the Depression on all

sectors of the Mexican economy can be found in Arnaldo Córdova, *La Politica de las Masas del Cardenismo* (México, D. F.: Ediciones Era, 1974), pp. 17–19.

5. Shulgovsky, *México en la Encrucijada*, p. 82.

6. Ibid. Also see Córdova, *La Politica de las Masas*, pp. 41–42.

7. Joe C. Ashby, *Organized Labor and the Mexican Revolution* (Chapel Hill: University of North Carolina Press, 1967), pp. 26–27.

8. Quoted in Verna Carleton Millan, *Mexico Reborn* (Boston: Houghton Mifflin, 1939), p. 94.

9. Ashby, *Organized Labor*, p. 26.

10. Raymond Vernon, *The Dilemma of Mexico's Development* (Cambridge: Harvard University Press, 1963), p. 71; Gerrit Huizer, "Peasant Organization and Agrarian Reform in Mexico," In *Masses in Latin America*, edited by Irving Louis Horowitz (New York: Oxford University Press, 1970), p. 469; Victor Alba, *Historia del Movimiento Obrero en América Latina* (México, D. F.: Libreros Mexicanos Unidos, 1964), p. 447; Nathaniel and Sylvia Weyl, *The Reconquest of Mexico: The Years of Lázaro Cárdenas* (New York: Oxford University Press, 1939), pp. 237–239.

11. Secretaría de Gobernación, *Seis Años de Servicio al Gobierno de México* (México, D. F.: La Nacional Impresora, 1940), pp. 95–96. According to Lieuwen, the workers' militia was eventually to become a determining force in Cárdenas's efforts to ward off a right-wing military coup. "On May Day, 1938, a newly organized and uniformed workers' militia, 100,000 strong, paraded en masse through the streets of the capital. Prior to the parade, Cárdenas had warned in a speech that if reactionary forces in the army revolted, they would be obliged to fight these proletarian defenders of his regime." Edwin Lieuwen, *Mexican Militarism: The Political Rise and Fall of the Revolutionary Army, 1910–1940* (Albuquerque: University of New Mexico Press, 1968), p. 127.

12. Confederación de Trabajadores de Mexico, *Informe del Comité Nacional* (México, D. F.; 1936–1937), p. 65.

13. Adalberto Tejeda in Veracruz, Saturnino Cedillo and Gonzalo N. Santos in San Luis Potosí, Emilio Portes Gil in Tamaulipas, Pedro Rodríguez Triana in the Laguna region, and others.

14. For example, the League of Agrarian Communities of Veracruz, a group of 40,000 armed peasants loyal to and controlled by Adalberto Tejeda, was one of the prime targets of the "unification" effort which preceded the formation by Cárdenas of the new peasant confederation. See Moises González Navarro, *La Confederación Nacional Campesina* (México, D. F.: Costa-Amic, 1968), pp. 134–141; and Emilio Portes Gil, *Autobiografía*, pp. 706–711.

15. Ashby, *Organized Labor*, pp. 33–34, 41.

16. Ministry of Foreign Relations, *The Mexican Government: Tour of the President*, p. 11, cited in Ashby, *Organized Labor*, p. 33.

17. Cárdenas's Fourteen Point Program, Monterrey, Feb. 11, 1936. Cited in Ibid., p. 34.

18. Arnaldo Cordova, *La Ideologia de la Revolución Mexicana: La Formación del Nuevo Regimen* (México, D.F.: Ediciones ERA, 1973), pp. 177–178.

19. Ibid.

20. State-owned development banks established under Cárdenas (the Banco Nacional de Crédito Ejidal, founded in 1935, and the Banco Nacional de Comercio Exterior, founded in 1937) along with other state banks which expanded their role during his administration, played a key part in the promotion and especially in the orientation of economic development in Mexico. Furthermore, the creation of these banking institutions was consistent with a policy of fostering "a private enterprise system in which the state role would complement, rather than supplant, that of private capital." Nora Louise Hamilton, "Mexico: The Limits of State Autonomy," *Latin American Perspectives*, 2, no. 2 (Spring 1975), 96.

21. Córdova, *La Ideologia de la Revolución*, p. 182. "That the Revolution recognized the collaboration of the capitalist class in the progress of Mexico was a principle accepted since the period of armed struggle. It formed part of the revolutionary ideology. Cárdenas said to a group of capitalists in May 1939, 'I cordially invite you to cooperate in the work of national reconstruction. . . . I value your knowledge, your experience and your entrepreneurial spirit; I see you as prominent factors of progress and proponents of our country's culture.' "

22. Albert L. Michaels, "The Crisis of Cardenismo," *Journal of Latin American Studies*, 2, no. 1, (May 1970), 59.

23. Michaels, "The Crisis of Cardenismo," pp. 53, 55, 70–72, 74.

24. The Mexican Right grew steadily more powerful during the Cárdenas years, financially supported in Mexico, as in virtually all Latin American countries, by the European fascist movements. In the mid-1930s the national press was heavily subsidized by German agents and was correspondingly sympathetic to the Nazi cause. The Mexican Sinanarchist movement modeled itself after the Spanish falange, and its influence throughout Mexico grew during this period. When Cárdenas came to power, large numbers of fascist sympathizers were holding office in the Chamber of Deputies—a fact reflected by the passage of immigration quotas excluding Jews. In 1937 and 1938 right-wing extremists burned property in Mexico City alleged to belong to Jews. See Nathan L. Whetten, *Rural Mexico* (New York: The Century Company, 1948), pp. 484–522; Weyl, *The Reconquest of Mexico*, pp. 353–366; and Friedrich Katz, ed. *Hitler sobre América Latina: El Fascismo Alemán en Latinoamérica, 1933–1943* (México, D.F.: Fondo de Cultura Popular, 1968), pp. 42–48.

25. Vernon, *Dilemma of Mexico's Development*, p. 70; L. Vincent Padgett, *The Mexican Political System* (Boston: Houghton Mifflin Company, 1966), p. 111; Robert J. Alexander, *Communism in Latin America* (New Brunswick: Rutgers University Press, 1957), p. 336; Betty Kirk, *Covering the Mexican Front* (Norman: University of Oklahoma Press, 1948), pp. 48, 86.

26. D. Scott, *Government in Transition*, p. 131.

27. Ibid.

28. Frank R. Brandenburg, *The Making of Modern Mexico* (Englewood Cliffs, N.J.: Prentice-Hall, 1964), p. 83.

29. Ibid.

30. Ibid.

31. Notably, the General Workers Confederation (Confederación General de

Trabajadores) plus one wing of the divided CROM and independent electricians and miners unions. Scott, *Government in Transition*, p. 132.

32. Padgett, *Mexican Political System*, p. 93.

33. Ibid.; Howard Handelman, "The Politics of Labor Protest in Mexico," *Journal of Interamerican Studies and World Affairs* 18, no. 3 (August 1976), pp. 269–270.

34. For example, in 1947 Lombardo Toledano left the organization he had helped to establish to form a new Marxist-oriented Popular Party with its own peasant and labor confederation, the General Union of Workers and Peasants of Mexico (Unión General de Obreros y Campesinos de México, or UGOCM).

35. Padgett, *Mexican Political System*, p. 99.

36. Susan Kaufman Purcell, *The Mexican Profit-Sharing Decision: Politics in an Authoritarian Regime* (Berkeley: University of California Press, 1975), p. 23.

37. Howard Handelman, "Politics of Labor Protest," p. 270.

38. Larissa Lomnitz, "Horizontal and Vertical Relations and the Social Structure of Urban Mexico," *Latin American Research Review* 17 no. 2 (1982) 57.

39. Padgett, *Mexican Political System*, p. 99.

40. See Roger D. Hansen, *The Politics of Mexican Development* (Baltimore: The Johns Hopkins Press, 1971), p. 116. ". . . the political weakness of labor vis-à-vis the government is also reflected by a wage structure that fluctuates more in accord with political factors than with economic ones." Purcell, *Mexican Profit-Sharing*, p. 23.

41. Evelyn P. Stevens, *Protest and Response in Mexico* (Cambridge, Mass.: MIT Press, 1974), pp. 103–104.

42. Ibid., p. 104; also see Handelman, "Politics of Labor Protest."

43. Robert J. Alexander, *Organized Labor in Latin America* (New York: The Free Press, 1965), p. 195.

44. The traditional relationship between landlord and peon has often been called a "patron-client" relationship. Characteristic of this relationship are arrangements whereby the peasant receives a tiny parcel of land to work for his family's subsistence in return for rendering services to the landlord. The peasant may be obliged to repay the landlord in cash by yielding a portion of his crop to the landlord, by paying rent for the land, or by farming a portion of the landlord's property for him. Typically, the peasant is also obliged to pledge his loyalty to the landlord and to support him in any political conflict that arises. The essential nature of the patron-client relationship is that it is formed by unequal parties: the peasant needs what the landlord provides, but the landlord does not need the services of any particular peasant because there are always other landless peasants ready to establish a patron-client relationship with the landlord. See John Duncan Powell, *Peasant Society and Clientelist Politics* (Cambridge, Mass.: Center for International Affairs, 1967), p. 5.

45. A *minifundista* is a peasant who owns a plot of land too small to provide for his family or to require the participation of all family members who are available to contribute their labor.

46. A *colono* is a peasant settled by the government on newly opened territory.

47. An *ejidatario* is a peasant who has received from the government a grant of land in a peasant community called an *ejido*. "The word *ejido* is derived from the Latin verb *exire, exitum,* 'to go out,' 'the way out.' As originally used in Spain, the term was applied to uncultivated land held collectively and located on the outskirts 'on the way out' of agrarian communities. In Mexico the word is used to refer to all types of land which have been restored to agricultural communities under the land reform initiated in 1915. By extension, the word is also used to designate the communities possessing such lands." Elyer N. Simpson, *The Ejido: Mexico's Way Out* (Chapel Hill: University of North Carolina Press, 1937), p. vii.

48. Gerrit Huizer, *The Role of Peasant Organizations in the Process of Agrarian Reform in Latin America* (Washington, D.C.: Inter-American Committee for Agricultural Development, 1968), p. 17.

49. On the "mentality" engendered in government officials by the *sexenio* system, that is, the six-year term of office followed by a clean sweep of personnel, see Merilee Serrill Grindle, *Bureaucrats, Politicians and Peasants in Mexico: A Case Study in Public Policy* (Berkeley: University of California Press, 1977), chapter 3; and Peter H. Smith, *Labyrinths of Power: Political Recruitment in Twentieth-Century Mexico* (Princeton: Princeton University Press, 1979).

50. For example, one of the obligations of the CNC State Leagues, according to the statutes of the organization is "to socially and politically orient the peasants in such a way that they invariably act in conformity with the national directives." Estatutos de la Confederación Nacional Campesina, Article 60, V. The model of the CNC as a mechanism for control rather than the articulation of demands is developed at length in an earlier study. See Judith Adler, "The Politics of Land Reform in Mexico" M.Ph. thesis, London School of Economics, 1970.

51. Leiuwen, *Mexican Militarism,* p. 85.

52. Ibid., pp. 119–120.

53. Cárdenas, quoted in Leiuwen, *Mexican Militarism,* p. 124.

54. "The present restrictions [against voting] which practically isolate the military from political life . . . are a grave error. . . . Henceforth the members of the army will have, constitutionally, political rights and the duty to exercise them" (Ibid.).

55. Cárdenas, quoted in Townsend, *Lázaro Cárdenas,* p. 216.

56. Scott, *Government in Transition,* p. 131.

57. Pablo González Casanova, *Democracy in Mexico* (New York: Oxford University Press, 1972), pp. 37–38.

58. Vernon, *Dilemma of Mexico's Development,* p. 74.

59. Padgett, *Mexican Political System,* p. 124.

60. Kenneth F. Johnson, *Mexican Democracy: A Critical View* (Boston: Allyn and Bacon, 1971), p. 67.

61. Evelyn P. Stevens, "Mexico's PRI: Institutionalization of Corporatism," in *Authoritarianism and Corporatism in Latin America*, edited by James M. Malloy (Pittsburgh: University of Pittsburgh Press, 1977), p. 241.

62. Scott, *Government in Transition*, pp. 169–170; Padgett, *Mexican Political System*, p. 123; Johnson, *Mexican Democracy*, p. 67.

63. Kevin J. Middlebrook, "Political Change in Mexico," in *Mexico-United States Relations*, edited by Susan Kaufman Purcell (New York: Praeger, 1981), p. 64.

64. Frank R. Brandenburg, "Mexico: An Experiment in One Party Democracy," Ph.D. dissertation, University of Pennsylvania, 1955, p. 188. More recent confirmation of these trends is provided by Smith, *Labyrinths of Power*, pp. 226–239.

65. Smith, *Labyrinths of Power*, p. 228.

66. González Casanova, *Democracy in Mexico*, p. 55.

67. José Luis Ceceña, *El Capital Monopolista y La Economía de México* (México, D.F.: Cuardernos Americanos, 1963), cited in González Casanova, *Democracy in Mexico*, pp. 49–50. Also see Richard S. Newfarmer and Willard F. Mueller, *Multinational Corporations in Brazil and Mexico: Structural Sources of Economic and Noneconomic Power* (Washington, D.C.: U.S. Government Printing Office, 1975), pp. 45–94.

68. Gonzales Casánova, *Democracy in Mexico*, p. 50.

69. Stevens, *Mexico's PRI*, p. 235.

70. Gonzales Casánova, *Democracy in Mexico*, p. 52.

71. Ibid.

72. John F. H. Purcell and Susan Kaufman Purcell, "Mexican Business and Public Policy," in *Authoritarianism and Corporatism in Latin America*, edited by James M. Malloy (Pittsburgh: University of Pittsburgh Press, 1977), p. 193. Lomnitz also notes:

> According to 1978 financial statements of the one hundred largest corporations in Mexico, twenty-nine decentralized state-owned corporations owned 68.3 percent of the total capital. More significantly,. among the fifty largest corporations with total assets of 2.3 billion pesos, seventeen large state-owned concerns controlled . . . 71.5 percent of the assets.

These state corporations include the state oil company, the national power commission, the telephone company, the national airlines, the national steel company, the Mexican federal reserve bank, the national finance corporation, and a variety of other financial organizations (Lomnitz, *Social Structure of Urban Mexico*, pp. 61–62).

73. Purcell, *Mexican Profit-Sharing*, p. 30.

74. Purcell and Purcell, Business and Public Policy, p. 193.

75. Lomnitz, *Social Structure of Urban Mexico*, p. 62.

76. Purcell, *Mexican Profit-Sharing*, p. 30, citing Clark W. Reynolds, *The Mexican Economy* (New Haven: Yale University Press, 1970), p. 186.

77. Purcell and Purcell, *Business and Public Policy*, p. 221.

78. Ibid.

79. Smith, *Labyrinths of Power*, p. 82.

80. Ibid., pp. 91–92.

81. Ibid., pp. 183–184.

82. Ibid., p. 201.

83. Ibid., p. 213. Stevens, *Mexico's PRI*, p. 237, provides a contrasting view:

Evidence of cordial relationships between business leaders and Party leaders has continued to accumulate. The social activities pages of Mexico's newspapers chronicle in news stories and pictures the delicate and complex process of cross-fertilizing loyalties through the ritual ties of *compadrazgo*, intermarriage, and secular festivities among Mexico's economic and political elites.

Both Smith's and Stevens's portrayals of these relationships or lack of relationships—seem to be based largely on anecdotal evidence. Smith, for example, writes: "Well-informed Mexicans have repeatedly told me that there is relatively little intermarriage between the two sectors: economic and political leaders do not, as a rule, strike alliances through the matching of their daughters and sons" (p. 213).

84. Ibid., pp. 202, 213. On the background of politicians also see Roderic Ai Camp, *Mexican Political Biographies, 1935–1975* (Tucson: University of Arizona Press, 1976) and Camp, "The National School of Economics and Public Life in Mexico," *Latin American Research Review* 10, no. 3 (Fall 1975).

85. Ibid., p. 215. Smith writes, ". . . the processes of political recruitment in Mexico may well have tended to foster the articulation of a relatively autonomous 'state interest.' "

86. Ibid. Weinert shares Smith's view and attempts to explain what he identifies as a peculiar "anomaly" of the Mexican system:

Although the business elite have obviously benefited enormously from state policies, they share a distaste and disdain for politicians. . . . An explanation might be that the Mexican business elite have received benefits without having to ally themselves politically with the State. The benefits were conferred by the State to further its own goal of maximizing control over the economy. The business elite and the State are therefore not as close as the coincidence of class interest and state policies would suggest (Richard S. Weinert, "The State and Foreign Capital," in *Authoritarianism in Mexico*, edited by José Luis Reyna and Richard S. Weinert [Philadelphia: Institute for the Study of Human Issues, 1977], p. 126.)

87.

In Mexico, the dominant [segment of the bourgeoisie] appears to be comprised of those individuals and families who control the so-called economic groups. These groups consist of industrial firms (often vertically integrated), commercial houses, financial institutions (in many cases integrated into powerful "financial groups"), and, sometimes, transportation firms, mines, or other economic firms, which are related through common ownership and interlocking directorates. Ownership of the firm in each economic group is generally concentrated in an "investment group" consisting of one or a few families or business associates, sometimes interrelated by marriage. (Nora Hamilton, *The Limits of State Autonomy: Post-Revolutionary Mexico* [Princeton: Princeton University Press, 1982], p. 33.)

88. Ibid., p. 34.

89. The term "revolutionary family" was probably first used by Brandenburg, *Making of Modern Mexico*, pp. 3–7.

90. Joseph C. Goulden, "Mexico: PRI's False Front Democracy," Alicia Patterson Fund Reprint, December 1966, p. 7.

91. Ibid.

92. Political leaders in Mexico often describe this process as "auscultation." Auscultation is really a medical technique in which the doctor uses a stethoscope to listen to sounds within the human body in order to detect those sounds which provide clues for a diagnosis. In Mexico, the term is used to describe the way the president listens for indications of the health of the body politic. In a way, auscultation is similar to a public opinion poll in which the only opinions that are registered are those of "opinion makers"—political bosses, the leaders of influential sectors of society, etc. (Jaime Plenn, *The News* [Mexico, D.F., January 3, 1969], p. 5).

93. Hansen, *Politics of Development*, p. 111.

94. Peter Lord, *The Peasantry as an Emerging Political Factor in Mexico, Bolivia and Venezuela* (Madison, Wisconsin: The Land Tenure Center, 1965), p. 25.

CHAPTER 3

1. Banco de Mexico, S.A., Departamento de Estudios Económicos, 1980.

2. In real terms.

3. Melvin J. Ulmer, "Who's Making It in Mexico?" *The New Republic*, September 25, 1971, p. 21.

4. Fernando Carmona et al., *El Milagro Mexicano* (Mexico, D.F.: Editorial Nuestro Tiempo, 1970), p. 20.

5. Ulmer, "Who's Making It?" p. 21.

6. Agriculture grew at about 5 percent per annum and industry at about 7 percent which added up to a gross domestic product growth rate fluctuating narrowly around 6 percent—"which as a *sustained* growth record must be almost unequalled in the post-war third world." E. V. K. FitzGerald, "The State and Capital Accumulation in Mexico," *Journal of Latin American Studies* 10, no. 2 (November 1978), 264.

7. Roger D. Hansen, *The Politics of Mexican Development* (Baltimore: The Johns Hopkins Press, 1971), p. 41.

8. *La Economia Mexicana en Cifras* (México, D.F.: Nacional Financiera, 1970).

9. Hansen, *Politics of Development*, p. 1.

10. David Barkin, "The Persistence of Poverty in Mexico: Some Explanatory

Hypotheses," paper delivered to the Latin American Studies Association, Washington, D.C., April 1970.

11. Ibid.

12. Hansen, *Politics of Development*, p. 3.

13. See Diego G. López Rosado and Juan F. Noyola Vásquez, "Los Salarios Reales en México, 1939–1950," *El Trimestre Económico* 18, no. 2, (abril/junio 1951). Ifigenia de Navarrete, "Income Distribution in Mexico," in *The Recent Development of Mexico's Economy* edited by Enrique Pérez López, (Austin: University of Texas Press, 1967). Figures on wage controls and consumer price index for the 1970s can be found in James L. Schlaghenck, "The Political, Economic and Labor Climate in Mexico," The Wharton School, University of Pennsylania, Multinational Industrial Relations Series no. 4, 1980.

14. Hansen, *Politics of Development*, p. 50. For example in 1979 workers' wages equaled only 15 percent of the gross product from manufacturing. See the discussion on this and other income indicators in Pablo González Casanova, "Economic Development in Mexico," *Scientific American* 243, no. 3 (September 1980), p. 196.

15. Banco Nacional de Comercio Exterior, *Informe*, September 1980; Euromoney, *Mexico: A Survey*. London, March 1981, p. 4; also see González Casanova, "Economic Development in Mexico," p. 202.

16. United States Agency for International Development, *A Review of Alliance for Progress Goals* (Washington, D.C.: U.S. Government Printing Office, 1969), p. 62. "In the late 1960s, Mexico ranked sixty-sixth of seventy-two countries in terms of the ratio of tax revenues to GNP—with 9.9 percent." See Robert E. Looney, *Mexico's Economy: A Policy Analysis with Forecasts to 1990* (Boulder, Colo.: Westview Press, 1978), p. 49. Looney cites figures from Jorge R. Lotz and Elliot R. Morss, "Measuring Tax Efforts in Developing Countries." International Monetary Fund Staff Papers no. 14, 1967.

17. International Advisory Services, "Intelligence Digest," Special Report no. 51, April 29, 1981, pp. 1–4. Sumiko Kusida, "Mexico Special Report: Growing Dependence," *South*, July 1981, p. 44. *Latin America Weekly Report* (WR-79-03), November 16, 1979, p. 32 notes that Mexico's rate of return on investment in 1978 was the highest in all of Latin America.

18. The proportion of government revenue raised by income tax was only 13 percent in 1980. "La Cuenta Publica 1980," *Comercio Exterior*, September 1980, p. 979. Looney links Mexico's low level of tax revenue to what he identifies as a highly problematic tendency of the Mexican government to resort to deficit financing. See Looney, *Policy Analysis with Forecasts*, p. 26. "The tax system had strong regressive features, and tax enforcement was inadequate. Furthermore, the low tax rates that resulted from this situation necessarily reduced the potential of fiscal policies and incentives and discouraged the efficient use of available economic and financial resources" (Ibid., p. 45). "In large part the authorities used the tax system as a means of providing incentives to investment rather than as a major source of revenues" (pp. 55–56).

19. Pablo González Casanova, *Democracy in Mexico* (New York Oxford University Press, 1970), p. 139.

20. According to Green, U.S. banks are the most important single source of external financing for the Mexican government. The six leaders in the field are Citibank, Chase Manhattan, Bank of America, Manufacturers Hanover Trust, Chemical Bank, and Morgan Guaranty Trust Company. Maria del Rosario Green, "Mexico's Economic Dependence," in *Mexico-United States Relations*, edited by Susan Kaufman Purcell (New York: Praeger, 1981), p. 111.

21. Ibid., p. 106.

22. Ibid., p. 107.

23. Ibid. FitzGerald's study confirms Green's evaluation: "Mexican investment relied upon the progressive skewing of the income distribution away from wages towards profits on the one hand and the progressively greater reliance on foreign finance, particularly in the form of official borrowing abroad, on the other" ("State and Capital Accumulation," p. 274).

24. Hansen, *Politics of Development*, pp. 48–49. Also see Rafael Izquierdo, "Protectionism in Mexico," in *Public Policy and Private Enterprise in Mexico*, edited by Raymond Vernon. Cambridge: Harvard University Press, 1964, pp. 243–289; and Adriaan Ten Kate and Robert Bruce Wallace, *Protectionism and Economic Development in Mexico* (New York: St. Martin's Press, 1980).

25. Barkin, "Persistence of Poverty", p. 10.

26. Hansen, *Politics of Development*, p. 49.

27. Barkin, "Persistence of Poverty," p. 8. Clark W. Reynolds, *The Mexican Economy* (New Haven: Yale University Press, 1970). Looney, *Policy Analysis with Forecasts*, pp. 27–42.

28. Barkin, "Persistence of Poverty," p. 10. See also International Advisory Services, "Intelligence Digest," pp. 2–3.

29. Preliminary results of a study of the psychology of Mexican businessmen, carried out by psychologists and psychiatrists of the Instituto Mexicano de Psicoanálisis, tend to confirm the existence of highly ambivalent feelings toward collaboration with American capitalists. The study, which included the analysis of the dreams of Mexican enterpreneurs, suggested that even among Mexicans whose business interests are strongly linked and intertwined with business interests of American capitalists, it is common to find overwhelming feelings of fear and repugnance for their foreign partners.

30. North American Congress on Latin America, *Mexico 1968: A Study of Domination and Repression* (New York: NACLA, 1968), p. 29.

31. Harvey Levenstein, "A Lesson in Foreign Control from Mexico," *Toronto Star*, April 4, 1973, p. 8.

32. Ibid.

33. North American Congress on Latin America, *Yanqui Dollar* (New York: NACLA, 1971), p. 29.

34. Ibid.

35. Ibid., p. 29. *Business in Latin America*, August 12, 1971, p. 250. On the "contradictions" of mexicanization policy from the point of view of Mexican development, see Douglas Bennett and Kenneth E. Sharpe, "El Control de las Multinacionales: Las Contradicciones de la Mexicanización," *Foro Internacional* 21, no. 4 (abril/junio 1981).

36. Carlos Fuentes, *The Death of Artemio Cruz* (New York: Noonday, 1971), pp. 20–21. See also pp. 53, 80, 111, 135.

37. Lawrence Rout, "Latin Labyrinth," *Wall Street Journal*, February 16, 1982. Rout notes that competition among foreign firms for reliable *prestanombres* became so fierce in the 1980s that "consultant" firms sprang up to match foreign investors with willing Mexican "partners." However, given the fraudulent nature of the activity in which all parties were engaged, it seems unsurprising that Rout would find, "The problem is that many of these consultants aren't legitimate. They charge thousands of dollars and don't do anything. Others simply disappear."

38. NACLA, *Yanqui Dollar*, p. 29; International Advisory Services, "Intelligence Digest," pp. 1–4; "Mexico has both imposed tough restrictions on foreign capital and attracted most of the foreign capital it has desired. Evidently, the most important determinants of capital flows are not the presence or absence of restrictions. . . . Rather, such fundamental factors as size, resources, economic potential, and political stability far outweigh the presence or absence of restrictive policies." Richard S. Weinert, "Foreign Capital in Mexico," in Purcell, *Mexico-U.S. Relations*, p. 121.

39. *Journal of Commerce*, April 26, 1971.

40. Weinert, "Foreign Capital in Mexico," p. 117.

41. Kusida, "Mexico Special Report," p. 44.

42. NACLA, *Domination and Repression*, p. 25. See figures for the 1970s and projections to 1985 in Gary Clyde Hufbauer, W. N. Harrell Smith IV, and Frank G. Vukmanic, "Bilateral Trade Relations," in Purcell, *Mexico-U.S. Relations*, pp. 136–145.

43. Between 1946 and 1965 the U.S. Export-Import Bank loaned Mexico $862 million at 12.6 percent interest. This loan, on which $108 million in interest was paid, was specifically earmarked for the purchase of U.S.-made machinery and equipment. Since 1945 this same bank loaned $270 million to finance the purchase of American equipment for the Mexican railways. Ibid., p. 26.

44. Barkin, "Persistence of Poverty," pp. 12–13. A hair-raising account of the consequences of the rush to buy foreign-made industrial equipment is provided by Leo Fenster, "At Twice the Price: The Mexican Auto Swindle," *The Nation*, June 2, 1970. In this article Fenster indicates that the new and expensive capital equipment supplied to the Mexican auto industry by American, British, French, Italian, German, and Japanese parent firms is, in fact, obsolete by advanced industrial standards.

45. René Villarreal, "The Policy of Import-Substituting Industrialization," in *Authoritarianism in Mexico*, edited by José Luis Reyna and Richard S. Weinert (Philadelphia: Institute for the Study of Human Issues, 1977), p. 76.

46. See Fernando Fajnzylber and Trinidad Martínez Tarrago, *Las Empresas Transnacionales: Expansión a Nivel Mundial y Proyección en la Industria Mexicana* (México: D.F.: Fondo de Cultura Económica, 1976); and Rhys Jenkins, "Transnational Corporations and their Impact on the Mexican Economy,"

NOTES TO PAGES 70–72 | 271

University of East Anglia, Development Studies Discussion Paper no. 43 (February 1979), pp. 30–31.

47. Weinert, "Foreign Capital in Mexico," p. 119.

48. Saul Trejo Reyes, "El Incremento de la Producción y el Empleo Industrial en México, 1950–1965," Demografía y Economía 4, no. 1 (1970), pp. 102–120.

49. Heberto Castillo, "El Programa de Energía Lava Conciencias," Proceso no. 215 (15 diciembre 1980), p. 28.

50. David Gordon, "Mexico: A Survey," The Economist, April 22, 1978, p. 26.

51. Schlaghenck, "The Political, Economic and Labor Climate," p. 165. Some sources cite figures as high as one million new entrants each year. See George Philip, "Mexican Oil and Gas: The Politics of a New Resource," International Affairs (Summer 1980), 477. Fixing the exact number of jobs needed at 800,000 or a million seems a somewhat questionable exercise since the Mexican economy, in any event, does not show signs of providing anywhere near that number of jobs in the short or medium run. In terms of actual performance, rather than projections, Mexican industry absorbed a total of 258,000 workers in 1965–1970, and 104,000 in 1970–1975. Latin America Economic Review 5, no. 18 (May 13, 1977).

52. James Flanigan, "North of the Border—Who Needs Whom?" Forbes, April 15, 1977, p. 37.

53. Rodolfo de la Torre, "Primeros Resultados del Censo, Razones 14 (July 1980), pp. 33–38.

54. Philip Russell, Mexico in Transition (Austin: Colorado River Press, 1977), p. 96.

55. David Barkin, "Education and Class Structure: The Dynamics of Social Control in Mexico," Politics and Society 5, no. 2 (1975), p. 193.

56. Barkin, "Persistence of Poverty," pp. 11–12.

57. Hansen, Politics of Development, pp. 43–45.

58. Barkin, "Persistence of Poverty," p. 7.

59. Ibid., p. 9.

60. Hansen, Politics of Development, p. 85.

61. "La Cuenta de la Hacienda Publica Federal 1980." Summary table in Francisco Carrada-Bravo, Oil, Money, and the Mexican Economy: A Macroeconometric Analysis (Boulder, Colo: Westview Press, 1982), p. 43. See also Statistical Abstract of Latin America, edited by James W. Wilkie and Stephen Haber (Los Angeles: UCLA Latin American Center Publications, University of California, 1981), pp. 638–643.

62. "Mexico was in this respect well below Latin American countries such as Cuba (100 percent coverage), Uruguay (97 percent), Chile (72 percent), Argentina (66 percent), Panama (41 percent), Peru (36 percent), and Costa Rica (32 percent)." Carmelo Mesa-Lago, "Social Security Stratification and Inequality in Mexico," in Contemporary Mexico, edited by James W. Wilkie et al. (Berkeley: University of California Press, 1976), p. 238. As we note in chapter 7,

the proportion of the population covered by social security rose slowly through the 1970s until roughly one-third was officially listed as benefiting from this system.

63. FitzGerald, "State and Capital Accumulation," p. 278.

64. For a discussion of the use of these terms in preference to "dependency," see James Caporaso, "Introduction: Dependence and Dependency in the Global System," *International Organization* 32, no. 1 (Winter 1978).

65. Richard S. Weinert, "The State and Foreign Capital," in Reyna and Weinert, *Authoritarianism in Mexico*, p. 116.

66. Pablo González Casanova, "The Economic Development of Mexico," *Scientific American* 243, no. 3 (September 1980), p. 200.

67. Fernando Fajnzylber, "Las Empresas Transnacionales y el Sistema Industrial de México," *El Trimestre Economico* 42, no. 4, (octubre/diciembre 1975), pp. 909–910.

68. González Casanova, "Economic Development of Mexico," 1980, p. 200.

69. Kusida, "Mexico Special Report," p. 44; Green, "Mexico's Economic Dependence," p. 110. See also Menno Vellinga, *Economic Development and the Dynamics of Class: Industrialization, Power and Control in Monterrey, Mexico,* (Assen, Neth: Van Gorcum, 1979), pp. 27–30.

70. González Casanova, "Economic Development of Mexico," p. 196.

71. Kusida, "Mexico Special Report," p. 44.

72. Clark Reynolds, "The Structure of the Economic Relationship," in Purcell, *Mexico-U.S. Relations*, p. 126.

73. To paraphrase Rosa Luxemburg, "Reform or Revolution," *Rosa Luxemburg Speaks* (New York: Pathfinder Press, 1977), p. 76.

74. George W. Grayson, "The Mexican Oil Boom," in Purcell, *Mexico-U.S. Relations*, pp. 146–147.

75. Grayson underscores the problem of obtaining reliable figures from a politically motivated government bureaucracy. See George W. Grayson, "Oil and U.S.-Mexican Relations," *Journal of Interamerican Studies and World Affairs* 21, no. 4 (November 1979), p. 431; Grayson, *The Politics of Mexican Oil* (Pittsburgh: University of Pittsburgh Press, 1980), pp. 71–73; and Grayson, "Oil and U.S.-Mexican Relations," p. 147. Philips notes that the discoveries were first hushed up to forestall an inflationary trend, and then broadcast widely to assist in the recovery from an economic slump in 1976. See George Philips, "Mexican Oil and Gas: The Politics of a New Resource," *International Affairs* (Summer 1980), p. 478.

76. George W. Grayson, "Oil and Politics in Mexico," *Current History* 80, no. 469 (November 1981), pp. 379–380.

77. Hugh O'Shaughnessy and Reginald Whitaker, *Financial Times of London.* Reprinted in the *Globe & Mail* (Toronto), January 28, 1980.

78. David J. Newton, "Mexico—The West's Latest Oil Well," *The World Today* 36, no. 7 (July 1980), p. 281.

79. Grayson, "Oil and U.S.-Mexican Relations," pp. 427–428.

80. Grayson, *Politics of Mexican Oil*, p. 24.

81. James Flanigan, "Why Won't the Mexicans Sell Us More Oil?" *Forbes*, October 29, 1979, p. 42.

82. On export substitution see Réne Villarreal and Rocio de Villarreal, "Mexico's Development Strategy," in Purcell, *Mexico-U.S. Relations*, pp. 98–100; and Sam Lanfranco, "Mexican Oil, Export-led Development and Agricultural Neglect," *Journal of Economic Development* 6, no. 1 (July 1981), pp. 125–151. See also Ignacio Cabrera, "Crisis Económica y Estrategia Petrolera en México," *Cuadernos Políticos* no. 28 (abril/junio 1981).

83. James H. Street, "Mexico's Economic Development Plan," *Current History* 80, no. 469 (November 1981), p. 376.

84. Ibid., pp. 376–377; Secretaria de Patrimonio y Fomento Industrial, *Plan Nacional de Desarrollo Industrial, 1979–1982*, México, D.F., 1979.

85. Flanigan, "Why Won't Mexicans Sell?", p. 46.

86. James Flanigan, "Pemex to Brown & Root: Yankee Come In," *Forbes*, August 15, 1977. Flanigan noted that even British Petroleum had to turn to Brown & Root for know-how adequate to meet the challenges of North Sea exploration and drilling.

87. Grayson, "Oil and U.S.-Mexican Relations," p. 430.

88. Laura Randall, "The Political Economy of Mexican Oil." Paper presented to the Santiago Conference on International Factors in Energy, Santiago, Chile, November 1979, p. 18.

89. Ibid., Roberto Gutierrez R., "La Balanza Petrolera de México, 1970–1982," *Comercio Exterior* 29, no. 8 (August 1979).

90. J. Antonio Pahnke, *Oil, Gas and Petrochemicals in Mexico, 1977–1982*, 2nd ed., (Mexico City: Commercial Division, Canadian Embassy, 1978), p. 20.

91. Grayson, "Mexican Oil Boom," p. 151.

92. *Latin America Weekly Report* 80, no. 47, November 28, 1980, p. 1.

93. Sofía Méndez Villarreal, *South*, July 1981, p. 45. Actual earnings from oil came to $311 million in 1976, $1 billion in 1978, $2.48 billion in 1979, $10.4 billion in 1980, and $18 billion in 1981. Oil enabled an economy which was floundering in the mid-1970s to increase its gross domestic product by 8 percent in 1979 and 7.4 percent in 1980. Grayson, "Oil and Politics," pp. 379–380; *Latin America Weekly Report* 81, no. 19, May 15, 1981, p. 3. Banco de México, December 1979.

94. In 1980 the value of manufactured imports from the United States was 12.6 billion while the value of Mexico's exported manufactures was only $3.4 billion. Grayson, "Oil and Politics," p. 380.

95. Ibid.

96. Lanfranco, "Mexican Oil, Export-led Development," p. 139.

97. Instituto Mexicano de Petróleo, *México y el Panorama Petrolero y Petroquímico Internacional*, México, D.F.: 1982, cited in *Latin America Weekly Report* 82, no. 6, February 5, 1982, p. 4.

98. David Morawetz, "Import Substitution, Employment and Foreign Exchange in Colombia," in *The Choice of Technology in Developing Countries: Some Cautionary Tales* edited by C. Peter Timmer et al. (Cambridge: Harvard

University Center for International Studies, 1975). Cited in John S. Evans and Dilmus D. James, "Conditions of Employment and Income Distribution in Mexico as Incentives for Mexican Migration to the United States: Prospects to the End of the Century," *International Migration Review* 13, no. 1 (1979), p. 14.

99. John G. Corbett, "Agricultural Modernization and Rural Employment in Mexico, 1980–1985: Implications for Mexican Migration to the United States." Paper presented to the XLIII International Congress of Americanists, Vancouver, August 1979, p. 18; *Unomásuno* (Mexico City), 13 abril, 1978, p. 13.

100. Randall, "Political Economy of Mexican Oil," p. 20. Randall argues that it would be better to pay a cash grant to firms settling in the new industrial zones rather than give them a discount on fuel, "because the present form of the subsidy (cheap hydrocarbon and electric power prices) leads to misallocation of resources by making capital intensive development cheaper than labor intensive development." p. 22.

101. Street, "Mexico's Development Plan," p. 376. See Secretaria de Patrimonó y Fomento Industrial. *Plan Nacional de Desarrollo Industrial, 1979–82*. México, D.F., 1979.

102. Grayson, *Politics of Mexican Oil*, 1980, p. 79.

103. Francisco Iracheta, World Bank biologist. Quoted Ibid. Citing *Excelsior* and *Proceso*, Grayson notes that while Pemex spends less than 1 percent of its development budget on environmental projects, irreparable damage has been done to marine spawning grounds, and the shrimp population of Campeche, once an important source of livelihood in that poor region, is all but extinct.

104. Since the mid-1970s Indians in Tabasco have resisted the intrusion of exploration and drilling crews. Chontales Indians have taken up arms against oil workers and construction crews and have blocked the access roads to wells near Villahermosa in protest against Pemex's failure to pay indemnities for damages to arable land and other property. Grayson, *Politics of Mexican Oil*, p. 75.

105. Corbett, "Agricultural Modernization and Rural Employment," p. 9.

106. Randall, "Political Economy of Mexican Oil," p. 12. Edward J. Williams, "Petroleum and Political Change in Mexico," in *Mexico's Political Economy: Challenges at Home and Abroad* edited by Jorge I. Dominguez, (Beverly Hills: Sage Publications, 1982), p. 47.

107. The population of Villahermosa, Tabasco, grew from 50,000 to 300,000 between 1976 and 1979. Randall, "Political Economy of Mexican Oil," pp. 12–13. On the social impact of the oil boom on the Southeast, see Leopoldo Allub and M. A. Michael, "Petróleo y Cambio Social en el Sureste de México," *Foro Internacional* 18, no. 4 (1978), pp. 691–709.

108. William A. Orme, Jr., "Ex-Pemex Chief's Ouster from Senate Sought," *Journal of Commerce*, October 20, 1982.

109. *Latin America Economic Report* 6, no. 45 (November 17, 1978), p. 354. On the "pervasive corruption and ineffective bureaucracy of Pemex," see Grayson, *Politics of Mexican Oil*, p. xvii; Grayson, "The Mexican Oil Boom," p. 155; Randall, "Political Economy of Mexican Oil," p. 16.

110. Grayson, *The Politics of Mexican Oil*, pp. 93–94.

111. *Unomásuno, Excelsior,* and *Proceso* are the periodicals which have focused on this issue. For detailed summary in English see Grayson, *The Politics of Mexican Oil*, pp. 93–102.

112. Orme, "Ex-Pemex Chief's Ouster"; Martha M. Hamilton and Merrill Brown, "Charge of Oil Payoffs to Mexico Probed," *Washington Post*, May 4, 1982.

113. Judith Adler Hellman, "Mexico in the Age of Petropesos," *Queen's Quarterly* 87, no. 2 (Summer 1980), p. 245.

114. Judith Adler, "The Politics of Land Reform in Mexico." M. Phil. thesis, London School of Economics, 1970. p. 90; Paul Nathan, "México en la Epoca de Cárdenas," *Problemas Agrícolas e Industriales de México*, 7, no. 3 (1955), p. 26; also see Nathaniel and Sylvia Weyl, *The Reconquest of Mexico: The Years of Lázaro Cárdenas* (New York: Oxford University Press, 1939), pp. 279–281.

115. Rodolfo Stavenhagen, "Social Aspects of Agrarian Structure in Mexico," In *Agrarian Problems and Peasant Movements* edited by Stavenhagen (Garden City: Doubleday, 1970), pp. 225–227.

116. The organization of the Laguna *ejidos* into collectives was only partially the result of Cárdenas's preference for collective forms of farming. It should be noted that the Laguna region became a principal site of land distribution under Cárdenas precisely because it had over the previous 30–35 years been the scene of a continuous political struggle for land, and the home of a large number and variety of socialist- and communist-led peasant leagues, unions, syndicates, and the like. These leftist *agraristas* played an important part in pressuring for collective forms of agricultural exploitation.

117. Shlomo Eckstein, "Collective Farming in Mexico," in *Agrarian Problems and Peasant Movements*, edited by Stavenhagen, p. 276.

118. Liga de Agrónomos Socialistas, *El Colectivismo Agrario en México: La Comarca Lagunera* (México, D.F.: Editorial Cultura, 1940), pp. 133–36. Salomón Eckstein, *El Ejido Colectivo en México* (México, D.F.: Fondo de Cultura Económica, 1967), p. 140; Eckstein, "Collective Farming in Mexico" pp. 292–294; Juan Ballesteros Porta, *¿Explotación Individual o Colectiva?: El Caso de los Ejidos de Tlahualilo* (México, D.F.: Centro de Investigaciones Agrarias, 1964), p. 46.

119. Ballesteros Porta, *¿Explotación Individual o Colectiva?* p. 46.

120. Eckstein, "Collective Farming in Mexico," pp. 277–281.

121. Ibid.; Nathan L. Whetten, *Rural Mexico* (New York: The Century Company, 1948), pp. 220–224.

122. Whetten, *Rural Mexico*, pp. 221–222.

123. Ibid.

124. The Decree of October 6, 1937.

125. Landowners were generally compensated for their land in government bonds, and for their capital goods (wells, pumps, etc.) in cash.

126. Jesús Silva Herzog, *El Agrarismo Mexicano y la Reforma Agraria* (México, D.F.: Fondo de Cultura Económica, 1959), p. 453.

127. Friedrich Katz, *Hitler sobre América Latina: El Facismo Alemán en Latinoamérica, 1933–1943* (México, D.F.: Fondo de Cultura Popular, 1968), pp. 42–48.

128. Vicente Lombardo Toledano, "Los Intentos de Revisión del Marxismo durante la Guerra," in *La CTAL ante la Guerra y ante la Post-Guerra* (México, D.F.: CTAL, 1945), pp. 65–80.

129. Manuel Avila Camacho, *Unidad Nacional: Pensamiento Político del Señor General de División Manuel Ávila Camacho, Presidente Constitucional de Los Estados Unidos Mexicanos* (México, D.F.: 1945), pp. 157–58.

130. *Compendio Estadístico*, Departmento Agrario, México, D.F., 1948.

131. Frank R. Brandenburg, *The Making of Modern Mexico* (Englewood Cliffs: Prentice-Hall, 1964), pp. 102–103.

132. Raymond Vernon, *The Dilemma of Mexico's Development* (Cambridge: Harvard University Press, 1963), pp. 102–103.

133. Ibid. See also Hansen, *Politics of Development*, p. 81.

134. Alemán's revision provided for legal holdings of 100 hectares (247 acres) of irrigated land, 200 hectares (494 acres) of seasonal rainfall land, 400 hectares (1,976 acres) of pasture land, and 800 hectares (3,952 acres) of arid mountain land. In addition, special exceptions to this formula were made to stimulate the production of certain cash crops. So-called small private properties given over to the cultivation of cotton were permitted to reach a legal 370 acres of prime irrigated land, while the limits on irrigated land devoted to bananas, sugar cane, henequen, vanilla, rubber, olives, cocoa, and fruit trees were revised upward to 740 acres.

135. Eckstein, "El Ejido Colectivo," pp. 146–47.

136. Even during the second half of the Cárdenas regime, an agrarian law was introduced which favored private commercial farmers over landless peasants and *ejidatarios*. The Law of Livestock Development issued 1 March 1937, declared unaffectable as much cattle land as was needed for the breeding of five hundred head of cattle or the equivalent in small livestock. The law intended to stimulate investments by cattle owners who, fearful of expropriation, had ceased to make further investments in cattle. In fact, the law stimulated neolatifundism, as large landowners stimulated cattle breeding on a large scale to protect illegally held large properties, some of which exceed 50,000 acres.

137. Edmundo Flores, *Tratado de Economía Agrícola* (México, D.F.: Fondo de Cultura Económica, 1968), p. 311.

138. François Chevalier, "The Ejido and Political Stability in Mexico," in *The Politics of Conformity in Latin America*, edited by Claudio Veliz (New York: Oxford University Press, 1967), p. 175.

139. Adler, "Politics of Land Reform," pp. 167–185.

140. Hansen, *Politics of Development*, p. 81.

141. Ibid.

142. Ibid.

143. Ibid.

144. Chevalier, "The Ejido and Political Stability," p. 179.

145. To the extent that the government brought a small number of

ejidatarios into the original green revolution program, the results were not happy for the peasants involved. Under the program, *ejidatarios* were forced to invest heavily in chemical and mechanical inputs, and the resulting increases in productivity did not cover the money laid out for equipment, wells, insecticide, fertilizer, etc. See Cynthia Hewitt de Alcántara, *Modernizing Mexican Agriculture: Socioeconomic Implications of Technological Change, 1940–1970* (Geneva: United Nations Research Institute for Social Development, 1976); and Hewitt de Alcántara "The 'Green Revolution' as History: The Mexican Experience," *Development and Change* 5, no. 2 (1973–1974).

146. Marc Edelman notes that stagnation in basic grain production was largely the consequence "of the capitalist sector's taking advantage of more profitable investment opportunities in the production and processing of luxury vegetable and fruit crops which are consumed by affluent Mexicans and North Americans." See Marc Edelman, "Agricultural Modernization in Smallholding Areas of Mexico: A Case Study in the Sierra Norte de Puebla," *Latin American Perspectives* 7, no. 4 (Fall 1980), p. 32. Changing diet as an aspect of the "modernization process" in Mexico was also noted by Corbett: "Changing patterns in consumer preferences also affect total demand . . . promotional efforts and higher incomes are shifting food consumption away from the traditional diet in favor of dietary styles prevalent in more industrialized countries. One aspect of this change is a greater emphasis on processed and "junk" foods, even where these are considerably more expensive than traditional or unprocessed items (p. 5). Corbett also points to a growing preference for animal protein reflected in a 6.7 percent annual increase in the demand for beef which has led, in turn, to conversion of land used for corn, beans, and wheat to livestock and poultry feed. Corbett, "Agricultural Modernization and Rural Employment," pp. 5–6. On this point see also Ruth Rama and Raúl Vigorito, *El Complejo de Frutas y Legumbres en México* (México, D.F.: Editorial Nueva Imagen, 1974). Also see Ernest Feder, *Strawberry Imperialism: An Enquiry into the Mechanisms of Dependency in Mexican Agriculture* (México, D.F.: Editorial Campesina, 1977); Feder, "Capitalism's Last-ditch Effort to Save Underdeveloped Agricultures: International Agribusiness, the World Bank and the Rural Poor," *Journal of Contemporary Asia* 7, no. 1 (1977), pp. 56–78; and Ruben Mújica Vélez, "Subempleo y Crisis Agraria: Las Opciones Agropecuarias," *Comercio Exterior* 27, no. 2 (1977), p. 1311.

147. Hewitt de Alcántara, *Modernizing Mexican Agriculture*, p. 53.

148. Edwin J. Wellhausen, "The Agriculture of Mexico," *Scientific American* 235, no. 3 (September 1976), p. 129.

149. *Razones* 7 (20 abril 1980), p. 3, cited in Richard L. Harris and David Barkin, "The Political Economy of Mexico in the Eighties," *Latin American Perspectives* 9, no. 1 (winter 1982), p. 5.

150. Street, "Mexico's Economic Development Plan," p. 375.

151. Banco Nacional de Mexico, *Review of the Economic Situation in Mexico* 57, no. 662 (January 1981), p. 9. Cited in Salvatore Bizzarro, "Mexico's Poor," *Current History* 80, no. 469 (November 1981), p. 372.

152. Banamex, *Examen de la Situación Económica de México* 55, (1979), p. 34.

153. Cynthia Hewitt de Alcántara, "Land Reform, Livelihood, and Power in Rural Mexico," In *Environment, Society and Rural Change in Latin America,* edited by D. A. Preston (New York: John Wiley & Sons, 1980), p. 33. Hewitt notes that the annual rate of growth of the agricultural product declined from a healthy 4.6 percent in 1942–1964 to a low of .2 percent in the 1970s.

154. Edelman, "Agricultural Modernization," p. 32.

155. Ibid.

156. Stavenhagen, "Social Aspects of Agrarian Structure," p. 251. Other studies that demonstrated the high productive capacity of ejidal and minifundist agriculture include: Salomón Eckstein, *El Marco Macroeconómico del Problema Agrario Mexicano* (México, D.F.: Centro de Investigaciones Agrarias, 1968); Sergio Reyes Osorio, "El Desarrollo Polarizado de la Agricultura Mexicana," *Comercio Exterior* 19 (March 1969); Hansen, *Politics of Development,* pp. 60–64.

157. Stavenhagen, "Social Aspects of Agrarian Structure," pp. 250–251.

158. Michael Redclift, "Agrarian Populism in Mexico—the 'Via Campesina,'" *Journal of Peasant Studies* 7, no. 4 (July 1980), pp. 494–498. See also Gustavo Esteva, "La Agricultura en México de 1950–1975: el fracaso de una falsa analogía," *Comercio Exterior* 25, no. 12 (December 1975); Esteva "En Pos de una Historia que Nunca Existió," *Comercio Exterior* 28, no. 11 (November 1978); and Arturo Warman, "El Problema del Campo," in *México, Hoy* edited by Pablo González Casanova and Enrique Florescano (México, D. F.: Siglo Veintiuno Editores, 1979), pp. 113–115.

159. Edelman, "Agricultural Modernization," p. 30.

160. Ibid. Also see Luisa Paré, "Inter-ethnic and Class Relations (Sierra Norte region; state of Puebla)," in *Race and Class in Post-colonial Society,* edited by John Rex. (Paris: UNESCO, 1977).

161. Nora Hamilton, "Introduction: Peasants, Capital Penetration and Class Structure in Rural Latin America," *Latin American Perspectives* 7, no. 4 (Fall 1980), p. 3.

162. *Comercio Exterior* 30, no. 3 (March 1980), pp. 200–202.

163. John J. Bailey, "Agrarian Reform in Mexico: The Quest for Self-Sufficiency," *Current History* 80, no. 469 (November 1981), pp. 359–360. Also see John Bailey and John Link, "Statecraft and Agriculture in Mexico: Domestic and Foreign Policy Considerations." Program in United States-Mexican Studies, University of California, San Diego, Working Paper in U.S.-Mexican Studies, no. 23, 1981; and Michael R. Redclift, "Development Policymaking in Mexico: The Sistema Alimentario Mexicano (SAM)." Program in United States-Mexican Studies; University of California, San Diego. Working paper in U.S.-Mexican Studies, no. 24, 1981.

164. Bolivar Hernández, "Las Contras del SAM," *Unomásuno* (Mexico City) 8 diciembre 1980. *Latin American Weekly Report* 81, no. 44 (November 6, 1981), p. 9.

165. Chevalier, "The Ejido and Political Stability", p. 167.

166. See Rodolfo Stavenhagen et al., *Neolatinfundismo y Explotación: De*

Emiliano Zapata a Anderson Clayton & Co. (México, D. F.: Editorial Nuestro Tiempo, 1968).

167. Hewitt de Alcántara, *Modernizing Mexican Agriculture*, p. 314.

168. Chevalier, "The Ejido and Political Stability," p. 189.

169. Ibid.

170. *Latin America Economic Report*, 7, no. 12 (March 16, 1979), p. 87. Estimates of foreign, mostly American, control of this sector run as high as 75 percent of industrial food production plants and 25 percent of all crops. Victor Bernal Sahagun, Instituto de Investigaciones Económicas, UNAM. Cited in Laurie Becklund and Robert Montemayor, "Land Reform: The Revolution that Failed," *Los Angeles Times*, July 15, 1979, p. 23.

171. Bailey, "Quest for Self Sufficiency," p. 360.

172. *Latin America Weekly Report* 81, no. 44 (November 6, 1981), p. 9. "The Ley de Fomento Agropequario reflects the bureaucracy's deep seated distrust of the peasantry. Local management committees *(comités directivos)* which are to be set up to administer the plans, will be organized by officials from the agriculture ministry and at least five other government bodies; those who work the land may be represented only at the invitation of ministry officials." *Latin American Weekly Report* 80, no. 47 (November 28, 1980), p. 7.

173. Hewitt de Alcántara, "Land Reform, Livelihood, and Power," p. 35.

174. Harris and Barkin, "Political Economy of Mexico in the Eighties," p. 7; Heberto Castillo, "Nunca los Pobres han estado Mejor," *Proceso*, no. 215, 15 diciembre, 1980, pp. 32–33; Sergio de la Peña, "Proletarian Power and State Monopoly Capitalism in Mexico," *Latin American Perspectives* 9, no. 1 (Winter 1982), pp. 31–33.

CHAPTER 4

1. David Felix, "Income Inequality in Mexico," *Current History* 72, no. 425 (March 1977), p. 112.

2. Pablo González Casanova, "The Economic Development of Mexico," *Scientific American* 243, no. 3 (September 1980), p. 202. The steady increase in the gap between rich and poor is shown by these data which express the income of the wealthiest 5 percent of Mexicans as a multiple of the income of the poorest 10 percent:

1958—22 times higher
1970—39 times higher
1977—50 times higher
1980—52 times higher

Expressed another way, we can say that the best-off 20 percent of Mexicans receive 60 percent of the national income while the poorest receive less than 3 percent.

3. Alan Riding, "The Mixed Blessing of Mexico's Oil," *New York Times Magazine*, January 11, 1981, p. 58. "Some industrialists have added homes in

New York or California or Padre Island, Texas, to their mansions in Mexico City, their rural haciendas and their villas by the beach—and, of course they've bought executive jets to fly between them."

4. González Casanova, "Economic Development of Mexico," p. 202.

5. Ibid.

6. Felix, "Income Inequality in Mexico," p. 113.

7. Centro de Investigaciones Agrarias, Estructura Agraria y Desarrollo Agrícola en México (México, D. F.: Fondo de Cultura Económica, 1979), p. 193. This study, completed in the early 1970s, is the most recent comprehensive survey of rural conditions, agriculture, and peasant life available, even in 1982.

8. Ibid.

9. Ibid.

10. Ibid.

11. Ibid.

12. Arthur Murphy and Henry Selby, "The City of Oaxaca," University of Texas—Institute of Latin American Studies, Indeco Working Paper no. 3, 1978.

13. Excelsior (Mexico City), November 30, 1971, pp. 1, 22. A study of employment carried out by the government Department of Hydraulic Resources in the 1970s indicated that 67 percent of the economically active population receive less than the minimum wage. Latin American Profile, CENCOS 1 Estructura Agraria 1973, p. 21.

14. Centro de Investigaciones Agrarias, Estructura Agraria, pp. 396–397. According to the 1960 census, in all of Mexico there were only 54,000 tractors and about three million handplows. By 1968 the number of tractors had increased to 70,000, but these were concentrated in the hands of large commercial producers. See R. S. Abercrombie, "Mecanización Agrícola y Ocupación en América Latina" in La Lucha de Clases en el Campo, edited by Ernest Feder (México, D. F.: Fondo de Cultura Económica, 1975), p. 230. Ironically, while peasants are seriously underequipped in most areas of Mexico, in the commercialized agricultural regions of the North and Northwest they are often "overequipped," i.e., they are encouraged or obliged by the government to buy on credit agricultural machinery which is too highly mechanized for their needs. Cynthia Hewitt de Alcántara, La Modernización de la Agricultura Mexicana, 1940–1970, (México, D. F.: Siglo Veintiuno Editores, 1978), pp. 71–78.

15. Centro de Investigaciones Agrarias, Estructura Agraria, pp. 396–397.

16. Philip Russell, Mexico in Transition, (Austin: Colorado River Press, 1977), p. 89.

17. World Bank figures cited in Financial Times (London), September 8, 1980.

18. Latin American Weekly Report 80, no. 31 (August 8, 1980), p. 9.

19. Salvador Zubirán et al., La Desnutrición del Mexicano, (México D. F.: Fondo de Cultura Económica, 1974), p. 21. Felix, "Income Inequality in Mexico," p. 113, notes that rural nutrition is so poor that even the urban shantytown dwellers have a "daily protein intake 17 percent higher than in the central and southern rural regions, although all are well below the national average."

20. Thomas G. Sanders, "The Plight of Mexican Agriculture," *American Universities Field Staff Report,* no. 3 (1979), pp. 1–2.

21. Marvin Alinsky, "Population and Migration Problems in Mexico," *Current History* 80, no. 469 (November 1981), p. 387.

22. For a discussion of the utility of census material as an indicator of social welfare in the period 1910–1960 see James W. Wilkie, *The Mexican Revolution: Federal Expenditure and Social Change since 1910* (Berkeley: University of California Press, 1967), pp. 204–232. A breakdown of the 1980 census, focused on population increases by state, is available in Richard W. Wilkie, "The Populations of Mexico and Argentina in 1980: Preliminary Data and Some Comparisons," in *Statistical Abstracts of Latin America* 21, edited by James W. Wilkie and Stephen Haber (Los Angeles: UCLA Latin American Center Publications, University of California, 1981), pp. 638–654.

23. Pablo González Casanova, *Democracy in Mexico* (New York: Oxford University Press, 1972), pp. 73–74.

24. Ibid. See also Julio Boltvinik, "Marginación: En la Base de la Pirámide," and Ignacio Almada Bay, "Salud: Muertos Que No Hacen Ruido," in *El Desafío Mexicano,* edited by Héctor Aguilar Camín (México, D.F.: Ediciones Oceano, 1982).

25. Carmelo Mesa-Lago, "Social Security Stratification and Inequality in Mexico," in *Contemporary Mexico,* edited by James W. Wilkie et al. (Berkeley: University of California Press, 1976), pp. 240–41.

26. González Casanova, *Democracy in Mexico,* 1972, pp. 72–74.

27. Ibid.

28. Felix, "Income Inequality in Mexico," p. 113.

29. Boletín Demografico—CELADE, "Población Total de la Region por Paises, 1920–2000," no. 23 (1979), p. 104. Only one-sixth of those entering the labor force during the 1970s found work in agriculture, indicating the limited capacity of agriculture to absorb new entrants into the job market. Fernando Rosenzweig, "Política Agrícola y Generación de Empleo," *El Trimestre Económico* 42, no. 4 (1975), p. 839; John G. Corbett, "Agricultural Modernization and Rural Employment in Mexico, 1970–1985: Implications for Mexican Migration to the United States." Paper presented to the XLIII International Congress of Americanists, Vancouver, August 1979.

30. There is an important and ongoing dispute in Mexico among politicians, agronomists, and economists as to just how far land resources might be stretched. On the one side are those who believe that the natural resources of Mexico would prove insufficient to support even the present agricultural population even if every square inch of land now held in illegally large land concentrations were distributed in accord with the land reform law. On the other side are agrarian experts who assert that the land resources of Mexico would be sufficient to support all future generations of peasants who wish to remain on the land *if* other models of agricultural development (particularly the labor-intensive model employed in the People's Republic of China) were applied in Mexico, while further industrialization draws surplus rural population into an urban job market. Either way, this dispute is over an essentially moot point.

The present Mexican government would not and could not institute a Chinese model in the agricultural sector. Therefore, in this discussion we have considered only the real-life effects of ongoing agricultural policy.

31. For a lengthy description and study of *bracero* working conditions see Ernest Galarza, "Trabajadores Mexicanos en Tierra Extranjera," *Problemas Agrícolas e Industriales de México* (January–June 1958), pp. 1–84. Also see Máximo Peón, *Como Viven los Mexicanos en los Estados Unidos* (México, D. F.: B. Costa-Amic, 1966); and Myrtle R. Reul, *Territorial Boundaries of Rural Poverty: Profiles of Exploitation* (East Lansing: Center for Rural Manpower and Public Affairs, Michigan State University, 1974), pp. 125–136, 459–472.

32. In 1958, for example, when an economic recession in the United States forced cuts of up to 60 percent in *bracero* contracting, this kind of violence occurred at the *bracero* induction centers in Enpalme, Sonora, and elsewhere throughout the North of Mexico.

33. "The seasonal emigration of *braceros* . . . far exceeds the number quoted in statistics. About 800,000 every year seems a likely figure." Chevalier, "The *Ejido* and Political Stability," p. 185. On the other hand, the figure 400,000 is cited by Cornelius as the peak number. See Wayne A. Cornelius, *Mexican Migration to the United States: Causes, Consequences and U.S. Responses* (Cambridge, Mass.: Center for International Studies, MIT, 1978), pp. 16–17.

34. The official estimate is $200 million for the period from 1958 to 1964. However, for political reasons this figure was set quite low and the actual remittance to Mexico during this time was probably more in the neighborhood of 750 million to one billion dollars. Donald D. Brand, *Mexico: Land of Sunshine and Shadow* (Princeton: D. Van Nostrand, 1966), p. 129.

35. The *bracero* remittances had been the third largest earner of foreign exchange after tourism (including border transactions) and cotton.

36. "The statistics for legal immigrants do not include Mexicans who are granted the so-called 'border crossing card' or 'shopping card,' which permits the holder to shop or do business (but not to work) in a zone within 25 miles of the border for a period of up to 72 hours." Also excluded from these figures are "commuter migrants" who live in Mexico and commute daily to jobs on the U.S. side. Cornelius, *Mexican Migration*, p. 7, fn.

37. See Charles B. Keely, "Counting the Uncountable: Estimates of Undocumented Aliens in the United States," *Population and Development Review*, 3, no. 4 (December 1977). Keely asserts that his "review of estimates of undocumented aliens leads to the undeniable conclusion that the estimates have been weak" (p. 479). Gordon writes: "The fluid nature of the population of the border needs to be understood to appreciate that what is not involved is a situation where a clear distinction can be made between Mexican citizens and United States citizens of Mexican or Indian background. . . . Population has moved quite freely back and forth across what is now this international border for hundreds of years." Wendell Gordon, "A Case for a Less Restrictive Border Policy," *Social Science Quarterly* 56, no. 3 (December 1975), p. 486.

38. Gary Clyde Hufbauer, W. N. Harrell Smith IV, and Frank G. Vukmanic,

"Bilateral Trade Relations," in *Mexico-United States Relations*, edited by Susan Kaufman Purcell (New York: Praeger, 1981), p. 140.

39. Cornelius, *Mexican Migration*, p. 7. Cornelius provides official figures on apprehensions as well as on legal migration and *bracero* contracts in the period 1930 to 1977. See pp. 4–6.

40. Since the Immigration and Naturalization Service began keeping records, the figure on apprehensions has fluctuated between 25 and 30 percent of the probable annual total of those who manage to cross. J. Craig Jenkins, "Push/Pull in Recent Mexican Migration to the U.S.," *International Migration Review* 11, no. 2 (1977), p. 181.

41. Cornelius, *Mexican Migration;* John S. Evans and Dilmus D. James, "Conditions of Employment and Income Distribution in Mexico as Incentives for Mexican Migration to the United States: Prospects to the End of the Century," *International Migration Review* 13, no. 1 (1979); Jenkins, "Push/Pull in Recent Migration"; and Jorge A. Bustamante, "Undocumented Immigration from Mexico: Research Report," *International Migration Review* 11, no. 2 (1977); Susan R. Walsh Sanderson, "Peasants and Public Policy: Social Change in Rural Mexico, 1916–1976." Unpublished Ph.D. diss., University of Pittsburgh, 1980, chapter 8; Francisco Alba, "Industrialización Sustitutiva y Migración Internacional: El Caso de México," *Foro Internacional* 18, no. 3 (enero/marzo 1978).

42. Cornelius, *Mexican Migration*, p. 40.

43. Jenkins, "Push/Pull in Recent Migration," pp. 183–185, writes: "In general, economic conditions in Mexico pushing emigrants out have had far more to do with migration than have pulls exercised by the U.S. agricultural economy. . . . Overall it seems to be changes in agricultural productivity and capital investment, not labor market conditions that have had the major impact on both illegal and bracero migration." Susan Sanderson's study correlates migration patterns with land distribution under the agrarian reform program in Mexico as well as with economic cycles in the United States. Sanderson, "Peasants and Public Policy," pp. 153–62.

44. C. Daniel Dillman, "Assembly Industries in Mexico: Contexts of Development," *Journal of Interamerican Studies and World Affairs* 25 (February 1983) pp. 38–42.

45. North American Congress on Latin America, "Hit and Run: U.S. Runaway Shops on the Mexican Border," *NACLA Report*, 9, no. 5, (July/August 1975), p. 7; Banco de México de Comercio Exterior, "La Industria Maquiladora: Evolución Reciente y Perspectivas." *Comercio Exterior* 28, no. 4 (April 1978).

46. Donald W. Baerresen, "Unemployment and Mexico's Border Industrialization Program," *Inter-American Economic Affairs* 29, no. 2 (Autumn 1975), pp. 81–82.

47. Linsey Hilsum, *Manchester Guardian Weekly*, March 28, 1982. On advantages to U.S. industry see also *Industry Week*, December 5, 1977, pp. 42–43 and April 16, 1979, pp. 26–27.

48. Mitchell A. Seligson and Edward J. Williams, "U.S.–Mexico Border In-

dustry Is Boon," *Los Angeles Times*, January 20, 1983. Dillman notes, "Devaluation quickly generated huge savings in production costs sufficient to restore much of the competitive advantage relinquished to other offshore sites in the hemisphere and in Asia." "Assembly Industries in Mexico," p. 51.

49. Anthony Spaeth, "The Maquila Boom," *Forbes*, December 10, 1979, p. 102.

50. Dillman, "Assembly Industries in Mexico," p. 44.

51. North American Congress on Latin America, "Hit and Run," pp. 8 and 21.

52. Robert M. Press, "US-Owned Plants in Mexico Produce Cheap Goods— and Controversy," *Christian Science Monitor*, February 5, 1982.

53. North American Congress on Latin America, "Hit and Run," p. 11.

54. Spaeth, "The Maquila Boom," p. 103.

55. Ibid., p. 104. Spaeth estimates that 65 percent of the wages are spent in the United States. Also see Baerresen, "Unemployment and Mexico's Border," p. 82.

56. Baerresen, "Unemployment and Mexico's Boom," p. 82. The depression which hit border towns like Douglas, Arizona, with the 1982 devaluation of the peso gives clear evidence of the degree to which the economy of the smaller American border towns had come to depend on Mexican spending. The various arguments in favor of the program, from both the Mexican and the American standpoints, are set out in Mitchell A. Seligson and Edward J. Williams, *Maquiladoras and Migration: Workers in the Mexican-United States* (Austin: University of Texas Press, 1982).

57. The oil boom towns of Coatzacoalcos, Minatitlan, Altamira, and Villahermosa have official growth rates of 6 percent yearly as compared with Mexico City, which slowed—according to official data—from 5.2 percent in 1972 to 4.3 percent in 1980. However, growth rates of 12 percent yearly are cited in other sources. See for example George Getschow, "Mexico Spends Billions to Foster Growth Outside Bursting Capital," *Wall Street Journal*, January 20, 1981. On relative rates of urbanization in the 1950s see Enrique Padilla Aragón, *Mexico: Desarrollo con Pobreza* (Mexico, D.F.: Siglo Veintiuno Editores, 1970), pp. 41–42.

The figures cited in this discussion refer to the "metropolitan zone of Mexico City," a term which encompasses the City of Mexico, the Federal District in which it lies (comparable to the District of Columbia), and those parts of the State of Mexico which have been engulfed by urban expansion. These various entities show different rates of growth. For example, while the core of the city, the colonial city built on the ruins of the Aztec's Tenochtitlan, expanded at a rate of 1.3 percent from 1950 to 1970, the general urban area grew by 5.6 percent in the same period. A detailed breakdown of the growth of the various urban entities is provided in Luis Unikel, "La Dinámica del Crecimiento de la Ciudad de Mexico," in *Ensayos Sobre el Desarrollo Urbano de México*, edited by Alejandra Moreno Toscano (México, D.F.: SepSetentas, 1974), pp. 175–206.

58. For very conservative estimates and projections see, Luis Unikel, *El*

Desarrollo Urbano de México: Diagnóstico e Implicaciones Futuras (Mexico, D.F.: El Colegio de México, 1976).

59. This figure compares with a world average of 35 years.

60. Alinsky, "Population and Migration Problems," p. 365.

61. Corbett, "Rural Employment in Mexico," p. 5; Alfredo Gallegos et al., "Recent Trends in Contraceptive Use in Mexico," *Studies in Family Planning* 8, no. 8 (1977), pp. 197–204.

62. Sanderson, "Peasants and Public Policy," p. 128.

63. Russell, *Mexico in Transition*, p. 156.

64. Ibid. On the total number of vehicles in Mexico City, 1939 to 1970, see Claude Bataillon and Hélène Rivière D'Arc, *La Ciudad de México* (Mexico, D.F.: SepSetentas, 1974), pp. 114–115. A recent study estimated that 97 percent of the vehicles in the capital transport only 21 percent of all passengers because so many cars carry only a driver. Alan Riding, "Problems of Mexico City: Warning to Third World," *New York Times*, May 15, 1983, p. 8.

65. Guy Guliotta, *Miami Herald*, February 26, 1981.

66. Ibid. See also Alinsky, p. 387.

67. Saul Trejo Reyes, "El Incremento de la Producción y el Empleo Industrial en México, 1950–1965," *Demografía y Economía* 4, no. 1 (1970), pp. 21–24.

68. *Unomásuno* (Mexico City), June 5, 1978, p. 26.

69. The tenement neighborhood described by Oscar Lewis in his study of the urban poor, *The Children of Sánchez* (New York: Vintage, 1961), was located in this area behind the National Palace and the main cathedral of Mexico.

70. Manuel Mejido, *México Amargo* (México, D.F.: Siglo Veintiuno Editores, 1974), pp. 328–29. Several detailed studies of the social and political life of the urban poor in Mexico City are available in English. See, especially, Wayne A. Cornelius, *Politics and the Migrant Poor in Mexico City* (Stanford: Stanford University Press, 1975); Susan Eckstein, *The Poverty of Revolution: The State and the Urban Poor in Mexico* (Princeton: Princeton University Press, 1977); and Larissa Lomnitz, *Networks and Marginality: Life in a Mexican Shanty Town* (New York: Academic Press, 1977).

71. Mejido, *México Amargo*, p. 326.

72. On the manipulation and exploitation of squatters and slum dwellers by *caciquillos* and others, see Jorge Montaño, *Los Pobres de la Ciudad en los Asentamientos Espontáneos* (México, D.F.: Siglo Veintiuno Editores, 1976), p. 207.

73. "México, uno de los cinco paises más matones del mundo," *Siempre!* (México, D.F.), October 28, 1970, p. 39. The *Siempre!* article was based on data from a 1970 United Nations report on criminality.

74. Mejido, *México Amargo*, pp. 327–28.

75. Bataillon and Rivière D'Arc, *La Ciudad de México*, p. 94.

76. Ibid.

77. *Excelsior*, November 4, 1975, p. 1a.

78. Carlos Perez Hidalgo, National Institute of Nutrition. Cited in Harry Nelson, "Chronic Malnutrition: 100,000 Children Die Yearly," *Los Angeles Times*, July 15, 1979, p. 18.

79. *New York Times*, News of the Week, June 11, 1972.

80. While there are some regulations that prohibit selling goods on city buses, the bus drivers, whose lot is extremely difficult and whose workday frequently runs fourteen hours, are usually sympathetic enough to allow hundreds of vendors to jump on and off their buses each day without paying the fare.

81. See Lourdes Arizpe, *Indígenas en La Ciudad de México: El Caso de las "Marías"* (México, D.F.: SepSententas, 1975), for a monographic study of the "Marías," the Indian women who move directly from traditional indigenous communities in the State of Mexico to a life as petty street vendors and sometime beggars in the downtown core of Mexico City.

82. *Journal of Commerce*, February 3, 1972.

83. Ibid. Mejido, *México Amargo*, pp. 340–42.

84. *Time*, October 8, 1979; and *Miami Herald*, February 26, 1981.

85. *Excelsior* (Mexico City), February 2, 1972.

86. The International Development Bank reported in 1980 that two million people had no access to piped water and those connected with the system received only intermittent service. Furthermore, even in the 1980s well over two-thirds of the urban population were still living in dwellings of one or two rooms. See International Development Bank, "Water for Mexico City," *International Development Bank News* 7, no. 6 (August 1980), p. 3; Cited in James H. Street, "Mexico's Economic Development Plan," *Current History* 80, no. 469. (November 1981), p. 390; and Alejandra Moreno Toscano, "La 'Crisis' en la Ciudad" in *México Hoy*, edited by Pablo González Casanova and Enrique Florescano (México, D. F: Siglo Veintiuno Editores, 1979), p. 168.

87. Alinsky, "Population and Migration Problems," p. 387.

88. González Casanova, "Economic Development of Mexico," p. 202.

89. Sergio Zermeño, "México: Estado, Pobreza y Democracia," *Foro Internacional* 19, no. 3 (enero-marzo 1979), pp. 443–444.

90. David Barkin and Gustavo Esteva, "Social Conflict and Inflation in Mexico," *Latin American Perspectives* 9, no. 1 (Winter 1982), p. 57. Only 14 percent of the economically active population is "actually" unionized. Raúl Trejo Delarbre, "El Movimiento Obrero: Situación y Perspectivas," in *México Hoy*, edited by Pablo González Casanova and Enrique Florescano (México, D. F.: Siglo Veintiuno Editores, 1979), p. 123.

91. *Gaceta UNAM* 18, *Nueva Epoca*, no. 3, March 1969. Only 2.8 percent of students enrolled at the National University come from peasant backgrounds.

92. David Barkin, "Education and Class Structure: The Dynamics of Social Control in Mexico," *Politics & Society* 5, no. 2 (1975), p. 188.

93. Fernando Carmona et al., *El Milagro Mexicano*, (México, D. F.: Editorial Nuestro Tiempo, 1970), back jacket.

CHAPTER 5

1. Pablo González Casanova, *Democracy in Mexico* (New York: Oxford University Press, 1972), pp. 23–24.

2. Ibid.

3. Ibid., pp. 17–18. For a discussion of the recruitment and brokerage (as opposed to the deliberative or representative) functions of Mexican legislators, see Alejandro Portes, "Legislatures Under Authoritarian Regimes: The Case of Mexico," *Journal of Political and Military Sociology* 5, no. 2 (Fall 1977), pp. 195–199.

4. Juan M. Vasquez, "Mexico—Press Freedom in Question," *Los Angeles Times*, June 28, 1982.

5. Ibid. An excellent analysis of the control and self-control of the various Mexican media is provided in Evelyn Stevens, *Protest and Response in Mexico* (Cambridge, Mass.: MIT Press, 1974), chapter 2; and in Daniel Levy and Gabriel Székely, *Mexico: Paradoxes of Stability and Change* (Boulder, Colo.: Westview Press, 1982), pp. 86–99.

6. González Casanova, *Democracy in Mexico*, p. 12.

7. Ibid.

8. For example, in an earlier study of electoral violence during the period 1957–1959, on the basis of newspaper reports *alone*, I noted 124 separate incidents of electoral violence, all associated directly or indirectly with the presidential elections of 1958. These incidents included the breakup of opposition party rallies, violence over disputed elections, physical attacks on the candidates and supporters of opposition parties, physical coercion at the polls, riots over the imposition of PRI candidates where an opposition party victory was generally believed to have occurred, and the destruction of opposition party headquarters by army and/or police forces. The figure 124 is probably low, given that it was based only on events reported in the Mexican press. These incidents occurred in twenty-three of the thirty-two federal states and territories, and were particularly frequent and virulent in the states of Baja California, Veracruz, Zacatecas, Chiapas, and Chihuahua.

9. González Casanova, *Democracy in Mexico*, p. 12.

10. Kevin J. Middlebrook, "Political Change in Mexico," in *Mexico–U.S. Relations*, edited by Susan Kaufman (New York: Praeger: 1981), p. 59.

11. Luis Villoro, "La Reforma Politica y Las Perspectivas de Democracia," in *México Hoy*, edited by Pablo González Casanova and Enrique Florescano (México, D. F.: Siglo Veintiuno Editores, 1979), pp. 352–353. See also John Foster Leich, "*Reforma Politica* in Mexico," *Current History* 80, no. 469 (November 1981), p. 362.

12. Ibid., and Middlebrook, "Political Change in Mexico," p. 59.

13. The significance of Rosario Ibarra's candidacy is explored in Nuria Fernández, "La Izquierda Mexicana en las Elecciones," *Cuadernos Políticos*, no. 33, (julio/septiembre, 1982), pp. 49–50. On the electoral fortunes of the

newly registered parties, see Rafael Segovia, "Las Elecciones Federales de 1979," *Foro Internacional*, 20, no. 3, (enero/marzo 1980).

14. Barry Carr, "Impressiones del XIX Congreso del PCM, 1981," *Cuadernos Politicos* 29 (julio/septiembre 1981), p. 84.

15. The Mexican Communists maintained excellent relations with the Italian, French, and Spanish Communist Parties and were much influenced by the development of these parties' growing rift with the Soviet Union and with the CPSU. At the celebration of the sixtieth anniversary of the October Revolution in Moscow in 1977, the secretary of the Mexican Communist Party, Arnoldo Martínez Verdugo, gave a speech, three paragraphs of which were omitted from the account provided in *Pravda*, a distinction generally accorded to the likes of Enrico Berlinguer, secretary of the Italian Communist Party, and a great thorn in Moscow's side. Berlinguer was the keynote speaker at Mexico's party congress in October 1981, a concrete gesture of his solidarity with and approval of the PCM's increasingly independent line.

16. There is wide agreement that the vote for the PCM, as for other opposition parties, was considerably higher than the official figures indicate. Only in the urban areas, where the minority parties were able to staff the election observer's posts at each polling place, were the reports from the polls even close to accurate. In the rural areas, in contrast, not only was the proportion of the vote given to the PRI much higher, but reports of abstentions were also much lower.

17. Carr, "Impressiones del XLX Congreso."

18. Judith Matloff, "Mexico's Juchitán: A Popular Challenge to PRI," *NACLA Report* 16, no. 6 (November–December 1982) p. 42.

19. Lawrence Rout, a reporter from the *Wall Street Journal* who traveled with the presidential entourage in the 1982 campaign, gives an idea of the dimensions of the PRI's campaign operations: "The PRI has a Boeing 727 and five large buses just for the press. Each journalist gets a private hotel room and three meals a day—courtesy of the PRI. The party also sets up a press room wherever the campaign goes, with six telexes, 77 typewriters, three modern photocopy machines and 28 telephones (direct-dial, long distance)—this in a country where it can take months, even years, for the average citizen to get one phone hookup. . . . The PRI pays for all this—in addition to privately giving a gift of $100 a day or more to many of the reporters."—Lawrence Rout, "Presidential Campaign in Mexico Shows Grip of Party over Nation," *Wall Street Journal*, April 22, 1982, p. 26.

20. Richard L. Harris and David Barkin, "The Political Economy of Mexico in the Eighties," *Latin American Perspectives* 9, no. 1 (winter 1982), p. 13.

21. Middlebrook, "Political Change in Mexico," pp. 62 and 65. Also see Leich, "*Reforma Politica* in Mexico," p. 393.

22. ALAI, "Mexico: López Portillo Define su Política Global," *Agencia Latino-Americana de Información*, no. 27 (29 septiembre, 1977).

23. *Punto Critico*, "Mexico: Class Struggle and 'Political Reform,'" *Contemporary Marxism*, no. 1 (Spring 1980), p. 75.

24. Harris and Barkin, "*Political Economy of Mexico in the Eighties*," p. 12.

25. Quoted in *The New York Times*, May 8, 1978.

26. Pablo González Casanova, "The Political Reform in Mexico," *LARU Studies* 3, no. 1 (January–April 1979), p. 30.

27. *Ibid.*, p. 29.

28. *Ibid.*

29. Sergio de la Peña, "El PRI—y las Fuerzas Proletarias en México," *Americalatina: Estudios y Perspectivas* no. 2 (1980), p. 219.

30. *Ibid.*, p. 220. See also Fernando Danel, "México: Crisis, Redespliegue Capitalista y Luchas Democráticas," *Americalatina: Estudios y Perspectivas* no. 2, (1980), pp. 190–191.

31. To the best of my knowledge the term was first used with specific reference to Mexico in James Cockcroft and Bo Anderson, "Control and Cooptation in Mexican Politics," in *Latin American Radicalism* edited by Irving Louis Horowitz et al. (New York: Random House, 1969), pp. 366–389, especially pp. 376ff. A second case study of co-optation in Mexican politics was developed by Robert F. Adie, "Cooperation, Cooptation and Conflict in Mexican Peasant Organizations," *Inter-American Economic Affairs* 24 (winter 1970), pp. 3–25. I am using the term in a broader sense than it is employed in either the Cockcroft and Anderson or Adie articles. See Judith Adler, "The Politics of Land Reform in Mexico." M. Phil. thesis, London School of Economics, 1970. pp. 228–232; and Judith Adler Hellman, "Social Control in Mexico," *Comparative Politics* 12, no. 2 (January 1980). For a use of the concept in a pre-1940 context, see the discussion of Obregón's skillful manipulation of peasant and labor masses in Richard Tardanico, "Revolutionary Nationalism and State Building in Mexico, 1917–1924, *Politics & Society* 10, no. 1, 1980.

32. Adler, "Politics of Land Reform."

33. A notable exception to this rule is the Catholic Universidad Ibero-americana in Mexico City which, from the late 1960s, was the site of a great flowering of critical thought in several different departments, such as anthropology.

34. Daniel Levy, "University Autonomy in Mexico: Implications for Regime Authoritarianism," *Latin American Research Review* 14, no. 3 (1979), p. 129.

35. Daniel Levy, *University and Government in Mexico: Autonomy in an Authoritarian System* (New York: Praeger, 1980), p. 23.

36. "There is evidence of greater presidential power to depose rectors than to select them. . . . The government may well manipulate . . . problems to depose rectors it does not like," as occurred in 1945, 1948, and 1965. Levy, "University Autonomy in Mexico," p. 138.

37. *Ibid.*, p. 134.

38. Larissa Lomnitz, "The Latin American University: Breeding Ground of the New State Elites." Paper presented to the American Anthropological Society, Houston, January 1979, p. 4.

39. Larissa Lomnitz, "Horizontal and Vertical Relations and the Social Structure of Urban Mexico," *Latin American Research Review* 18, no. 2 (1982), p. 55.

40. See Peter H. Smith, *Labyrinths of Power: Political Recruitment in Twentieth-Century Mexico* (Princeton: Princeton University Press, 1979), pp. 82–87; Roderic Ai Camp, *Mexican Political Biographies, 1935–1975*, (Tucson: University of Arizona Press, 1976); Roderic Ai Camp, "The National School of Economics and Public Life in Mexico," *Latin American Research Review* 10, no. 3 (Fall 1975); and Larissa Lomnitz, "Conflict and Mediation in a Latin American University," *Journal of Interamerican Studies and World Affairs* 19, no. 3 (August 1977).

41. Smith, *Labyrinths of Power*, p. 86. Smith explains, "Being near the seat of the national government and near the center of the decision-making apparatus, UNAM has provided its students with opportunities to observe and meet national leaders (and vice versa). It has been a place where students have developed their political sensitivities, where they have formed crucial friendships and alliances, and where they have taken part in overt action (most notably through strikes). Frequently, too, political leaders have held part-time positions on the UNAM faculty, and used the opportunity to recruit students to their teams, machines or *camarillas*." Ibid.

42. The reasons for this situation, Wionczek asserts, are "the anti-intellectual attitude . . . of the postrevolutionary elites which is the result of the rise to national, regional and local power of poorly educated leaders, the incorporation into the political apparatus of 'cooptable' intellectuals, and the profound suspicion of this apparatus toward those who are not disposed to sell their independence in exchange for immediate political gain." Miguel S. Wionczek, "El Subdesarrollo Científico y Technológico: Sus Consecuencias," In *Disyuntivas sociales*, edited by Wionczek (México, D.F.: SepSetentas, 1971), pp. 185–86.

43. Lomnitz, "Horizontal and Vertical Relations," p. 55.

44. Roderic Ai Camp, "Intellectuals and the State in Mexico, 1920–1980: The Influence of Family and Education." Paper presented to the Sixth Conference of Mexican and United States Historians, Chicago, September 1981, p. 2. Camp found that more than half of all Mexican intellectuals worked in appointed or elected positions in the federal government for at least five years and of the full-time careers chosen by Mexican intellectuals, the largest group, 28 percent, followed lifelong government careers.

45. Ibid., pp. 20–23.

46. Henry A. Landsberger and Cynthia N. Hewitt, "Ten Sources of Weakness and Cleavage in Latin American Peasant Movements," in *Agrarian Problems and Peasant Movements in Latin America*, edited by Rodolfo Stavenhagen, (Garden City: Doubleday and Company, 1970), pp. 569–573.

47. Ibid., p. 573.

48. Hobart A. Spalding, Jr., *Organized Labor in Latin America: Historical Case Studies of Urban Workers in Dependent Societies* (New York: Harper & Row, 1977), p. 134.

49. Ibid.

50. A work that makes this same important distinction between individual and group co-optation is Susan Eckstein, "The Irony of Organization: Resource

and Regulatory," *The British Journal of Sociology* 27, no. 2 (June 1976), pp. 150–164.

51. For example, the UGOCM, an independent peasant organization led by Jacinto López, agitated throughout the late 1950s to focus attention on illegal land holdings in the states of Sonora, Sinaloa, Nayarit, and Colima. In 1957 and 1958 the peasant movement carried out a series of land invasions on huge estate illegally owned by foreign nationals, including the million-acre Cananea Cattle Company of the American Greene family. The invasions of the Greene estates began in late spring of 1957, and UGOCM members tell of being removed by federal troops and returning to occupy the land as many as eighteen times. Finally the government responded and the estate was expropriated and divided into seven huge cattle-raising *ejidos*. However, among the 853 peasant families who formed part of the new *ejidos*, less than one-third were UGOCM members. The rest were CNC-affiliated peasants who had not participated in the land invasions.

52. Steven E. Sanderson, *Agrarian Populism and the Mexican State: The Struggle for Land in Sonora* (Berkeley: University of California Press, 1981), p. 142.

53. *Charro* ("cowboy") is the term popularly used to describe corrupt union leaders. For a full explanation of the derivation of this term, and its application to unionists, see Stevens, *Protest and Response in Mexico*, pp. 103–106.

54. *Tamales* are baked corn meal cakes, often prepared with a filling of hot chili peppers. They are a typical peasant dish.

55. The full name of the organization is the Unión Central de Sociedades de Crédito Colectivo Ejidal (Central Union of Collective Ejidal Credit Societies).

56. Gerrit Huizer, *The Role of Peasant Organizations in the Process of Agrarian Reform in Latin America* (Washington, D.C.: Comité Inter-Americano de Desarrollo Agricola, 1968), p. 132.

57. The Ejidal Bank acts as an agent in the sale of crops produced by most of the *ejidatarios* affiliated with the CNC. As the Ejidal Bank in most regions of Mexico is notorious for its corruption, peasants who are forced to rely on the Bank to act as their sales agent normally receive lower profits than peasants, like the Central Union members, who are able to avoid dealing with the Ejidal Bank representatives. Even when the Central Union sells its members' cotton on the world market at exactly the same price obtained by the Ejidal Bank, members come out ahead financially because they have not had to underwrite or subsidize the kickbacks, rake-offs, etc., enjoyed by Ejidal Bank functionaries.

58. Dionisio Encina, who worked as a carpenter and blacksmith in Torreón in the period leading up to the general strike, was one of the Communist youth militants who took an active role in organizing the countryside. By the time the strike broke out, Encina, then in his late twenties, had gained sufficient status to be elected president of the strike committee. Four years later he was secretary general of the Mexican Communist Party.

59. For a comparative analysis of a non-ideological, personalistic independent peasant organization and the Central Union see Judith Adler Hellman, "The Role of Ideology in Peasant Politics: Peasant Mobilization and Demobili-

zation in the Laguna Region." *Journal of Interamerican Studies and World Affairs*, 25, no. 1 (February 1983).

60. "Ideology may be viewed as the polar opposite of exchange in the specific sense that exchange subjects the person to an instrumental logic which facilitates the social and political control over him, while ideology gives an individual autonomous ends on which material and immediate rewards have no hold. . . ." Luigi Graziano, "A Conceptual Framework for the Study of Clientelism." Center for International Studies, Cornell University. Western Societies Occasional Paper no. 2, April 1975, p. 46.

Many analysts have noted the irrelevance of ideology to the formation of political affiliations in Mexico. See, for example, Merilee S. Grindle, "Patrons and Clients in the Bureaucracy: Career Networks in Mexico," *Latin American Research Review* 12, no. 1 (1977), p. 39, and Susan Eckstein, *The Poverty of Revolution: The State and the Urban Poor in Mexico* (Princeton: Princeton University Press, 1977), p. 137.

61. The difficulty in making this distinction is highlighted in this statement from a longstanding Central Union member from the Ejido "El Cuije" who asserted, in an interview in 1976, that he had never been a Communist. "In this ejido we have always been with Orona. We gave him support in everything. We participated in the *caravanas*. But we were never communist. Just Orona and a few of the leaders were. We liked the collectivism that Orona always pushed and we went along with the rest—with solidarity campaigns, with support for the Soviet Union—out of respect for him, even though we were persecuted as a consequence."

62. "Rapid industrialization, an Alemán fetish, required low wages and the sacrifice of the labor force to capital accumulation. . . . Continuous protests from . . . labor made no perceptible change in Alemán's philosophy or conduct. . . . For Alemán, the sacrifice of a generation of workers and peasants was a small price for making his nation materially strong, industrialized, modernized, advanced." Frank R. Brandenburg, *The Making of Modern Mexico* (Englewood Cliffs, N.J.: Prentice-Hall, 1964), pp. 102–103.

63. Ruíz Cortines received 74 percent of the vote. By PRI standards of those times, he had only just "squeaked by."

64. Gustavo Díaz Ordaz, quoted in *La Opinión* (Torreón, Coahuila), Feb. 24, 1947.

65. The full page advertisement in a local or national daily is a political tactic employed with great frequency by Mexican organizations of every political coloration. Full page ads are used to promulgate political manifestos, the proceedings of party or union congresses, to applaud or denounce legislative initiatives or newly announced policies, and so forth. Often they are used to declare an organization's solidarity with the president and his party. In the height of the student movement crisis in 1968, Mexican newspapers were bursting with paid announcements of solidarity with the president and his regime, placed there by official party organizations such as unions and associations affiliated with the CTM, CNC, or CNOP, as well as by certain opposition organizations that wished to disassociate themselves from the "disorders."

66. *Oposicio*, 3, no. 43 (June 1972), p. 13.

67. "Informe que rinde la Unión Central al quinto congreso, febrero 1947," Archives of the Central Union, Torreón, Coahuila.

68. The creation of parallel and competing organizations designed to sap strength from hard-to-control or co-opt organizations and institutions is a technique employed by the state not only with regard to peasant unions but at every level and in all sectors of the society. For example the establishment of the Universidad Metropoletana, the Metropolitan University, in the 1970s can be seen as an effort to draw students, resources, prestige, etc., away from the often unruly UNAM. See Levy, "University Autonomy in Mexico," p. 147.

69. On the shift in public investment priorities from industrial to agricultural development and the overall expansion of state activities in the countryside under Echeverría, see Merilee S. Grindle, "Policy Change in an Authoritarian Regime: Mexico Under Echeverría," *Journal of Interamerican Studies and World Affairs* 19, no. 4 (November 1977).

70. Included in this figure are the *socios delegados* of each ejidal credit union, that is, the *ejidatarios* whose agricultural labor is taken over by their fellows so that they can devote full time to representing the credit group's interests. Gustavo del Castillo Vera, "Reflexiones sobre el proyecto de La Laguna," CIS-INAH, 22 marzo 1977.

71. Here is a typical example of this approach from the archives of the Central Union: "It is known to all that the widespread desire for liberation made possible the Revolution of 1910. Emiliano Zapata, with profound wisdom pointed out the necessity of giving land to those who had none, and in 1917 defeated the usurpers who had risen up against our Revolution, motivated by the same interests as those who today ask for the revision of Article 27 of the Constitution. . . . Is it inconsequential that after the loss of so much blood, after so many vicissitudes and sacrifices have been endured for the country, a group of playboys [señoritos] attempt with one feather, to wipe away the entire Agrarian Reform, and, in so doing, to halt all progress in the agrarian field?"

72. Militant movements of the left are not the only organizations that claim Zapata as their inspiration. The CNC has appropriated Zapata as their symbol, and they play on the Zapata image continually. Zapata's face and words appear on the cover or letterhead of a large proportion of CNC publications, and his portrait is prominently displayed in CNC headquarters. Often CNC artists go so far as to use drawings and woodcuts of the *agrarista* hero with gun in hand and a murderous expression in his eyes.

In 1971 an "urban guerrilla group" called the Zapatista Urban Front, kidnapped Julio Hirschfeld, a wealthy businessman, and held him for $240,000 ransom. However, it now appears that these latter-day *zapatistas* may have been right-wing extremists trying to provoke a government crackdown on the left.

With so many different organizations simultaneously claiming Zapata as their inspiration, a certain amount of confusion develops in the minds of many Mexicans as to what it was that Zapata really stood for. But nonetheless, most opposition organizations continue to identify their struggle with that of Zapata.

73. Rubén Jaramillo was a leader of peasants in Morelos State from his youth, fighting under Emiliano Zapata, to his death on May 23, 1962, when he was taken from his home by soldiers and assassinated along with his wife, two stepsons, and a nephew. Their disfigured bodies were riddled with bullets marked with the symbol of the National Munitions Factory, which produces arms and ammunition exclusively for the army and police forces. See Froylan Manjarrez, "Matanza en Xochicalco," in Rubén Jaramillo: Autobiografía y Asesinato edited by Jaramillo and Manjarrez. (México, D.F.: Editorial Nuestro Tiempo, 1967), pp. 126–131. Jénaro Vázquez, a rural schoolteacher turned guerrilla, was killed in an auto accident while fleeing army troops on February 2, 1972. Lucio Cabañas, another rural schoolteacher, likewise led a peasant band in the mountains of Guerrero State and evaded capture for almost a decade until he was shot and killed by army troops in the Sierra Madre near Acapulco in December 1974. See José Natividad Rosales, ¿Quién es Lucio Cabañas? (México, D.F.: Posada, 1975). Efraín Calderón Lara was a law student from Yucatan who organized city bus drivers and shoe workers into unions independent of CTM control. He was seized by local police in Merida on February 13, 1974, and his mutilated body was found shortly thereafter. See Philip Russell, Mexico in Transition, (Austin: Colorado River Press, 1977), p. 99.

74. By 1979, human rights groups had compiled lists of about 450 political activists who had "disappeared" in recent years. Robert Montemayor and Laurie Becklund, "The Dead Aren't Counted or Listed," Los Angeles Times, July 15, 1979, p. 24.

75. Sergio Alcántara Ferrer, quoted in Ibid.

76. Ibid. On torture and assassinations of priests who championed radical peasant or labor causes see IDOC, "Growing Repression in Mexico," LADOC 8, no. 2, (Nov./Dec. 1977), pp. 19–22.

77. On the railroad workers' movement see Stevens, Protest and Response in Mexico, Chapter 4.

78. See José Santos Valdes, Madera (México, D. F.: Imprenta Laura, 1968).

79. "The Mexican Struggle," NACLA's Latin America and Empire Report 6, no. 3 (March 1972), p. 5.

80. Michael Klare, "The Pentagon's Counterinsurgency Research Infrastructure," NACLA Newsletter 4, no. 9 (June 1971), p. 9.

81. U.S. Department of Defense, Military Assistance Facts (Washington, D.C., 1969), pp. 16–17.

82. Ibid., p. 21.

83. U.S. Agency for International Development, Statistics and Reports Division, Operations Report, June 30, 1961–July 30, 1969.

84. For example, the total U.S. Military Assistance Program expenditures for the fiscal years 1950–1969 was $425.6 million for Brazil, $163 million for Chile, $128.8 million for Argentina, and $105.4 million for Venezuela. U.S. Department of Defense, Office of the Assistant Secretary of Defense for International Security Affairs, Military Assistance and Foreign Military Sales Facts

(Washington, D.C.: 1970). Cited in Michael T. Klare, *War Without End* (New York: Random House, 1972), p. 376.

85. For a survey and critical analysis of this debate see Hellman, "Social Control in Mexico."

86. From the famous Almond and Verba study carried out in the 1960s onward, there is no systematic survey of even the most modest scientific pretensions which does other than confirm Almond and Verba's findings that the vast majority of Mexicans are profoundly alienated from their government, and generally characterize government as corrupt, discriminatory, and unresponsive. See Gabriel A. Almond and Sidney Verba, *The Civil Culture* (Boston: Little, Brown & Company, 1965), especially pp. 67–70. For a full discussion of these and other social scientists' findings, see Hellman, "Social Control in Mexico."

87. Spaulding, *Organized Labour*, p. 135.

88. Arturo Warman, "El Problema del Campo," in González Casanova and Florescano, *México Hoy*, pp. 117–118.

CHAPTER 6

1. A good English source on these events is NACLA, *Domination and Repression*. NACLA also marked the tenth anniversary of the movement with a retrospective analysis: North American Congress on Latin America, "Schooled in Conflict: Mexican and Chicano Students, 1968–1978," *NACLA Report on the Americas* 12, no. 5 (September –October 1978), pp. 8–23. In his study, Kenneth F. Johnson, *Mexican Democracy: A Critical View* (Boston: Allyn and Bacon, 1971), pp. 148–164, the author provides an analysis that focuses on behind-the-scenes, inter-elite maneuverings in high political circles. A more recent publication, Evelyn P. Stevens, *Protest and Response in Mexico* (Cambridge, Mass.: The MIT Press, 1974), pp. 185–240, provides an excellent, detailed analysis of the events in comparative perspective with other Mexican protest movements. In writing this account, I relied on contemporary newspaper accounts, interviews with participants, an unpublished report by Cuauhtemoc Reséndez Nuñez, the NACLA documents cited above, and, in particular, my own experience with the movement.

2. Jean Louis M. de Lannoy, "Student Political Activism in Mexico." Paper presented to the Canadian Sociology and Anthropology Association, May 30, 1973, p. 5.

3. Ibid.

4. The most important groups represented in Mexican high schools and universities at the time were the Communists, Christian Democrats, Trotskyists, Maoists, Sparticus League, Guevarists, and Socialists. Ramón Ramírez, *El Movimiento Estudiantil de México*, vol. 1 (México, D. F.: Ediciones ERA, 1969), p. 24.

5. The unification of these groups was particularly significant because the

government had long promoted division, if not direct confrontation between liberal arts and technical students as a means of containing potential political opposition on the campuses. Hiber Conteris, "The New Outbreak of the Student Rebellion" in NACLA, "Schooled in Conflict," p. 8.

The preparatory schools and the UNAM into which they channel their graduates are the prestige institutions of Mexican education. "The UNAM complex, with headquarters at the specially constructed University City, consumes three quarters of the total federal budget assigned to Mexican universities. Its student body is drawn primarily from the urban middle and upper classes. Since 1928, the campus has enjoyed 'autonomy,' i.e., freedom from military and police intervention.

"The technical schools, on the other hand, draw their students primarily from worker and peasant backgrounds, enjoy a much lower budget, do not have 'autonomy' and are consequently from time to time the scenes of brutal military and police intervention.

"These and other differences, coupled with PRI manipulations have tended to produce antagonisms and rivalries which had traditionally divided the Mexican student movement." NACLA, "Schooled in Conflict," p. 24.

6. Jean Louis M. de Lannoy, "Student Political Activism in Mexico," p. 17.

7. Ibid., p. 18.

8. "In order to practice direct democracy, the students organized multiple seminars and meetings, assemblies, teach-ins and mass demonstrations. In all those forms of meeting the principle of free speech was strictly enforced; no regulation on speech was accepted. . . . But the refusal of any organizational restraint leaves the door open to all possible manipulations. The paradox is that the principle of direct democracy gets defeated when it allows the least democratic minded people to take advantage of it at the expense of the majority. Appeals to collective enthusiasm for all prepared motions do not favor the formation of a responsible, accountable electorate at the grass root level." Ibid., p. 22.

9. In the period when Daniel Cohn-Bendit ("Dany the Red") and other student leaders were turned into international celebrities almost overnight by media anxious to reduce ideological movements to individual personalities, this concern on the part of the Mexican students is understandable.

10. This account is based on personal observation, interviews, and Mexico City daily newspapers for the period July–October, 1968.

11. See Luís González de Alba, Los Díaz y los Años (México, D. F.: Biblioteca ERA, 1971); and Ramón Ramírez, El Movimento Estudiantil de México.

12. University and secondary school faculty formed their own organization, the Coalition of Middle and Higher Education Teachers for Democratic Freedom.

13. CTM Bulletin, September 3, 1968.

14. Labor and peasant organizations that came out in support of the movement were some of the electricians'; telephone workers', taxi drivers' and railroad workers' unions, and the Independent Peasant Central, affiliated with the Communist Party.

15. John Womack, Jr., "The Spoils of the Mexican Revolution," *Foreign Affairs* 48, no. 4 (July 1970), p. 683.

16. Jean Louis M. de Lannoy, "Student Political Activism in Mexico," p. 11.

17. Articles 145 and 145[b] defined the crime of "social dissolution," providing sentences of two to twelve years for any Mexican or foreigner who met with a group of three or more individuals (Mexican or foreign) to discuss ideas or programs that tend to disturb the public order or affect Mexican sovereignty. Sentences of up to twelve years were given those convicted to spreading ideas that "tend to produce rebellion, sedition, riot, or insurrection," and sentences of up to twenty years to any Mexican or foreigner convicted of carrying out acts "which prepare morally or materially for the invasion of national territory or the submission of the country to any foreign government."

Articles 145 and 145[b] were passed during World War II when it appeared that stiff legislation was needed to control the rampant activities of Nazis and fascists sympathizers in Mexico. However, since their passage, the articles were almost exclusively employed to persecute figures on the left: communists, socialists, and radical student, labor, and peasant leaders.

18. Hiber Conteris, "New Outbreak," p. 9.

19. In 1971, the existence of paramilitary shock troops was finally publicly acknowledged, although the government refused to take responsibility for their acts, which cost hundreds of lives in 1968 and hundreds more since that time.

20. Hiber Conteris, "New Outbreak," p. 9.

21. In the Plaza of the Three Cultures the sixteen century Spanish colonial Church of the Apostle Santiago stands directly adjacent to the recently excavated Aztec ruins and the ultra-modern headquarters of the Ministry of Foreign Relations. Hence the plaza is named for the Aztec, Spanish, and modern Mexican Cultures.

22. Oriana Falacci, the Italian journalist, received four bullet wounds, was dragged by her hair from a balcony overlooking the plaza, and was left bleeding on the ground after having been robbed of her watch and all her money. An English journalist was forced to lie under fire for two hours with a gun at his head. These experiences are recounted in *The Sunday Times* and *London Observer*, London, October 6, 1968.

23. National Strike Council, Bulletin, October 6, 1968, reproduced in NACLA, "School in Conflict," p. 19. For good coverage of these events in English, see the *Sunday Times* and the *Observer*, both October 6, 1968. For further detail see, Jorge Carrión et al, *Tres Culturas en Agonía* (México, D. F.: Editorial Nuestro Tiempo, 1969); and Elena Poniatowska, *La Noche de Tlatelolco* (México, D. F.: Ediciones ERA, 1971).

24. There is little agreement on the precise number of people killed on 2 October. Some estimates go as high as 500, while naturally the official government figures are very low: some thirty-seven killed and wounded. My own estimate coincides with the figures given by John Womack, Jr., "Spoils of the Revolution," p. 684. Although I was in Tlatelolco on the night of the massacre, I am in no position to supply accurate details based on my own observations. I was approaching the plaza at the moment when the soldiers surrounded the

area. I managed to reach one of the buildings facing the plaza when the shooting commenced. When the plaza had been "cleared" the buildings came under fire. Several direct hits were scored killing at least two people on the lower floors of the building. Thus, given the precarious nature of the observation point, my experience is more that of an earwitness than an eyewitness.

25. The government claimed that the students had been armed and offered the army fatalities as evidence that the "exchange" of the fire had been initiated by the students. However, autopsies on the army casualties later confirmed that the soldiers had been shot by military-issued weapons.

26. Typical of the abuses was the 1 January 1970, assault at Lecumberi Prison in Mexico City. Fifty-odd "common" prisoners armed with clubs and chains were turned loose by the warden in the political prisoners' wing of the penitentiary. The political prisoners were beaten and their cells sacked while the jailers looked on.

Another abuse vigorously protested by the students was the fact that after more than a year in jail, the political prisoners were neither offered bail nor brought to trial. The Mexican Constitution guarantees a fair and open trial within one year of arrest.

27. Everyone was in accord that the movement had to agitate for the release of the prisoners, but conflicts arose between whose who insisted that the political prisoners be absolved of all guilt at an open trial, and others (including a majority of the prisoners themselves) who were content to see the prisoners released under a general amnesty, even though they realized that the government would score valuable propaganda points from this sort of "humanitarian gesture."

28. The word literally means "cheerleaders." The different paramilitary groups go under a variety of names: the Falcons (halcones), the Pancho Villas, the Olympic Battalion (active since 1968), and others.

CHAPTER 7

1. John Womack, Jr., "The Spoils of the Mexican Revolution," *Foreign Affairs* 48, no. 4 (July 1970), pp. 684–685.

2. Ibid.

3. This is often framed in terms of a "clean sweep" or a cleanup of the corruption tolerated or even promoted by the preceding president. The clearest case was the cleanup campaign of Adolfo Ruíz Cortines, who succeeded Miguel Alemán in 1952. Ruíz Cortines faced a grave problem upon assuming office. The dignity of the presidential office had deteriorated so rapidly during the last years of Alemán's incumbency that Ruíz Cortines was hard pressed to restore its prestige. Flagrantly corrupt activities of Alemán and of *alemanistas* at all levels of the government had been carried on in a manner so cavalier as to become distressing if not to say intolerable to even the least idealistic of their countrymen. "Exposures of graft and fraud during the Alemán administration," wrote Clarence Senior, "started exploding immediately after it went out of

office in the fall of 1952. The amounts pocketed by the government clique must be astronomical for a poverty-stricken country like Mexico, even if they do not reach the frequently quoted figure of $800 million." Clarence Senior, *Land Reform and Democracy* (Gainesville: University of Florida Press, 1958), p. 141.

4. Porfirio Muñoz Ledo, undersecretary of the ministry of the presidency, from a speech delivered April 27, 1971. Quoted in *Excelsior* (Mexico City), April 28, 1971.

5. Ibid., and *Excelsior* (Mexico City), August 7, 1971, p. 1.

6. See Echeverría's State of the Nation Address, Sept. 1, 1972.

7. *Excelsior* (Mexico City), April 18, 1971.

8. Ibid.

9. *Excelsior* (Mexico City), May 25, 1971.

10. Carlos Fuentes, *Tiempo Mexicano* (México, D.F.: Cuadernos de Joaquín Mortiz, 1973), p. 166.

11. León Roberto García, "Democracia: real o fascismo?" *Excelsior* (Mexico City), April 1971, p. 13.

12. *Latin America* (London), March 19, 1971.

13. Lawrence Whitehead, "La Política Economica del Sexenio de Echeverría: "¿Qué Salió Mal y Por Qué?" *Foro Internacional* 20, no. 3 (enero/marzo 1980), p. 499.

14. Douglas Bennett et al., "National and International Constraints on the Exercise of Power by the State: The Echeverría *Sexenio* in Mexico." Paper presented to the Latin American Studies Association, Pittsburgh, April 1979, p. 11.

15. Bennett et al., "Echeverría *Sexenio* in Mexico," p. 11. Apart from expanding the number and range of educational facilities, Echeverría's policy on education tended to strengthen the legal concept of "university autonomy," the right of the national and state universities to remain independent of outside political control. To give greater force to the "organic law" that protected university autonomy, in 1971 Echeverría threw his weight behind the students and faculty of the University of Nuevo León in their fight to oust a university rector imposed on them by the industrial bourgeoisie of Monterrey and the politicians in their service. *Excelsior* (Mexico City), May 4, May 19, 1971.

16. Jorge Eduardo Navarrete, ed., *México: La Politica Económica del Nuevo Gobierno* (México, D.F.: Banco Nacional de Comercio Exterior, 1971), pp. 16–18, 83–86.

17. Ibid., pp. 71, 87.

18. Robert E. Looney, *Mexico's Economy: A Policy Analysis with Forecasts to 1990* (Boulder, Colo.: Westview Press, 1978), p. 88. "Taxes on business incomes were imposed cautiously for fear of adverse effects on investment, and generous exemptions were given for reinvested earnings. The "fiscal reforms" of the Echeverría administration consisted largely in tightening up business tax deductions, raising marginal tax rates on personal incomes in the highest brackets, imposing taxes on luxury consumption, raising real estate property taxes and emphasizing improvements in the administration of budgeting and

tax collection procedures. Tax officials admit that there was no basic reform."
p. 65.

19. August Schumacher, "Agricultural Development and Rural Employment: A Mexican Dilemma." Program in United States–Mexican Studies, University of California, San Diego. Working Papers in U.S.–Mexican Studies no. 21, 1981, pp. 8–13.

20. Merilee S. Grindle, "Official Interpretations of Rural Underdevelopment: Mexico in the 1970s." Program in United States–Mexican Studies, University of California, San Diego, Working Papers in U.S.–Mexican Studies, no. 20, 1981, p. 10. Also see Grindle, "Policy Change in an Authoritarian Regime: Mexico Under Echeverría," Journal of Interamerican Studies and World Affairs, 19, no. 4 (November 1977), pp. 539–540.

21. Address of the chief of the Department of Agrarian Affairs to the Chamber of Deputies, February 2, 1971, quoted in El Nacional (Mexico City), February 3, 1971.

22. Grindle, "Interpretations of Rural Underdevelopment" 1981, p. 11.

23. Ibid., pp. 95–100, 119–122.

24. Jorge Eduardo Navarrete, ed., México: La Política Económica para 1972 (México, D.F.: Banco Nacional de Comercio Exterior, 1972), pp. 26–33.

25. Merilee S. Grindle, "Power, Expertise and the 'Tecnico': Suggestions from a Mexican Case Study," The Journal of Politics, 9, no. 2 (November 1977), pp. 422–423.

26. Navarrete, La Política Económica, pp. 127–128.

27. Richard S. Weinert, "The State and Foreign Capital," In Authoritarianism in Mexico, edited by José Luis Reyna and Richard S. Weinert (Philadelphia: Institute for the Study of Human Issues, 1977), pp. 120–122.

28. Navarete, La Política Economica, pp. 127–128.

29. The U.S. buys two-thirds of Mexico's exports and provides three-fourths of Mexico's imports. Mexico is the United States' largest trading partner in Latin America. U.S. investment represents 80 percent of the $3.5 billion worth of foreign investment in Mexico.

30. Mexico established relations with the Peoples Republic of China in February 1972. Notwithstanding the huge potential of the Chinese market, in Asia Mexico's most promising trade agreement was made with Japan, a country whose economy is nearly perfectly complementary to Mexico's, a country eager to supply Mexico with technicians and know-how, and a country whose interests in expanding its economic influence in Latin America coincide perfectly with Mexico's desire to move away from dependency on the United States.

31. Luís Echeverría, "The President of Mexico's Report on his Trip to Three Continents," Comercio Exterior 19, no. 6 (June 1973), pp. 7–11; and Navarrete, La Política Ecónomica, pp. 145ff.

32. George W. Grayson, "Mexican Foreign Policy," Current History 72, no. 425 (March 1977), pp. 98–99.

33. Ibid.; Yoram Shapira, "Mexico's Foreign Policy Under Echeverría: A Retrospect," Inter-American Economic Affairs 31, no. 4 (spring 1978), p. 51.

34. Ibid., p. 47.

35. Ibid, pp. 47, 51.

36. Whitehead, "¿Qué Salío Mal y Por Qué?," p. 495.

37. Guy Poitras, "Mexico's 'New' Foreign Policy," *Inter-American Economic Affairs* 28, no. 3 (winter 1974), pp. 66–70.

38. Whitehead, "¿Qué Salío Mal y Por Qué?", p. 495 notes that in the case of the charter, as in the leading role played by Echeverría in the UN Conference on the Rights of the Sea, the president "achieved some victories on paper which however proved unsubstantial in practice, thus reinforcing the criticism that the President specialized in rhetoric, sermons, and the dispatch of optimistic decrees, more than in realistic evaluations of power and interests that would be affected if his proposals would be taken seriously. Although the General Assembly of the UN adopted the Mexican proposal for a Charter, the principal industrialized countries objected, which meant that they remained without practical effect to a degree even greater than the majority of UN resolutions" (pp. 495–496). Echeverría may have failed in his "Third Worldist" initiatives, but, as Whitehead notes, he was hardly alone as this was the same period which witnessed the development of splits between OPEC and oil-poor Third World nations, and the breakdown of multinational compacts in general. The ultimate humiliation, however, came for Echeverría when, after six years of posing himself as a primary spokesman for Third World interests, he received not even one vote in his bid for the secretary general's post at the United Nations.

39. Bennett et al., "Echeverría Sexenio in Mexico," p. 20.

40. Francisco José Paoli Bolio, "Petroleum and Political Change in Mexico," *Latin American Perspectives* 9, no. 1 (winter 1982), p. 68. Whitehead, "¿Qué Salío Mal y Por Qué?" p. 502 estimates that as much as $7 billion may have fled the country in this period.

41. Ifigenia de Navarrete. Study cited in CENCOS, National Center for Social Communication, Mexico, May 15, 1974.

42. Mexico's purchases from the United States rose to $2.6 billion in 1973, while her sales to the United States were only $1.7 billion. This trade deficit represented an increase of 90 percent over 1972.

43. Alan Riding, "Recession Interrupts Mexico's 20 Years of Growth," *Globe and Mail* (Toronto), February 1972.

44. Roger Bartra, "Capitalism and the Peasantry in Mexico," *Latin American Perspectives* 9, no. 1 (winter 1982), p. 37.

45. Ibid.

46. The injunctions served their purpose which was to buy time until Echeverría's successor would be installed as president. In the end only 42,416 acres were expropriated for which indemnification was promptly paid out. Ibid., p. 38.

47. The expansion of the state in this period, however, represents only the culmination of a long-term trend. Bailey notes that in 1930 the state employed 48,730 public servants in 21 agencies to serve a population of 17 million. By the time Echeverría left office in 1976, 1.3 million officials were employed in 1,018

agencies to serve 62 million Mexicans. John J. Bailey, "Presidency, Bureaucracy, and Administrative Reform in Mexico: The Secretariat of Programming and Budget," *Inter-American Economic Affairs* 34, no. 1 (Summer 1980), p. 33. Also see Alejandro Carrillo Castro, *La Reforma Administrativa en México* (México, D.F.: Ediciones INAP, 1978).

48. E.V.K. FitzGerald, "The State and Capital Accumulation in Mexico," *Journal of Latin American Studies* 10, no. 1 (November 1978), p. 278.

49. Ibid.

50. Looney, *Policy Analysis with Forecasts*, p. 71.

51. Ibid. p. 99.

52. Ibid. pp. 102, 99.

53. Ibid. Sanders gives some suggestion of the malfeasance to which the swift expansion and proliferation of government agencies gave rise. "Though Luis Echeverría, more than any recent Mexican president, drew attention to the backwardness of the rural sector and promoted a variety of stimuli to increase production, his efforts were neutralized by the profligacy and corruption of his administration. . . . The principal government institutions concerned with food such as the Secretariat of Agriculture and Livestock, the Secretariat of Agrarian Reform, the Companía Nacional de Subsistencias Populares (CONASUPO), and the Banco Nacional de Crédito Rural are all centers of corruption and inefficiency that lose millions of dollars annually. They publish only the most minimal financial data, refuse to grant interviews, and evade any form of public accountability." Thomas G. Sanders, "The Plight of Mexican Agriculture," *American Universities Field Staff Report* no. 3 (1979), pp. 15, 5.

54. For analyses of the limitations imposed on Echeverría by these exogenous factors see Whitehead, "¿Qué Salío Mal Y Por Qué?", p. 492; Looney, *Policy Analysis with Forecasts* pp. 77–78, 81–82, 96; and Bennett et al., "Echeverría Sexenio in Mexico," pp. 21–23.

55. The role of *porristas* is confusing for precisely this reason. Since the 1940s, provocateurs and shock troops in the pay of local, regional, or national politicians, or responsible directly to certain ministries and departments within the government, have been used on occasion in place of conventional law enforcement agents to squelch leftist activities in labor and peasant movements or on the university campuses. By the same token, hired thugs controlled by conservative capitalists have attacked the same sectors of the population, but have done so as much to undermine government authority as to repress leftist movements. It is often difficult to determine who controls or commands any particular band of political gangsters. These troops may be directed by political strongmen within the official party, by elements of the national bourgeoisie, or by both acting in concert. Often it is equally hard to tell if the left is under attack from political forces intent on simply suppressing leftist activities, or if the attack is also an attempt to embarrass the government. Obviously, from the point of view of the left-wing group under attack, the effect is the same in either case. It is important to note, however, that in whatever country they are found, it is the nature of such political thugs, recruited as they are from the ranks of unemployed and unemployable street toughs, that they

can be bought and utilized as political tools by any sector of the society that has the money necessary to sponsor paramilitary operations.

56. Martínez Domínguez was named president of the official party in 1968, a post from which he hoped to launch a campaign to win his party's nomination for the presidency of the republic. Díaz Ordaz himself may well have preferred to name the conservative Martínez Domínguez as his successor, but was forced by internal party pressures to give the nod to Echeverría. When Echeverría edged him out for the PRI nomination for president, Martínez Domínguez was "kicked upstairs" to the post of regent (in effect, mayor) of the Federal District. On both personal and ideological grounds, Martínez Domínquez regarded Echeverría with implacable hostility.

57. *Excelsior* (Mexico City), June 11, 1971.

58. As is usual in these events there are no absolutely reliable figures on the number of casualties, but the estimates given here are gleaned from newspaper reports and eye-witness accounts.

59. *Excelsior* (Mexico City), June 11, 12, 13, 1971. The fact that journalists themselves were physically assaulted by the *halcones* probably contributed, together with a temporary lifting of press censorship, to the accuracy of the report on this event.

60. *Excelsior* (México City), June 16, 1971.

61. Ibid.

62. For example, in August 1971, Carlos Fuentes wrote an article expressing qualified approval of the new president and his policies. Even then, however, Fuentes noted that Echeverría, "had not complied with one basic condition without which the policy of democratization could not be carried out: He did not dismantle the repressive apparatus created in 1968." Only two months later Fuentes had joined poet and essayist Octavio Paz, university leaders Heberto Castillo and Cabeza de Vaca, railraod workers' union leader Demitrio Vallejo, and electricians' union leader, Rafael Galvan, in the formation of what they hoped would become the core of an opposition movement of the Left. See Fuentes, *Tiempo Mexicano*, pp. 166, 192–193.

63. In July 1976, the progressive group of editors who had brought the Mexican daily *Excelsior* to hemispheric prominence as the leading independent newspaper in Latin America, was ousted from control of the paper in a rigged general assembly of the cooperative that owns the daily. Led by Julio Srherer, the progressive editors had pursued an editorial line of critical support for Echeverría. Toward the end of the Echeverría regime, as *Excelsior's* support on domestic issues turned increasingly to criticism, the *Excelsior* editors lost their access to high government officials and came under attack for their "lack of patriotism." The conservative takeover of *Excelsior* is generally seen as a significant turn to the right in the Echeverría regime. However, the question of who might have engineered it—Echeverría, a large investor in *Organización Editorial Mexicana*, which owns a chain of 27 newspapers in competition with *Excelsior*, or president-elect José López Portillo, who had not enjoyed *Excelsior's* endorsement during his precandidacy—remains unclear. For details see *Latin America* 10, no. 29 (July 23, 1976), pp. 229–230; and Daniel Levy and

Gabriel Székely, *Mexico: Paradoxes of Stability and Change* (Boulder, Colo.: Westview Press, 1982), pp. 93–99.

64. *Latin America* (London), August 30, 1974.

65. Ibid.

66. In 1971 Echeverría gave the word to the Ministry of Labor to recognize Rafael Galván's independent (non-CTM affiliated) electricians' union as a legitimate representative of the workers in contract negotiations.

67. For example, in 1974, Velázquez "won" a 20 percent across the board wage hike for CTM members, but the cost of living was up 42 percent in the same year, and the original demand had been for a 35 percent wage increase.

68. David F. Ronfeldt, "The Mexican Army and Political Order since 1940," in *Armies and Politics in Latin America*, edited by Abraham F. Lowenthal (New York: Holmes & Meier, 1976), argues that the Mexican army "may not be so inactive nor the political system as highly demilitarized as it often appears" (p. 294). Ronfeldt asserts that the army has important "residual political roles" which should not be overlooked "just because they are exercised in subordination to civilian ruling groups and strong political institutions" (ibid.). I believe that the significance of Echeverría's appeal to army leaders lies not in the fact that he recognized the army's importance, but in the open and effusive quality of the courtship he pressed.

69. Alan Riding, "Mexican Army, Amid Rumors, Insists It Steers Clear of Politics," *New York Times*, Feb. 5, 1974.

70. *Latin America* (London), July, 1974.

71. *New York Times*, November 7, 1973.

72. *Excelsior* (Mexico City), October 23, 1973.

73. As potential allies in his reform efforts, Echeverría possibly could have counted upon the support of Sergio Mendes Arceo, powerful bishop of Cuernavaca as well as other progressive churchmen. However the constitutional prohibition on political activity by the clergy was successfully invoked by the right to neutralize the potential alliance between the reformist *echeverristas* and the leaders of the Catholic left.

74. Looney, *Policy Analysis with Forecasts*, p. 65.

75. Ibid., pp. 118–119.

76. On the fiscal crises of 1976 see FitzGerald, "The State and Capital Accumulation," pp. 268–69; Whitehead, "¿Qué Salío Mal y Por Qué?"; and Looney, *Policy Analysis with Forecasts*, chapter 8.

CHAPTER 8

1. Donald D. Holt, "Why the Bankers Suddenly Love Mexico," *Fortune*, July 16, 1979, pp. 138–45.

2. David Gordon, "Mexico: A Survey," *The Economist*, April 22, 1978, p. 18.

3. Echeverrías's 18-hour workday was mentioned in virtually every early analysis of his administration.

4. Holt, "Bankers Suddenly Love Mexico," p. 139.

5. Ibid.

6. Lawrence Whitehead, "La Política Económica del Sexenio de Echeverría: ¿Qué Salio Mal y Por Qué?," *Foro Internacional* 20, no. 3 (enero/marzo 1980), p. 503.

7. George W. Grayson, "The Mexican Oil Boom," in *Mexico–U.S. Relations*, edited by Susan Kaufman Purcell (New York: Praeger, 1981), p. 156.

8. CONASUPO and INFONAVIT, however, continued to expand their operations even under López Portillo although the overall thrust of his policy was clearly away from social spending.

9. *Financial Times*, April 27, 1982. See also Jaime Ros, "La Encrucijada del Corto Plazo," *Nexos*, Issue 59, 5 (noviembre 1982), pp. 35–39.

10. Although television is nationally controlled, a large proportion of the broadcast time is given over to American mass audience programming which is dubbed into Spanish and sold, prepackaged, with advertisements for the products of transnational corporations slotted into the intervals in the show designed for commercials.

11. *Journal of Commerce*, February 18, 1982.

12. Claudia Dziobek, "Mexican Economy: Creative Financing to the Rescue," *NACLA Report on the Americas*, 17, no. 1 (January–February, 1983), p. 40.

13. *Proceso* (Mexico City) 14 septiembre 1982.

14. Ibid. Estimates on the value of the land and houses in this family compound vary from $8 million (*Washington Post*, September 9, 1982) to $50 million (*Los Angeles Times*, December 10, 1982). Attention and outrage have focused on the opulence of the materials used in construction, the foreign origin of the furnishings and appointments, and the use of government workers and equipment in construction of the four mansions and library.

15. The wage increases gave a 30 percent raise to those earning less than $430 a month, 20 percent to those earning between $430 and $650 a month, and 10 percent to workers earning more than $650.

16. *Financial Times*, April 27, 1982.

17. At one stage, when the price of oil was hovering around $34 per barrel, figures approaching $80 per barrel were confidently predicted in confidential U.S. government documents.

18. Dziobek, "Creative Financing," p. 42. Citibank was reported to have loaned half of its capital base to Mexico, a situation which obviously made this bank highly vulnerable.

19. Ibid. According to Dziobek (p. 41), the resources made available to Mexico included $1.85 billion through BIS, half of which was to be provided by the U.S. Federal Reserve; $1 billion in advanced payments from the American government for oil deliveries to its "Strategic Petroleum Reserve"; $1 billion in loans guaranteed by the U.S. Commodity Credit Corporation to finance food exports to Mexico; $300 million in prepaid oil shipments from Spain; and $4 to 5 billion from the IMF contingent upon agreements on an austerity plan.

20. José López Portillo, "State of the Nation Address," September 1, 1982.

21. Carlos Tello, "The Nationalized Banking System: First Specific Measures," *Commercio Exterior* 28, no. 10 (October 1982), p. 358.

22. *Latin America Weekly Report*, December 3, 1982, p. 6.

23. As of January 1983.

24. Tello, "Nationalized Banking System." Unfortunately the discretionary powers given to the executive to classify currency exchanges under either the preferential or the ordinary rate also opened a whole new range of opportunities for corrupt practices in the administration of the new system. For an analysis of this and other aspects of the nationalization, see *Nexos*, nos. 58 and 59 (October and November 1982).

25. Roger Bartra, "El Reto de la Izquierda," *Nexos*, no. 59 (noviembre 1982), p. 15.

26. Carlos Monsiváis cited Ibid., p. 18. Ross, a long-time observer of Mexican politics, notes that rumors of coup d'état reached genuinely alarming levels in both 1976 and 1982. See Stanley R. Ross, "LEA and Don Pepe, 1976 and 1982: Divergent Approaches to the Presidential Succession," *The Mexican Forum* 3, no. 1 (January 1983), p. 11.

27. The bulk of the López Portillo administration was equally in the dark, for the nationalization plan had been formulated by a secret committee struck for that purpose.

28. In this period of López Portillo's shaky lame duck administration, the director of the Bank of Mexico, Miguel Mancera, a man opposed to nationalization was replaced by Carlos Tello, the leftist architect of the bank nationalization scheme. Tello's overall concept of economic development was unacceptable to the incoming president. Predictably, de la Madrid, upon assuming office, fired Tello and replaced him with Mancera.

29. Although he is committed to reducing protectionist barriers, at this writing Miguel de la Madrid seems unable to bring his country into GATT, the General Agreement on Tariffs and Trade, because of the strong opposition in Mexico to such a move, based on nationalist sentiment.

30. See Enrique Krauze, "Mexico: The Rudder and the Storm," *The Mexican Forum*, 3 (January 1983), pp. 1–9.

31. See, for example, the opening sentence to a chapter on the military in Robert F. Adie and Guy Poitras, *Latin America: The Politics of Immobility* (Englewood Cliffs, N.J.: Prentice-Hall, 1974), p. 189. "The military in Latin America, except in countries like Costa Rica and Mexico, plays a pivotal role in the various political systems of the area."

32. Pablo González Casanova, *Democracy in Mexico* (New York: Oxford University Press, 1972), p. 37.

33. Ibid., pp. 36–37. Also see David F. Ronfeldt, "The Mexican Army and Political Order since 1940," in *Armies and Politics in Latin America*, edited by Abraham P. Lowenthal (New York: Holmes & Meier, 1976).

34. Susan Kaufman Purcell, "The Future of the Mexican System," in *Authoritarianism in Mexico*, edited by José Luis Reyna and Richard S. Weinert (Philadelphia: Institute for the Study of Human Issues, 1977), p. 187. Also see

Roger Bartra, *El Reto de la Izquierda* (México, D.F.: Editorial Grijalbo, 1982), pp. 38–39.

35. Ronfeldt, "Army and Political Order," pp. 294–299.

36. Ibid., p. 296. Granados Roldán argues that the military is assuming greater importance because of its expanded role in the Southeast of Mexico. Here the army is increasingly involved in guarding the oil fields and the border (against spillover of the conflicts in Central America). See Otto Granados Roldán, "Ejercito: ¿Regreso a las Armas?" in *El Desafio Mexicano*, edited by Héctor Aguilar Carmín (Mexico, D.F.: Ediciones Oceano, 1982), pp. 126–130.

37. Marlise Simons, "Mexico Trains a Quick-Reaction Force," *Washington Post*, February 18, 1982.

38. Héctor Islas, "The 1982 Elections: Many Votes and Some Figures," *Commercio Exterior* 28, no. 8 (August 1982), p. 263.

39. Nuria Fernández, "La Izquierda Mexicana en las Elecciones," *Cuadernos Políticos* no. 33 (julio-septiembre 1982), pp. 51–52.

40. Evelyn P. Stevens, "Mexico's PRI: The Institutionalization of Corporatism?" in *Authoritarianism and Corporatism in Latin America*, edited by James M. Malloy (Pittsburgh: University of Pittsburgh Press, 1977), p. 227.

41. Alex M. Saragoza, "El Grupo Monterrey and Mexican Popular Culture." Paper presented to the VI Conference of Mexican and United States Historians, Chicago, September 1981, p. 3. (*Charros* are Mexican cowboys, *mariachis* are musicians, and *adelitas* are the women who followed the revolutionary troops). The leftist periodical, *Punto Critico*, notes that even the left is to some degree taken in by the "ambiguous, nationalistic and apparently revolutionary ideology" of the political elite. See *Punto Critico*, "Mexico: Class Struggle and 'Political Reform'," *Contemporary Marxism*, no. 1 (Spring 1980), pp. 77–78.

42. "Social banditry, a universal and virtually unchanging phenomenon, is little more than endemic peasant protest against oppression and poverty: a cry for vengeance on the rich and the oppressors, a vague dream of some curb upon them, a righting of individual wrongs. . . . Social banditry, though a protest, is a modest and unrevolutionary protest. It protests not against the fact that peasants are poor and oppressed, but that they are sometimes excessively poor and oppressed." Eric J. Hobsbawm, *Primitive Rebels* (New York: W. W. Norton, 1959), pp. 5, 24. See also Hobsbawm, *Bandits* (New York: Dell, 1969), p. 16. In the period of heightened guerrilla activity in Guerrero State, the *Los Angeles Times* (December 19, 1971) reported: "Federal officials estimate that Guerrero's 1.5 million people account for at least 2,500 homicides a year but admit that the figure is only an estimate. None but the more sensational killings attract attention outside the lawless backlands."

43. For an analysis of the class base and national character of the Vietnamese NLF, see Eric Wolf, *Peasant Wars of the Twentieth Century* (New York: Harper and Row, 1969), chapter four.

44. Marlise Simons, *Washington Post*, June 30, 1974. The political program of Jénaro Vázquez and Lucio Cabañas can be found in English in NACLA, "The Mexican Struggle," *Latin America and Empire Report* 6, no. 3 (March 1972). Also see ¿Porqué? no. 160 (July 22), 1971 and no. 161 (July 19, 1971).

45. Kevin J. Middlebrook, "International Implications of Labor Change: The Automobile Industry," in *Mexico's Political Economy: Challenges at Home and Abroad*, edited by Jorge I. Domínguez (Beverly Hills: Sage Publications, 1982), p. 158.

46. Richard L. Harris and David Barkin, "The Political Economy of Mexico in the Eighties," *Latin American Perspectives* 9, no. 1 (winter 1982), p. 13. Raúl Trejo Delarbre, "El Movimiento Obrero: Situación y Perspectivas," in *Mexico Hoy* edited by Pablo González Casanova and Enrique Florescano (Mexico, D. F.: Siglo Veintiuno Editores, 1979), pp. 135–136.

47. *Solidaridad*, May 1978. Cited in Howard Handelman, "Organized Labor in Mexico: Oligarchy and Dissent," *American Universities Field Staff Reports* no. 18 (1979), p. 11.

48. Trejo Delarbre, "El Movimiento Obrero," p. 138.

49. Ibid., pp. 131, 139.

50. Ibid., p. 131.

51. For the history of struggle of the electricians' unions see Mark Thompson, "The Development of Unionism among Mexican Electrical Workers." Ph.D. diss., Cornell University, 1966; Silvia Gómez Tagle and Marcelo Miquet, "Integración o Democracia Sindical: El Caso de los Electricistas," in *Tres Estudios Sobre el Movimiento Obrero en México*, edited by José Luis Reyna et al (México, D. F.: El Colegio de México, 1976); and Howard Handelman, "The Politics of Labor Protest in Mexico: Two Case Studies," *Journal of Interamerican Studies and World Affairs* 18, no. 3 (August 1976).

52. These demonstrations included one in July 1972 which mobilized 100,000 workers (Handelman, "Politics of Labor Protest," 1976, p. 285) and another in November 1975 which drew 200,000 to the center of Mexico City (Peter Baird and Ed McCaughan, "Labor and Imperialism in Mexico's Electrical Industry," *NACLA Report on the Americas*, 11, no. 6 [September–October 1977], p. 35).

53. Trejo Delarbre, "El Movimiento Obrero," p. 140.

54. Antonio Gershenson, quoted in Baird and McCaughan, "Mexico's Electrical Industry," p. 38.

55. Arnaldo Córdova, "Mass Politics and the Future of the Left in Mexico," *Latin American Perspectives*, 9, no. 1 (winter 1982), p. 100.

56. Trejo Delarbe, "El Movimiento Obrero," pp. 143, 148.

57. Pablo González Casanova, "Mexico: The Most Probable Course of Development," *Latin American Perspectives* 9, no. 1 (Winter 1982), p. 84.

58. Barry Carr, "The Development of Communism and Marxism in Mexico—A Historiographical Essay." Paper presented to the VI Conference of Mexican and United States Historians, Chicago, September 1981.

59. Jorge Montaño, *Los Pobres de la Ciudad en los Asentamientos Espontáneos*, (Mexico, D. F.: Siglo Veintiuno Editores, 1976), chapter 3.

60. Nuria Fernández, "La Izquierda Mexicana en las Elecciones," *Cuadernos Políticos* no. 33 (julio–septiembre 1982), p. 57. The most important of these coordinating organizations are: the Coordinadora Nacional Plan de Ayala

(CNPA) which groups independent peasant organizations; Coordinadora Nacional del Movimiento Urbano Popular (CONAMUP), which coordinates the struggles in slums, *ciudades perdidas*, and squatters' settlements; the Coordinadora Nacional de Trabajadores de la Educación (CNTE), which carries forward the struggle for a nationwide teachers' and university workers' organization; the Coordinadora Sindical Nacional (COSINA), which attempts to coordinate the efforts of independent trade unions and democratic currents within official trade unions; and the Frente Nacional Contra la Represión (FNCR), organized to coordinate resistance to repression everywhere in the republic. At this writing the most recent such grouping to emerge is the Frente Contra la Austeridad, the anti-austerity front which incorporates the five *coordinadores* listed above.

BIBLIOGRAPHY

Abercrombie, R. S. "Mecanización Agrícola y Ocupación en América Latina." In Ernest Feder, ed., *La Lucha de Clases en el Campo*. Mexico, D. F.: Fondo de Cultura Económica, 1975.

Adie, Robert F. "Cooperation, Cooptation and Conflict in Mexican Peasant Organizations." *Inter-American Economic Affairs* 24 (Winter 1970).

Adie, Robert F., and Guy E. Poitras. *Latin America: The Politics of Immobility*. Englewood Cliffs, N.J.: Prentice-Hall, 1974.

Adler, Judith. *The Politics of Land Reform in Mexico*. M. Phil. Thesis, London School of Economics, 1970.

Aguilar Camín, Héctor., ed. *El Desafio Mexicano*. México, D. F.: Ediciones Oceano, 1982.

Aguilar M., Alonso et al. *Política Mexicana Sobre Inversiones Estranjeras*. México, D. F.: Instituto de Investigaciones Económicas, 1977.

Aguilar Mora, Manuel. *La Crisis de la Izquierda en México: Orígenes y Desarrollo*. México, D. F.: Juan Pablos, 1978.

Alba, Francisco. "Industrialización Sustitutiva y Migración Internacional: El Caso de México." *Foro Internacional* 18, no. 3 (enero–marzo) 1978.

———. *The Population of Mexico: Trends, Issues, and Policies*. New Brunswick: Transaction Books, 1982.

Alba, Victór. *Historia del Movimiento Obrero en América Latina*. México, D. F.: Libreros Mexicanos Unidos, 1964.

Alcántara Ferrer, Sergio. *La Organización Colectivista Ejidal en la Comarca Lagunera*. México, D. F.: Centro de Investigaciones Agrarias, 1967.

Alexander, Robert J. *Communism in Latin America*, New Brunswick, N.J.: Rutgers University Press, 1957.

———. *Organized Labor in Latin America*, New York: The Free Press, 1965.

Alinsky, Marvin. "Population and Migration Problems in Mexico." *Current History* 80, no. 469 (November 1981).

Allub, Leopoldo, and M. A. Michael. "Petróleo y Cambio Social en el Sureste de México." *Foro Internacional* 18, no. 4 (1978).

Almada Bay, Ignacio. "Salud: Muertos Qui No Hacen Ruido." In Héctor Aguilar Camín, ed. *El Desafio Mexicano*. México, D.F.: Ediciones Oceano, 1982.

Almond, Gabriel A., and Sidney Verba. *The Civic Culture*. Boston: Little, Brown and Company, 1965.

Alonso, Antonio. *El Movimiento Ferrocarrilero en México*. México, D. F.: Ediciones ERA, 1975.

Alonso, Jorge, ed. *El Estado Mexicano*. México, D. F.: Editorial Nueva Imagen, 1982.

Alonso, Jorge et al., *Los Campesinos de la Tierra de Zapata: Subsistencia y Explotación*. México, D. F.: CIS-INAH, 1974.

Alvarez, Alejandro, and Elena Sandoval. "Industrial Development and the Working Class in Mexico." *LARU Studies no. 1* (October 1976).

Araiza, Luis. *Historia de la Casa del Obrero Mundial.* México, D.F.: 1963.

Arizpe, Lourdes. *Indígenas en la Ciudad de México: El Caso de las 'Marias.'* México, D. F.: SepSetentas, 1975.

Arriola, Carlos. "Los Grupos Empresariales Frente al Estado (1973–1975)." *Foro Internacional* 16, no. 4 (abril–junio 1976).

Ashby, Joe C. *Organized Labor and the Mexican Revolution Under Lázaro Cárdenas.* Chapel Hill: University of North Carolina Press, 1967.

Ávila Camacho, Manuel. *Pensamiento Político.* México, D. F.: 1945.

Baerresen, Donald W., "Unemployment and Mexico's Border Industrialization Program." *Inter-American Economic Affairs* 29, no. 2 (Autumn 1975).

Bailey, John J. "Agrarian Reform in Mexico: the Quest for Self-Sufficiency." *Current History* 80, no. 469 (November 1981).

———. "Presidency, Bureaucracy, and Administrative Reform in Mexico: The Secretariat of Programming and Budget." *Inter-American Economic Affairs* 34, no. 1 (Summer 1980).

Bailey, John, and John Link. "Statecraft and Agriculture in Mexico: Domestic and Foreign Policy Considerations." *U.S.–Mexican Studies* (Program in United States–Mexican Studies, University of California, San Diego), no. 23 (1981).

Baird, Peter, and Ed McCaughan. *Beyond the Border: Mexico and the U.S. Today.* New York: North American Congress on Latin America, 1979.

———. "Power Struggle: Labor and Imperialism in Mexico's Electrical Industry." *NACLA Report on the Americas* 11, no. 6 (September–October 1977).

Ballesteros Porta, Juan. *¿Explotación Individual o Colectiva?: El Caso de Los Ejidos de Tlahualilo.* México, D. F.: Centro de Investigaciones Agrarias, 1964.

Banco de México. *Encuesta Sobre Ingreso y Gastos Familiares en México.* México, D. F.: Banco de México, 1967.

Banco de México de Comercio Exterior, "La Industria Maquiladora: Evolución Reciente y Perspectivas." *Commercio Exterior* 28, no. 4 (April 1978).

Banco Nacional de México. *Review of the Economic Situation in Mexico* 57, no. 662 (January 1981).

Barkin, David. *Desarrollo Regional y Reorganización Campesina.* México, D. F.: Nueva Imagen, 1978.

———. "Mexico's Albatross: The U.S. Economy." *Latin American Perspectives* 2, no. 2 (Summer 1975).

———. "Education and Class Structure: The Dynamics of Social Control in Mexico." *Politics & Society* 5, no. 2 (1975).

———. "The Persistence of Poverty in Mexico: Some Explanatory Hypotheses." Paper delivered to the Latin American Studies Association, Washington, D.C., April 1970.

Barkin, David, and Gustavo Esteva. *Inflación y Democracia: El Caso de México.* México, D.F.: Editorial Siglo Veintiuno, 1979.

_____. "Social Conflict and Inflation in Mexico." *Latin American Perspectives* 9, no. 1 (Winter 1982).

Bartra, Roger. "Capitalism and the Peasantry in Mexico." *Latin American Perspectives* 9, no. 1 (Winter, 1982).

_____. *Estructura Agraria y Clases Sociales en México*. México, D.F.: Ediciones ERA, 1974.

_____. *El Reto de la Izquierda*. México, D.F.: Editorial Grijalbo, 1982.

Basáñez, Miguel. *La Lucha por la Hegemonía en México 1968–1980*. México, D.F.: Siglo Veintiuno Editores, 1981.

Bataillon, Claude, and Hélène Rivière D'Arc. *La Ciudad de México*. México, D.F.: SepSetentas, 1973.

Beals, Carleton. *Mexico: An Interpretation*. New York: 1923.

Becklund, Laurie, and Robert Montemayor. "Land Reform: The Revolution that Failed." *Los Angeles Times*, 15 July 1979.

Bejar Navarro, Raúl. "La Cultura Popular en los Setentas." Paper presented at the VI Conference of Mexican and United States Historians, University of Chicago, Chicago, Illinois, September 1981.

Bennett, Douglas, and Kenneth E. Sharpe. "El Control de las Multinacionales: Las Contradicciones de la Mexicanización." *Foro Internacional* 21, no. 4 (abril–junio 1981).

Bennett, Douglas et al. "National and International Constraints on the Exercise of Power by the State: The Echeverría Sexenio in Mexico." Paper presented to the Latin American Studies Association, Pittsburgh, April 1979.

Bermúdez, Antonio J. *The Mexican National Petroleum Industry: A Case-Study in Nationalization*. Stanford: Institute of Hispanic-American and Luso-Brazilian Studies, Stanford University, 1963.

Bizzarro, Salvatore. "Mexico's Poor." *Current History* 80, no. 469 (November 1981).

Boletín Demográfico–CELADE. "Población Total de la Region por Paises, 1920–2000," no. 23 (1979).

Boltvinik, Julio. "Marginación: En la Base de la Piramide." In Héctor Aguilar Camín, ed. *El Desafio Mexicano*. México, D.F.: Ediciones Oceano, 1982.

Brading, David A., ed. *Caudillo and Peasant in the Mexican Revolution*. Cambridge: Cambridge University Press, 1980.

Brand, Donald D. *Mexico: Land of Sunshine and Shadow*. Princeton: D. Van Nostrand, 1966.

Brandenburg, Frank R. *The Making of Modern Mexico*. Englewood Cliffs, N.J.: Prentice-Hall, 1964.

_____. *Mexico: An Experiment in One Party Democracy*, Ph.D. Dissertation, University of Pennsylvania, 1955.

_____. "Organized Business in Mexico." *Inter-American Economic Affairs* 12 (Winter 1958).

Briggs, Vernon Jr., "Labor Market Aspects of Mexican Migration to the United States in the 1970s." In Stanley R. Ross, ed., *Views Across the Border: The*

United States and Mexico. Albuquerque: University of New Mexico Press, 1978.

Bustamante, Jorge A. "Undocumented Immigration from Mexico: Research Report." *International Migration Review* 11, no. 2 (1977).

Cabrera, Ignacio. "Crisis Económica y Estrategia Petrolera en México." *Cuadernos Politicos,* no. 28 (abril–junio 1981).

Calvert, Peter. *The Mexican Revolution, 1910–1914: The Diplomacy of Anglo-American Conflict.* Cambridge: Cambridge University Press, 1968.

Camp, Roderic Ai. "Intellectuals and the State in Mexico, 1920–1980: The Influence of Family and Education." Paper presented to the VI Conference of Mexican and United States Historians, Chicago, September 1981.

――――. "Mexican Governors since Cárdenas: Education and Career Contracts." *Journal of Interamerican Studies and World Affairs* 16, no. 4 (November 1974).

――――. *Mexican Political Biographies, 1935–1975.* Tucson: University of Arizona Press, 1976.

――――. "The Middle-Level Technocrat in Mexico." *Journal of Developing Areas* 6, no. 4 (July 1972).

――――. "The National School of Economics and Public Life in Mexico." *Latin American Research Review* 10, no. 3 (Fall 1975).

Camposeco, Miguel Angel. "El Proceso Político de Renovación en México." *Nueva Sociedad,* no. 35 (marzo–abril 1978).

Caporaso, James. "Introduction: Dependence and Dependency in the Global System." *International Organization* 32, no. 1 (Winter 1978).

Carlos, Manuel L. "State Policies, State Penetration and Ecology: A Comparative Analysis of Uneven Development in Mexico's Micro Agrarian Regions." *Working Papers in US–Mexican Studies* (Program in United States–Mexican Studies, University of California, San Diego), no. 19 (1981).

Carmona, Fernando et al. *El Milagro Mexicano,* México, D.F.: Editorial Nuestro Tiempo, 1970.

Carr, Barry. "The Development of Communism and Marxism in Mexico—A Historiographical Essay." Paper presented to the VI Conference of Mexican and United States Historians, Chicago, September 1981.

――――. "Impresiones del XIX Congreso del PCM, 1981." *Cuadernos Políticos,* no. 29 (julio–septiembre 1981).

――――. "The Peculiarities of the Mexican North, 1880–1928: An Essay in Interpretation." *Occasional Paper* (Institute of Latin American Studies, University of Glasgow), no. 4 (1971).

Carrada-Bravo, Francisco. *Oil, Money, and the Mexican Economy: A Macroeconometric Analysis.* Boulder, Colorado: Westview Press, 1982.

Carrillo Castro, Alejandro. *"La Reforma Administrativa en México."* México, D.F.: Ediciones INAP, 1978.

Carrión, Jorge. "Retablo de la Política 'a la Mexicana.' " In Fernando Carmona et al., *El Milagro Mexicano,* México, D.F.: Editorial Nuestro Tiempo, 1970.

_____ et al. *Tres Culturas en Agonía*, México, D.F.: Editorial Nuestro Tiempo. 1969.

Castillo, Heberto. "Comprometer Nuestro Petroleo es Comprometer México." *Proceso* (20 June 1977).

Ceceña, José Luis. *El Capital Monopolista y la Economía de México*. México, D.F.: Cuadernos Americanos, 1963.

_____. *México en la Orbita Imperial*. México, D.F.: Ediciones El Cabillito, 1970.

Centro de Investigaciones Agrarias. *Estructura Agraria y Desarrollo Agrícola en México*. México, D.F.: Fondo de Cultura Económica, 1979.

Centro Latinoamericano de Demografía. "América Latina: Indice de Crecimento de la Población en el Periodo 1950–2000." *Boletín Demográfico* (Santiago, Chile) 7 (January 1974).

Centro Operacional de Vivienda y Poblamiento. *Investigación Sobre Vivienda* 11. México, D.F.: COVP, 1977.

Chance, John R. "Recent Trends in Latin American Urban Studies." *Latin American Research Review* 15, no. 1 (1980).

Chevalier, François. "The *Ejido* and Political Stability in Mexico," in Claudio Veliz, ed., *The Politics of Conformity in Latin America*. New York: Oxford University Press, 1967.

Clark, Marjorie Ruth. *Organized Labor in Mexico*. Chapel Hill: University of North Carolina Press, 1934.

Clavijo, Fernando. "Reflexiones en Torno a la Inflación Mexicana 1960–1980." *El Trimestre Económico* 47, no. 4 (octubre–diciembre 1980).

Cline, Howard F. *The United States and Mexico*. New York: Atheneum, 1965.

Cockcroft, James, and Bo Anderson. "Control and Cooptation in Mexican Politics," in Irving Louis Horowitz et al. , eds., *Latin American Radicalism*. New York: Random House, 1969.

El Colegio de México. *Estudio Demográfico del Distrito Federal*. México, D.F.: El Colegio de México, 1975.

Coleman, Kenneth M., and Charles L. Davis. "Preemptive Reform and the Mexican Working Class." *Latin American Research Review* 18, no. 1 (1983).

Confederación de Trabajadores de México. *Informe del Comité Nacional*. México, D.F.: 1936–1937.

Consejo Nacional de Ciencia y Technología. *National Program for Science and Technology, 1978–1982*. México, D.F.: CONACYT, 1978.

_____. *El Petróleo en México y en el Mundo*. México, D.F.: CONACYT, 1979.

Corbett, John G. "Agricultural Modernization and Rural Employment in Mexico, 1980–1985: Implications for Mexican Migration to the United States." Paper presented to the XLIII International Congress of Americanists, Vancouver, August 1979.

Cordera, Rolando, and Carlos Tello. *México la Disputa por la Nación: Perspectivas y Opciones del Desarrollo*. México, D.F.: Siglo Veintiuno Editores 1981.

Córdova, Arnaldo. *La Ideologia de la Revolución Mexicana: la Formación del Nuevo Régimen*. México, D.F.: Ediciones ERA, 1973.

_____. "Mass Politics and the Future of the Left in Mexico." *Latin American Perspectives* 9, no. 1 (Winter 1982).

_____. *La Política de las Masas del Cardenismo*. México, D.F.: Ediciones ERA, 1974.

Cornelius, Wayne A. *Mexican Migration to the United States: Causes, Consequences, and U.S. Responses*. Cambridge: Center for International Studies, Massachusetts Institute of Technology, 1978.

_____. *Politics and the Migrant Poor in Mexico City*. Stanford: Stanford University Press, 1975.

Cosío Villegas, Daniel. *El Estilo Personal de Goberar*. México, D.F.: Editorial Joaquín Mortiz, 1974.

_____. "The Mexican Left," in Joseph Maier and Richard W. Weatherhead, eds., *The Politics of Change in Latin America*. New York: Praeger, 1964.

_____. *El Sistema Político Mexicano*. México, D.F.: Editorial Joaquín Mortiz, 1972.

Cumberland, Charles Curtis. *The Mexican Revolution: Genesis Under Madero*. New York: Greenwood Press, 1969.

_____. *Mexico: The Struggle for Modernity*. New York: Oxford University Press, 1968.

Danel, Fernando. "México: Crisis, Redespliegue Capitalista y Luchas Democráticas." *Americalatina: Estudios y Perspectivas*, no. 2 (1980).

de Lannoy, Jean Louis M. "Student Political Activism in Mexico." Paper presented to the Canadian Sociology and Anthropology Association, May 1973.

de la Peña, Sergio. "El PRI y las Fuerzas Proletarias en México." *Americalatina: Estudios y Perspectivas*, no. 2 (1980).

_____. "Proletarian Power and State Monopoly Capitalism in Mexico." *Latin American Perspectives* 9, No. 1 (Winter 1982).

de la Torre, Rodolfo. "Primeros Resultados del Censo." *Razones* 14 (July 1980).

del Castillo Vera, Gustavo. "El Desarrollo de la Hacienda Algodonera en la Laguna en el Siglo XIX." Paper presented at the Seminario sobre Haciendas en México, CIS-INAH, Tlalpan, February 1977.

_____. "Reflexiones sobre el Proyecto de la Laguna." CIS-INAH, 22 marzo 1977.

del Villar, Samuel I. "Estado y Petróleo en México: Experiencias y Perspectivas." *Foro Internacional* 20, no. 1 (julio–septiembre 1979).

Díaz Serrano, Jorge. "La Mayor Riqueza Petrolera Jamás Imaginada en México." *Económica* (16 November 1977).

Dillman, C. Daniel. "Assembly Industries in Mexico: Contexts of Development." *Journal of Interamerican Studies and World Affairs* 25, no. 1 (February 1983).

Domínguez, Jorge I. *Mexico's Political Economy: Challenges at Home and Abroad*. Beverly Hills: Sage Publications, 1982.

Dovring, Folke. "Land Reform and Productivity: The Mexican Case, Analysis of Census Data." Madison: The Land Tenure Center, 1969.

Dziobek, Claudia. "Mexican Economy: Creative Financing to the Rescue." NACLA Report on the Americas 17, no. 1 (January–February, 1983).

Eckstein, Salomón. El Ejido Colectivo en México. México, D.F.: Fondo de Cultura Económica, 1967.

_____. El Marco Macroeconómico del Problema Agrario Mexicano. México, D.F.: Centro de Investigaciones Agrarias, 1968.

Eckstein, Shlomo. "Collective Farming in Mexico." In Rodolfo Stavenhagen, ed., Agrarian Problems and Peasant Movements in Latin America. Garden City: Doubleday and Company, 1970.

Eckstein, Susan. The Poverty of Revolution: The State and the Urban Poor in Mexico. Princeton: Princeton University Press, 1977.

Edelman, Marc. "Agricultural Modernization in Smallholding Areas of Mexico: A Case Study in the Sierra Norte de Puebla." Latin American Perspectives 7, no. 4 (Fall 1980).

Edelman, Murray. The Symbolic Uses of Politics. Urbana: University of Illinois Press, 1967.

Erb, Richard D., and Stanley R. Ross, eds. United States Relations with Mexico: Context and Content. Washington, D.C.: American Enterprise Institute, 1981.

Escudero, Roberto, and Salvador Martínez Della Rocca. "Mexico: Generation of 68." NACLA Report on the Americas 12, no. 5 (September–October 1978).

Evans, John S., and Dilmus D. James. "Conditions of Employment in Mexico as Incentives for Mexican Migration to the United States: Prospects to the End of the Century." International Migration Review 13, no. 1 (1979).

Fagen, Richard R., and William S. Tuohy. Politics and Privilege in a Mexican City. Stanford: Stanford University Press, 1972.

Fajnzylber, Fernando. "Las Empresas Transnacionales y el Sistema Industrial de México." El Trimestre Económico 42, no. 14 (octubre–diciembre 1975).

Fajnzylber, Fernando, and Trinidad Martínez Tarrago. Las Empresas Transnacionales: Expansión a Nivel Mundial y Proyección en la Industria Mexicana. México, D.F.: Fondo de Cultura Económica, 1976.

Feder, Ernest. "Capitalism's Last-ditch Effort to Save Underdeveloped Agricultures: International Agribusiness, the World Bank and the Rural Poor." Journal of Contemporary Asia 7, no. 1 (1977).

_____. Strawberry Imperialism: An Inquiry into the Mechanisms of Dependency in Mexican Agriculture. The Hague: Institute of Social Studies, 1977.

Felix, David. "Income Inequality in Mexico." Current History 72, no. 425 (March 1977).

Fenster, Leo. "At Twice the Price: The Mexican Auto Swindle." The Nation, 2 June 1970.

Fernández, Nuria. "La Izquierda Mexicana en las Elecciones." Cuadernos Políticos, no. 33 (julio–septiembre 1982).

_____. "Lucha de Clases e Izquierda en México." *Cuadernos Políticos*, no. 30 (octubre–diciembre 1981).

FitzGerald, E.V.K. "A Note on Capital Accumulation in Mexico: The Budget Deficit and Investment Finance." *Development and Change* 11, no. 3 (July 1980).

_____. "The State and Capital Accumulation in Mexico." *Journal of Latin American Studies* 10, no. 1 (November 1978).

Flanigan, James. "North of the Border—Who Needs Whom?" *Forbes*, 15 April 1977.

_____. "Pemex to Brown and Root: Yankee Come In." *Forbes*, 15 August 1977.

_____. "Why Won't the Mexicans Sell Us More Oil?" *Forbes*, 29 October 1979.

Flores, Edmundo. *Tratado de Economía Agrícola*. México, D.F.: Fondo de Cultura Económica, 1968.

Flores Caballero, Romeo, and María de los Ángeles Moreno. "El Endeudamiento de México, 1970–1974." *El Trimestre Económico* 43, no. 3 (julio–septiembre 1976).

Frank, Andrew Gunder. "Mexico: The Janus Faces of Twentieth Century Bourgeois Revolution." *Monthly Review* 14, no. 7 (November 1962).

Friedrich, Paul. *Agrarian Revolt in a Mexican Village*. Englewood Cliffs, N.J.: Prentice-Hall, 1970.

Fuentes, Carlos. *The Death of Artemio Cruz*. New York: Noonday Press, 1971.

_____. *Tiempo Mexicano*. México, D.F.: Cuadernos de Joaquín Mortiz, 1973.

_____. *Where the Air Is Clear*. New York: Noonday Press, 1971.

Galarza, Ernest. "Trabajadores Mexicanos en Tierra Extranjera." In *Problemas Agrícolas e Industriales de México*. (enero–junio, 1958).

Galeano, Eduardo. *Open Veins of Latin America*. New York: Monthly Review Press, 1973.

Gandará M., Leticia. "Las Haciendas en la Comarca Lagunera." Paper presented at the Seminario sobre Haciendas en México, CIS-INAH, Tlalpan, February 1977.

Glade, William P., and Charles W. Anderson. *The Political Economy of Mexico*. Madison: University of Wisconsin Press, 1968.

Goldfrank, Walter. "World System, State Structure, and the Onset of the Mexican Revolution." *Politics & Society*, vol. 5, no. 4, 1975.

Gómez Tagle, Silvia. "La Reforma y el Problema de la Representación Política de las Clases Sociales." In Jorge Alonso, ed., *El Estado Mexicano*. México, D.F.: Nueva Imagen, 1982.

_____. *Organización de las Sociedades de Crédito Ejidal en La Laguna*. Tesis profesional, UNAM, 1968.

González Casanova, Pablo. "Las Alternativas de la Democracia." In Pablo González Casanova and Enrique Florescano, eds., *México Hoy*. México, D.F.: Siglo Veintiuno Editores, 1979.

_____. *Democracy in Mexico*. New York: Oxford University Press, 1972.

_____. "The Economic Development of Mexico." *Scientific American* 243, no. 3 (September 1980).

_____. "Mexico: The Most Probable Course of Development." *Latin American Perspectives* 9, no. 1 (Winter 1982).

_____. "The Political Reform in Mexico." *LARU Studies* 3, no. 1 (January–April 1979).

González Casanova, Pablo, and Enrique Florescano. *México Hoy*. México, D.F.: Siglo Veintiuno Editores, 1979.

González de Alba, Luis. *Los Días y Los Años*. México, D.F.: Ediciones ERA, 1971.

González Navarro, Moisés. *La Confederación Nacional Campesina*. México, D.F.: Costa-Amic, 1968.

González Ramírez, Manuel. *La Revolución Social de México*. Vol. 3, *El Problema Agrario*. México, D.F.: Fondo de Cultura Económica, 1966.

Gordon, David. "Mexico: A Survey." *The Economist* 267, no. 7025 (22 April 1978).

Gordon, Wendell. "The Case for a Less Restrictive Border Policy." *Social Science Quarterly* 56, no. 3 (December 1975).

Goulden, Joseph C. "Mexico: PRI's False Front Democracy." *Alicia Patterson Fund Reprint*. December 1966.

Graciarena, Jorge. *Poder y Clases Sociales en el Desarrollo de América Latina*. Buenos Aires: Editorial Paidós, 1967.

Granados Chapa, Miguel Angel. "El Reformismo se Reforma." *Cuadernos del Tercer Mundo* 2., no. 14 (julio 1977).

Granados Roldán, Otto. "Ejercito: ¿Regreso a las Armas?" In Héctor Aguilar Camín, ed. *El Desafio Mexicano*. México, D.F.: Ediciones Oceano, 1982.

Grayson, George W. "Mexican Foreign Policy." *Current History* 72, no. 425 (March 1977).

_____. "The Mexican Oil Boom." In Susan Kaufman Purcell, ed., *Mexico-United States Relations*. New York: Praeger, 1981.

_____. "Oil and Politics in Mexico." *Current History* 80, no. 469 (November 1981).

_____. "Oil and U.S.-Mexican Relations." *Journal of Interamerican Studies and World Affairs* 21, no. 4 (November 1979).

_____. *The Politics of Mexican Oil*. Pittsburgh: University of Pittsburgh Press, 1980.

Graziano, Luigi. "A Conceptual Framework for the Study of Clientelism." *Western Societies Occasional Paper* (Center for International Studies, Cornell University), no. 2 (April 1975).

Grindle, Merilee S. *Bureaucrats, Politicians and Peasants in Mexico: A Case Study in Public Policy*. Berkeley: University of California Press, 1977.

_____. "Patrons and Clients in the Bureaucracy: Career Networks in Mexico." *Latin American Research Review* 12, no. 1 (1977).

_____. "Policy Change in an Authoritarian Regime." *Journal of Interamerican Studies and World Affairs* 19, no. 4 (November 1977).

_____. "Power, Expertise and the 'Tecnico': Suggestions from a Mexican Case Study." *The Journal of Politics* 39, no. 2 (May 1977).

Gruening, Ernest. *Mexico and Its Heritage*. New York: The Century Company, 1928.

Guevara Niebla, Gilberto. "El Movimiento Estudiantil de 1968." *Cuadernos Políticos*, no. 17 (julio–septiembre 1978).

Gutierrez R. Roberto. "La Balanza Petrolera de México, 1970–1982." *Comercio Exterior* 29, no. 8 (August 1979).

Hamilton, Nora, "Introduction: Peasants, Capital Penetration and Class Structure in Rural Latin America." *Latin American Perspectives* 7, no. 4 (Fall 1980).

———. *The Limits of State Autonomy: Post-Revolutionary Mexico*. Princeton: Princeton University Press, 1982.

Handelman, Howard. "Determinants of Working-Class Political Ideology: A Mexican Case Study." *Studies in Comparative International Development* 11, no. 3 (Fall 1976).

———. "Organized Labor in Mexico: Oligarchy and Dissent." *American Universities Field Staff Reports*, no. 18 (1979).

———. "The Politics of Labor Protest in Mexico: Two Case Studies." *Journal of Interamerican Studies and World Affairs* 18, no. 3 (August 1976).

Hansen, Roger D. *The Politics of Mexican Development*. Baltimore: The Johns Hopkins Press, 1971.

Harris, Charles H. *A Mexican Family Empire: The Latifundio of the Sánchez Navarros, 1765–1867*. Austin: University of Texas Press, 1975.

Harris, Richard L., and David Barkin. "The Political Economy of Mexico in the Eighties." *Latin American Perspectives* 9, no. 1 (Winter, 1982).

Hart, John M. "Agrarian Precursors of the Mexican Revolution: The Development of an Ideology." *The Americas* 29, no. 2 (October 1972).

Hellman, Judith Adler. "Capitalist Agriculture and Rural Protest." *LABOUR Capital and Society* 14, no. 2 (November 1981).

———. "Mexico in the Age of Petro-pesos." *Queen's Quarterly* 87, no. 2 (Summer 1980).

———. "Notes on the Failure of Reformist Capitalism in Mexico." *LARU Working Paper*, no. 18 (1976).

———. "Social Control in Mexico." *Comparative Politics* 12, no. 2 (January 1980).

———. "The Role of Ideology in Peasant Politics: Peasant Mobilization and Demobilization in the Laguna Region." *Journal of Interamerican Studies and World Affairs* 25, no. 1 (February 1983).

Hewitt de Alcántara, Cynthia. *Ensayo Sobre la Satisfacción de Necesidades Básicas del Pueblo Mexicano entre 1940 y 1970*. México, D.F.: Centro de Estudios Sociológicos, El Colegio de México, 1977.

———. "The 'Green Revolution' as History: the Mexican Experience." *Development and Change* 5, no. 2 (1973–74).

———. "Land Reform, Livelihood and Power in Rural Mexico." In D. A. Preston, ed., *Environment Society and Rural Change in Latin America*. London: John Wiley and Sons, 1980.

_____. *La Modernización de la Agricultura Mexicana, 1940–1970.* México D.F.: Siglo Veintiuno, 1978.

_____. *Modernizing Mexican Agriculture: Socioeconomic Implications of Technological Change, 1940–1970.* Geneva: United Nations Research Institute for Social Development, 1976.

Hilsum, Lindsey. "Uncle Sam's Jobs South of the Border." *Manchester Guardian Weekly,* 28 March 1982.

Hobsbawm, Eric J. *Bandits.* New York: Dell, 1969.

_____. *Primitive Rebels.* New York: W. W. Norton, 1959.

Horton, D. E. "Land Reform and Economic Development in Latin America: The Mexican Case." *Illinois Agricultural Economics* 8, no. 9 (January 1968).

Hufbauer, Gary Clyde, W. N. Harrell Smith IV, and Frank G. Vukmanic. "Bilateral Trade Relations." In Susan Kaufman Purcell, ed., *Mexico-United States Relations.* New York: Praeger, 1981.

Huizer, Gerrit. "Emilano Zapata and the Peasant Guerrillas." In Rodolfo Stavenhagen, ed., *Agrarian Problems and Peasant Movements in Latin America.* Garden City: Doubleday and Company, 1970.

_____. "Peasant Organization and Agrarian Reform in Mexico." In Irving Louis Horowitz, ed., *Masses in Latin America.* New York: Oxford University Press, 1970.

_____. *The Role of Peasant Organizations in the Process of Agrarian Reform in Latin America.* Washington, D.C.: Comité Inter-Americano de Desarrollo Agrícola, 1968.

IDOC. "Growing Repression in Mexico." *LADOC,* 8, no. 2 (November-December 1977).

Iturriaga, José E. *La Estructura Social y Cultural de México.* México, D.F.: Fondo de Cultura Económica, 1951.

Izquierdo, Rafael. "Protectionism in Mexico." In Raymond Vernon, ed., *Public Policy and Private Enterprise in Mexico.* Cambridge: Harvard University Press, 1964.

Jaramillo, Ruben. *Autobiografía.* México, D.F.: Editorial Nuestro Tiempo, 1967.

Jenkins, J. Craig. "Push/Pull in Recent Mexican Migration to the U.S." *International Migration Review* 2, no. 2 (1977).

Jenkins, Rhys. "Foreign Firms, Manufactured Exports and Development Strategy: the Case of Mexico." *Boletín de Estudios Latinoamericanos y del Caribe,* no. 23 (Diciembre 1977).

_____. "Transnational Corporations and their Impact on the Mexican Economy." *Development Studies Discussion Paper* (University of East Anglia), no. 43 (February 1979).

Johnson, Kenneth F. *Mexican Democracy: A Critical View.* Boston: Allyn and Bacon, 1971; New York: Praeger Publishers, 1978.

Joseph, Gilbert M. "Mexico's 'Popular Revolution': Mobilization and Myth in Yucatan, 1910–1940." *Latin American Perspectives* 6, no. 3 (Summer) 1979.

_____. "Revolution from Without: The Mexican Revolution, 1910–1940." In

Edward H. Moseley and Edward D. Terry, eds., *Yucatan: A World Apart.* Tuscaloosa: University of Alabama Press, 1980.

Kaplan, Marcos. "Petróleo y Desarrollo: El Impacto Interno." *Foro Internacional* 21, no. 1 (julio-septiembre) 1980.

Katz, Friedrich. "Agrarian Changes in Northern Mexico in the Period of Villista Rule, 1913–1915." In James W. Wilkie et al., eds., *Contemporary Mexico.* Berkeley: University of California Press, 1976.

———, ed. *Hitler Sobre América Latina: El Fascismo Alemán en Latinoamérica 1933–1943.* México, D.F.: Fondo de Cultura Popular, 1968.

———. "Labor Conditions on Haciendas in Porfirian Mexico: Some Trends and Tendencies." *Hispanic American Historical Review* 54, no. 1 (February 1974).

———. "Peasants in the Mexican Revolution of 1910." In Joseph Spielberg and Scott Whiteford, eds., *Forging Nations: A Comparative View of Rural Ferment and Revolt.* East Lansing: Michigan State University Press, 1976.

———. *The Secret War in Mexico: Europe, the United States and the Mexican Revolution.* Chicago: University of Chicago Press, 1981.

Kautsky, John H. "Patterns of Modernizing Revolutions: Mexico and the Soviet Union." *Sage Professional Papers in Comparative Politics* 5, no. 01-056 (1975).

Keely, Charles B. "Counting the Uncountable: Estimates of Undocumented Aliens in the United States." *Population and Development Review,* 3, no. 4 (December 1977).

Keesing, Donald B. "Employment and Lack of Employment in Mexico, 1900–1970." In James W. Wilkie and Kenneth Ruddle, eds., *Quantitative Latin American Studies: Methods and Findings.* Los Angeles: Latin American Center, University of California at Los Angeles, 1977.

Keremitsis, Dawn. *La Industria Textil Mexicana en el Siglo XIX.* México, D.F.: SepSetentas, 1973.

Kirk, Betty. *Covering the Mexican Front.* Norman: University of Oklahoma Press, 1942.

Klare, Michael. "The Pentagon's Counterinsurgency Infrastructure." *NACLA Newsletter* 4, no. 9 (June 1971).

———. *War Without End.* New York: Random House, 1972.

Krauze, Enrique. "Mexico: The Rudder and the Storm." *The Mexican Forum* 3, no. 1 (January 1983).

Kusida, Sumiko. "Mexico Special Report: Growing Dependence." *South* (July 1981).

Landsberger, Henry A., and Cynthia N. Hewitt. "Ten Sources of Weakness and Cleavage in Latin American Peasant Movements." In Rodolfo Stavenhagen, ed., *Agrarian Problems and Peasant Movements in Latin America.* Garden City: Doubleday and Company, 1970.

Lanfranco, Sam. "Mexican Oil, Export-led Development and Agricultural Neglect." *Journal of Economic Development* 6, no. 1 (July 1981).

Leal, Juan Felipe. "The Mexican State: 1915–1973, A Historical Interpretation." *Latin American Perspectives* 2, no. 2 (Summer 1975).

Leich, John Foster. "Reforma Política in Mexico." *Current History* 80, no. 469 (November 1981).

Lerner, Sigal, Berta et al. *Mexico: Realidad Política de Sus Partidos, México,* D.F.: Instituto Mexicano de Estudios Políticos, 1970.

Levenstein, Harvey. "A Lesson in Foreign Control from Mexico." *Toronto Star.* 4 April 1973.

Levy, Daniel C. *University and Government in Mexico: Autonomy in an Authoritarian System.* New York: Praeger Publishers, 1980.

Levy, Daniel, and Gabriel Székely. *Mexico: Paradoxes of Stability and Change.* Boulder, Colo.: Westview Press, 1982.

Lewis, Oscar. *The Children of Sanchez.* New York: Vintage, 1961.

_____. *Pedro Martínez.* New York: Vintage, 1967.

Lieuwen, Edwin. *Mexican Militarism: The Political Rise and Fall of the Revolutionary Army, 1910–1940.* Albuquerque: University of New Mexico Press, 1968.

Liga de Agrónomos Socialistas. *El Colectivismo Agrario en México: La Comarca Lagunera.* México, D.F.: Liga de Agrónomos Socialistas, 1940.

Lombardo Toledano, Vicente. "Los Intentos de Revisión del Marxismo Durante La Guerra." In *La CTAL Ante La Guerra y Ante La Post-Guerra.* México, D.F.: 1945.

Lomnitz, Larissa. "Conflict and Mediation in a Latin American University." *Journal of Interamerican Studies and World Affairs* 19, no. 3 (August 1977).

_____. "Horizontal and Vertical Relations and the Social Structure of Urban Mexico." *Latin American Research Review* 17, no. 2 (1982).

_____. "The Latin American University: Breeding Ground of the New State Elites." Paper presented to the American Anthropological Society, Houston, Texas, January 1979.

_____. "Mechanisms of Articulation between Shantytown Settlers and the Urban System." *Urban Anthropology* 7, no. 2 (Summer 1978).

_____. *Networks and Marginality: Life in a Mexican Shantytown.* New York: Academic Press, 1977.

Looney, Robert E. *Mexico's Economy: A Policy Analysis with Forecasts to 1990.* Boulder, Colorado: Westview Press, 1978.

López Montjardin, Adriana. "La Lucha Popular en los Municipios." *Cuadernos Políticos,* no. 20 (abril–junio 1979).

López Rosado, Diego G., and Juan F. Noyola Vásquez. "Los Salarios Reales en México, 1939–1950." *El Trimestre Económico* 18, no. 2 (abril–junio, 1951).

Lord, Peter, *The Peasantry as an Emerging Factor in Mexico, Bolivia and Venezuela.* Madison: The Land Tenure Center, 1965.

Maccoby, Michael. "Love and Authority in a Mexican Village." In Jack M. Potter et al., eds., *Peasant Society.* Boston: Little, Brown and Company, 1967.

Manzanilla Schaffer, Victór. *Reforma Agraria Mexicana*. Colima: Universidad de Colima, 1966.

Marshall, F. Ray. "Economic Factors Influencing the International Migration of Workers." In *Stanley R. Ross, ed., Views Across the Border: The United States and Mexico*. Albuquerque: University of New Mexico Press, 1978.

Martínez Saldeña, Tomás. *El Costo Social de un Exito Político*. Chapingo: Colegio de Postgraduados, 1980.

Matloff, Judith. "Mexico's Juchitán: A Popular Challenge to PRI." *NACLA Report on the Americas* 16, no. 6 (November–December 1982).

Mejido, Manuel. *México Amargo*. México, D.F.: Siglo Veintiuno Editores, 1974.

Mesa-Lago, Carmelo. "Social Security Stratification and Inequality in Mexico." In Wilkie et al., eds., *Contemporary Mexico*. Berkeley: University of California Press, 1976.

Metz, William D. "Mexico: The Premier Oil Discovery in the Western Hemisphere." *Science*, 22 December 1978.

Meyer, Jean. "Periodización e Ideología." In James Wilkie, et al., eds., *Contemporary Mexico*. Berkeley: University of California Press, 1976.

Meyer, Michael, C. *Huerta: A Political Portrait*. Lincoln: University of Nebraska Press, 1972.

_____. *Mexican Rebel: Pascual Orozco and the Mexican Revolution*. Lincoln: University of Nebraska Press, 1967.

Meyer, Michael C., and William L. Sherman. *The Course of Mexican History*. New York: Oxford University Press, 1979.

Meyers, Frederick, "Party, Government and the Labour Movement in Mexico; Two Case Studies." In Arthur Ross, ed., *Industrial Relations and Economic Development*. London: Macmillan, 1966.

Meyers, William K. "Politics, Vested Rights, and Economic Growth in Porfirian Mexico: The Company Tlahualilo in the Comarca Lagunera, 1885–1911." *Hispanic American Historic Review* 57, no. 3 (August 1977).

Michaels, Albert L. "The Crisis of Cardenismo." *Journal of Latin American Studies* 2, no. 1 (May 1970).

Middlebrook, Kevin J. "International Implications of Labor Change: The Automobile Industry." In Jorge I. Domínguez, ed., *Mexico's Political Economy: Challenges at Home and Abroad*. Beverly Hills: Sage Publications, 1982.

_____. "Political Change in Mexico." In Susan Kaufman Purcell, ed., *Mexico–United States Relations*. New York: Praeger, 1981.

_____. "State Structure and Labor Participation in Mexico." Paper presented to the Latin American Studies Association, November 1977.

Millan, Verna Carleton, *Mexico Reborn*. Boston: Houghton Mifflin Company, 1939.

Miller, Solomon. "Hacienda to Plantation in Northern Peru: The Processes of Proletarianization of a Tenant Farmer Society." In Julian H. Steward, ed., *Contemporary Change in Traditional Societies*, Vol. 3. Urbana: University of Illinois Press, 1967.

Montaño, Jorge. *Los Pobres de la Ciudad y los Asentamientos Espontáneos.* México, D.F.: Siglo Veintiuno Editores, 1976.

Montavon, Remy et al. *The Role of Multinational Companies in Latin America: A Case Study in Mexico.* Westmead, Farnborough, G.B.: Saxon House, 1979.

Montemayor, Robert, and Laurie Becklund. "The Dead Aren't Counted or Listed." *Los Angeles Times,* July 15, 1979.

Montes de Oca, Rosa Elena. "The State and the Peasants." In José Luis Reyna and Richard S. Weinert, eds., *Authoritarianism in Mexico.* Philadelphia: Institute for the Study of Human Issues, 1977.

Moreno Toscano, Alejandra. "La 'Crisis' en la Ciudad." In Pablo González Casanova and Enrique Florescano, eds., *México Hoy.* México, D.F.: Siglo Veintiuno Editores, 1979.

Mújica Velez, Ruben. "Subempleo y Crisis Agraria: Las Opciones Agropecuarias." *Comercio Exterior* 27, no. 12 (1977).

Nacional Financiera. *La Economía Mexicana en Cifras.* México, D.F., 1970.

Nathan, Paul. "México en La Epoca de Cárdenas." *Problemas Agrícolas e Industriales de México* 7, no. 3 (1955).

Navarrete, Ifigenia M. de. "Income Distribution in Mexico." In Enrique Pérez López, ed., *Mexico's Recent Economic Growth.* Austin: University of Texas Press, 1967.

Navarrete, Jorge Eduardo, ed. *México: La Política Económica del Nuevo Gobierno.* México, D.F.: Banco Nacional de Comercio Exterior, 1971.

Needler, Martin C. *Mexican Politics: The Containment of Conflict.* Stanford: The Hoover Institution Press, 1982.

Newfarmer, Richard S., and William F. Mueller. *Multinational Corporations in Brazil and Mexico: Structural Sources of Economic and Noneconomic Power.* Report to the Subcommittee on Multinational Corporations of the Committee on Foreign Relations, U.S. Senate, Washington, D.C.: Government Printing Office, 1975.

Newton, David J. "Mexico—the West's Latest Oil Well." *The World Today* 36, no. 7, (July 1980).

Niemeyer, E. V., Jr. *Revolution at Queretaro: The Mexican Constitutional Convention of 1916–1917.* Austin: University of Texas Press, 1974.

Niering, Frank E., Jr. "Mexico—A New Force in World Oil." *Petroleum Economist* 46, no. 109 (March 1979).

North American Congress on Latin America. "Del Monte: Bitter Fruits." *NACLA Report* 10, no. 7 (September 1976).

North American Congress on Latin America. "Harvest of Anger: Agro-imperialism in Mexico's Northwest." *NACLA Report* 10, no. 6 (July–August 1976).

North American Congress on Latin America. "Hit and Run: U.S. Runaway Shops on the Mexican Border." *NACLA Report* 9, no. 5 (July–August 1975).

North American Congress on Latin America. *Mexico 1968: A Study of Domination and Repression.* New York: NACLA, 1968.

North American Congress on Latin America. "Schooled in Conflict: Mexican and Chicano Students 1968–1978." *NACLA Report on the Americas* 12, no. 5 (September–October 1978).

North American Congress on Latin America. *Yanqui Dolar.* New York: NACLA, 1971.

Ojeda, Mario. "El Poder Negociador del Petróleo: El Caso de México." *Foro Internacional* 21, no. 1 (julio–septiembre, 1980).

Orme, William A., Jr. "Ex-Pemex Chief's Ouster from Senate." *Journal of Commerce,* 20, October 1982.

Olizar, Maryoka. *Guía de los Mercados de México.* México, D.F.: 1974.

Padgett, L. Vincent. *The Mexican Political System.* Boston: Houghton Mifflin Company, 1966.

Padilla Aragón, Enrique. *México: Desarrollo con Pobreza.* México, D.F.: Siglo Veintiuno Editores, 1970.

Pahnke, J. Antonio. "Oil, Gas and Petrochemicals in Mexico 1977–1982." Commercial Division, Canadian Embassy, Mexico City, May 1978.

Paoli Bolio, Francisco José. "Petroleum and Political Change in Mexico." *Latin American Perspectives* 9, no. 1 (Winter 1982).

Paré, Luisa. "Inter-ethnic and Class Relations (Sierra Norte region; state of Puebla)." In John Rex, ed., *Race and Class in Post-colonial Society.* Paris: UNESCO, 1977.

Parkes, Henry Bamford. *A History of Mexico.* London: Shenval Press, 1962.

Paz, Octavio. *Labyrinth of Solitude: Life and Thought in Mexico.* New York. Grove Press, 1961.

———. *The Other Mexico.* New York: Grove Press, 1972.

Peón, Máximo. *Como Viven los Mexicanos en los Estados Unidos.* México, D.F.: B. Costa-Amic, 1966.

Pereyra, Carlos. "Estado y Movimiento Obrero." *Cuadernos Políticos,* no. 28 (abril–junio 1981).

———. "Estado y Sociedad." In Pablo González Casanova and Enrique Florescano, eds., *México Hoy:* México, D.F.: Siglo Veintiuno Editores, 1979.

Pérez López, Enrique, ed. *The Recent Development of Mexico's Economy.* Austin: University of Texas Press, 1967.

Philip, George. "Mexican Oil and Gas: The Politics of a New Resource." *International Affairs* (Summer 1980).

Poitras, Guy. "Mexico's 'New' Foreign Policy." *Inter-American Economic Affairs* 28, no. 3 (Winter 1974).

Pontiatowska, Elena. *La Noche de Tlatelolco.* México, D.F.: Ediciones ERA, 1971.

Population Reference Bureau. "1978 World Population Data Sheet." Washington, D.C., March 1978.

Porfirio Hernández, Alfonso. "Analisis de la Rentibilidad Generada por el Cultivo del Algodonero." *CIANE Seminarios Técnicos* 2, no. 1 (mayo 1975).

Portes, Alejandro. "Legislatures Under Authoritarian Regimes: The Case of Mexico." *Journal of Political and Military Sociology* 5, no. 2 (Fall 1977).

Portes Gil, Emilio. *Autobiografía de la Revolución Mexicana*. México, D.F.: Instituto Mexicano de Cultura, 1964.

———. "Novecientos Mil Campesinos en una Sola Confederación." In *La Unificación Campesina*. México, D.F.: Ediciones del PNR, 1935.

Powell, J. Richard. *The Mexican Petroleum Industry: 1939–1950*. New York: Russell & Russell, 1972.

Powell, John Duncan. *Peasant Society and Clientelist Politics*. Cambridge: Center for International Affairs, 1967.

Press, Robert M. "U.S.-Owned Plants in Mexico Produce Cheap Goods—and Controversy." *Christian Science Monitor* 5, February 1982.

Punto Crítico. "Mexico: Class Struggle and 'Political Reform.'" *Contemporary Marxism*, no. 1 (Spring 1980).

Purcell, John F. H., and Susan Kaufman Purcell. "Mexican Business and Public Policy." In James M. Malloy, ed., *Authoritarianism and Corporatism in Latin America*. Pittsburgh: University of Pittsburgh Press, 1977.

Purcell, Susan Kaufman. *The Mexican Profit-Sharing Decision: Politics in an Authoritarian Regime*. Berkeley: University of California Press, 1975.

Quirk, Robert. *The Mexican Revolution 1914–1915*. Bloomington: University of Indiana Press, 1960.

Raat, W. Dirk. *Revoltosos: Mexico's Rebels in the United States, 1903-1923*. College Station: Texas A & M Press, 1981.

Rama, Ruth, and Raúl Vigorito. *El Complejo de Frutas y Legumbres en México*. México, D.F.: Editorial Nueva Imagen, 1979.

Ramírez, Ramón. *El Movimiento Estudiantil de México*, Vols. 1, 2. México, D.F.: Ediciones ERA, 1969.

Ramos, Samuel. *Profile of Man and Culture in Mexico*. Austin: University of Texas Press, 1962.

Ramos Uriarte, Guillermo. *El Mercado de Algodón en la Comarca Lagunera*. México, D.F.: Banco Nacional de Crédito Ejidal, 1954.

Randall, Laura. "The Political Economy of Mexican Oil." Paper presented to the Santiago Conference on International Factors in Energy, November 1979.

Redclift, Michael. "Agrarian Populism in Mexico—the 'Via Campesina.'" *Journal of Peasant Studies* 7, no. 4 (July 1980).

Reed, John. *Insurgent Mexico*. New York: Appleton and Company, 1914.

Restrepo, Iván, and Salomón Eckstein. *La Agricultura Colectiva en México*. México, D.F.: Siglo Veintiuno, 1975.

Reul, Myrtle R. *Territorial Boundaries of Rural Poverty: Profiles of Exploitation*. East Lansing: Center of Rural Manpower and Public Affairs, Michigan State University, 1974.

Reyes Osorio, Sergio. "El Desarrollo Polarizado de la Agricultura Mexicana." *Comercio Exterior* (marzo 1969).

Reyna, José Luis. "El Movimiento Obrero en una Situación de Crisis: México 1976–1978." *Foro Internacional* 19, no. 3 (enero—marzo 1979).

——— et al. *Tres Estudios Sobre el Movimiento Obrero en México*. México, D.F.: Jornadas 80, 1976.

Reynolds, Clark W. *The Mexican Economy*. New Haven: Yale University Press, 1970.

———. "Why Mexico's 'Stabilizing Development' Was Actually Destabilizing." *World Development* 6, no. 7/8 (1978).

Richmond, Patricia McIntire. *Mexico: A Case Study of One-Party Politics*. Ph.D. dissertation, University of California, 1965.

Riding, Alan, "The Death of the Latin American Guerrilla Movement," *World*, 3, July 1973.

———. "The Mixed Blessing of Mexico's Oil." *New York Times Magazine*, 11, January 1981.

———. "Problems of Mexico City: Warning to Third World." *The New York Times*, May 15, 1983.

Roman, Richard. *Ideology and Class in the Mexican Revolution: A Study of the Convention and the Constitutional Congress*. Ph.D. dissertation, University of California, Berkeley, 1973.

Ronfeldt, David F. *Atencingo: The Politics of Agrarian Struggle in a Mexican Ejido*. Stanford: Stanford University Press, 1973.

———. "The Mexican Army and Political Order Since 1940." In Abraham F. Lowenthal, ed., *Armies and Politics in Latin America*. New York: Holmes and Meier Publishers, 1976.

Ros, Jaime. "La Encrucijada del Corto Plazo." *Nexos* 5, no. 5 (noviembre 1982).

Rosales, José Natividad. *¿Quién es Lucio Cabañas?* México, D.F.: Posada, 1975.

Rosenzweig, Fernando. "Política Agrícola y Generación de Empleo." *El Trimestre Económico* 42, no. 4 (octubre–diciembre 1975).

Ross, Stanley R. *Francisco I. Madero: Apostle of Mexican Democracy*. New York: Columbia University Press, 1955.

———. "LEA and Don Pepe, 1976 and 1982: Divergent Approaches to the Presidential Succession." *The Mexican Forum* 3, no. 1 (January 1983).

———, ed. *Views Across the Border: The United States and Mexico*. Albuquerque: University of New Mexico Press, 1978.

Russell, Philip. *Mexico in Transition*. Austin: Colorado River Press, 1977.

Salamini, Heather Fowler. "Adalberto Tejeda and the Veracruz Peasant Movement." In James Wilkie et al., eds., *Contemporary Mexico*. Berkeley: University of California Press, 1976.

———. *Agrarian Radicalism in Veracruz, 1920–38*. Lincoln: University of Nebraska Press, 1978.

Sandeman, Hugh. "Pemex Comes Out of Its Shell." *Fortune*, 10, April 1978.

Sanders, Thomas G. "The Plight of Mexican Agriculture." *American Universities Field Staff Report*, no. 3 (1979).

Sanderson, Steven E. *Agrarian Populism and the Mexican State: The Struggle for Land in Sonora*. Berkeley: University of California Press, 1981.

Sanderson, Susan R. Walsh. *Peasants and Public Policy: Social Change in Rural Mexico, 1916–1976*. Ph.D. dissertation, University of Pittsburgh, 1980.

Santos Valdes, José. *Madera*. México, D.F.: Imprenta Laura, 1968.

Saragoza, Alex M. "El Grupo Monterrey and Mexican Popular Culture: The Origins, 1930–1958." Paper presented to the VI Conference of Mexican and United States Historians, Chicago, September 1981.

Schlagheck, James L. *The Political, Economic and Labor Climate in Mexico.* Multinational Industrial Relations Series, no. 4. Philadelphia: The Wharton School, University of Pennsylvania, 1980.

Schmitt, Karl M. *Communism in Mexico.* Austin: University of Texas Press, 1965.

Schryer, Frans J. *The Rancheros of Pisaflores: The History of a Peasant Bourgeoisie in Twentieth-Century Mexico.* Toronto: University of Toronto Press, 1980.

Schumacher, August. "Agricultural Development and Rural Employment: A Mexican Dilemma." *Working Papers in U.S.–Mexican Studies,* no. 21. San Diego: Program in United States–Mexican Studies, University of California, San Diego, 1981.

Scott, Robert E. *Mexican Government in Transition.* Urbana: University of Illinois Press, 1964.

———. "Mexico: The Established Revolution." In Lucien W. Pye and Sidney Verba, eds., *Political Culture and Political Development.* Princeton: Princeton University Press, 1965.

———. "Politics in Mexico." In Gabriel Almond and G. Bingham Powell, eds., *Comparative Politics Today: A World View.* Boston: Little, Brown and Co., 1980.

Secretería de Gobernación. *Seis Años de Servicio al Gobierno de México.* México, D.F.: La Nacional Impresora, 1940.

Secretaría de Industria y Comercio. *Censo General de Población 1970: Resumen General.* México, D.F.: Dirección General de Estadística, 1972.

Secretería de Patrimonio y Fomento Industrial. *Plan Nacional de Desarrollo Industrial, 1979–1982.* México, D.F.: March, 1979.

Segovia, Rafael. "Las Elecciones Federales de 1979." *Foro Internacional* 20, no. 3 (enero–marzo 1980).

Seligson, Mitchell A., and Edward J. Williams. *Maquiladoras and Migration: Workers in the Mexican-United States.* Austin: University of Texas Press, 1982.

Senior, Clarence, *Land Reform and Democracy.* Gainesville: University of Florida Press, 1958.

Sepúlveda Amor, Bernardo, et al. *Las Empresas Transnacionales en México.* México, D.F.: El Colegio de México, 1974.

Sepúlveda Amor Bernardo, and Antonio Chumacero. *La Inversión Extranjera en México.* México, D.F.: Fondo de Cultura Económica, 1973.

Shapira, Yoram. "Mexico's Foreign Policy Under Echeverría: A Retrospect." *Inter-American Economic Affairs* 31, no. 4 (Spring 1978).

Shulgovsky, Anatol. *México en la Encrucijada de su Historia.* México, D.F.: Fondo de Cultura Popular, 1968.

Sierra, José Luis. *El 10 de Junio y la Izquierda Radical.* México, D.F.: Editorial Heterodoxia, 1972.

Sigmund, Paul E. *Models of Political Change in Latin America.* New York: Praeger, 1970.

Silva Herzog, Jesús. *El Agrarismo Mexicano y La Reforma Agraria.* México, D.F.: Fondo de Cultura Económica, 1959.

Simpson, Eyler N. *The Ejido, Mexico's Way Out.* Chapel Hill: University of North Carolina Press, 1937.

Singelmann, Peter. "Rural Collectivization and Dependent Capitalism: The Mexican Collective Ejido," *Latin American Perspectives* 5, no. 3 (Summer 1978).

Smith, Peter H. *Labyrinths of Power: Political Recruitment in Twentieth-Century Mexico.* Princeton: Princeton University Press, 1979.

Solis, Leopoldo M. *Controversias sobre el Crecimiento y la Distribución.* México, D.F.: Fondo de Cultura Económica, 1972.

Spaeth, Anthony. "The *Maquila* Boom." *Forbes,* 10 December 1979.

Spalding, Hobart A., Jr. *Organized Labor in Latin America: Historical Case Studies of Urban Workers in Dependent Societies.* New York: Harper and Row, 1977.

Stavenhagen, Rodolfo. "Capitalism and the Peasantry in Mexico." *Latin American Perspectives* 5, no. 3 (Summer 1978).

————. "Social Aspects of Agrarian Structure in Mexico." In Rodolfo Stavenhagen, ed., *Agrarian Problems and Peasant Movements in Latin America.* Garden City: Doubleday and Company, 1970.

Stavenhagen, Rodolfo et al. *Neolatifundismo y Explotación: De Emiliano Zapata a Anderson Clayton & Co.* México, D.F.: Editorial Nuestro Tiempo, 1968.

Stevens, Evelyn P. "Mexico's PRI: The Institutionalization of Corporatism?" In James M. Malloy, ed., *Authoritarianism and Corporatism in Latin America.* Pittsburgh: University of Pittsburgh Press, 1977.

————. *Protest and Response in Mexico.* Cambridge, Mass.: The MIT Press, 1974.

Street, James H. "Mexico's Economic Development Plan." *Current History* 80, no. 469 (November 1981).

Tannenbaum, Frank. *The Mexican Agrarian Revolution.* New York: Macmillan, 1929.

Tardanico, Richard. "Revolutionary Nationalism and State Building in Mexico, 1917–1924." *Politics & Society* 10, no. 1 (1980).

Tello, Carlos. *La Política Económica en México.* México, D.F.: Siglo Veintiuno Editores, 1979.

Ten Kate, Adriaan, and Robert Bruce Wallace. *Protection and Economic Development in Mexico.* New York: St. Martin's Press, 1980.

Thompson, Mark. "Collective Bargaining in the Mexican Electrical Industry." *British Journal of Industrial Relations* 8, no. 1.

_____. *The Development of Unionism among Mexican Electrical Workers.* Ph.D. dissertation, Cornell University, 1966.

Thompson, Mark, and Ian Roxborough. "Union Elections and Democracy in Mexico: A Comparative Perspective." Paper presented to the Latin American Studies Association, April 1979.

Torres, Gaytán, Ricardo. *Un Siglo de Devaluaciones del Peso Mexicano.* México, D.F.: Siglo Veintiuno Editores, 1980.

Townsend, William Cameron. *Lázaro Cárdenas, Mexican Democrat.* Ann Arbor: George Wahr Publishing Company, 1952.

Trejo Delarbre, Raúl. "The Mexican Labor Movement: 1917–1975." *Latin American Perspectives* 3, no. 1 (Winter 1976).

_____. "El Movimiento Obrero: Situación y Perspectivas." In Pablo González Casanova and Enrique Florescano, eds., *México Hoy.* México, D.F.: Siglo Veintiuno Editores, 1979.

Trejo Reyes, Saúl. "Expansión Industrial y Empleo en México: 1965–1970." *El Trimestre Económico* 43, no. 1 (enero–marzo 1976).

_____. "El Incremento de la Producción y el Empleo Industrial en México, 1950–1965." *Demografía y Economía* 4, no. 1 (1970).

_____. *Industrialización y Empleo en México.* México, D.F.: Fondo de Cultura Económica, 1973.

_____. *Industrialization and Employment Growth: Mexico 1950–1965.* Ph.D. dissertation, Yale University, 1971.

Tucker, William. *The Mexican Government Today.* Minneapolis: University of Minnesota Press, 1957.

Unikel, Luís. *El Desarrollo Urbano de México: Diagnóstico e Implicaciones Futuras.* México, D.F.: El Colegio de México, 1976.

_____. "La Dinámica del Crecimiento de la Ciudad de México." In Alejandra Moreno Toscano, ed., *Ensayos Sobre el Desarrollo Urbano de México.* México, D.F.: SepSetentas, 1974.

_____. "Urbanización y Urbanismo: Situación y Perspectivas." In Miguel S. Wionczek, ed., *Disyuntivas Sociales: Presente y Futuro de la Sociedad Mexicana.* México, D.F.: SepSetentas, 1971.

Ulmer, Melville J. "Who's Making It in Mexico?" *The New Republic,* 25 September 1971.

United Nations Economic Commission for Latin America. "Income Distribution in Latin America." *Economic Bulletin for Latin America* (October 1967).

United States Agency for International Development. *A Review of Alliance for Progress Goals.* Washington, D.C.: U.S. Government Printing Office, 1969.

United States Agency for International Development, Statistics and Reports Division. *Operations Report.* June 30, 1961–June 30, 1969.

United States Department of Defense. *Military Assistance Facts.* Washington, D.C.: 1969.

United States Department of Defense. Office of the Assistant Secretary of Defense for International Security Affairs. *Military Assistance and Foreign Military Sales Facts.* Washington, D.C.: 1970.

Urquidi, Victor L., "La Carta de Derechos y Deberes Económicos de los Estados: La Cuestion de su Aplicación." *Foro Internacional* 20, no. 2 (octubre–diciembre 1979).

Velasco-Suárez, Jesús. "México en el Mercado Internacional del Petróleo." *Ciencia y Desarrollo,* no. 27 (marzo-abril 1981).

Velázquez Toledo, José. "Sumario Estadístico," *Comercio Exterior* 35, no. 9 (September 1981).

Vellinga, Menno. *Economic Development and the Dynamics of Class: Industrialization, Power and Control in Monterrey, Mexico.* Assen, Neth: Van Gorcum, 1979.

————. *Industrialización, Burguesía y Clase Obrera en México.* México, D.F.: Siglo Veintiuno Editores, 1979.

Vernon, Raymond. *The Dilemma of Mexico's Development.* Cambridge, Mass.: Harvard University Press, 1963.

Villarreal, René. "El Petróleo Como Instrumento de Desarrollo y de Negociación Internacional: México en los Ochentas." *El Trimestre Económico* 48, no. 1 (enero–marzo 1981).

————. "The Policy of Import-Substituting Industrialization, 1929–1975." In José Luis Reyna and Richard S. Weinert, eds., *Authoritarianism in Mexico.* Philadelphia: Institute for the Study of Human Issues, 1977.

Villarreal, René, and Rocio de Villarreal. "Mexico's Development Strategy." In Susan Kaufman Purcell, ed., *Mexico–United States Relations.* New York: Praeger, 1981.

Villaseñor García, Guillermo. "Reformar la Reforma Política." *Proceso,* no. 215 (15 diciembre 1980).

Villoro, Luis. "La Reforma Política y las Perspectivas de Democracia." In Pablo González Casanova and Enrique Florescano, eds., *México, Hoy.* México, D.F.: Siglo Veintiuno Editores, 1979.

Warman, Arturo. *Los Campesinos: Hijos Predilectos del Regimen.* México, D.F.: Editorial Nuestro Tiempo, 1972.

————. "El Problema del Campo." In Pablo González Casanova and Enrique Florescano, eds., *México Hoy.* México, D.F.: Siglo Veintiuno Editores, 1979.

————. *"We Come to Object": The Peasants of Morelos and the National State.* Baltimore: Johns Hopkins University Press, 1981.

Weinert, Richard S. "Foreign Capital in Mexico." In Susan Kaufman Purcell, ed., *Mexico–United States Relations.* New York: Praeger, 1981.

————. "The State and Foreign Capital." In José Luis Reyna and Richard S. Weinert, eds., *Authoritarianism in Mexico.* Philadelphia: Institute for the Study of Human Issues, 1977.

Wellhausen, Edwin J. "The Agriculture of Mexico." *Scientific American* 235, no. 3 (September 1976).

Weyl, Nathaniel and Sylvia Weyl. *The Reconquest of Mexico: The Years of Lázaro Cárdenas.* New York: Oxford University Press, 1939.

Whetten, Nathan L., *Rural Mexico*, New York: The Century Company, 1948.

Whitehead, Lawrence. "La Política Económica del Sexenio de Echeverría: ¿Qué Salió Mal y Por Que?" *Foro Internacional* 20, no. 3 (enero–marzo 1980).

Wilkie, James W. *The Mexican Revolution: Federal Expenditure and Social Change Since 1910*. Berkeley: University of California Press, 1967.

Wilkie, Raymond. *San Miguel: A Mexican Collective Ejido*. Stanford: Stanford University Press, 1971.

Wilkie, Richard W. "The Populations of Mexico and Argentina in 1980: Preliminary Data and Some Comparisons." In James W. Wilkie and Stephen Haber, eds. *Statistical Abstract of Latin America* 21. Los Angeles: UCLA Latin American Center Publications, University of California, 1981.

Williams, Edward J. "Mexican Hydrocarbon Export Policy: Ambition and Reality." In Robert M. Lawrence and Martin O. Heisler, eds., *International Energy Policy*. Lexington, Mass.: D. C. Heath and Company, 1980.

———. "Oil in Mexican–U.S. Relations: Analysis and Bargaining Scenario." *Orbis* 22, no. 1 (Spring 1978).

———. "Petroleum and Political Change." In Jorge I. Domínguez, ed., *Mexico's Political Economy: Challenges at Home and Abroad*. Beverly Hills: Sage, 1982.

Wionczek, Miguel S. "El Subdesarrollo Científico y Tecnológico: Sus Consecuencias." In Miguel S. Wionczek, ed., *Disyuntivas Sociales: Presente y Futuro de la Sociedad Mexicana*. México, D.F.: SepSetentas, 1971.

Witte, Ann Dryden. "Employment in the Manufacturing Sector of Developing Economics: A Study of Mexico and Peru." *Journal of Development Studies* 10, no. 1 (October 1973).

Wolf, Eric R. "Fases de la Protesta Rural en América Latina." In Ernest Feder, ed., *La Lucha de Clases en el Campo*. México, D.F.: Fondo de Cultura Económica, 1975.

Wolf, Eric R. *Peasant Wars of the Twentieth Century*. New York: Harper and Row, 1969.

Wolf, Eric R. and Sidney Mintz. "Haciendas and Plantations in Middle America and the Antilles." *Social and Economic Studies* 6, no. 3 (1957).

Womack, John, Jr. "The Spoils of the Mexican Revolution." *Foreign Affairs* 48, no. 4 (July 1970).

———. *Zapata and the Mexican Revolution*. New York: Vintage, 1970.

Yunez-Naude Antonio. "Los Dilemas del Desarrollo Compartido: La Política Económica de 1971 a 1976." *El Trimestre Económico* 48, no. 2 (abril–junio 1981).

Zermeño, Sergio. "Mexico: Estado, Pobreza y Democracia." *Foro Internacional* 19, no. 3 (enero–marzo 1979).

Zubirán, Salvador et al. *La Desnutrición del Mexicano*. México, D.F.: Fondo de Cultura Económica, 1974.

INDEX